Precarities of 21st Century Childhoods

CRITICAL CHILDHOOD & YOUTH STUDIES: THEORETICAL EXPLORATIONS AND PRACTICES IN CLINICAL, EDUCATIONAL, SOCIAL, AND CULTURAL SETTINGS

Mission Statement

Critical Childhood & Youth Studies is a scholarly series that is concerned with understanding the lived experiences of children and youth in economic, social, cultural, political and historical contexts, and addresses complex experiences only knowable through multidisciplinary lenses. The series seeks to address the following core questions: How do notions of childhood & youth differ across time and space? What new theories and methodologies can we employ to enhance our understanding and wellbeing of young people? What position and meaning is attributed to children and childhoods in/across different societies, and what are the public and political discussions concerning children's general position in society? Is agency possible, or must children live in states of exception? What can it mean to theorize the conditions and processes through which children and young people embody a meaningful existence in light of the histories they inherit?

Books in Series

Precarities of 21st Century Childhoods: Critical Explorations of Time(s), Place(s), and Identities Edited by Michael O'Loughlin, Carol Owens, and Louis Rothschild

Critiquing Social and Emotional Learning: Psychodynamic and Cultural Perspectives by Clio Stearns

Precarities of 21st Century Childhoods

Critical Explorations of Time(s), Place(s), and Identities

Edited by Michael O'Loughlin, Carol Owens, and Louis Rothschild

LEXINGTON BOOKS
Lanham • Boulder • New York • London

Published by Lexington Books
An imprint of The Rowman & Littlefield Publishing Group, Inc.
4501 Forbes Boulevard, Suite 200, Lanham, Maryland 20706
www.rowman.com

86-90 Paul Street, London EC2A 4NE

British Library Cataloguing in Publication Information Available

Library of Congress Cataloging-in-Publication Data

Names: O'Loughlin, Michael, editor. | Owens, Carol (Psychoanalyst), editor. | Rothschild, Louis, editor.
Title: Precarities of 21st century childhoods : critical explorations of time(s), place(s), and identities / edited by Michael O'Loughlin, Carol Owens and Louis Rothschild.
Other titles: Precarities of twenty-first century childhoods
Description: Lanham : Lexington Books, [2023] | Series: Critical childhood & youth studies: theoretical explorations and practices in clinical, educational, social, and cultural settings | Includes bibliographical references and index. | Summary: "This interdisciplinary collection of essays explores internal and external precarities in the lives of children. The goal of the book is to illuminate, promote, and help situate subjectivities that are often blotted out for both the child and society"-- Provided by publisher.
Identifiers: LCCN 2022054380 (print) | LCCN 2022054381 (ebook) | ISBN 9781666907773 (cloth) | ISBN 9781666907780 (epub)
Subjects: LCSH: Child psychology. | Child development. | Children--Social conditions.
Classification: LCC BF721 .P69 2023 (print) | LCC BF721 (ebook) | DDC 155.4--dc23/eng/20221114
LC record available at https://lccn.loc.gov/2022054380
LC ebook record available at https://lccn.loc.gov/2022054381

∞™ The paper used in this publication meets the minimum requirements of American National Standard for Information Sciences—Permanence of Paper for Printed Library Materials, ANSI/NISO Z39.48-1992.

This book is dedicated to the memory of Rosiane Cristina dos Santos (1976–2021) of State University of Campinas in São Paulo State, Brazil, coauthor of Chapter 2, who sadly passed away prior to the completion of this book.

Contents

List of Figures xi

Foreword xiii

Acknowledgments xvii

Introduction: Meditations on Precarity in Childhood 1
Michael O'Loughlin, Carol Owens, Louis Rothschild

PART I: TIMES 17

Chapter 1: Found Objects of/as Re-Membering Through the Lens of Child as Method 19
Erica Burman

Chapter 2: "School Is a Time-Out in My Tough Life!": Use of Pause, Bridge, and Intermittence as Resources for Student Development in School 37
Ana Archangelo, Fabio Camargo Bandeira Villela, and Rosiane Cristina dos Santos

Chapter 3: Making Space for the Unfathomable: Liminality in Inner City Schools 51
Aileen Schloerb

Chapter 4: Psychoanalyzing "From Both Sides Now": At the Extremities of Adolescence—"The Tweenies" and "The Twenties" as New Geo-Psychical Positions 63
Carol Owens and Jamieson Webster

Chapter 5: Childhood and Adolescence: The Familiar Strangeness of Virtuality 79
Liora Stavchansky

PART II: PLACES 93

Chapter 6: "***I Love You More***": Making Childing Visible—Children's Emotional Labor in Affluent Libidinal Economies 95
Anne-Marie Cummins

Chapter 7: The Precarity of Children's Mental Wellness in Aotearoa New Zealand 109
Kaye P. Cederman

Chapter 8: Storying: Re-Writing History of Children and Families in Migration 125
Elizabeth Quintero

Chapter 9: States of Nowhere-Ness in Children and Adolescents 143
Ionas Sapountzis

Chapter 10: Inconspicuous Precarity: The Impossibility of the Inherently Creative Child 159
Katherine Martin

PART III: IDENTITIES 173

Chapter 11: The Weaponization of Childhood in Mussolini's Ethiopian Laboratory and Its Revenants in Present Day Italy 175
Paula Salvio

Chapter 12: Necrophobia as a Nihilistic Preoccupation in Paternal Fantasies of Maturation Gone Awry 193
Louis Rothschild

Chapter 13: Re-Finding Lost Boys: Lessons from Literature and the Clinic 209
Marilyn Charles

Chapter 14: Fractional Distillation: On Psychoanalysis' (Mis) Formulation of Autistic Children 225
Ben Morsa

Chapter 15: Negotiating Agency in the Formation of Subjectivity: The Child, the Parental Other, and the Sovereign Other 241
Michael O'Loughlin

Index 261

About the Contributors 269

List of Figures

Figure 11.1: Children in uniforms painting a map of Ethiopia, Eritrea colonial postcard (Aurelio Bertiglia, colonial postcard, 1936). 177

Figure 11.2: Italian soldiers "feeding" weak and hungry natives (Aurelio Bertiglia, colonial postcard, 1936). 180

Figure 11.3: *Genti del Tigrai Tacazze* (The People of Tigrai) (Aurelio Bertiglia, colonial postcard, 1936). 182

Figure 11.4: Ethiopian female and Italian soldiers singing *Faccetta Nera* (Aurelio Bertiglia, colonial postcard, 1936). 186

Foreword

Psychoanalysis looks to childhood origins, but goes further; it rewrites childhood, it rewrites memory, it rewrites the body, and it rewrites desire. This is a writing that goes on writing itself in the unconscious all our lives. What remains of childhood, of origins, is often unsayable, therefore of the Real, and perhaps the most precarious aspect of our lives.

Before I remark on my reading of this crucial book, I want to reconsider my childhood and say something about my approach to working with children clinically over many years. Childhood is a creation in language, shadowed by the unsayable. In my clinical work the unsayable expresses a link between language, the signifier, and traumatic experience, experience that introduces a gap in time, place, and memory (Rogers, 2006). Another way to say this, and the several authors of this book do so very well, is that precarities are omnipresent in childhood and beyond; missed encounters in childhood return to us in unexpected moments as adults.

Recently, in a visit to see my sister in St. Louis, Missouri, I reencountered my mother and our different precarious childhoods with her. Our mother died some time ago, in 1988. Mary had kept the documentation of her life in boxes for thirty-four years when we opened them. First, we opened her banking statements, bills to be paid, handwritten in blue, crossed out in red, and refigured to fit her budget. Our mother kept holy cards, train tickets, our letters from camp, report cards, arts awards. As we unpacked the boxes, there was no present, no past, only an unprecedented mixing of times. When we opened the box of her dresses, "the Ma's" scent rushed out and there she was—all around us in the room, every dress empty and every dress inhabited. Much of what we found my sister re-boxed, although perhaps in better order.

My response to opening the boxes was to find something new of my mother and myself. I had been leaving her for much of my life, disappearing in childhood into nothingness, nowhere; in adolescence into psychosis; later into books she could not read; eventually completing my education and leaving her in St. Louis, moving to Cambridge, Massachusetts. Yet in her yearning to keep us alive and with her, I realized she had been alone, raising us in the aftermath of my father's suicide when she was still young, and we were only five and six. What came to me out of those boxes was a sense of her love, imperfect as it was. That realization changed my childhood, a childhood fraught with fear, neglect, abuse, and loss. Those words are poor placeholders for what I have written elsewhere, and they say so little. It was curious to me, this love that was transmitted from my mother to me, that changed childhood itself, made of childhood a palimpsest of memories, moments in time like clouds in motion.

Reading *Precarities of 21st century childhoods: Critical explorations of time(s), place(s), and identities* is refreshing and deeply gratifying. This book adumbrates the experiences of children and our conception of childhood in new and surprising ways. I appreciate in particular the plurality of positions signaled to the reader in every part of this book; there are many precarities, likewise times, places, and identities, that children encounter and experience in the 21st century. The book challenged me to consider more acutely and honestly the cruel markers of structural trauma, prohibitions that cross generations and geo-political borders, and the failure of language by adults to convey the singular subjective experiences of children and adolescents, rendering them all but invisible to us and to themselves.

Reading this book allows me to see some of the limitations of my own lifetime of work with children and their families. My published writing carries my own peculiar preoccupations, preoccupations that were already present in the notes on which I relied as a source. My focus has been on the clinic, the inner life of a child unfolding in play and in speech. Too often what fell away was the wider context, that envelop of *life at scale* in various times, places, cultures, that has rendered this or that childhood particularly and acutely precarious.

This book invites us as readers to consider and situate subjectivities in various contexts of childhood, for example, to question the place of the child in parental fantasy in light of parental desire and its limitations. To consider, too, missed encounters in childhood, the experience of disappearing from view, situated in a particular place such as a school clinic designed to create a space of liminality for speaking and knowing. Not least, this book opens our minds and hearts to see and consider refugee childhoods, children living in peril of their lives, as well as childhoods lived under affluent conditions of fragmented social bonds and immersive technologies. Importantly, the authors of this book point toward and create in words specific markers of their own childhoods. As I read the book, including its introduction by the editors, it became an ethical imperative to bear in mind that these writers were once children, and that their lived childhoods have shaped their work.

Among the definitions the on-line Oxford English Dictionary offers concerning the word "precarious" is the following: "Dependent on chance or circumstance; uncertain; liable to fail; exposed to risk, hazardous; insecure, unstable." This certainly strikes me as an apt word for the experience of childhoods conveyed in this book. Yet I also want to say that reading many of these chapters brings alive the creative work that children themselves undertake to make childhood bearable, even to make an unbearable childhood yield something rich and useful. Another word that shapes this book is "critical." Again, the OED offers me an angle into my experience of reading. Critical carries many possibilities: "a decisive point turning point, a crisis with an effect, a close, skilled reading, and an investigation." The field of physics refers to "critical" as "the value of the frequency of variation of a regularly varying light source at which it passes between being seen as flickering and being seen as steady." This last definition spoke to me as an experience of reading. Moving along from chapter to chapter, and even within chapters, following closely each of the writers' words, I would think I "had" what was being said, only to have it questioned, flickering along the horizon of thought, something in words near to me, near to my own thought, yet infinitely receding. It made me want to read again, re-read passages, read between the lines, follow that which flickered.

There are as many reasons as readers to open this book and return to it often as a reference. For anyone interested in psychoanalysis, whether with children, adolescents, or adults, the experience of childhood we find here, including many ways to think of it, can inform and inflect clinical practice. I cannot think of another book with the scope and depth of this one as a current reference. Foremost for me is that each and every writer keeps alive the subjective experiences of children rooted in their own particular childhood, while not turning from the very real unprecedented challenges facing children of the 21st century.

Annie G. Rogers, PhD
Lismore, Ireland

Acknowledgments

The opportunity to collaborate with colleagues is a pleasure and privilege, and for me, who always loved books, the opportunity to create books is a very special pleasure. Sincere thanks to Carol and Louis, who made the work of creating this book both a joyful and creative experience. Thanks to all our authors for their scholarly work, creativity, and passion for bettering the lives of children. Thanks too to Annie Rogers, who graciously wrote the Foreword. I am grateful to my series co-editors, Awad Ibrahim from Toronto, Gabrielle Ivinson from Manchester, and Marek Tesar from Auckland, who graciously accepted this work in our Critical Childhood and Youth Studies series. Thanks to Kasey Beduhn, Acquisitions Editor at Lexington Books at the time this book was contracted. She helped shepherd this work through its early stages. I am also deeply grateful to Judith Lakamper, Acquisitions Editor, Mark Lopez and the team at Lexington Books, who have graciously seen this book through production. Finally, my thanks for assistance with preparation of the index to Chloe Civin, Mila Kirstie Kulsa, and Breanna Vizlakh, doctoral students at Adelphi University, New York.

—Michael O'Loughlin

I want to thank Michael and Louis for inviting me to work with them on this volume; what a gift and honor it has been for me to work alongside such dedicated and generous scholars. In addition I'd like to acknowledge the labor of creativity and passion each individual author has brought, to the work and completion of their essays for this volume; the courage and resilience of all children and adolescents in places and times of precarity; and in particular, the courage and resilience of the young Danish flutist Camilla Egholm whose own singular struggle with precarity I have found both inspirational and magnificent.

—Carol Owens

The genesis for this volume may be traced through meetings of the Association for the Psychoanalysis of Culture and Society. There, in 2006, Marilyn Charles's kindness landed me on a panel with Howard Covitz where metaphorical discussion of fish kindled friendship and return. Almost a decade later, the publication of a volume edited by Angie Voela and others led to a 2015 panel which in turn led to a round table with Michael in the following year. Through conversation with Richard Ruth, Michael and I began to envision what eventually became this volume. Working with Michael, Carol, and the other contributors has, I think, yielded transformative fruit. Hopefully, for the reader, the pages that follow reflect creative time passages with the satisfaction found in a good bottle of wine.

—Louis Rothschild

Introduction

Meditations on Precarity in Childhood

Michael O'Loughlin, Carol Owens, Louis Rothschild

For this book we wished to locate internally focused, critical perspectives regarding the social, political, emotional, and mental growth of children. Through the radical openness afforded by psychoanalytic and related frameworks, the goal of this book is to illuminate, promote, and help situate subjectivities that are often blotted out for both the child and society. To that end, we sought writing that would open up thought to challenge developmental and linear assumptions, hegemonies, and a bias toward homogeneity about children and childhood in order to help us to re-imagine childhoods otherwise. As such we welcomed proposals for chapters that addressed the challenges involved in thinking about, and working with children who have experienced traumas of dis-location that do not fit neatly into normative theories of development (children who are poor, migrant, trans, of color, etc.). The emphasis throughout the volume is upon motifs of lostness and foundness, in terms of the geographies of the psycho-social, and how such motifs govern and regulate what have come to count as the normative indexes of childhood as well as how they exclude other real childhoods. For example, the notion of childhood innocence written into law powerfully legitimates regulatory as well as protective measures in societies. As psychoanalysis attests, what is "lost" in childhood finds its way into narratives of loss in adult functioning and these narratives are of interest since they allow us to re-theorize ideas of child, family, and society. To that end, we have curated essays that focus in and on dissociated places and moments across varied childhood(s). In addition to clinical and other writing on children, we also welcomed contributions in the form of autobiographical inquiry, historical, and literary exploration that interrogates un-corralled, refugee states with respect to post-colonial discourses of child-development. In keeping with this intent, and consistent with our belief in the importance of locatedness in scholarship, we decided to devote a substantial part of our introduction to interrogating the genealogies of our own concerns about childhood, and the inevitable rootedness of these concerns in our own sociohistorical and familial backgrounds and experiences.

MICHAEL'S STATEMENT

When I teach my undergraduate course, *Childhood Development*, a key organizing principle is the notion of life chances. What enhances a child's prospects, and what are the personal, familial, and societal factors that serve as what Paulo Freire would call *limit situations* that inhibit or foreclose the possibility of freedom? Policymakers often use the technical term *risk factors* and *protective factors* to describe some of these constraints, while the psychologized term *adverse childhood experiences* [ACES] has gained wide popularity as a means of putatively quantifying a potential degree of risk from trauma for any child. A problem with the discourses of both risk and adversity is an essentialization of childhood experience and a rather fatalistic determinism. This is particularly true for groups of children who already risk relegation to what Giorgio Agamben (2005) called *states of exception* because of their essentialized status as poor, or undocumented, or because of their perceived membership in particular racial, ethnic, gender, religious, or ability categories. The shadow of Senator Daniel Patrick Moynihan's ascription of "a tangle of pathology" to "the Negro family" in the United States in 1965 serves as a salutary reminder of the hazards of such categorical thinking.

My training as a psychoanalyst causes me to reach to my origins for an explanation of my interest in childhood precarity. As my story illustrates, while precarity can produce foreclosure, sometimes it can also engender new possibility. Extensive hospitalizations during the first two years of my life—so severe that my parents were advised to prepare for my death—caused me to grow up feeling sickly and fragile. My mother's persistent preoccupation with my potential death no doubt contributed to my fragility and caused me to develop a parentifying impulse as I sought to take care of her and ease her worry. On the other hand, my father's insistence on transferring me to another hospital in town, and his successful insistence that I live, undoubtedly infused me with a desire for life. The precarity of my institutionalized hospital stays—where my parents were forbidden to visit often and were commanded to view me through a window because the staff insisted that their in-person visits upset me—were mitigated by one Nurse O'Halloran, who "adopted" me during my hospital stays and undoubtedly provided me with the kind of holding and containment that my fretting parents were forbidden to provide even if they had the capacity to do so.

And then I went to school. Having been planted in a rural community in a "council house," a distinctively red-roofed structure that marked our family as recipients of government aid and members of an underclass, my family and others like us were treated as outsiders. My elementary education was punctuated by exclusion, physical punishment, and unremitting anxiety, and the pedagogical milieu was decidedly *anti-thought*. Secondary schooling required fees and I only managed to earn a space at secondary school by winning a scholarship. In my senior year, after my parents had scraped up enough money for the coach fare, I visited a local university with my class only to be castigated on my return by my guidance counselor for wasting my time as college was not in my future. He brusquely advised me to apply for jobs in banks or the civil service. In seeking to understand my persistence in the face of such negation I am drawn to another childhood memory. When I was just seven years old a visiting school inspector, apparently impressed with my performance, took me aside, and despite asking the inevitable questions to assess my family's economic condition—and hence my life chances—urged me to consider university as part of my future. As surely as my father's insistence on my living, and my mother's lifelong passion for books, this singular intervention by a generous man was formative in my capacity to imagine myself otherwise. As Boris Cyrulnik (2010) would have it, a "silent but deeply meaningful encounter" can be mutative and can help mitigate occlusions and the foreclosure they may portend.

It goes deeper, of course. I grew up in Ireland, a society that had been colonized for perhaps 1,000 years and had suffered through endless wars and conflicts. The Cromwellian War of 1649–1653 was a genocide that eliminated perhaps 40 percent of the indigenous population and led to the enslavement of others. The poorest people, from whom I am descended, suffered a catastrophic famine in 1845–1852 that left a million people dead and that, through death and forced migration, halved the population from 8 million to 4 million within 25 years. The Irish language, which embodied millennia of history in its *bealoideas* (folklore and myth), was practically eliminated through a systematic linguistic and cultural genocide in the nineteenth century, a century which also saw the prohibition of education and the enforcement of sharecropping on the poorest people. What effect did these prohibitions have on the development of subjectivity of succeeding generations? In discussing the struggles of Aboriginal Australians, Judy Atkinson (2002) suggests that *lorelessness*—the absence of lore or cultural patrimony (*coimcne* in Gaelic), is catastrophic to the development of future generations as embodied and located subjects. Davoine and Gaudillière (2004) argue, similarly, that severance of social linkages can lead to intergenerational trauma transmission and potentially even to psychosis in future generations. Ruptures of genealogical filiation and the intentional severance of links to cultural patrimony are inherent in all wars, and inherent, also, in the very mission of colonization. These severances affect not only the approximately 100 million people currently displaced in the world, but also all who are descended from peoples who have suffered such ruptures and dislocations.

In my own family, the consequences for my parents' generation in a now ostensibly liberated Republic of Ireland was unremitting poverty, denial of education, foreclosure of hope, disconnection from cultural patrimony, an unremitting fatalism, and a very Catholic belief that suffering was "the will of God." Above all, there was a silence about these living conditions, a silence that produced a resistance to looking inward, and a pervasive powerlessness. Karima Lazali's (2021) clinical documentation of emotional constriction and indeed wordlessness among indigenous Algerians due to the catastrophic consequences of the colonial conquest in that country is eerily familiar to me from the emotional milieu of my childhood.

My struggle to come to be—what Judith Butler (in Butler and Athanasiou, 2013) calls "the vexed thematics of agency"—has been a struggle with the occlusions and erasures in my family, occlusions that are necessarily embedded in larger ancestral, sociopolitical, and sociohistorical contexts. The invitation of this book for me, therefore, is to illuminate, promote, and help situate subjectivities that are often blotted out for both the child and society. I have long questioned developmental and linear assumptions and hegemonies and sought to re-imagine childhoods otherwise. In contrast to developmental theorists who conceptualize growth uncritically as linear and normative, and in contrast to some psychoanalysts who conceptualize growth as exclusively intrapsychic, acknowledging only the narrowest parameters of maternal or familial influence, I locate my understanding of child subjectivity in sociohistorical circumstance, mediated through familial and cultural socialization. The complexity of entering into subjectivity, of experiencing agency and the possibility of freedom, must be understood in terms in terms of family dynamics, the genealogical inheritances that suffuse the family, and the role the family and societal institutions such as schools have as conduits for ideological and political socialization. The question, then, is how a child can acquire familial and cultural elements of subjectivity without, as André Green put it, being "forbidden to be" (1972).

It would be remiss of me not to acknowledge that the capacity to experience being and agency is a privilege reserved for the world's elite, an elite that often imposes perpetual and even intergenerational precarity on those who are destined to live in states of exception. Of the 100 million people currently displaced or in refugee status, some 36 million are children according to UNICEF. In just one conflict, the war in Yemen, the death toll among children is in excess of 10,000. In the current war in Ukraine, UNICEF estimates that two thirds of all children are either internally displaced or are refugees. Much of this precarity is defined by a world order based on a realpolitik demanded by neoliberal capitalism, struggles over resource allocation, and a colonial legacy that simply values certain categories of children over others, and prizes the appropriation of resources over the self-determination of peoples. What we are dealing with then is not an abstract concept of child precarity, but a political problem of understanding how historical and contemporary geopolitical forces deprive some children permanently of agency and the possibility of freedom.

CAROL'S STATEMENT

I spend about 25 hours a week listening to adolescents speaking about their lives, hearing about the ups and downs, the ins and outs, the highs and lows of this odd, liminal time, this strange seemingly interminable place, this ridiculously precarious identity. The rest of the time I'm listening to grown-ups. Sometimes they are remembering, repeating, and working-through the residues and lost chances, the missed encounters, the regrets and losses of their childhood and adolescences. A near 80-year-old man has been speaking with me for a couple of years now, and he says with a sob, "my God, my mother, she really hated me when I was a little child. How can I bear this?" It is still to be borne, still to be reckoned with, after all these years. Indeed, for much of the time, the childhood precarity I am most often bearing witness to with my patients is the one Lacan referred to as that which is coordinated with the desire and/or rejection of the parents for the child (Lacan, 1975). The precariousness of this parental desire weighs heavily on the one who is the child; the child insofar as they occupy the place in the parental fantasy as a necessary supplement, or its opposite; a problem, an afterthought. When I started my formation as a psychoanalyst almost 25 years ago here in Dublin with Cormac Gallagher, he would encourage us to try to hear in our patients' speech the place they occupy in their parents' desire.

Myself, I was a "love child," an expression which my lovely mother would chastise my sweet father for using in public, denoting as it did, in Ireland in the seventies when I was a little girl, a child born outside of marriage. I wasn't as it happens. But, Ireland in the seventies would not have been smilingly benevolent towards a "love child." What my father meant by this mis-use of a tricky signifier was that I was the result of an act of love, highly desired. My unfortunate much older siblings (14, 18, and 19 years older) were the result of, well, let us say, something more urgent, less loving, and on my mother's part, less welcome. The precarities of my older siblings' childhood were associated with low-income, and poor cramped housing; my parents and their three young children shared a two-room flat in a tenement house divided into many cramped, cold over-populated flats. My mother came to hate my father for his ability to add to this already precarious situation by having his desire for untrammeled sexual expression with her sanctioned by the Church; at one point my mother went to the priest to ask how she could avoid getting pregnant again and was unceremoniously told to go home and "do her duty."

By the time I came along, the three oldest were all grown, the eldest two on scholarships in secondary school, my sister at the convent school, my brothers working at the nearby jam factory and bringing in small incomes, and although my father's income was still low, it was easier all around. Like Michael, we had a council house and although looked down upon when we mentioned where we lived, the street was friendly, safe, and hospitable to our childhood games and goofing around. Although the worst thing I could have done to my mother when I was an adolescent was to "get pregnant," in fact the actually worst thing I did was to move to England (sometimes going to England was the consequence of "getting pregnant" during the time of my adolescence, in the absence of accessible birth control and abortion in the place of my adolescence, Ireland). England, oh England, where anything could happen to an Irish girl in the eighties! After goofing around for another couple of years and picking up work, boys, and drugs from time to time, I eventually wound up studying Psychology at the University of Reading. There I met one of the most influential people of my life, Rex Stainton Rogers; my undergraduate dissertation supervisor, my teacher, my PhD supervisor, my mentor, my friend. Rex saw something in me that I had not seen in myself, and he nurtured my intellect and my passion for learning. He was one of the leading critical thinkers of his generation and a key part of the whole critical psychology and critical developmentalism movement in the UK in the late eighties. With his partner, the great educationalist Wendy Stainton Rogers, he created a "home" for nerdy "orphans"; they fed us (real food), and often housed us (real beds), but also fed us on scholarship, on reading, on the necessity to trouble and challenge prevailing hegemonies, critically examining the warrants and essentializing practices of mainstream psychology. For the first time in my life I understood that childhood was not a given, but a construct, a set of stories, practices, ideological warrants, serving distinct political and economical operations (Stainton Rogers and Stainton Rogers, 1992). Schooled in this critical tradition, me and my fellow "orphans" read Freud with Lacan, with Winnicott, with Derrida, with Baudrillard, with Deleuze and Guattari, with Butler, with Haraway, and with Spivak.

Unsurprisingly, perhaps, Freud had me at the first mention of repression. For it was to Freud I would return after having my own babies and to begin my study of psychoanalysis. And it was to Ireland I would return to pursue my own formation as a psychoanalyst. As an analyst, as an Irish woman, as a mother, I am deeply mindful of how the times of our lives are correlated with the places in our lives, and who we are, and who we may become. I am passionate about working with adolescents for this very reason; where and when, and how we come of age becomes key in our narratives of becoming. The Ireland I came of age in, was a very different Ireland to the one Michael grew up in, to the one my parents grew up in, and very different again to the one in which 21st century Irish adolescents are growing up in. I have written elsewhere about the changes in the social and cultural landscape of Ireland today (Owens, 2020). On the one hand constitutional amendments permitting divorce (1996), same-sex marriage (2015), and abortion (2018) have created grounds for the perception that Ireland is progressive, liberal, or at least catching up with the rest of advanced Western societal models. On the other hand, lingering effects of post-Tiger austerity, an unprecedented housing crisis, the rise of violent drug and gang crimes, new family structures, and inadequate provision for young people suffering poor mental health, together and interdependently, mobilize an array of new social, cultural, and psychical symptoms

The massive changes in the Irish constitution over the past two decades have created the conditions for new family complexes, and new social bonds. It is entirely significant that the various changes to the constitution leading to lawful divorce, same-sex marriage, and abortion in Ireland have entered the constitution as "amendments." Etymologically speaking, the term "amendment" from its early thirteenth century use through to its later sixteenth century expansion includes notions of rectitude: to correct, to set right, to improve, and the fact that each of these amendments was the result of a referendum indicates the push for rectitude and improvement of the Irish socio-familial order by the Irish themselves. But after Lacan, and the research and clinical contributions of psychoanalysts during the past couple of decades, we are also seeing that these changes to the Symbolic order mobilize the invention and experience of new social, cultural, and psychical topographies, and new social, cultural, and psychical effects and symptoms. I believe that the precious chapters in this volume that Michael, Louis, and I have assembled, each and together, testify to how childhoods are themselves both the effects as well as the symptoms of our social order(s). We need to continue to understand childhoods as manifesting precarity, since the subjects of childhood continue to bear the experiences of those manifest precarities in their lived lives.

LOUIS'S STATEMENT

In considering some introductory remarks, one obvious thought occurs to me: Due to asymmetry, much of the writing about and for children is done by adults. As adult selves, we attempt to make sense of children's utterances in what is drawn, verbal, and felt, in order to share our sense in a re-illustration of another's perspective. Some of the writing assembled here is fittingly critical of this practice. Frequently, the stated motivation in sense making is that of aiding child development while also laboring to make the world safer for children. In keeping with basic feelings of empathy and compassion, there is often good in this desire to be of help. However, as clinicians who have resonated with the posts of post-structural and post-colonial if not also of thinking considered post-humanist, we know that what occupies and preoccupies is not one sided in simplicity. Part of professional and adult humility or maturity entails a capacity to situate fault lines or breakdowns in one's own and others development in a manner that affirms the assault of misreadings and promotes the rebirth found in recovery. There, in appreciation of breakdown and recovery as a rhythmic cycles in life (Eigen, 1999), our own histories are awakened. As therapists in clinical encounters, we speak of counter-transference as a patient's cries stimulate our own. In his dedication to *Playing and Reality*, Donald Winnicott (1971/2005) thanks his patients for paying to teach him. Indeed such work entails sitting with profound and challenging states of mind on a daily basis, and in that Winnicott's peer, Wilfred Bion (1981) recommends cultivating a relationship to awe, while adding that appreciation through awe is a state easily lost. With similar concern, Erik Erikson (1976) considers that a capacity for play needs to be integrated into each stage of adult development. Simply, if dissociated, a loss of being, an attitude considered an essence of childhood, leaves us poorer. Freud (1925) considered that educational and clinical work have similar ends, as each works to afford an enrichment that helps a child settle in and find a way to keep on keeping on. In the interminable project of reclaiming and reworking, I am reminded of some moments in my own development that dovetail with my interest in this volume.

While in graduate school, I made the trip uptown to the New York Psychoanalytic Institute to hear Elizabeth Young-Bruehl present a paper where afterwards, another member of the audience asked if she was in fact arguing that pre-Oedipal development mattered. She replied that she had been well understood. I was taken aback by the idea that such a thought still warranted discussion but pressed on because I had been reading her work for my dissertation on essentialism and prejudice, and was hopeful to meet a former student of Hannah Arendt. After the talk I had a chance to speak with her, and as our brief exchange concluded, she pinched my cheek exclaiming, "Keep the faith, kid." Such a sharing in faith is at the core of this book. Keeping or rekindling faith is no simple matter, and for me, associations to Arendt awaken that challenge. There, in keeping with my pinched face, and in the spirit of childhood, I will remain concrete: As an undergraduate, I returned to my parent's home and found a volume of some of Arendt's writing on one of their bookshelves. I was shocked that in travel across the country, what was new to me, was known to them. That volume among many others was lost to Hurricane Katrina, and decades later, the fragmentation and displacement related to that storm is still being felt. In and though its damp walls, New Orleans knows that themes of rebirth are found in jazz (cf., Rothschild, 2021), and this knowledge harmonizes in professing that we find a way to sing "in the gnarled center of ourselves" (Eigen, 2007, p. 92). As many of the chapters in this volume show, we come to our work finding children in search of a song or a capacity from which to sing.

Some years after I found Arendt in my parent's home, on another visit, I ran a 5K race at a local park. It turned out that the cross country team from my former school was volunteering to help out with the organization of that race. As I crossed the finish line, I encountered my old coach who knew me as an asthmatic kid who would in addition to inhalers, require a back brace for scoliosis before graduating high school. He was happy to see me, a former student who around age 12, after flying through the air and briefly blacking out in response to a rather gentle practice block, left American football for track and soccer. Beside an adult marathon medal is a childhood fourth place ribbon that I earned on the track in middle school. I cherish both. I was not a great athlete, but I do remember seeing excitement in my coach's face on the day I found my stride in practice. Then, I too was smiling. Decades later, we were smiling again. As an adult, sport has been a site of rejuvenation, affirming that sometimes, what we need is time, and an engaged witness who is willing to take development seriously. As a mid-life adult, a triathlon coach taught me how to do flip turns in the pool. That process was fun, but also stressful enough as to afford a profound experience of my attachment issues regarding faith in continuity. Writing during the COVID pandemic, I'm grateful to my wife who was finally able to teach me how to play tennis during lockdown. Taken literally and as a metaphor, possibilities present like shards of light in what otherwise could be a dark time.

Sometime in my early 40s while shopping, I came across a pair of tan oxford saddle shoes with reddish soles that struck my fancy. I thought of them as so conservative as to be ironic, and purchased the saddle shoes from a catalog with that sense of enjoyment in mind. Upon seeing these shoes on my feet, a patient reminded me of the distinction between an internal reverie and external translation when he jokingly wondered if I would next arrive in my consulting room wearing a zoot suit. Indeed, there is precarity in simply showing up, and in that I am grateful for good humor. However, my intent in writing about these funny shoes points to another location and subjective experience. Upon first putting these saddle shoes on, I was transported to my five-year-old self. While tying the laces, I suddenly remembered having once owned a much smaller pair. The memory that took hold of me was of my smaller self putting that first pair of saddle shoes on with dress pants and a turtleneck because my mother had told me that I was missing school for an important appointment. I had dressed up for what started as an X-ray of my lungs and quickly turned into a hospital admission for acute asthma. Sitting on the side of my adult bed, remembering tying shoes from my childhood bed there was sadness. As an adult in my now larger shoes, I could grieve the state of mind of a little boy who despite pulmonary dysfunction, did not know that he was sick. This, in part, is what is frightening about precarity. How could one have such distress at such a young age and manage to, like a frog in water heated slowly, to miss or dissociate not only from a song, but from the air needed to express it? Considerations of an as-if mode of functioning come to mind, and I am fortunate and grateful that this level of distress was impossible to maintain. The occasional wearing of these shoes as an adult affords a sense of play that may have been harder to come by in years past. Yet, childhood memories of wrestling, running, and laughing co-occur with those of distress. Indeed, to embrace psychoanalytic work is to recognize complexity while betting on the possibility of transformations that are uncertain and have no clear end point. Awareness of my childhood precarity was not unknown to my adult self. In my own development, I had worked with my feelings around that hospital admission long before purchasing these shoes, and was aware of the significance of my then alienation from my own body beyond the physiological. Good psychological treatment alters becoming an adult and a therapist. Still, the attraction to and experience with those saddle shoes facilitated increasing depths. Some years before this new pair of shoes transported me into a traumatic grief-struck reverie, a massage therapist became agitated while working on me. She said that my breathing was off due to what I heard as her interpretation of unresolved pre-Oedipal issues that she had located near my hip. An experience like that is well worth a trip to California and was thoroughly enriched through my earlier work in psychotherapy. Over time, I have learned that there is still a need to discuss the pre-Oedipal, and that going for a run, swim, or round of tennis feels a bit better if I can remember to use my inhaler and remember to breathe.

A Note on Organization

The reader will already have noticed the appearance of three key signifiers in our individual statements; time, place, identity. These were also the signifiers that beckoned to us again and again as we read through the essays that now form the contents of this book. As such, it seemed to us that certain essays "spoke" more to one of these signifiers than to another and so we grouped them into three sections, but, as time, place, and identity are overdetermined, non-singular, and non-extant with respect to childhood, we have thus rendered each signifier in the plural form. The title of the volume also deals with pluralities: *precarities, childhoods*. What follows via our organization of this material is one distillation among others, which we are aware nonetheless may inflect the reader's parsing of the contents. There were no doubt, countless other ways we could have organized the essays. This one, felt good for all three of us.

So, let's take a look at the first section, which we've called *times* . . .

We lead with Erica Burman's beautiful chapter which finds her noticing objects on or near the streets of Manchester (UK) where she lives and works; discarded and/or lost objects of childhood—mittens, dolls, shoes, school reports, pushchairs—which she photographs and thinks about. Coining the concept "Found Childhood" as illustrative of some of the ways childhood is bound up with notions of temporality and memory (as well as hegemonic ideals about the child and its fragility), Erica goes on to contemplate how the these found objects of childhood mobilize considerations of the temporary matter of childhood, and the places where it meets its cultural correlate of childhood as a state, a biologically marked psychosocial condition. Her arguments allow her to reflect upon Found Art as well as her own key invention of the notion of Child as method, an approach that reads children and childhood as key axes and dynamics (both psychic and material) of the geopolitical (Burman, 2019).

We follow with the co-written piece by Ana Archangelo, Fábio Camargo Bandeira Villela, and Rosiane Cristina dos Santos. Their chapter considers the ways that time operates in the experience of the child as pause, as gap, and as "time-out"; and how the "times" offered by schools function as inimitable resources for a child in times of precarity. In particular they reflect upon and argue sympathetically for an understanding of how schools in Brazil offered to children returning after the pandemic lockdowns the opportunity for pause, but also what they call bridge and intermittence, all scansions of time allowing children to manage time-space, relations with others and "return to digesting what was to be digested."

The third chapter here also asks us to think about school and time. This time though, it is the kind of intervention that can be positioned in a school—understood by Aileen Schloerb—as the creation of a liminal space aimed at allowing a child to work through what is unfathomable (in her history, in her experiences) with a psychoanalytically informed clinician. This remarkable account of a clinical case in the school clinic (run by The City Project, itself an initiative of the local Psychoanalytic Institute), asks us to consider how the installation of a liminal time makes certain things possible in the world of a child.

By contrast, the fourth chapter in this section jointly authored by Carol Owens and Jamieson Webster focuses upon the stretching out of the liminal in adolescence. Looking at adolescence from "both sides now," Carol and Jamieson examine first of all the group of young speaking beings called "tweenies" who jump into adolescence as an apparent flight from the precarities of childhood, and secondly the group of older speaking beings at the recently expanded perimeter of adolescence, who, in their early 20s, appear to tarry in the liminal in an effort to defer entry into the precariousness of adulthood. Carol and Jamieson comment on the effects of neo-liberal ideology and capitalism upon the times and symptoms of adolescence, via the examination of a number of clinical vignettes.

The last chapter in the section we call "times" is also a reflection on the changing time(s) of adolescence especially with regard to the rise of what author Liora Stavchansky calls the "virtual bond," and which she coordinates with the pandemic effects of social distancing together with its correlative experience of the *unheimlich*. Arguing for an interpretation of the adolescent as a foreigner of time, as a "familiar stranger," Liora examines adolescence as a frontier-space for indefinite stays of time, within which the territories of waiting, transition, and boredom dialogue. Far from being the radical anomaly so often conjured up by scientific narratives, Liora situates adolescence as the time par excellence of irruption and rupture, as event in the sense of Badiou.

Our next section is called *places*. The key preposition we are dealing with here is "in"; in "affluent libidinal economies," in "Aotearoa," in "migration," in "nowhereness," in "conspicuous." Each of our authors is profiling a certain type of precarity associated with a certain place, state of existence, or state of inexistence, invisibility, or being(s) hidden.

First up is Anne-Marie Cummins's piece on the emotional labor carried out by children in affluent libidinal economies. Describing what she defines as the hidden subject of the emotional load carried by children on behalf of their parents' happiness, she examines this emotional work and the ways in which (she argues) children have become responsible for that parental happiness. The corresponding parental anxiety which exists as a contingent effect of the failure to produce perfect childhoods for their children is also analyzed.

Chapter 7 in this section is an examination of the state of child and adolescent mental health in Aotearoa in New Zealand. Reflecting on the *pahekeheke* (precariousness) of children's mental wellness against the utopian ideals of recent government aspirations to create the "best place in the world for children and young people," Kaye P. Cederman argues that this utopian vision needs to be critically assessed. Ruminating upon the effects of intergenerational trauma, racism, marginalization and disadvantage on the one hand, and the fragmentation of social bonds and values, degradation of familial roles, hyper-individualism and immersion in digital technology on the other hand, Kaye envisages a long and protracted journey towards that utopia.

Betsy Quintero's chapter 8 looks to the dissociated places and experiences across varied childhoods during several global refugee crises in recent decades. She describes instances and stories from her varied experiences of working in Bilingual Family Literacy programs from as early as the 1980s on the El Paso border, to the 1990s working with recently migrated families and children from Laos, Vietnam, and Somalia. From there, she takes us to a primary school in Northeast London whose population is comprised 97 percent of Asian and Black children, and finally to listening to asylum seekers in Southern California. Her use of story as method is compellingly rich, reminding us that stories make meaning, but also interrogate meaning.

From somewhere, or anywhere, in the cases of the young migrants in Betsy's chapter, we move with our next author in chapter 9 to read about the child and adolescent who withdraws or retreats to *nowhere*. Ionas Sapountzis describes what he calls "states of nowhere-ness" in children and adolescents who experience inner turmoil and negativity that engulfs their lives like a psychic envelope. Children who exist without the validating presence of the other or for whom the other's gaze is deeply threatening try to cope—Ionas theorizes—by not seeing and by not thinking. Such a strategy for survival leaves children without the internal and external links they need, and results in them feeling "nowhere" as subjects. Once there is what Ionas calls a facilitating Other, one who determines to find the nowhere-child, such a child can evolve into a state of somewhere-ness.

The last of the chapters in this section (chapter 10) also deals with a hidden place of childhood precarity, hidden, that is, by inconspicuousness. Katherine Martin deconstructs the notion of the inherently creative child revered as a natural attribute and situated as an emblem of modern Anglo-American youth identity. In her essay she questions how children can embody both the malleable, imaginative individual brimming with creativity and, what she calls the "every-child" posited as a linear development model. This line of critical enquiry leads Katherine to ask where the children identified outside of the inherently creative ideal fit and how our thinking can be encouraged to shift to include these children in histories of childhoods as opposed to viewing such children as an abstraction.

We have called the last section *identities*.

What do we make of children? What do we make of our children? How do we think of their formation/de-formation? How shall we speak of their identities as subjects? How shall we speak about their identities as subjects of fascism, reductionism, authority, and fantasy (literary, parental, sovereign . . .)?

Paula Salvio examines the Italian fascist imaginary via the scenes depicted on Italian colonial postcards (especially those of Aurelio Bertiglia) circulated during the second Italo-Ethiopian war in order to mobilize a critical reading of what she nominates as the weaponization of childhood and childhood innocence. These postcards depicted Italian soldiers and Ethiopians as children but as Paula demonstrates (and illustrates with images) vividly in her chapter, the child, and its apparent innocence served various meanings and purposes; children drawn as cherubs representing Italian soldiers could be read as performing divine fascist duties for Mussolini, whereas Ethiopian children were rendered with racialized facial features resonant of the picaninny, an anti-Black caricature circulating in the United States and British Empire in the nineteenth and early twentieth centuries.

In chapter 12, Louis Rothschild examines two monographs written as letters from fathers to teenage sons as revealing what he calls "a dire press" to break out of a dehumanized frame of dissociative indifference in order to cultivate loving bonds between fathers and sons. The question: What is a father to do to protect his son from other men, or from the horrors of the ideals of masculinity is immanent in both. Louis detects in Coates' *Between the World and Me* and Black's *A Better Man: A (Mostly Serious) Letter to my Son* a common position; a shared sense of the real and imagined dangers their sons face in light of the prevailing ideals of toxic masculinities and masculinist bravado practices under neo-liberalism. Reading the fear that he detects in both monographs as a necrophobia of sorts (the nightmare of present-day terror), Louis compares and contrasts the two monographs and reads their fears and their pessimism with Freud, with Fanon, and within the context of his own embodied, Jewish boyhood, and that of his consulting room.

Chapter 13 is also concerned with what happens to boys, how their identities are developed and shaped, how they become the subjects they later become. Taking her lessons from literature and the psychoanalytic clinic, Marilyn Charles comments extensively on the complexities of young male identity development in A. S. Byatt's *The Children's Book* from her understanding of the theories of Bion, Klein, Winnicott, Lacan, Fonagy, and Levinas. The whole business of the mother and child relationship is examined for what can be made available to the one by the other; suffering denied, destructive fantasmatic entanglements. From there, and by way of contrast with the stories of *The Children's Book* Marilyn goes on to illustrate how in the psychoanalytic clinic, a young man may be given the opportunity of a "different ending," one in which both parent and child can each survive and perhaps finds themselves and one another in the process.

Chapter 14 considers the identity-formation of the Autist per-formed as a gross categorization (by the field of mental health) which author Ben Morsa compares—chillingly—to the process known as fractional distillation. This process by which crude oil is salvaged by its subjection to iterative cycles of intense heat and pressure in a fracking column, also yields mixtures of oils distilled and siphoned off at various levels of purity/impurity. The parallel Ben is making immanent here is between this distillation process and the one he claims is deployed by Applied Behavioral Analysis and Psychoanalysis; regarding autism as a panoply of developmental deficits/gifts and endeavoring to remove/remediate a child's autism as if the two were separate. This view, Ben argues, identifies autistic people as fractional humans, and leads to the fostering of treatment approaches which seek to "rescue" children from the sticky crude of autism by distilling their higher functioning parts.

The final chapter in this section, and in the volume as a whole, is Michael O'Loughlin's. Michael's focus and purpose in his chapter is to consider how the child constructs subjectivity—becomes a subject—through perilous encounters with the parental and sovereign Other. On the one hand, the child faces the potential perils of an encounter with a parent whose—perhaps—unconscious occlusions, foreclosures and misrecognitions can greatly complicate the construction of subjectivity and limit the child's "going on being." On the other hand the child who is indigenous, refugee, orphaned by war or genocide, trafficked for child or sexual labor, othered by caste, class, ethnicity, race, and/or religion, suffering from (after Arfuch) the radical disparity of the gaze, fails to attain the status of the human. From the writings and observations of André Green to those of Maurice Sendak, from Kristeva to Bion, and from his own autobiography (O'Loughlin, 2009), Michael compels us to interrogate precarities of identity and subjectivity in childhood writ both large and small.

It is our hope that the reader will be surprised, stimulated, and intrigued to discover for themselves the treasures which we feel are waiting to be found within the pages of these richly critical accounts and interrogations of the precarities of 21st century childhoods.

REFERENCES

Agamben, G. (2005). *State of exception*. K. Attell (Trans.). University of Chicago Press.

Atkinson, J. (2002). *Trauma trails: Recreating song lines: The transgenerational effects of trauma in Indigenous Australia*. Spinifex Press.

Bion, F. (1981). Memorial Meeting for Dr. Wilfred Bion. *International Review of Psycho-Analysis*, *8*: 3–14.

Burman, E. (2019). *Fanon, education, action: child as method*. Routledge.

Butler, J. and Athanasiou, A. (2013). *Dispossession: The performative in the political*. Polity Press.

Cyrulnik, B. (2010). *The whispering of ghosts: Trauma and resilience*. Other Press.

Davoine, F. and Gaudillière, J-M. (2004). *History beyond trauma: Whereof one cannot speak, thereof one cannot stay silent*. Other Press.

Eigen, M. (2007). *Feeling matters*. Karnac Books.

Eigen, M. (1999). *Toxic nourishment.* Karnac Books.

Erikson, E. H. (1976). Play and actuality. In: J. S. Bruner, A. Jolly, K. Sylva (Eds.), *Play—its role in development and evolution*, pp. 688–704. Basic Books.

Freud, S. (1925). Preface to Aichhorn's *Wayward Youth. S. E., 19*: 271–76. Hogarth.

Green, A. (1972). The dead mother. In *On private madness* (pp. 142–73). International Universities Press.

Lacan, J. (1975). *Conférence à Genéve sur le symptôme*. Translated by R. Grigg. Geneva Lecture on the Symptom. In *Analysis*, (1), Melbourne: Centre for Psychoanalytic Research.

Lazali, K. (2021). *Colonial trauma.* M. W. Smith (Trans.). Polity Press.

O' Loughlin, M. (2009). *The subject of childhood.* New York: Peter Lang Publishing.

Owens, C. (2020). The Torso is Missing: Coming of Age in 21st Century Ireland. In, *Psychoanalysis, Culture & Society*. 25: 376–93.

Rothschild, L. (2021). Breakdown and recovery: Going *Berserk* and other rhythmic concerns. In: K. Fuchsman and K. S. Cohen (Eds.): *Healing, Rebirth and the Work of Michael Eigen: Collected Essays on a Pioneer in Psychoanalysis*, pp. 53–64. Routledge.

Stainton Rogers, R. and Stainton Rogers, W. (1992). *Stories of Childhood: Shifting Agendas of Child Concern*. New York and London: Harvester Wheatsheaf.

Winnicott, D. W. (1971/2005). *Playing and reality.* Routledge.

PART I

Times

Chapter 1

Found Objects of/as Re-Membering Through the Lens of Child as Method

Erica Burman

In this chapter I offer some reflections arising from a project that I have entitled Found Childhood as illustrative of some of the ways childhood is bound up with notions of temporality and memory. Such temporalities and memories are constructed by adults as well as, correspondingly, by and for children. Questions of desire and loss, of possibility and its disavowal, emerge as central in this project: the desire for childhood, the loss of childhood, the possibilities—whether realized or thwarted—of childhood. All these are very much part of the cultural baggage adults in the Global North bring to their understandings of children and childhoods, and which—through the global hegemonic power accorded Northern gendered and class-specific notions reverberate far beyond.

What is less obvious, perhaps, until more closely analyzed, is how unstable or even contradictory the supposedly (at least in mainstream popular discourse) near sacred commitment to children and childhood is. In this sense, it is precarious, and still more so when its under-interrogation arises (to a psychodynamic eye) as a psychic defense of brittle refusal to tolerate questioning. This refusal is, as I have discussed elsewhere (Burman 2019a), a version of the psychoanalyst Octave Mannoni's (2003) analysis of the structure of ideology, where the confrontation with contradiction is overlooked, or, even when fleetingly acknowledged, somehow put aside; that is, disavowed.

Commitments to and about children seem especially subject to this dynamic; for example, that children should be protected and cared for etc., but such claims coexist with the patent, even banal, actuality that a major proportion of the world's children—including those most local to Global Northern commentators—precisely are not. If we add into the mix the kinds of reactions surrounding ideas of what can and cannot be spoken of in the presence of children (sex, sexuality, violence etc.), then it becomes clear (again, from a psychoanalytic perspective) that the fragility attributed to children is a displaced version of the adults' vulnerabilities who, in supposedly protecting children, are instead defending themselves against challenge to their own social investments and commitments. These commitments concern children but also highlight how the matrix of communicational relations to and about children not only reiterates, but even precisely provides, a key crucible of wider culturally sedimented meanings demanding urgent interrogation.

As *The Simpsons'* meme "Won't somebody please think of the children?" parodically highlights, claims to act on behalf of, or for, children function as an unquestionable imperative or social good, that pre-empt rather than prompt critical thinking about what should be thought about children, what children might think (for and about themselves, and about others), and indeed which children are included and excluded from the generalized category of (presumed incapable and in need of protection) childhood. As has often been commented upon, childhood seems to function separately as a moral entity beyond specific, live, embodied, racialized, and classed children, a disjunction which can then be turned against children to assess the extent to which they qualify for the indulgences or privileges of its status (if such indeed exist).

The reflexive empirical project of Found Childhood (Burman, 2019b) offers a different way into these discussions, circumventing overt challenge to but nevertheless subverting hegemonic yet patently partial (in the dual senses of being motivated and incomplete) constructions of children and childhood. As an analysis of material objects discarded during children's trajectories across the over-developed post-industrial and post-imperial city in the Global North where I currently reside, the objects themselves animate stories of desire as well as loss. These objects—large and small, weather booties, mittens, school reports, toy packaging or even rocking horses and pushchairs—are left behind, perhaps dropped accidentally, or discarded willfully—for the intentions giving rise to their presence in public space cannot be known. In both physical and psychodynamic senses, then, such objects may be lost as well as found (by me). They may be part objects, whether rejected or treasured, but we cannot know. Indeed rather than (over)humanize, essentialize or indeed sentimentalize children, or even the adults or others accompanying them, I attend to what remains after. While this focus on space and place could be situated within a posthuman frame, and I hope also an ecological one (see Andreotti 2011; Payne and Wattchow 2009), my focus is less on what can be read from the presence or intra-actions of the objects left behind by child-human-plus (perhaps)-adult assemblages on streets, pavements, hedges or in parks, than on what affective resources come to mind in interpreting these scenes. Rather than visualizing the children, then, I attempt to explore what can be discerned from the records of their traversal across everyday public space. Such space is too often considered as a non-place in Augé's (1995) sense, as devoid of meaning or social significance notwithstanding having been created by (what he calls) supermodernity. Augé's examples of the airport and shopping mall perhaps highlight the fluidity of such categorizations—for these nonplaces appear to have acquired the status of places in their own right. Nevertheless, the ambiguity or instability of meaning generated by these objects found in such settings is fruitful, productive in a psychoanalytic sense, indicating cultural imaginaries that both enact and transgress dominant narratives of childhood, whose projections invite divergent interpellations across national and cultural contexts.

This last point is important since, both when observing everyday practices in different countries and also discussing this project with other childhood scholars across a range of national contexts, it is evident that those different geopolitical and cultural conditions give rise to very different scenes, as well as interpretations of those scenes. Indeed, many countries generate almost no such debris or stuff of childhood to be dropped or left behind. There are likely many intersecting reasons for this, some concerning the ways childhood functions in postindustrial economies, and others around the more biodegradable character of childhood toys, clothing and equipment outside the overdeveloped plastic-centric North. What can be seen here obviously concerns exhibitions or displays of class and cultural positioning, but also community—since colleagues from cultural-national contexts different from my own have pointed out that typically lost clothing or equipment would be quickly returned to the child or family. That is, community relationship comes to the fore.

While this may sound like a romanticist orientalist gaze of a viewer from the Global North (which of course it also is), I should emphasize what my key point is here: while I have seen horrific amounts of debris, rubbish, and mess in many poor, as well as rich, countries, I have seen little obvious childhood-marked "mess." Perhaps Found Childhood, then, might be thought of as a particular lens on the peculiarly English character of individualism that Marilyn Strathern identified in her book *After Nature* (1992), in which family organization and especially (small) numbers of children conceived and reared form a key topic. When showing the archive of photographs to colleagues some years ago, those in my locality responded with a sense of recognition; such scenes had, it seems, become second nature; while across other national-cultural contexts they evoked a sense of abandonment, urban decay, desolation and social alienation.

I will return to alienation and its alternatives later. For now, perhaps these strong responses arose in part from the absence of people, or humans of any age or generational status, in the images generated. This was in part a practical decision to avoid "ethical" complications, or rather not exactly a decision but something I realized after I had started collecting these images, which somehow drew me in and preoccupied me. But the strong sense of haunting, of the shadow of the object (so to speak) seems to resonate widely, albeit in different ways to different viewers. Hence this is a project concerning memory in various ways, both individual and specific as also cultural-historical. I willfully mobilize my own associative capacities, considering these as culturally constructed repositories wrought from my particular (but also shared) class, gendered, cultural, and geopolitically located positioning. The remembrance, therefore, also concerns absences as well as presences; both what is overlooked and what is presumed or normalized. In this chapter I reflect on the process of collecting these images as well as the kinds of narratives prompted by photographs I have taken, photos of discarded material remnants of children's lives. The objects are themselves a kind of pictorial memory, a spatial representation that fixes time in the moment (Barthes, 1981) and so matter that will in time become (more) soiled, battered, weather-beaten, or decomposed, is preserved in this image. Childhood, here, is therefore membered as well as remembered, maintained or even constructed as a material record even as the embodied child(-adult assemblage) has passed on. The temporary matter of childhood, that is childhood as a developmental chronological life stage, as a transient state to be navigated through as best possible on the way to adulthood, here meets its cultural correlate of childhood as a state, a biologically marked psychosocial condition that all humans powerfully resonate to, whatever the retrospectively recalled reality of what our own lived childhoods were like.

In terms of conceptual and procedural reference points, motley conceptual resources inform the hybrid project of Found Childhood. In the next section I outline two key inspirational perspectives, also outlining how I have adapted, appropriated and interpreted them for my own purposes. On the way, I will also indicate how as well as why the archive of Found Childhood images was generated.

FOUND CHILDHOOD AND FOUND ART

Like the art movement—Found Objects—that inspired its name, there is a strong psychoanalytic influence. The Surrealists and Da Daists who insisted on according art object status to everyday objects, even abandoned or apparently natural (unfabricated) items, were making two key interventions.

Firstly, they highlighted how it is the act of recognition, a particular (cultural and classed) gaze that elevates an object to art status, and in particular they were drawing attention to the commercial, marketized as well as classed and cultural specificities structuring such evaluative processes. Hence Found Art is sometimes an everyday object (as in Marchel Duchamp exhibiting a urinal, a *readymade*), or something supposedly "natural"—such as driftwood or other flotsam and jetsam (Waldman and Matisse 2012).

My practice, for Found Childhood, has been to document the object and its context, its surrounding; the better to reflect and consider its complex associations and imbrications. The rationale here (though this is a retrospective construction, I cannot claim to have thought this through when I embarked on this practice), is that I have not touched or removed the objects; doing so would seem to recapitulate the cultural abstraction associated with children and childhood that (in my view) forms a key aspect of how and why both they, and other marginalized groups, are oppressed. The boundary between object and environment literally comes into focus here (particularly as the items sometimes are in the process of disintegrating, and also because I am not a skilled photographer!). But this is of course also a relationship between object and subject. Rather than physically collecting it or bringing the object into a gallery, instead what is documented is my own movement toward, alongside and around the objects that drives the changes of perspective, shape, and size of the object.

The photos, therefore, are a virtual gallery but also a record of my journey, from my perspective clearly—and sometimes (on a rare sunny day in Manchester) my shadow literally appears in the scene too. And since I am now being reflexive, even "confessional," I should declare that this project began incidentally, as a hobby, a personal practice of amusement that has (as yet, anyway!) no institutional or financial support. Over the past decade and more that—on and off—I have been doing this, it has simply been a ruminative if also playful process, without (as theories of play emphasize) instrumental purpose. Just as the speaking process of "free association" forces the analysand to encounter their own inhibitions and become aware of the bodily, affective and interpersonal dynamics structuring what they (cannot) say, so each time my attention is caught by, attracted to, some piece of debris in the street or park as I walk along I am confronted by the arbitrary workings of my thinking and decision processes. Why photograph this, and not that? Why today and not yesterday? Is it because I'm not in such a hurry? Or because I'm feeling in a more expansive, reflective mood? Then, later, other considerations kick in: in what sense is this scene or object "about" children or childhood, and what might this evaluation disclose about wider cultural-political understandings of the place of children and (their) others?

This brings me to a second important point. The practitioners of Found Object art were explicitly influenced by psychoanalysis (Iversen 2004), in particular exploring how placing familiar objects in unfamiliar contexts (and vice versa) disturbs received meanings and interpretations, both of the object and of our relations to these artefacts. Freud's (1919) notion of "the uncanny" concerns how the familiar and unfamiliar are much more closely connected that is typically appreciated; indeed, it is precisely when the familiar unaccountably (until we consider it more closely) morphs into the unfamiliar that we encounter the discomfort, or unsettled affect, that is the uncanny.

While the project of Found Childhood does not aim to provoke psychic disturbance, it certainly tries to invite unsettling of received meanings or assumptions, both around children and childhood and beyond. Given how children and childhood are symbolically and culturally configured within discourses of family, the question of familiarity or unfamiliarity seems particularly apposite. Specifically, here childhood is a considered a public practice, enacted in everyday urban spaces of streets and pavements and, occasionally, alleyways and parks. The point here is that childhood is not, or not only, a property of the family, practiced in interior, domestic (sometimes called personal or private) space, just as the familiar has to be recognized—correspondingly—as sociohistorical and geopolitical. Familiar discourses, that is, discourses of family, suffuse developmental theories of childhood to the neglect of sociopolitical contexts. This is not only the only reason why the child so often functions as an index of abstraction outside culture and community, but it is certainly part of this complex (see Burman 2021; 2015). Rather, returning the child to its context, literally noting its litter or waste as embodied trace, asserts children's lives as lived in specific national-cultural geospatialities and temporalities. These temporalities include not only, for example, the speed at which the child moved (or was moved) through this space, or the interval between when its object was lost and then "found" and photographed (by me), but also multiple other velocities and fixations prompted by the associative meanings set in play.

I have already indicated how the material records of childhood trajectories comprising the archive of Found Childhood clearly reflect the historical period and political affects of their time. One reading of the project of Found Childhood would be to see this as claiming the position of child as consumer (and indeed a burgeoning literature addresses this question, Cook 2013). Clearly children are as much sites and surfaces for the consumer display as they are also agents in commodity accumulation (or, in this case, of loss—since the material documented is what has been lost or surpassed). A political economist might also reflect on what a focus on the makers of the object, rather than the (former) bearers or owners, might bring to this analysis. Indeed the whole question of possessive individualism, to which relations around children are especially subject (Lesnik-Oberstein, 2008), speaks of capitalism and its extraction of surplus value from labor. This line of thinking is one I want to maintain, to keep in mind, as also the key significance of the absent presence of those makers. Goods (as objects are sometimes called) travel far, while the humans who make them are often disallowed, deported, kept out of sight.

Further, the separation between owner and object is not only spatial but also temporal. I have many photos of abandoned pushchairs, some left in parks, others on street corners as if the child who was being carried has outgrown this mode of transport (or, in a more sinister reading, has otherwise departed from that specific state/situation). The objects tell stories of changing, growing bodies. But they also resonate with 21st century eco-anxiety around consumption and decay, and invite commentary upon the ways discourses of childhood function to promote or mitigate such considerations—whether the landfill mountains of disposable nappies or eco futurity of planetary stewardship now personified or projected onto children. While Found Childhood might offer a childhood-focused segue into the recent interest in ruins in social geography (Edensor 2008) as well as mobile methodologies (Payne and Wattchow 2009; Warren 2017), I do not think it suffers from the melancholic affect that sometimes suffuses such work. Perhaps this is because my "attachment" to the objects documented is often fleeting, a momentary noticing and quickly snapped photo—sometimes as I first saw it, then a close-up, then a wider view; while also that they are in the main (what appear to me) very ordinary, typical, scenes. Many of the images in the archive of Found Childhood elicit humor as well as being puzzling and sometimes disturbing.

FOUND CHILDHOOD AS A PRACTICE OF CHILD AS METHOD

As already highlighted, a key feature of Found Childhood, then, is to ward off the separation of childhood from the social. This is a reflection of a wider project of Child as method, an approach that reads children and childhood as key axes and dynamics (both psychic and material) of the geopolitical (Burman 2018, 2019a, b). Children and childhood both exemplify the geopolitical but also enact and contribute in key (economic, ideological, psycho-affective) ways to this. While both Chen's (2010) *Asia as method* and Mezzadra and Nielson's (2013) *Border as Method* had little to say about children, these influential texts in postcolonial studies nevertheless identified some useful analytical strategies that can be re-interpreted or appropriated to address analyses of the relations between childhood and colonialization, including decolonizing childhood. In particular, Chen resists the essentializing binary between east and west (which, like other commentators, he sees as reproducing the very problem it names) by calling instead for an attention to regional, proximal relations. This strategy of "inter-referencing" can be thought of as historical and cultural, as a disinvestment from the orientation towards the colonial center (as in the postcolonial analytic invitation to "provincialize Europe," Chakrabarty 2009). Significantly, Chen insists that the project of decolonization is as much a psychic process of disinvestment from imperial desires as also economic and political matters. Like Asia as method, Child as method is a generative analytical framework to help pose fruitful questions about the meanings and functions of childhood within specific geopolitical dynamics and relations.

Inter-referencing can be thought as contemporaneous (re-)connection or attention to contiguous and adjacent relations (many of which, in the Asian context—as other regions—involve shifting colonial histories and dynamics). But, importing a biopsychoaffective sensibility, this could also be thought of in temporal terms: tropicalizing how memories are invoked by generational orders as well as also crossing generations. This brings us to another psychoanalytic resource.

To any post colonially attuned ear, Freud's famous description of narcissism as evoking "His majesty the baby" signals the heteronormative, gendered, classed and racialized (imperialist) exclusions that are structured into adult investments in children and childhoods. To the primary narcissism of the small child, the infant, is added a secondary form produced by the relation with the symbolic, the social order. This social order is, under current capitalist conditions, racist, (hetero)sexist, colonial, and much more. What might it mean to de-imperialize "His Majesty the Baby"? The phrase, which characterizes Freud's account of narcissism, is said to have been inspired by a painting Freud had seen exhibited at the Royal Academy (since he cited its title in English) depicting two policemen stopping traffic to allow a woman, a nursemaid or nanny, lead a child across a busy road.[1] Here we have a perfect enactment of the classed character of state and family relationships along with capitalism and development, which is taken as the groundwork of the narcissism of the parents attempting to create for their progeny a happier and more materially comfortable childhood than they themselves had experienced. The proxy of the state is, most obviously, the policemen; while the nursemaid or nanny is the proxy of the (rich) parents (especially, under dominant conditions of gendered relations, the mother). These key parties are recruited, mobilized, literally to open the way for the privileged child to cross the road.

Heteropatriarchal authority trumps generational orders such that the (boy) child is the focal point around which the others act. It is a visual representation of how cisgendered reproductive futurism, as Edelman (2004) put it, spans feudal and capitalist relationships, while more recent conceptions of childhood also are subject to such tropes (including environmental movements, Taylor 2013). The colonial archive of the Dutch East Indies discussed by Stoler (2002) comes to mind here. This included images as well as documents many of which record the complex intimacies of servant-child relations, with the children appearing confident, large, entitled, and the women servants—who, Stoler notes, might even be their biological mothers—caring for them but not allowed to touch them as part of the colonial policy to racialize these mixed heritage children, the products of colonial domination, as white(ned) imperial subjects and future leaders.

In *Black Skin, White Masks* Frantz Fanon, the political revolutionary and psychoanalytically informed psychiatrist as well as philosopher, expounds a psychosocial, psychoaffective account of the material basis of subjectivity, through the lens of colonial violence. From this, he explores and evaluates forms of anticolonial resistance. In the famous encounter with the white woman and boychild who hails Fanon as black, and so racializes him as other, blackened and apart, Fanon's account grounds phenomenology in the body, and psychic responses to intersubjective encounters in which the body's racialized characteristics instigate traumatic fixation and rumination. It is a psychoaffective account of the subjective introjection of a toxic social unconscious—in Fanon's terms, sociogeny. In the iconic encounter with these—significant—representatives of the white symbolic order—the mother and (boy) child who put Fanon in his abjected, diminished, and racialized place, Fanon portrays a subject trapped in memory, or association and fantasy. Narrative stops and lists of vilified characteristics attributed to the racialized other replace reflection and argument. In this way, Fanon presents how history as the continuity of lived, embodied experience is suspended, and instead a secondary alienation is installed, cutting off the subject's connection with the body, with the social bond, and with the sense of its own being and agency. This is what oppression does.

Found Childhood sits in the wake of such imperial, racialized capitalist (Bhattacharyya 2018) histories. It discloses the material everyday cultural practices that rely on these legacies and actualities, as part of the assumed order and ordinariness of daily life in the Global North, and in which children and childhood figure in vital—if also ambiguous—ways. It is this in ambiguity that perhaps we may find some possibilities of resistance or alternative vistas.

THE (AN-)ARCHIVE: ON (NARRATING) GLOVES, HATS, TOYS, AND MORE

There are many discussions about archives and their forms and functions. History, as Walter Benjamin (1986) noted, tells the story of its winners. Archives are composed to convey a particular representation of the past, usually to legitimate the past and to interpellate approving future assessments. By contrast, an-archives are said to offer resources for the generation of counter-narratives (Millei et al. 2019; Pogačar 2016; Gökarıksel 2020), that resist political or institutional standardization (Phillips and Willis 2014). I am unsure whether the pictures comprising Found Childhood could be considered archival or an-archival, as they remain quite opaque and invite multiple readings.

Perhaps, drawing on Benjamin again, this time his Arcades project (Benjamin 1999) and other writings (as in his essay on book collecting, Benjamin, 1986), the less formal and technical notion of "collection" suits better, implying less planning or purpose and foregrounding instead more open questions about inclusion and exclusion, and motivation. When I had planned this chapter, I had intended to present some images and offer examples of the narrative associative process this, as I will now call it, collection has generated for and in me. Yet even as space seems to limit this (but see Burman, 2019b), I also wonder if the material literalness of the image might distract from some of the conceptual and interpretive issues already posed here. Yet, dear reader, I feel you are owed some more straightforwardly descriptive account of what it is I am talking about.

The collection is composed of several hundred photos of scenes that have—at some point as I have encountered them on the streets near where I live, or (especially) on my walking route to work—over the past years—piqued my attention and interest as something to do with children and childhood. Typically, these are images of shoes, booties, mittens, hats marked by size or design as being for children, or (remnants) of toys, toyboxes, including balls, hospital sets, toddler tricycles, and baby play stations. Some of the clothing has obviously been picked up by a conscientious passer-by and placed on a gatepost or a hedge, in the hope that the owner will return to retrieve it. Given the very extensive cultural literacies around dolls (e.g., Quintieri 2021), including their functions in racialization (Khawaja et al. 2021), the many whole and parts of dolls are particularly evocative. But other images I think of as referencing "schooled childhood," with pens and pencils scattered on pavements mingling with autumn leaves, and test sheets for SATS (Schools Attainment Tests) and whole or parts of school reports that drift into gutters, or progressively mush into the mud, along with the occasional article of school uniform (usually a tie). There are also well arranged and cared for objects (bicycles, balls, and other larger activity toys) that I think of "curated childhood," visible but guarded and secured behind gates and fences near houses, as well as broken items left in "waste" spaces or corners between buildings, that include two rocking horses, and cots, as well as the various pushchairs and prams already mentioned.

Aside from playing with such crude classifications, and their limits, I have not done any systematic analysis in the sense of quantifying the proportion of debris that I categorize as child vs. adult-oriented, for example. Rather, so far, I have attempted to explore single objects in more depth, considering how each sits in its context (as in the baby or toddler shoe strapped onto cemetery railings, or the decapitated teddy bear in a neglected front garden), discussed in Burman 2019b. That is, I explore what the juxtaposition of images solicits. The images dwell in my mind, but more often as I work with them they bring wider cultural-material connections to the fore that had not been consciously in my mind at the outset. Most (but not all) are not particularly startling, and as with memorywork in general (Haug 2008; Hamm 2021), it is perhaps the very ordinariness that confirms the sense that these childhood practices are the very stuff of our (well, my, anyway) geopolitical living, offering traces of normalized assumptions and exclusionary conditions and effects.

Not least among such normalized assumptions is the privilege structured into my own geopolitics of place and movement: that I can afford to live close enough to be able to walk to my workplace (albeit that is a considerable distance); that I have the security of a job that permits such regularity of (daytime) hours of work; that I have the luxury of stable (indeed owner-occupied) accommodation. I am reminded here of Vassallo's (2020) critique of the psychological concept of emotional regulation, as structured around a classed positioning that presumes stability and predictability of daily life. His argument is that the impulsivity that is seen as a problem in children from poor and marginalized backgrounds may well be adaptive to being able to respond to rapidly changing and precarious circumstances (while the culturally sanctioned qualities of regulation in fact promote compliance and dependence, Vassallo 2013). All such considerations also, of course, qualify the classed spaces I traverse on my journeys, and indeed—to my eyes—the scenes often do appear messy, disorganized, chaotic. But they also speak of another order at play.

BACK TO FANON: OPACITY, LOSS, AND PRECARITY IN FOUND CHILDHOOD

If Found Childhood highlights the provisional and situated character of childhood and, in that sense, both its fragile and retroactively animated aspects, then this also invites the critical (re)construction and evaluation of some of its key conceptual resources. The child that is found is (of course) created from the epistemic and affective resources of the finder, as also inscribed by their cultural-political frames. This returns us to reconsider what else Fanon had to say about childhood, as recalled and renegotiated in our lives.

The principal child associated with Fanon is indeed the whiteboychild who is the agent of, or (depending on your interpretation) cypher for, the racialized and racist symbolic order. But (as I discuss elsewhere), this is not the only "child" to be read in Fanon's writings (Burman 2019c). Fanon in fact opens and ends *Black Skin, White Masks*, with a claim about childhood, this time from the vantage point of the generalized human subject. He writes: "Man's tragedy, Nietzsche said, is that he was once a child" (p. 9), while on the final page he reiterates: "The tragedy of the man is that he was once a child" (p. 165). It appears that he is acknowledging how legacies of earlier fears that remain present or evoked in the adult work to forge our unique, specific "tragedies," in the sense that they continue to affect us and distort or impair our capacities for (political) action. Discussing this, McCall (2015) proposes that it is this fear that ushers in vulnerability to dominant social norms, including the vulnerability to accepting or complying with those norms. This point also speaks to the dominant cultural imaginary of nostalgia structured into the recollection of *having been* a child, a recollection which becomes retrospectively reconfigured as a particularly treasured or creative period of life that came before one's awareness of current constraints and limitations. From Freud we know this to be narcissism and, from Winnicott (1994) we also know that the sentimentality with which many adults approach children, and which infuses dominant representations of childhood, is a form of disengagement that is of no use to them.[2]

Interestingly, the phrase that Fanon initially attributes to Nietzsche appears to have actually originated from Simone de Beauvoir (Adkins 2013). For Beauvoir, this was about gender-specific modes of embodiment and identities while Fanon took this point up in terms of racialization. Common to both projects was the attempt to grapple with what happens to the sense of being thwarted, or displaced, and how this threatens to shape and limit the subjective and political possibilities. As Gordon (1995) notes:

> Beauvoir and Fanon argue that gender and racialization raise problems of a social condition that impedes human development: Man's unfortunate nostalgia

> for childhood makes sense where adulthood is realizable. But what is there to do in a world that offers nothing beyond imposed childhood? As women are not men, what are the consequences of some men being a standard by which other males are denied manhood? How do those latter men relate to women? (p. 32)

In Fanon's account of his encounter, and then confrontation, with the white mother and (boy)child, he portrays the immediate (and insufficient) response on his part via a performance of (verbal) masculinist aggression in the face of the mother's (ineffectual) efforts at appeasement. This is despite the fact that, by the end of the book, Fanon is proposing a very different route for creating a transformed world without racialized categorizations. Still, his temporary resolution (of rage—"I had incisors to test. I was sure they were strong . . . " [p. 81]) remains the one most often cited. Yet—in the light of the claims about childhood framing the book as a whole—a wider question arises: How do we avoid claiming the victim position of suffering an "imposed childhood" (as Gordon puts it)? Discussions of decolonization and de-imperialization (which must include, as I have suggested above, de-imperializing "His Majesty the Baby"), call for the privileged to acknowledge their access to power and in particular not to retreat either into willful ignorance or (white) fragility (Alcoff 2007; Bailey 2007; DiAngelo 2018; Applebaum 2017).

Echoing dominant cultural imaginaries of (ontogenetic as also transnational) development, Fanon's radical humanism, influenced by Sartre and Beauvoir as also Merleau Ponty (Laubscher et al. 2022), mobilized a rather conventionally developmental model of maturity proposed as a question of facing up to political and personal responsibilities. Gordon (1995) explicates the connection with Fanon's existentialist philosophical commitments as follows:

> It is only human beings who are capable of tragedy, and in the unfolding of a tragic version of a particular institutionalized version of human reality is the accountability of human beings who maintain structures that militate against human *being*. In effect, then, Fanon's theory of violence—in both its cathartic and organizing forms—is connected to his critical anthropology in a provocative way: it reveals the implications of a humanity that tries to evade the challenge and responsibility of growing up. (p. 83)

This "maturity" (the dominant developmentalist trope recapitulating linear, masculinist and colonial nuances of "mastery") was something that Fanon knew intimately—in both its partiality and frailty. It was rooted in his own biography, growing up in Martinique where French rule both displaced African matrilineal authority and, even as it offered men patriarchal power, undermined and denied this via the racialized interiorization of colonial relations.

If the fact that Fanon took up Beauvoir's phrase, without acknowledging Beauvoir as its source, is—as Gordon (1995) puts it—suggestive of epistemic sexism (p. 32), it surely also indicates how gender and racialization are interwoven in their construction and elaboration.[3] At the very least this example highlights how resonances of our own specific histories cannot but be at play.

Yet, importantly, Fanon's mobilization of childhood as the source of man's [sic] "tragedy" is also an acknowledgment of the weight of history, rather than advocating for its inevitability. Here he engages a psychoanalytic reading of how biographical, embodied experiences accumulate to shape and distort subjectivity. Having been a child involves experiences of dependency, helplessness, vulnerability, anxiety, and fear, all of which mark us and structure our capacities for subjective relational engagement and agentic capacities in the world.

In his account Fanon mobilizes this precisely to argue that this "tragedy" can be overcome, even though it so powerfully enters into our sense of who are, often in very limiting ways. Indeed Fanon cites a psychoanalyst (Charles Odier) referring to how "the neurotic's fate lies in his own hands" (p. 9). This (psychoanalytically-informed) conviction highlights that psychological obstacles are not insuperable. Indeed, the final reference to "the tragedy of childhood" is preceded by the sentence: "At the beginning of his life a man is always clotted, he is drowned in contingency." Leaving aside, or perhaps notwithstanding, the presumed gendered positioning of the subject as masculine, Fanon's reference to "contingency" as well as "clottedness" fits well with the concerns of this volume. Evocative, if also cryptic, this claim (of being "clotted") mobilizes the sense that not only is the child not yet fully formed as well as being vulnerable, but the clottedness[4] also suggests a kind of opacity or resistance to legibility. As Applebaum (2017) and other feminist antiracist philosophers note, in relation to social justice pedagogies, vulnerability is something to be open to, as a route towards solidarity and critical hope. "Clottedness" is also a substance that has been forged through material intra-active practices of human and more-than-human labor (as in the churning of milk to make clotted cream).

What Fanon, and Child as method, bring to Found Childhood, therefore, is an attention to how memories of and about children and childhood are membered as well as remembered. That is, they are geopolitically inscribed material, embodied and performed histories, in terms of both the material specificity of the moment of collection and of recollection, including the complex and shifting desires of the recaller. In this sense, Found Childhood is forged (in a double sense); not in fact "found" at all—albeit that this recognition may in itself be a kind of "finding." For what emerges from such speculations, and analysis of their processes, is how we both create and deceive ourselves in any commitment to fixedness, completion, or closure.

Instead, as Fanon argues, the child's fate is contingent, not fixed, and forged through socio-material practices. It is this statement the precedes Fanon's call for critical reflexivity as necessary and central both to personal and political transformation.

REFERENCES

Adkins, A. V. (2013). Black/feminist futures: Reading Beauvoir in Black skin, white masks. *South Atlantic Quarterly*, *112*(4): 697–723.

Alcoff, L. M. (2007). Epistemologies of ignorance: Three types. In Sullivan, S., and Tuana, N. (Eds.), *Race and epistemologies of ignorance* (pp. 39–58). Suny Press.

Andreotti, V. (2011). *Actionable Postcolonial Theory in Education*. Palgrave Macmillan.

Applebaum, B. (2017). Comforting discomfort as complicity: White fragility and the pursuit of invulnerability. *Hypatia*, *32*(4): 862–75.

Augé, M. (1995). *Non*-Places: *Introduction to an Anthropology of Supermodernity.* Verso.

Bailey, A. (2007). Strategic ignorance. In S. Sullivan and N. Tuana (Eds.). *Race and epistemologies of ignorance* (pp. 77–94). State University of New York Press.

Barthes, R. (1981). *Camera lucida: Reflections on photography*. Macmillan.

Benjamin, W. (1986). *Illuminations*. Random House.

Benjamin, W. (1999). *The arcades project*. Harvard University Press.

Bhattacharyya, G. (2018). *Rethinking racial capitalism: Questions of reproduction and survival*. Rowman & Littlefield.

Burman, E. (2015). "'It shouldn't happen here': cultural and relational dynamics structured around 'the poor child.'" In L. Hopkins and A. Sriprakash (Eds.), *The 'Poor Child': The cultural politics of education, development and childhood* (pp. 23–42). Routledge.

Burman, E. (2017). *Deconstructing Developmental Psychology.* 3rd Edition. Routledge.

Burman, E. (2018). Child as method: anticolonial implications for educational research. *International Studies in the Sociology of Education* DOI: http://dx.doi.org/10.1080/09620214.2017.1412266.

Burman, E. (2019a). *Fanon, education, action: child as method.* Routledge.

Burman, E. (2019b). Found childhood as a practice of child as method, Children's Geographics, DOI. 10.1080/14733285.2019.1566518.

Burman, E. (2019c). Child as method: implications for decolonising educational research. *International Studies in Sociology of Education*, *28*(1): 4–26.

Burman, E. (2021). *Developments: child, image, nation.* Routledge.

Butz, D. and Cook, N. (2017). The epistemological and ethical value of autophotography for mobilities research in transcultural contexts. *Studies in Social Justice*, *11*(2): 238–74.

Chakrabarty, D. (2009). *Provincializing Europe*. Princeton University Press.

Chen, K. H. (2010). *Asia as method: Toward deimperialization.* Duke University Press.

Cook, D. T. (2013). Taking exception with the child consumer. *Childhood, 20*(4): 423–38.

DiAngelo, R. (2018). *White fragility: Why it's so hard for white people to talk about racism*. Beacon Press.

Edelman, L. (2004). *No future*. Duke University Press.

Edensor, T. (2008). Walking through ruins. In T. Ingold and J. L. Vergunst (Eds.), *Ways of walking: Ethnography and practice on foot* (pp. 123–41). Routledge.

Fanon, F. (1952/1970). *Black skin, white masks* (Translated by C. L. Markmann). London: Paladin.

Fanon, F. (1959/1965). *A Dying Colonialism* (Translated by H. Chevalier). New York: Grove Press.

Fanon, F. (1961/1963). *The Wretched of the Earth.* (Translated by C. Farrington). Penguin.

Freud, S. (1957). On narcissism: An introduction. In *The Standard Edition of the Complete Psychological Works of Sigmund Freud, Volume XIV (1914–1916): On the History of the Psycho-Analytic Movement, Papers on Metapsychology and Other Works* (pp. 67–102).

Freud, S. (1919). The uncanny. In J. Strachey (Ed.) *Standard Edition of the Complete Psychological Works of Sigmund Freud, Vol XVII* (pp. 219–32). Hogarth Press.

Gökarıksel, S. (2020). Beyond transparency: the communist-era secret police archives in postsocialist Eastern Europe. *Archives and Records, 41*(3): 236–53.

Gordon, L. (1995). *Fanon and the crisis of European man*. Psychology Press.

Hamm, R. (Ed.) (2021). *Reader: collective memory-work.* BeltraBooks.

Haug, F. (2008). Memory work. *Australian Feminist Studies, 23*(58): 537–41.

Iversen, M. (2004). Readymade, Found Object, Photograph. *Art Journal,* 63(2): 44–57.

Khawaja, I. Staunæs, D. and Vertelyte, M. (2021). How racial matter comes to matter: memory work, animacy and childhood dolls. Paper presented to the Recollect/Reconnect/Reimagine Conference, Tampere, October.

Laubscher, L., Hook, D. and Desai, M. (Eds.) (2022). *Fanon, phenomenology and psychology.* Routledge.

Lesnik-Oberstein, K. (2008). *On having an own child: Reproductive technologies and the cultural construction of childhood.* Karnac.

Mannoni, O. (2003). I know well, but all the same. In M. A. Rothenberg, D. A. Foster, and S. Žižek (Eds.), *Perversion and the Social Relation* (pp. 68–92), trans. G. M. Goshgarian. Duke University Press. First published in O. Mannoni (1969). *Clefs pour l'imaginaire ou l'Autre Scène*. Seuil.

McCall, C. (2015). Nietzsche, Fanon and the question of fear, unpublished paper presented at the Caribbean Philosophical Association (June).

Mezzadra, S., and Neilson, B. (2013). *Border as Method, or, the Multiplication of Labor*. Duke University Press.

Millei, Z., Silova, I., and Gannon, S. (2019). Thinking through memories of childhood in (post) socialist spaces: ordinary lives in extraordinary times. *Children's Geographies*, 1–14.

Payne, P. G., and Wattchow, B. (2009). Phenomenological Deconstruction, Slow Pedagogy, and the Corporeal Turn in Wild Environmental/Outdoor Education. *Canadian Journal of Environmental Education, 14*(1): 15–32.

Phillips, L. G., and Willis, L. D. (2014). Walking and Talking with Living Texts: Breathing Life against Static Standardization. *English teaching, practice and Critique, 13*(1): 76–94.

Pogačar, M. (2016). *Media Archaeologies, Micro-Archives and Storytelling*. Palgrave Macmillan.

Quintieri, R. (2021). *Dolls, photography and the late Lacan: Doubles beyond the uncanny*. Routledge.

Stoler, A. L. (2002). *Carnal knowledge and imperial power: Race and the intimate in colonial rule*. Berkeley: University of California Press.

Strathern, M. (1992). *After nature: English kinship in the late twentieth century*. Cambridge University Press.

Surkis, J. (2010). Ethics and violence: Simone de Beauvoir, Djamila Boupacha, and the Algerian war. *French Politics, Culture & Society, 28*(2): 38–55.

Taylor, A. (2013). *Reconfiguring the natures of childhood*. Routledge.

Vassallo, S. (2013). Critical pedagogy and neoliberalism: Concerns with teaching self-regulated learning. *Studies in Philosophy and Education, 32*(6): 563–80.

Vassallo, S. (2020). *Neoliberal Selfhood*. Cambridge University Press.

Waldman, D., and Matisse, H. (1992). *Collage, assemblage, and the found object*. Phaidon.

Warren, S. (2017). Pluralising the walking interview: researching (im)mobilities with Muslim women. *Social & Cultural Geography, 18*(6): 786–807.

Winnicott, D. (1994). Hate in the Counter-Transference. *Journal of Psychotherapy Practice and Research 3*(4): 350–56.

NOTES

1. Interestingly there are competing theories about precisely which picture it was that inspired Freud's account, since there is also a French version too.

2. "Sentimentality is useless for parents, as it contains a denial of hate, and sentimentality in a mother is no good at all from the infant's point of view" (Winnicott, 1994, 356).

3. On the other hand, there is some evidence that Beauvoir was inspired politically by Fanon, to the extent that she mobilized her status in support of campaigns to free Algerian women activists. Specifically she wrote publicly in support of a particular campaign for the FLN militant, Djamila Boupacha, against French state violence and

torture as a particular and particularly gendered strategy of brutalization and torture, see Surkis (2010).

4. Clotted, derived from "clot"—a portion of a substance adhering together in a thick nondescript mass (https://www.merriam-webster.com/dictionary/clot).

Chapter 2

"School Is a Time-Out in My Tough Life!"

Use of Pause, Bridge, and Intermittence as Resources for Student Development in School

Ana Archangelo, Fabio Camargo Bandeira Villela, and Rosiane Cristina dos Santos

Having returned to school after the suspension of classes due to the pandemic, William, a Brazilian student, says to his teacher: "School is a time-out in my tough life, school is a pause." What was William trying to say?

We all are aware that intense effort and continuous fixation of the mind on a task or a challenge that is arduous and impossible to complete at a certain moment will possibly result in the exhaustion and eventual damage or collapse of some mental processes or of the psychic apparatus itself. This is why one benefits when able to change focus temporarily, without necessarily activating some more drastic defensive psychic mechanism, to then take up the task or challenge later, with new perspectives or more favorable contexts. Everybody recognizes this interval as a "pause." So, William has faced something so arduous outside school that it has been impossible for him to cope with it on his own. We cannot know what this is precisely, although we can assume that the pandemic and its consequences were among the possible problems. What we do know is that in addition to missing Math, Portuguese, and Science classes, he missed something else during those months of school absence. Furthermore, we also know that he did not find what he was missing elsewhere. So, what was that pause he mentioned?

In reference to Schroder, a character in Amity Gaige's (2013) novel who is interested in the demarcating gaps between thoughts, Alcorn (2013) differentiates the pauses of gaps and silences, stating that pauses "reveal a certain slowness in the digestive process of thought" (Alcorn, 2013, p. ix). Therefore, pause is not only the interval itself, a blank, but also a momentary withdrawal of attention previously focused on highly charged external and internal demands. It gives time and creates mental space for the processing of an emotional experience or a thought in a less hurried way; and in doing so, pause is also the processing itself. It tends to be an important resource for the protection of the psychic apparatus, of which the subject can avail. It is, however, still far from substituting for other defensive mechanisms, such as repression, denial and projective identification. The function of the pause at school has already been briefly highlighted by Winnicott:

> The nursery school has obvious important functions. One such is the provision for a few hours a day of an emotional atmosphere that is not the highly-charged one of the home. This gives the child breathing-space for personal development. (1991, pp. 191–92)

Although the pause indicates the presence of a certain degree of anguish and some risk of obstruction in the activity of thinking, it does not imply very powerful or drastic defensive mechanisms. This permits it, paradoxically, to be constituted as an interstice, in-between one intense experience and another, a free space where dynamic and creative processes can occur (Bion, 2014a/1962). In sum, a pause offers a good atmosphere that contrasts with emotional turbulence and, simultaneously, creates time-space for the turbulence to be dealt with (Bion, 2014d/1976). In this sense, pauses carry in them the potential for development. The central idea of pause is to expand time-space for the "digestive process of thought" to which Alcorn made reference. This is a time-space for the mind to both temporarily deflect some pressure, tension or pain and borrow from another mind to create additional resources to metabolize intense experiences, as Bion (2014a/1962) points out. A phenomenon such as this can be the result of conscious or unconscious intrapsychic factors.

In the first case, we could take, for example, a young child who, experiencing anxiety at not being able to fit a cube into a box with holes of various shapes, temporarily ignores the task, while silently watching another child actively who faces the same difficulty, without giving up the challenge. This child vigorously returns for further attempts to solve the problem. In the second case, that same child struggling with anxiety at not being able to fit the cube, finds an educator who recognizes some degree of suffering and kindly plays with them as if struggling with the same difficulty, with a view to both sharing the attention previously directed towards the child's pain. This adult offers them additional time-space and mental resources to process their experience.

Pauses are of utmost importance for the mind's activity. However, the pandemic led Brazilian children and adolescents to immerse themselves in an unpausable exclusive co-existence with overwhelmed family members, in stressful routines and affective dynamics. In many cases they occurred within precarious and insufficient physical spaces and lacked the opportunity for the creative exchanges usually favored by circulation in such diverse environments as school, for instance. Given the importance of environmental factors for beneficial pauses, we need to explore more deeply the nature of what children and young people, like William, lost during the pandemic, experienced, so we can offer it to all whenever they are in need of it.

We argue that, among other things, their loss can be considered in terms of time-space for the "digestive process" mentioned earlier, that is, loss of pauses, which were jeopardized or made unavailable by the absence of school. Additionally, we believe that pause is not the only loss. School also provides what we call bridge and intermittence, which, alongside pause, play an important role in modulating the means by which students relate to others and by which they cope with their own minds and move towards independence. We also advocate that pause, bridge and intermittence offered by school are particularly imperative for the most vulnerable, poor and stigmatized populations for whom supportive mechanisms or institutions outside family and school tend to be rare, if not absent entirely.

THE FOUR TYPES OF PAUSES WILLIAM MISSED DURING THE PANDEMIC

One of the pauses may be described as time-space to tolerate some extreme frustration, to be momentarily distanced from intense anxieties that obstruct the flow of thinking, associations, and actions. Extreme frustration tends to color the objects[1] with a more menacing face and to trigger more omnipotent mechanisms to deal with them. Who has never seen a student rejecting their teacher's help by saying "I know it; I don't need your help!" and immediately giving up their task? This is the point when a pause would be useful: it would momentarily separate the subject from the internal threatening object (the task they have failed to accomplish), and help them to avoid permanent withdrawal from thinking, from the processing of an emotional experience or a meaningful action. The pause decants the object and the anxiety, providing something analogous to what Bion (2014d/1976, p. 116) describes as part of "an artificial splitting of the total situation into various elements." By doing so, further mental effort can be made to cope with the experience and the subject is able to integrate what was artificially and temporarily separated—"an ordering of these elements, and a reintegration to bring these perceptions together again" (Bion, 2014d/1976, p. 116).

A second category of pause is that which offers time-space to marshal existing, more integrated internal resources. It comes as no surprise when we see students who give up on a task without even trying, claiming not to know how to do it. It is also not uncommon to find out that, if calmly asked about the activity, step by step, students demonstrate that they have the resources to finish it successfully. In cases like this, the pause is time-space for the student to recognize if they have the resources, and what these are, to deal with the pressure which prevents them from activating such resources at that determined moment. We are aware that, in some situations, there are no useful resources available. However, in many others, the resources are there, and yet not available, solely due to the lack of time-space to deal with anxiety and to harness these resources.

When internal resources are unavailable, a third kind of pause is the time-space for the subject to identify external resources in the environment, to search for them as a source of aid. External resources can refer to the adult mind of the Other, to what Bion (2014a/1962) calls the alpha function of this Other, which might be available and on which they might be able to count for the processing of anxiety and of thinking.

Finally, pause can be time-space to distance oneself from the state of confusion. There are real situations of major destructivity that demand time-space for the subject to separate themselves, including physically, from violent, mindless relationships, which provoke distress resulting in an inability to think, which Bion called *attacks on linking* (Bion, 2014c/1967). Family violence is an example of this. Social exclusion and societal symbolic violence are others. Humiliation, competitiveness, harassment, and physical abuse are generally crossed by power relations and often come in emotionally charged relationships. The aggressors tend to be loved ones or those by whom the subject would like to be recognized and/or loved, which trigger what Meltzer calls a "confluence of good and bad" (1989, p. 61), in such a way as to create a state of confusion. The subject is stuck between the need for subservience to and transgression against the "other." The pause can allow a temporary distancing from the state of confusion and time-space for a later search for and co-existence with stable others that are endowed with goodness.

In short, pauses promote time-space for students to be able to mobilize the necessary conditions to expand their capacity to imagine and create ways of thinking, feeling, acting, relating and ultimately of being. However, if the necessary pause is not provided, we may see a mere withdrawal being installed, that is, an apparent pause, but without the "digestive process." In this case, the student becomes paralyzed in a state of non-thinking, non-digesting, or what Bion (2014c/1967) calls *no K*, a condition more associated with evasion than modification, learning and growth. Therefore, one must ask whether during the pandemic, and in the absence of time-space provided by school or other social resources, have young people become more vulnerable to risks of being more evasive, or even of making use of more drastic psychic processes?

If a person places themselves in pause, the environment, including school, can and must offer itself as a resource to wait for the person's time-space to have other experiences, marshal resources and return to digesting what was to be digested. School and other social resources must be a companion in this process and offer themselves as emotional support and thoughtful repertoire, and in doing so they function as a bridge.

DOES SCHOOL HAVE SOMETHING TO DO WITH WILLIAM'S NON-SCHOOL-RELATED TOUGH LIFE?

Without necessarily being aware of this bridge-function, the teacher—with pedagogical resources and, above all, with their own internal resources, that is, their own personality—often contributes to the elaboration of some students' internal conflicts.

In general, it is not a matter of specific teacher intervention, nor of being outside the context of didactic activities in the classroom, although this may occur. On the contrary, the student extracts important elements to rethink and elaborate their non-school-related conflicts using what is offered by the content, the activity, and the personality of the teacher. Planned activities which expand the possibilities for the student to perceive themselves as part of historical and social contexts, which instigate the capacity to problematize human production and the destinies designed by a history marked by domination and subjection, tend to promote internal resources that can come to be transferred from the school and academic environment to the ambit of personal and affective experiences.

In addition, by their attitudes, by their way of teaching and conducting activities, by their availability to talk and to be attuned to students, the teacher represents models of adult relatedness and these models favor experimentation with new ways of approaching and confronting conflicts. It is from this perspective that we define bridge as the non-direct connecting link between the child or adolescent and whatever they consider to be family or society, by means of which conflictive non-school situations gain space for elaboration.

In the bridge, the environment is deliberately active, because it offers resources which, indirectly, will be of use for new forms of experimentation in emotional life also outside school. Some of these resources refer to what

Bion (2014a/1962) calls alpha function: the capacity to mentally process sensory elements of experience. On offering alpha function and promoting a student-teacher relation in which its development is possible, the school is a bridge because it reinforces the good, understanding object, and re-guarantees its existence when it appears fragile or threatened by attacks proffered by bad objects.

The existence and survival of a good and stable object allows for a richer relationship with reality, less alienated regarding the historicity of the self and others. This is the path to more tranquil relationships and to a return to non-school experience with less threatening bases, as this makes the student feel encouraged to grow and not to feel threatened when trying to make contact with what motivated the pause. There are at least three types of bridge.

First, school can be a bridge when it provides space for a necessary counterpoint to the culture of the family or the prejudices disseminated socially. The counterpoint is fundamental for students to deal with tensions, rivalry, jealousy, love and hatred between them and their parents and siblings, as it provides a diversity of others (several teachers, friends of different ages, school staff), new models of triangular relations and of authority, and spaces for elaborating them outside the family environment (Winnicott, 1991, p. 191). School can also be a counterpoint when and if it problematizes hegemonic discourses, narratives and mentalities (Villela and Archangelo, 2014) forged in a white, socially excluding Eurocentric culture, and when it confronts meritocratic, racist, homophobic, transphobic behavior. In other words, the bridge built by counterpoint gives voice to minorities or discriminated groups and provides an environment that helps to overcome what De Decca (1986) called the "silence of the beaten."

Second, school also builds a bridge by stimulating encounters with adult minds. This is about thinking of school as a space to meet adults who can recognize "how often situations of unprocessed loss can be the cause of disruption in the life of the individual" (Maltby, 2008, quoted in O'Loughlin, 2020, p. 48) and that the unprocessed losses are not only of an individual order, but are often collective, of groups that historically suffer and inherit losses related to gender, ethnicity, social class, educational level and job, among others. On doing this, adults can help to create "emotionally facilitative spaces in which children can grow to [. . .] 'imagine themselves otherwise'" (O'Loughlin, 2013, p. 28); and engage in "healing work" (O'Loughlin, 2019, p. 213), which "creates a sense of social cohesion, community and belonging and creates a space where children can narrate their experiences and process their feelings" (O'Loughlin, 2020, p. 49).

Finally, a bridge may also be provided by the offer of an other endowed with authority, not badness. Domestic or social violence against children and adolescents tends to be understood by the actors as something used as an educative strategy, as a resolution for problems provoked by the victims (Elsen, Próspero, Sanches, Floriano, and Sgrott, 2011). Caretakers endowed with the function of protecting and raising gain a dubious quality of aggression and threat, which makes it difficult for the child and adolescent to constitute a good and understanding internal object, as well as apprehending the distinction between one who cares and one who hurts. It is common for the adolescent to state that the aggression suffered is for their "own good," the same statement parents and others involved in child-rearing usually allege when practicing what Miller (2002) calls "poisonous pedagogy," that is, humiliation and silencing the pain, which leads children to the destruction of their vitality. Where there is violence, the affective bases are confused with destructivity. At school, the bridge can offer experiences with rich, good others, in which learning is not confused with competitiveness or rivalry; dissent and generational divergence are not confused with authorization for retaliation; existential questionings and physical changes are not subjected to moralizing, normalizing scrutiny. The rich and good others are endowed with authority that is not confused with badness, in such a way as to guarantee some hope in the confluence of authority and protection, without the contamination of cruelty and destructivity.

An example of how to do or not to do that in schools follows. A teacher organizes a learning dynamic for the students where they have to be in groups and role-play characters who approach and discuss important subjects chosen by them. They have to study extra material, prepare their presentation and present it to their classmates and families. Students are deeply involved in reading and writing autonomously, in cooperating with each other, in preparing oral presentations. School is providing them with care, cooperative relationships, and support towards intellectual independence. They are having a very exciting and meaningful experience, with good objects—with the teacher, with knowledge and with classmates. But everything can turn upside down if the purpose is to compete and see which group is the best. Classmates who have worked as partners, suddenly have to work as rivals. Knowledge which has been shared is now to be kept in secret. What should have been an enriching and good time is converted into a time for anxiety, for pressure. Only five of them have the right to feel like winners. Meanwhile, thirty-five out of forty students are suddenly considered losers. And the authority is now in charge of delivering this verdict, which may be discouraging and occasionally damaging for many. Bridges can be easily built when one of the school's main objectives is to be inclusive, to welcome and favor a field for the signification and re-signification of the student's experiences. That is what we call meaningful school. A school strongly based on discipline, meritocracy, and competitiveness will find it much more difficult to offer reasonable bridges to students.

The bridge can be experienced vividly and silently by the student, with mental work that can even be unconscious, provided only by new, healthy relations offered at school, be it through knowledge, people who transmit it, or those who give support to the functioning of the institution. The bridge needs to be significant, but not necessarily directive: it places the subject and object in a commensal relationship (Bion, 2014a/1962, p. 357), where one stimulates and enriches the other, and from which the subject-object pair produces something new and beneficial to both and to the group. As Cyrulnik (2010) points out, by telling the moving story of the unspoken but powerful relationship between a working boy and his teacher, "the [. . .] effect occurred thanks to a mute but deeply meaningful encounter in which the man and the boy became important to each other" (p. 63). The relationship expands the resources of the pair to think, feel and act. Analogous to the process of pollination, the pair cannot have absolute control over what is to be fertilized or how far the seeds will be carried by the wind. However, they experience that something alive is produced creatively from this expansion.

The bridge allows for the construction of another level for the student's experience that refers to family relations, another level of awareness of their social place, their historicity and the transgenerationality of their personal experience, as well as the possibilities and limits for the transformation of the status quo.

If it is correct to affirm the important role that the teacher and school can play in the life of the student on offering this bridge, then it is possible to presume that, inversely, the suspension of contact between the student, the school, and the teachers, for example, due to the pandemic, but also due to exclusion from or dropping out of school, has most likely interfered in the formerly possible paths to the elaboration of family conflicts and those experienced collectively. It is from this hypothesis that we thus formulate the concept of intermittence.

INTERMITTENCE: A SPECIAL PROTECTION AGAINST EXCESSIVE ADHESIVENESS AND AGGRESSIVE ATTACKS

Intermittence supposes a period of phatic suspension of an encounter, or co-existence, or a relationship in the encounter. The conjecture that the phenomenon of intermittence has clinical importance resulted from a curious observation in a school toy library whose function was therapeutic. Given that the children helped there were, in Winnicott's (2000d) terms, living in deprived conditions, many of them presenting unequivocal and accentuated anti-social behavior directed towards classmates and the teacher, it was to be expected that they would present some destructive or threatening behavior in relation to those responsible for the work. Surprisingly, however, almost none of the students presented challenging, aggressive or hostile behavior in relation to the adult in attendance. On the contrary, the students soon demonstrated a bond with the adult, and sought to maintain a tender, collaborative relationship, even when aware that they could freely express feelings including even their anger, disappointment or destructive impulses (Villela and Hosokawa, 2012).

Something paradoxical took place: similar to what Winnicott observed in the child's adaptation moments in hostels or substitute family homes, the children directed their anger and challenging behavior towards the teacher and classmates. However, nothing like this manifested itself in the toy library. The hypothesis put forward, corroborated over time, was that, in contrast with daily contact—and in this sense, continuous—between the student and teacher, the experience in the toy library had introduced intermittence.

The instance related above makes it clear that the temporal aspect is crucial for the understanding of what went on. We can differentiate a continuous phenomenon (daily classes) from an intermittent one (weekly sessions). Our hypothesis is that the children experienced care and affection as continuous in the former and as discontinuous in the latter. Hence, the stability of the object-relation varied accordingly. In the former, the object-teacher was permanent, stable, and capable of reassuring the children of his or her strength and capacity to tolerate aggressiveness by their constancy and real presence. It was a kind of "No matter what, I'll be here for you tomorrow!" On the other hand, in the latter, the contact with the person who had become relevant for the child in their search for care and affection was suspended. Because of its discontinuity, the permanence and integrity of the external object strongly depended on the child's own efforts to keep the relationship alive and stable for a relatively long period while waiting for the next session. An aggressive or destructive attack on the other during the sessions would probably have produced a depreciated or hateful internal object ("I hate him/her"), and occasionally persecutory thoughts ("He/she hates me"), with which the child would need to deal in the absence of the person.

In this scenario, there are two determining factors. First, there is the internal condition of the child to conceive certain non-continuous events as intermittent or not over time. This is close to what Winnicott and Britton (2000/1947) point out on the efficacy of the transitional object in the absence of the mother: it depends on the moment of the child's development and on the contingencies given during separation.

Second, there is how much the child is able to contain part of their aggressive and destructive impulses against the object. The capacity to keep both the other and the image of the good and vitalized internal object alive makes it possible for the child to benefit from it by transiting in other activities, thoughts, and emotional experiences, even in the absence of the person. On not feeling the integrity or existence of the object at risk, they can be forgotten and remembered (Bion, 2014a/1962) and kept internally safe. Meanwhile, the child can cope with destructive impulses against them (Klein, 1997; Meltzer, 1989) and look forward to re-encountering them. It seems to us that this dynamic prevents destructive impulses from being presented intensely in periodic meetings, as was expected previously.

Intermittence is thus an interesting phenomenon and material for further investigation, for it tends to promote an object-relation in which aggressiveness and destructivity appear in an attenuated and symbolized form. At the same time, more destructive content does not fail to be present and elaborated, albeit gradually, throughout the development of the learning and relationship activities, allowing an evident evolution in the psychic condition and in the emotional development of the subject.

The manifestation of destructivity is part of any relationship and something that deserves to be examined and unfolded. However, it is difficult for any professional to work with a person who manifests intense aggressive and destructive feelings towards them. In schools, destructive attitudes usually wreck the teacher's connection with the student, which challenges the potentiality of the teacher-student relationship. If intermittence introduces a facilitative element in this challenge, it raises the importance of thinking about its applicability in wider school or non-school services.

As for temporal limits, intermittence lies in the interval between an initial point at which the subject stops perceiving their experience with the other as continuous, and a limit point, from which trust in the alternation between presence and absence of the other is replaced by the sensation of rupture, or, in a more drastic sense, of abandonment.

Winnicott (2000b) repeatedly discusses what we call here a limit point, which corresponds to the threshold of the capacity of the child to bear the absence of the mother or other object who is cherished or central in their life. We know from Winnicott's studies that the baby depends on their mother deeply and generally needs and wants to stay with her. However, how tolerable and beneficial would it be, theoretically speaking, for them to remain exclusively with her, with no pauses or interruptions? If such a question seems irrelevant when applied to a baby or very small child, what if it is considered for older children and adolescents?

What psychic consequences can we infer from the hypothesis of a scenario of exclusive relationship, without pauses or bridges, of a young person with their mother or caregiver? And complementarily, how beneficial, pleasurable, and salutary for such a relationship could a momentary suspension of this relationship be, with the possibility of new experiences, contact with distinct people, unusual subjects and problems?

The unfoldings of the pandemic, of isolation and temporary suspension of face-to-face lessons have obliged us to think that the intermittence of relationships occupies a place of distinction in the good emotional development of the child and adolescent.

In the case of the toy library, for example, the children bore the separation well during intervals of a week. Nevertheless, when the interval between sessions exceeded this time, what became evident were manifestations of insecurity and rage, the refusal to have contact with the adult, even when the child themselves, in the case of illness for example, or school, in the case of vacation, had motivated the more prolonged separation.

We can thus confirm that intermittence occupies a place of distinction in good emotional development. It promotes a special condition that protects the object-relation from excessive adhesiveness and from excessively aggressive attacks, which facilitates sublimation. In what Meltzer (1989) considers to be Klein's terms, these are mental activities intended "to prevent the damage of assault on the objects, or reverse the damage" (p. 70). Furthermore, one can affirm that intermittence avoids the risk of what Bion calls a "parasitic relationship" being established (Bion, 2014a/1962, p. 357) between the subject and object, in which one extracts so much from the other that the former "is left without substance" (Bion, 2014b/1966, p. 28). However, this is possible only when such intermittence is endowed with predictability and a time period suited to the subject.

SOME FINAL CONSIDERATIONS

Satisfactory development begins with the care the child receives from their primary caretakers, which they will probably recognize at some moment in their life and for which, eventually (but not necessarily), they will be grateful.

Family relationships are both intense and impossible to be fully realized. Thus, external mediations—direct or indirect, intentional or fortuitous, conscious or unconscious—introduce pause and bridge to conflicts, which promotes time-space for the expansion of the emotional and interpersonal life of the child, as well as the creative re-encounter with their love objects. Such a re-encounter is not only a motive of joy for the child; it re-ensures the possibility of preserving the loved and esteemed other as a good, stable internal object. The good, stable other does not impose the oppressive need for physical inseparability as a condition of security in relation to the love object, an imposition which, according to Winnicott (2000c), so deeply affects children and adults marked by a strongly depressive condition.

The phenomena of pause, bridge, and intermittence, for the most part favored or provided by the environment, act in a complementary, less definitive way than the classic defense mechanisms utilized to avoid displeasure or to maintain the integrity of the ego. Even so, such phenomena seem to guarantee important aspects for healthy coexistence inside the family, in extended groups and at school. In their absence, one can verify an effect of saturation in relationships and of anxiety that is hardly individually processed. This can result in emotional difficulties that set off and intensify the classic defense mechanisms discussed by Freud (1915, 1925).

The temporary deprivation of school launched many of the students into excessively, intensively continuous, un-pausable and unbridgeable relationships with their family. For those who were able to feel the absence of school and other social environments as intermittence, keeping the object of past experience alive and vitalized, the return to classes, even in hybrid format (face-to-face and online) was marked by the hope for new pauses, bridges and intermittence. However, many of those who went over the limit point of intermittence, who experienced the period of suspension of activities as abandonment or as the death of the internal object, did not return to school. We cannot as yet measure with precision whether there will be effective public policies to cause them to return. But we suspect that they will be insufficient—perhaps deliberately.

Just as the evacuation of children from London and the large industrial centers in England shed light on the phenomenon of deprivation and on correlated anti-social behaviors, social isolation during the pandemic will allow us to examine the psychic consequences of the absence of school in Brazilian society, a society that is particularly unequal in the provision of essential services and opportunities for young people from families with low-income or low levels of education.

Although historically omnipresent, inequality has become more visible in the pandemic and has revealed another facet of marginalization of children and adolescents from socially vulnerable families. It is impossible to ignore that the absence of pause, bridge and intermittence has had a different impact on children and adolescents who have not had the same resources during this period. Inequality has infiltrated deeply and widely in socially excluded environments in terms of access to digital platforms, school activity plans, housing, overwork, and unemployment. Hence, it has also profoundly affected the care for those who have become sick, and even the right to mourn those who have died.

Pause, bridge and intermittence were certainly missed by everyone. However, unequal conditions of confinement in physical and emotional environments oblige us to continue thinking about the psychic and social effects of their absence. Above all, it is necessary to investigate the psychic effects of exceeding the limit point of intermittence, after which the subject, deprived of living, vitalized objects, begins to co-exist with dead internal objects, at the same time being launched unprotected into a historically unequal, violent, and increasingly deadly society for poor and marginalized groups.

In place of a time-space for working through conflictive aspects of primary relationships, or a time-space for transition between family experience and the adult world of work, the fate of the young in these conditions will be left to luck. This is a problem for which we will need to find a solution.

REFERENCES

Alcorn Jr., M. W. (2013). *Resistance to Learning: Overcoming the Desire-Not-To-Know in Classroom.* Palgrave.

Bion, W. R. (2014a). Learning from experience. In *The Complete Works of W. R. Bion* (pp. 247–366). Karnac. (Originally published in 1962.)

Bion, W. R. (2014b). Catastrophic Change. In *The Complete Works of W. R. Bion* (pp. 19–44). Karnac. (Originally published in 1966.)

Bion, W. R. (2014c). Second Thoughts. In *The Complete Works of W. R. Bion* (pp. 45–202). Karnac. (Originally published in 1967.)

Bion, W. R. (2014d). Emotional turbulence. In *The Complete Works of W. R. Bion*. Karnac (pp. 113–22). (Originally published in 1976.)

Cyrulnik, B. (2010). *The whispering of ghosts: trauma and resilience.* Other Press.

De Decca, E. (1986). *1930: O Silêncio dos Vencidos.* [The silence of the Beaten]. Brasiliense.

Elsen, I., Próspero, E. N. S., Sanches, E. N., Floriano, C. J., and Sgrott, B. C. (2011). Escola: Um espaço de revelação da violência doméstica contra crianças e adolescentes. [The school as a revealing space of home violence against children and teenagers]. *Psicol. Argum*, *29*(66): 303–14.

Freud, S. (1953a). Repression. In *The Standard Edition of the Complete Psychological Works of Sigmund Freud, vol XIV* (1914–1916): *On the History of the Psycho Analytic Movement, Papers on Metapsychology, and Other Works* (pp. 141–58). The Hogarth Press. (Originally published in 1915.)

Freud, S. (1953b). Negation. In *The Standard Edition of the Complete Psychological Works of Sigmund Freud, vol XIX (1923–1925): The Ego and The Id and Other Works* (pp. 235–43). The Hogarth Press. (Originally published in 1925.)

Gaige, A. (2013). *Schroder: A Novel.* Hachett Book Group.

Hinshelwood, R. D. (1991). *A Dictionary of Kleinian Thought*. Aranson.

Klein, M. (1997). *Envy and Gratitude—and Other Works.* Vintage Books.

Meltzer, D. (1989). *O desenvolvimento kleiniano II*: desenvolvimento clínico de Melanie Klein. [*The Kleinian Development*—Part II: Richard Week by Week: Melanie Klein's Narrative of a Child Analysis]. Escuta.

Miller, A. (2002). *For your own good: hidden cruelty in child-rearing and the roots of violence.* Ferrar, Straus and Giroux.

O'Loughlin, M. (2013). The uses of psychoanalysis. In M. O'Loughlin (Ed.), *The uses of psychoanalysis in working with children's emotional lives* (pp. 27–46). Jason Aronson.

O'Loughlin, M. (2019). Engaging children in healing work. In M. Charles and J. Bellinson (Eds.), *The importance of play in early childhood education: Building lives* (pp. 213–27). Rowman & Littlefield.

O'Loughlin, M. (2020). Preparing for a Return to School After Covid 19: Creating Emotionally Healing Spaces for Children in Brazilian Schools. *Linha Mestra, 41*.

Villela, F. C. B., and Archangelo, A. (2014). *Fundamentos da escola significativa.* [Fundamentals of meaningful school] (4th ed). Loyola.

Villela, F. C. B., and Hosokawa, R. R. (2012). Brinquedoteca escolar e intervenções lúdicas destinadas a alunos com dificuldades emocionais. [The School Playroom and Ludic Interventions Geared Towards Students With Emotional Difficulties]. In S. Z. de Pinho and J. B. B. de Oliveira (Org.). *Núcleos de ensino da UNESP: artigos 2011 - Tecnologias da informação e comunicação e material pedagógico* (vol. 3, p. 175–96). Cultura Acadêmica.

Winnicott, D. W. (1991). *The child, the family and the outside world.* Penguin. (Originally published in 1957.)

Winnicott, D. W. (2000a). Evacuation of small children. In D. W. Winnicott. *Deprivation and delinquency.* Routledge. (Originally published in 1939–1940.)

Winnicott, D. W. (2000b). The return of the evacuated child. In D. W. Winnicott. *Deprivation and delinquency.* Routledge. (Originally published in 1945.)

Winnicott, D. W. (2000c). Some psychological aspects of juvenile delinquency. In D. W. Winnicott. *Deprivation and delinquency.* Routledge. (Originally published in 1946.)

Winnicott, D. W. (2000d) Children's hostels in war and peace. In: D. W. Winnicott. *Deprivation and delinquency.* Routledge. (Originally published in 1948.)

Winnicott, D. W., and Britton, C. (2000). Residential management as treatment for difficult children. In D. W. Winnicott. *Deprivation and delinquency.* Routledge. (Originally published in 1947).

NOTE

1. The term "object" is employed here as a component in the mental representation tinged with good or bad impulses and with which the self establishes an unconscious relationship. There are object-relations from birth and they may evoke intense love and gratitude or hatred and envy (Hinshelwood, 1991).

Chapter 3

Making Space for the Unfathomable

Liminality in Inner City Schools

Aileen Schloerb

AN ILLUSTRATION OF THE PREDICAMENT

The Vietnamese-American poet Ocean Vuong tells the story (Vuong, 2016) of how as a "poor," small, fourth grade ESL student of color he got into trouble for his imagination. Having taken to hiding in the elementary school library during recess so as to avoid getting beaten up on the playground, he began listening to "Great American Speeches" on a tape player—powerful words that set aflame his own agile imagination. This experience eventually risked its way into his invention of a poem, *If a Boy Could Dream*, that he ventured to show a teacher who immediately accused him of plagiarism and dumped over his desk in search of the "original." Standing amidst its contents now strewn across the floor, Ocean was terrified but also realized what his teacher could not perceive or even imagine: that this young mind and body possessed something "unfathomable"—a power that could make an adult afraid to the point of "losing it."

The socio-cultural lenses through which "poor" children of color are usually perceived in our country blind us to their "unfathomable" potential, living as they do in certain neighborhoods where material resources are low and structural violence is high. Adjectives most frequently used to describe these children emphasize "lack" rather than "limitless possibility." But contrary to what such terms as "disadvantaged," "underprivileged," "low-performing," and "under-resourced" suggest or what can be observed on the outside, *all* children contain unfathomable creative potential on the inside whose boundlessness is rarely perceived. It is less threatening for adults to imagine children as less developed versions of themselves rather than as forces of power in their own right. Yet every child is born with the capacity to imagine and see beyond what society has constructed as a "receivable" reality. Not only is our society often incapable of perceiving children in this way but, tragically, they are often punished for the limitations of the adult imagination. The unfathomability of the child becomes an object of fear that the adult must ward off and interpret in terms of criminality or, more problematically, simply ignore.

Ocean Vuong's story lays out what is at the heart of a child's predicament: his subjective experience comes into confrontation with a perception on the part of an other that misidentifies and frames it not as a sacred experience of creation, but as a transgression of the social order. Such experiences are frequent in the lives of children, especially in neighborhoods where perceptions of criminality and the effects of mass incarceration are prevalent. Children whose acts are consistently misperceived have an endless series of accusations waged against them and are consequently mis-labeled "problematic." Internalizing this externally produced image, children express themselves in whatever forms they have access to and reproduce reactions of violence from those who cannot tolerate the ruptures they produce in society's system of perceptions, ideals, values, and prohibitions. This is not to say that rules must be ignored, but rather that those in a position to "respond" to a child's act must recognize what is at stake.

The adult knows nothing of the child's own singular experience. Ocean Vuong's teacher reinforced rather than recognized the effects of the bullying that sent him seeking refuge in the library where he found a box of cassettes and a headset through which to hear "a robust male voice" surging forth and "emptying into his body." This voice found its way into his inner world to mix with the words of the women who raised him; its inflections invoked "waves on the sea" striking this child who thinks it "must possess the power of a moon"—a power that goes beyond his grasp. Ocean imagines that because this voice of Dr. Martin Luther King is the voice of a doctor, there must be medicine in his words, and they knit themselves together with the names of flowers from his grandmother's gardening shows to produce: "If a boy could dream of golden fields, full of lilacs, tulips, marigolds . . . " The word "pansy" inflicted on him as a form of bullying is thereby transformed into loveliness. What does his teacher know of any of this rich and moving experience? The adult has the perception that the poem on paper, an object he can observe, is fake and, operating within the reality of what he can only see, he holds it up to the light as if it is counterfeit money. This insistence on the "observable" blinds him to the infinite invisible universe behind it and leads him to shrink the creation of the child into a crime fabricated by his own limited perception.

THE CITY PROJECT

How can we best understand this unfathomable dimension of a child and, more importantly, engage with it and facilitate its flourishing? Through my work with The City Project, which provides psychoanalytically informed individual and group therapy for elementary and middle school students who have been exposed to trauma, I have found that one answer is the creation of a shared liminal space in which children can safely discover and invent the solutions they need. Run under the auspices of a Child and Adolescent Clinic at the local Psychoanalytic Institute, The City Project was formed over a decade ago with the mandate of bringing psychoanalytic services to children traumatized by gun violence and the effects of poverty and social neglect that plague their neighborhood in a large North American city. Its theoretical frame is founded on a core belief that engaging the creative resources of the child is essential to any significant analytically informed work, and that this requires a liminal space in which to manifest. I will describe an intervention with one child that highlights the salient features of the psychoanalytic frame constructed around these core assumptions, the nuts and bolts of such an intervention, and, most importantly and compellingly, the response of the child to the possibilities mobilized thereby. Of particular interest are the position of the clinician, the specific conditions that create this liminal space which allows the innate creative potential of a child to drive the process, and an example of the singular solutions this child produces to the problems that she defines for herself.

A PSYCHOANALYTIC CONCEPTUALIZATION

Lacan's theorization of the *mirror-stage* in early childhood (Lacan, 1966) captures what is at stake when the unfathomable lived experience of the child encounters a misrecognition coming from the other that skews this experience and confronts the child with a radical gap between what they have experienced and what can be said about it both by themselves and others. What is at stake here is the expression of two fundamental dimensions of human experience—one that is grounded in the human quest that is beyond what can be put into language, and the other grounded in what can be said about it by an other anchored to the social link. So as to better understand what is needed from a liminal space in which this lived experience of the child can reveal itself, let us examine further the nature of these two fundamental dimensions that undergird the lives of children and entail a particular way of working with the possibilities inherent within them.

In his essay "The Limit" (Apollon, 2010), Willy Apollon describes these two primary facets of human experience. As illustrated by Ocean Vuong's story, the first belongs to the realm of "the observable" and is linked to what can be named and thus perceived by the external gaze of an other. This corresponds with the realm of scientific observation which locates the human subject in the position of object, "one thing among others in a space that is defined and controlled" (Apollon, 2010, para. 3). All that science and any other external observer can access in the human subject is that which can be measured and observed from the outside. Science does not have access to the internal subjective experience of the human, to one's mental representations, fantasies, or multiple levels of the unconscious. Just as the child's image in the mirror reduces their inner world to what is externally observable, this objective perception reduces the child to a construction that is radically dissociated from the truth of their existence.

In contrast, the lived experience of the child engenders questions that go beyond the sphere of what can be perceived and named within a shared reality with others. It begins before the advent of the mirror-stage when the child is "barely able to distinguish forms in the masses of light and shadow" (Apollon, 2010, para. 5). This fundamental experience is not grounded in a perception that can be replaced by a name, but rather in a mental representation that marks an encounter with something it cannot fathom. For example, the temporal form of the audible sound of the voice of the father enters and ruptures the homeostatic intrauterine environmental space defined by the voice of the mother and inscribes an effect both in the mother and the fetus growing within her. This conceptualization builds on Freud's notion of trauma as set forth in *Beyond the Pleasure Principle* (Freud, 1920/1955), where trauma is defined as "any excitations from outside which are powerful enough to break through the protective shield—a breach in an otherwise efficacious barrier against stimuli" (Freud, 1920/1955, p. 29). Furthermore, the less able a system is to bind the influx of external stimuli, "the more violent must be the consequences of such a breach" (Freud, 1920/1955, p. 30). In Apollon's view, this experience of that which ruptures the capacity of the psyche to function properly induces it to produce a mental representation for what cannot be seen or found in the environment so as to bind the trauma. The mental representation which eventually finds expression as a fantasy sets the being in search of something in the external environment that cannot be perceived or named. In other words, what is unfathomable in the child is engendered by its encounter with something it cannot fathom—that which has a singular impact on the child and overdetermines the child's existence as it unfolds.

This encounter with something that possesses "the power of the moon" (Vuong, 2016), something that takes the being beyond its grasp—its "little life," leads to a surging forth of energy in the subversion of the biological being. This forms the basis for what the child will later experience as an absence of boundaries between the spiritual and the biological and constitutes the body as distinct from a purely biological organism (Apollon, 2010, para. 8). Ocean Vuong's story illustrates the way in which the surging forth of a voice breaks into the world he inhabits and ignites his imagination, an experience he succeeds in managing through his construction of a poem.

In contrast, children captured within the social link via an identification with the misperceptions of others situated within it have more difficulty accessing the unfathomable dimension within them on their own. It is in a commitment to supporting this dimension of the child and to making a space for its expression that The City Project organizes itself. Let us turn now to a description of the psychoanalytic work that constitutes a liminal space in between the social link of the school and the dimension of the child beyond the perimeters of what it can perceive and name.

A LIMINAL SPACE IN AN INNER CITY SCHOOL

In the etymology of *liminal*, the noun *limen* refers to the point at which a physiological or psychological effect begins to be produced, and *liminal* is the adjective used to describe things associated with that point (Encyclopedia Britannica, n.d.) This evokes the possibility of a transitional point or intermediary zone in between two others. Likewise, an effective clinical stance in schools involves positioning the clinician in between the two aforementioned spheres of human experience: the social link and what lies beyond it. On the one hand, the child exists in a social surround and must find a place for themselves within it. The school is a social institution that has been constructed within the particular culture in which it exists so as to reproduce its beliefs, values, and ideals. As such, a school, as any social institution, will actively determine what is receivable within it and what must be kept out of it. However, as an individual human subject, the child is constituted of experiences, thoughts, feelings, and actions that originate beyond the social. In order to exist, the child must access a liminal space through which to discover what determines who they are on their own terms. Our project is organized around the construction of such a space so as to make such discoveries possible.

To date, The City Project has operated in six different schools in which children are referred by their teachers, other school personnel, parents, and often themselves. Once referred to our program, the children meet individually with a clinician and are invited to participate in the project either with a group or individually. They are asked if they would be interested in meeting to invent activities of their choice, to talk about "things that matter to them" and to figure out what they'd like to know more about. Most often the children are not sure what this is all about but are curious to give it a try and their own investment in the process comes when they find a way to make the time and space of the meetings their own. Without a desire of their own to participate in the process, the work does not happen. The Project is designed to help children deal with the impact of their exposure to trauma by helping them to gain some awareness and understanding of themselves through the engagement of their capacity to represent and reflect on their thoughts, feelings, behaviors, and experiences. We do this by establishing a reliable time and place to come together once a week where both real and the imagined, actual, and unformulated experiences that children carry inside them can find a place of expression.

I have selected an example of an individual intervention which began when the girl I will call C was in fourth grade and ended when she was in eighth grade to illustrate the conditions of possibility that allowed an unfathomable dimension of her existence to emerge in our work. When I first met C, she was presented by the school as a playground bully and as having trouble with math and writing. Then nine years old, she was the biggest fourth grader in the class "and the strongest," she assured me. She could beat up anyone at school. C was able to let me know that her guardian had died suddenly and unexpectedly when she was a young child. What she lost then was the person that organized and held together her already fragile existence. In addition to troubles with learning and on the playground, she had been diagnosed with ADHD and the intermittent presence of trance states which did not appear to have a physiological basis.

The early experience of trauma as an effraction in one's being engages the child's capacity to imagine that which does not exist in the form of a mental representation that forms the basis for the elaboration of a blueprint for interacting with the world at an unconscious level. This unconscious material constitutes an important source of "unknown knowledge" that builds up with regard to oneself and to the world. Thus, in a critical way, the locus of "knowledge" is not in the clinician but rather in the child, even if it is unconscious. Such an assumption is at odds with the notion of the clinician as an "expert" who can diagnose and treat a problem without engaging the knowledge in the other. Here, we are proposing the opposite—that in order for real work to be done, the clinician must elicit the conditions of possibility for this "knowledge" in the child to communicate itself.

THE POSITION OF THE CLINICIAN

In other words, the assumption that a child's behavior is a form of communication of that which has not found its way into words entails a particular position in the clinician. It is one thing to listen and another to hear. What the clinician is able to hear and receive in the communications coming from a child are related to the work she has done on her own unconscious. Resistance can exist more strongly on the side of the clinician than on the side of the child. What is it that comes up for an adult working with a child? To what extent does a child feel able to risk speaking about what may be not only rejected in the social link but not even heard? It is important not to assume that one could know in the place of the child anything of their thoughts, feelings, or experiences. The presence of surprise and awe in the clinician are a sign of something new that has emerged into the liminal space of the work, something that was not imagined by the clinician and that was brought by the child's capacity to imagine and create something that they needed to exist.

In working with C, I tried to position myself as an ally in her searches (Davoine and Gaudillière, 2004). We played endless seeking games in the first part of our work together, searching for something side by side or hiding something for the other to find. I tried to keep the space safe enough for C to engage in her searching and open enough so that she could create whatever she needed in order to discover and represent that for which she had no words. Once she came to trust that the space and time of our work was her own and unbeholden to any other imperative, she began to risk communicating heretofore unnamed and unshared inner representations of herself and the world. I tried to hold open the possibilities of putting words and play to something as yet unspoken and also to recognize the points at which it resisted being put into words. The clinician's belief in the integrity of that which C was trying to express and the importance of communicating about it together allowed her to hold something in her mind, to think about it and to give form to it in a way that she could make use of it. Beyond the "problem" defined in terms of the socio-cultural surround or within what is defined as problematic, what is it that C was truly seeking to communicate?

The Emergence of the Unsayable

It wasn't until three years into our work together that one day C could announced, in an act fraught with anxiety and courage, that she was going to tell me who she really was.

> In her true state, C had a sleek coat of fur, dark as the night, and golden eyes. A long time ago, she had begun to reveal what eventually manifested as the

> sharpness of her teeth by showing me enigmatically how she had to hide something in her mouth and without words she would sometimes draw the eyes and the paws. Following that, she slowly began to elaborate what she knew of this form of herself and what she was in the process of discovering. The name she gave herself in this form metaphorically evoked one of the symptoms she had presented with at the beginning of our work together. Often she was unable to put descriptors into words and wished on many occasions that I could just see her, directly, as she was. What she could say was that she was made up of different parts. In her words, some were nice and some not so nice. The part just evoked was the Coyote part into which she felt herself beginning to transform at times in the midst of a session. She felt she had to fight against this for fear of some vaguely sensed consequences. This Coyote part (and she saw me in my Coyote state as a gray-furred one) was good-sized—long enough, she said, to carry an adult on its back, and tall—with a head that reached up to my waist. It was strong and powerful, able to leap from one building to another and to fly through the air. She felt exhilarated when in this form but also subject to a ruthless bloodlust. She could smell it in the air and felt, along with her pack, that it was time for a kill. C worried about this because she also loved animals and was very protective of them. She also worried what might happen if a transformation were to occur during the course of our meetings. In addition to the Coyote part, she was something associated with blood. For lack of another word, she called this a "Bloodsucker" though she didn't think that's really what it was. There was another part called "Demon," and a fourth part of which she was only vaguely aware which had to do with being a "Half" creature whose species was made extinct when at war with her Coyote pack. She associated the vague part with her uncertainty about her true paternity. She knew that she had another father than the one she had been told about but did not know more than that about him and was curious to know.

The assumption that a young girl has the capacity to imagine that which does not exist and to need it enough to create it means that she has the capacity to find her way on her own terms for what she is seeking to know. What was needed were the conditions through which she was able to mobilize this creativity and desire necessary to give a form to her quest. In this work with a child, the position of the clinician and assumptions about what is at stake within the child and how to work together led to the construction of this liminal space in between the social link and the unsayable through which what mattered to her could be shared. Fragments from her work reported here convey something of C's mental representation embodied as a fantasy and the way in which voices from inside her interrupt and sometimes protest against her attempts to communicate this. The clinician's remarks are indicated within parentheses.

> C often came in with a scowl and feelings of agitation and I would ask what was going on. She would feel irritated about talking and apologized for this saying that she didn't want to talk about it. I'd wait and acknowledge how hard it felt to talk. She came in one day and said something about how hard it was for her to act "regular" and how exhausting it was to put on "an act." She'd had a headache for three days because a lot had been going on (what?) she didn't want to talk about it she said again but then did—voices were telling her not to and we talked about how hard it was to want to talk about it but also feel like she should not. She talked about "blood lust" and how they all feel that—the smell of blood leads them to want to kill. She fears for her pets. She sometimes felt like something was coming in the window and she picked up her cats and held them inside her shirt to protect them (sometimes you feel blood lust but you struggle with this because you love animals too). She shared that she could see things in a special way—see people even when they are not in front of her—zoom in on them as if her eyes are a microscope and see things about them. She said the pack was telling her that she shouldn't tell me these things. They didn't like that she used these powers because it took her away from following the blood lust. She said as she was talking to me she had a glimpse of me as an alpha. The alpha of her pack didn't want her doing things—there was this idea that she would be the alpha one day and he didn't want her to take his place.

This brief clinical fragment illustrates how, given the chance, a child can risk finding the words needed in the presence of an other, despite the difficulty in doing so. What words could possibly be imagined and uttered by anyone else to give sense to what C was experiencing, how could anyone have known how she, herself, experienced it? Once C had perceived that what she can say about her own experience will be received in our shared liminal space, she was moved to elaborate further.

> C would speak about having to act "all smiley and fine" so the adults at school wouldn't worry but this was tiring. She wasn't sleeping. (What's going on at night?) "Everything," (Tell me about it.) She says she doesn't know. She speaks of how she likes to play with her cats. The little one eats so much! And she's getting so big! Once she accidentally bit C because she was hungry and she thought C's finger was food. C's finger bled and the little one looked up as if she were sorry. C knew that she didn't mean to hurt her. She has talked before about how she can understand what animals are thinking. She hears what they say—not in words but in their thoughts. She looks distracted and I ask what she is thinking. She says that she hears the voices. She has to struggle with them. They come and try to get her to go with them. (What is that like for you?) She kept hearing from them—it was the alpha now talking to her. He says—"you've told her enough—come with me now." She has found a way to fight it off (how?). They get into your mind by repeating the same thing over and over and then suddenly they take over and it's like she's not there anymore (they take over your mind and it's no longer yours) yes, I guess [strange look on her face] (what do you think?) she

> has found a way to keep it from happening (how?) "I think of things like flowers and ice cream, nice things." In the midst of this she stops (what?) and says there was a "pause" (what do you mean?) I don't know—just like a pause (a pause in your mind? Like something stopped? What was it like?) She begins to draw (what are you doing?) drawing you a picture (of?) I don't know. She draws and shrugs then asks, "Do you want to see?" (yes) She shows me a picture of a paw and gets up—feeling exhilarated—reaches for the basket of animals and holds up a black panther asking me what it would feel like to be one (you'll have to help me imagine it). She wants to know what I imagine and I say speed and grace—the ability to run fast and jump. She says that it is like being very strong physically and mentally—she is able to hear the tiniest sounds—like a tiny mouse walking across the floor. She can also touch something, like this table and know who touched it last (your senses are very sensitive—you can pick up a lot of information through them). It makes her happy to be in this state she says, "but you have to be able to control it. You hear so many sounds—you would go crazy if you heard them all so you have to be able to control what you hear." She looks at the underside of some of the animals and notices the genitalia and says "eew, why do they do that? A kid might see that" (what would they think?) "it's nasty" (what's nasty?) "don't want to say—in the pack, the alpha has a p . . . " (penis?) "oh, don't say that" (you don't like that word) "I don't want to talk about it" (it makes you feel uncomfortable to say it or think it—it feels nasty). "The males in the pack can pull that in so that it's just smooth—you don't see anything—and the girls don't have a . . . for them it's just smooth" (those words make you feel anxious—things that kids begin to think about as they grow up).
>
> She said there was a man at school who put the ideas of these things into people's minds. "He puts these bad ideas into peoples' heads—like 'kill this'" (who is he?) "maybe the father of one of the kids at the school—I don't really know. He's from this place in between. I don't know about my other father—I don't really know."

CONCLUSION

There is a homophonic link between a signifier for one of the symptoms C had at the beginning of our work and a name she had given herself which evoked both her image of her body and a moment of suspended time and disjointed mental functioning. It was associated in my mind with a dream she had reported about a year into our work in which she imagined herself joining someone she had lost *in a place of death depicted as 'boring' without a heaven or hell.* This "boring" in-between place also evokes the game she initiated called "Monster Freeze" in which one of us would close our eyes and count to twenty while the other person had to move during this interval of frozen time and take a pose. We talked about how something changed when she wasn't looking and was stuck in frozen time. To find what she was looking for C needed to access this in-between space, beyond what could be "said" or "heard" in the social link, that could receive what was beyond what she could say so as to evoke it in the presence of an ally.

At the beginning of our meetings there was often a downcast look on C's face, sometimes a scowl. As we got further into the work, there was a back and forth at the beginning of the session between feeling like she was not going to talk about "it" and then finding a way to communicate. There was something inside of her that she could not manage, something which led her to have difficulty sleeping at night. Adults called it ADHD or "unexplained trance states." C found a way to begin to communicate through her body that for which she had no words. When she began to talk about her private world we both became highly absorbed and animated by it. There was a liveliness and excitement that accompanied her telling of what she knew of it and her searching to communicate unknown parts of it.

For both Ocean Vuong and C, the child's creative production allows them to exist in a way that feels vital. In order to exist in such a way, they must be able to find a form and a place to communicate what feels real for them within. During the months when C began to communicate more directly about the "unsayable" within her, the school became concerned that she was "off in her own world" and "isolated in the lunchroom." With C's permission, I was able to let school personnel know that she was aware of this and working out her own solution for it. In the months following her revelation about her sense of herself and the many sessions spent playing out scenarios around this part of herself in our work, her "social isolation" began to shift. C began to speak about her interest in other young people her age and began to want to get together with others. Her school reported that her academic and social engagements were improving. As she moved through eighth grade, she expressed an interest in wanting to be herself but also in figuring out how to get along with others and to have friends. In addition to these changes, she decided that she wanted to go to a selective high school in the city and surprised everyone by taking charge of successfully making it happen. With this in place, and after several months of feeling she had nothing more to work on, we decided to conclude our work together.

It is because a child encounters something that cannot be "fathomed" that an unfathomable dimension opens up within them. In its attempt to communicate itself, it can take the form of violence or creation. In order to create a form by which to manage this dimension within, we have seen how a liminal space within the social institution of the school offers what is beyond ordinary language and common reality a chance to express itself. C positioned me both as a fellow coyote and as a human, in short, as an ally that could accompany her within the different realms she inhabited. The extent to which

I could straddle both worlds *on her terms* rather than on the terms of the cultures and civilizations which format social beings allowed her to create a form for the unbound energy within her that could be shared in the world aesthetically rather than through the violence she had previously employed. It is important to note that any words coming from a clinician linked to their own socio-cultural formatting could block expressions from deeper levels of the unconscious that exist beyond such formatting. C's encounter with a space that could allow her to express elements of her own unconscious mental representations gave her the experience of herself on her own terms in the company of another subject. The child leads—the clinician follows. Sometimes it takes more than one human playing alone. The presence of two subjects can create this liminal space—in between the social and the real beyond it—through which one can begin to know something about unspoken and unthought but lived experience.

Self-driven play or play animated by what is unspoken and unspeakable depends on a liminal space in which one can engage in the act of creating—a form for one's own experience which no other could ever name, represent, or explain—an act that founds the being on its own terms. This experience of creation is central to the sense that something matters. From the beginning of a human life, it is the experience of creation that brings one into existence and that offers access to a space and time outside of the social link defined by a shared reality. The focus of the work is led by the quest of the child to find something which they may only intuit. It is the responsibility of the clinician to listen for, receive and follow the lead of this quest so that the child may begin to make it their own.

REFERENCES

Apollon, W. (2010, December). *The Limit: A Fundamental question for the subject in human experience*. Konturen. journals.oregondigital.org/index.php/konturen/article/view/1391/1531.

Davoine, F. and Gaudillière, J-M. (2004). *History beyond trauma*. The Other Press.

Freud, S. (1955). *Beyond the pleasure principle, Group psychology and other works*. In *The Standard edition of the complete psychological works of Sigmund Freud, (Vol. 18):* (J. Strachey trans.). The Hogarth Press. (Original work published 1920–1922.)

Lacan, J. (1966). *Ecrits*. Editions du Seuil.

Encyclopedia Britannica (n.d.) Liminal. *Merriam-Webster Dictionary*. Retrieved October 5, 2021 from www.merriam-webster.com/dictionary/liminal.

Vuong, O. (2016). Surrendering. *The New Yorker*. June 6 and 13, 2016 Issue. www.newyorker.com/magazine/2016/06/06/ocean-vuong-immigrating-into-english.

Chapter 4

Psychoanalyzing "From Both Sides Now"

At the Extremities of Adolescence— "The Tweenies" and "The Twenties" as New Geo-Psychical Positions

Carol Owens and Jamieson Webster

The time of adolescence is expanding. According to a wide variety of sources, adolescence currently starts around nine years of age and extends to twenty-five and even beyond (for example, Cottone, 2021; Sawyer et al., 2018). The capacity of a category to change shape, expand, and contract is an index of its socio-discursive constructedness. As with the category of childhood, the invention of adolescence to denote a discrete time in the life span of a human being is always conditioned by, and indexed upon, the way that human youth is figured, in a given time and location (cf. Aries, 1965; Stainton Rogers and Stainton Rogers, 1992). It is though worthy of our interest as psychoanalysts and theorists of the psycho-social to consider what this pushing out of the borders of adolescence is about now, both at the level of the social bond, and for the lived subjectivity of young speaking beings.

As a new social grouping, the tweenies are in Lacanian terms an S2, the product of (pseudo) scientific knowledge, conditioned by capitalism as a product which simultaneously consumes (Lacan, 1978; 2007). One might even say that to be a tween is to mark through capitalism the paradoxical status of being produced as an object and being born as a subject of desire. Tweens might tell us something about this contradictory experience as a speaking being in the 21st century.

At the other extreme, the cohort of young people previously thought to be "all grown up" by nineteen or twenty are now revealed in their twenties as late-stage adolescents. If the tweenies are regarded as "new" consumers, the older group is often regarded as reluctant consumers; they stay at home for longer, delaying separation from their parents and hometowns, and appear to reject the outward traditional "signs" of adulthood—cars, houses, serious intimate relationships, marriage, babies, and so on (cf. Danniger and Rouse, 2008; Twenge and Park, 2017).

In what follows we look at adolescence from *both sides now*—in the words of Joni Mitchell's beautiful song of ambivalence—at these newly populated borders of liminal existence (Mitchell, 1966), and by way of our clinical work as psychoanalysts working with clients from these two groups consider the symptoms and *sinthomes* constituted by both, commenting upon the particular conditions of being that these new psycho-social (politico-consumerist) groups address to the Other. Since our work as psychoanalysts takes place on opposite sides of the Atlantic Ocean, our remarks and observations here reflect our situated knowledge(s) of, and practice(s) in the social bond of which we each are a member. In the first part of our chapter Jamieson discusses her work with tweenies in New York city and reflects upon the discourses and legitimating practices at work in the production and circulation of these discourses. In the second part of the chapter Carol considers the promotion of (new) ideals in neo-liberalism in her discussion of her work with late-stage adolescents in Dublin.

SIDE ONE: THE TWEENIES—DIVING INTO THE LIMINAL

I consulted at a local private middle school after a suicide by an eleven-year-old girl and some copy-cat attempts by friends. This wasn't the first suicide in recent times by a pre-teen or tween girl in New York City, nor the presence of ripple effects in a kind of hysterical contagion. Parents and school were obviously alarmed by this spate of suicides in tweens, and confused by the growing "evidence" that this age group, particularly girls, seem incredibly vulnerable to suicide, suicidal ideation, self-harm, and forms of depression and anxiety (Curtin, 2020; Curtin et al., 2021; Appleby et al., 2021; Ghandour et al., 2019; Twenge et al., 2019).[1]

Some feel there is, in fact, nothing new here; the beginning of teen angst has always been felt in the years leading up to adolescence proper, and middle school has often been seen as more brutal than high school—"middle" seemingly doubling down on the signification of the liminal state of tweens, at least in the United States. Tween could simply be the name for the turbulent entry into adolescent turbulence. Perhaps then these statistics follow significations, especially those that come in the wake of increased marketing to this age group to the tune of a multi-billion-dollar industry of products designed for "tweenies." This includes, importantly, psychopharmacology, where a large increase in anti-depressant prescriptions is in the ten–fifteen-year-old age group (Cuddy and Currie, 2020).

As well, the wide-spread use of screen time and social media has consistently been reported to effect tweens the most adversely (Alonzo et al., 2021; Keles, McCrae, and Grealish, 2019; Lissak, 2018; Schrobsdorff, 2016). there has been an increase in acute crises for this age group, with increased visits to psychiatric emergency facilities (Office of the Surgeon General, 2021). Importantly there are also new forms of education for teachers who are taught to understand warning signs surrounding the "emotional vulnerability" of tweenagers (Swanbrow Becker, 2021; Rusch et al., 2021). So one thing we might say is the degree to which tweens are under observation, even under surveillance, has increased.

While kids have immemorially observed their peers or the intricacies of their own families, I felt the degree of surveillance was exponentially greater (Office of the Surgeon General, 2021; Hickok, 2021; Schrobsdorff, 2016). It is inarguable that there is a hyper-focus on tweens, as if to monitor them for the early signs of adolescence, or any supposed "emotional instability" or other forms of corruption (Bailen et al., 2019; Mendo-Lázaro et al., 2019; Schrobsdorff, 2016). Important also was how this information was a currency within a shared discourse at school and at home that tweens are well aware of (Schrobsdorff, 2016).

Psychoanalysis theorizes that shifts in discourse have real effects, and this is often a hidden cause. Moreover, this makes tweens not a subject or group of subjects to be addressed, but in fact an object—of knowledge, speculation, and certainly of anxiety, not to mention the fact that they are an object in the form of consumer capital. So what then is this hyper-focus on tweens, or monitoring of the limits and boundary of childhood and entryway into adolescence?

As a psychoanalyst, it was their "status" as object—to be worried about or to cash in on—that I began to think about. To be an object in an "in-between" space was really to be cast into a limbo, neither child nor true adolescent. These young people found themselves in a space that was signified as a no-where, saturated by negative judgments about adolescence and adulthood communicated by this vigilance over its onset. What were the adults so afraid of? Tweens also spoke with one another about their mutual feelings of hopelessness facing the world which felt ruined. This was then confirmed by the adults, rather than be told that adult life is a realm of new possibilities. Tweens are thus given a message concerning the impossibility of living once an adult, especially with the imminent death of the natural world a la tween sensation Greta Thunberg.

One patient turned parental vigilance of her sexuality on herself through anorexia which postponed menstruation and other biological markers of puberty. A twelve-year-old girl described picking and scratching at herself as a way of creating a container, a boundary, that her parents seemed to be unable to locate in their fears of her adolescence, and it was as if she repeated *and* tried to undo their attention to the beginning changes in her body. Lastly, a patient of mine spoke about her "gender dysphoria" and identity as "trans" as stabilizing an ambiguous, painful, feeling of separating from her parents and concerns about *their* emotional well-being, a fate she wanted to avoid which she felt she could do by changing genders. Indeed "trans" becomes an interesting signifier with respect to the liminal aspects and need for passage that exemplify adolescence.

We see here the contagion of anxiety that is openly shared, articulated, and enacted; a state of emergency that is given room, marketed, and even sanctioned by an Other. Interestingly, one popular marketing strategy for tweens was to find the object that appealed to the tween but could be sanctioned by the adults who were still monitoring their choices. Lacan writes about the eruption of anxiety in the shift between pre-oedipal and oedipal childhood in Seminar IV on *The Object Relation*:

> In short, the instant when the subject is suspended between a moment at which he no longer knows where he is, and shift towards a moment when he will become something in which he will never be able to find himself again. That is anxiety. (Lacan, 2020, p. 218)

I think it's important to remember that for Freud the Oedipal complex is repeated after latency in the transition to adolescence; and here, Lacan emphasizes it precisely as the problem of being in-between, suspended, at a threshold when a new order needs to be established (see Freud 1905). The infant needs to become a subject in their own right with what he calls a "title" for their future (See, Lacan, 2020). But it becomes a problem of "the devil that you know" versus the devil you don't.

EITHER WAY I LOSE

I worked with a young girl at two points in her life, when she was eleven and again when she was seventeen. She also had been seen as a baby by a psychoanalyst since she had a rare case of infant anorexia, needing a feeding tube.

This analyst told me the birth of this child led the parents to split up and he realized the feeding tube acted as a kind of prop, holding this infant together in a family that was falling apart. They were eventually able to keep the feeding tube, but begin to feed her regularly. After this point, she seemingly progressed well through childhood until age of eleven when she developed symptoms of anxiety.

What she came to articulate during that time had been a crisis surrounding her father's break up with a girlfriend. The father had many girlfriends over the years so what was different this time? Well, this girlfriend was friends with the mother, and had verbally attacked the mother during the time the relationship was breaking down. In fact, the mother was often over-involved in her ex-husband's love life. Once the relationship was over, however, the mother revealed the details of her difficulties with this woman to her daughter—I suspect, out of jealousy, since this woman was younger and my tween patient enjoyed going to the nail salon with her, going shopping, listening to music, and other things she didn't share with her older mother.

This information had a retro-active effect, making my patient revise her feelings about the girlfriend, bringing to the surface a question about all that she "did not know." She suddenly felt herself to be in the midst of chaos and violence. She had several anxiety attacks, developed fears of vomiting in public, beginning with confronting bureaucratic tasks having to do with school that normally a parent would handle, but which she often handled because her parents weren't "good at that kind of thing." But she had been handling this for quite some time.

As with infancy, something that was propping her up—the girlfriend, a certain image of her parents—fell apart and anxiety erupted. Being able to articulate and pinpoint the moment of confusion and panic eased her anxiety and allowed her to begin to ask some important questions about the father's many relationships and his volatility, the mother's lack of relationships, why they remained so tied to one another despite separating when she was born, and the mother's depression often spoken about to her daughter. Her question was certainly a question about the familial *jouissance* and to be a tween meant becoming aware of its sexual and aggressive dimensions without the protections of childhood, but also without the potential rush for independence in adolescence.

When I saw her again at seventeen, on the other side of adolescence, she had a more extreme moment of collapse. One evening while smoking marijuana, while very "stressed out," she looked in the mirror and couldn't recognize herself. She became so confused she had to go to the emergency room. She subsequently developed severe stomachaches—almost a return of her infant anorexic symptoms. She spoke once again about her parents, separation from them. She wanted to know that she could avoid their fate in the future, bet kept re-encountering them in herself, causing the breakdown of certain imagistic constructions that had secured a tolerable position for her.

I saw an eleven-year-old who was at a school where one of her peers had committed suicide. The parents spoke very concretely about how adolescent hormones adversely affected their two daughters—the older daughter having a very difficult adolescence requiring a whole team of therapeutic helpers, and now, they were seeing the signs of "hormones" in their youngest daughter. Oddly, they had little else to say about their children.

In fact, it didn't take long in speaking with the girl to see that much of the symptoms at home were symptoms of the difficulties of the parents in their life and marriage. She spoke passionately, and in a very mature way, about not wanting to grow up, that the world was rotten and poisoned by toxic waste, that getting married and having children was disgusting and perpetuating the problems, and she only could see getting a job or going to school as a lot of work and stress that made everyone unhappy. What she wanted most in the world, she told me, was to live alone and have as many dogs as possible. She loved her dog more than anything—at which point she would suddenly become like a very young child squealing about how cute and fluffy her dog is and then would often insist on looking at pictures of dogs for the rest of the session, as if to obliterate the misery of her prior speech.

There was something very moving about this overly adult discourse, somewhat cynical and depressive at times, and the lineaments of such a young girl, turning back to what was almost a "transitional object" for comfort. Something about the idea her parents had of the toxicity of adolescent hormones, and her idea of their toxic marriage, toxic work and school environments, toxic planet, mirrored one another in fascinating ways, including a hidden ideal of innocence. Where is my nice, innocent child? I love the innocence of animals!

In treatment she tried to address difficult topics that were barely tolerable to her: puberty, menstruation, sexuality, her sister's "mental illness," and being a woman. What came to the surface was a question about why her mother tolerated what she saw as bad treatment by her father who was a stressed out high powered that took it out on his wife. In fact, a lot of her "hormonal" emotional behavior was her fighting her father on behalf of her mother—something she didn't even quite know she was doing.

Much of this came out because of a dream she had of a clock that said 11:11—of course signifying her age. She also told me that it was the time that you make a wish, and that it reminded her of her and her mother on one side, and her sister and her father on the other. She then spoke about one of the reasons she can't sleep (something her parents endlessly complained about as this pre-teen symptom)—she compulsively goes to check on her mom in the night to see if she's in bed with the father or on a couch outside the room where she sometimes goes.

On the other side of this obsessive concern for her mother—with the close to the surface wish to abscond from this family with her—was a feeling that nothing good comes of being an adult woman. This is where the thoughts turned quite dark and had their own suicidal edge, idealizing the little girl who succeeded in her act at school. What she began to say was that her hopelessness was, in part, because her mother was none too receptive to her daughter's sympathy with her. She always took the father's side.

What is interesting is that the picture of this family is quite conventional, almost the 1950s American heteronormative nuclear family, and yet, we have the contemporary tween who doesn't quite rebel against or conform to this family, but goes from acting-in (within the family frame) to acting-out (on the world stage but as collapse into isolation and suicidal feelings), aided, in part, by a discourse worried about adolescence, and another discourse worried about forms of toxicity run amok. How could she find a position? Sadly, she wanted to confront the mother more forcefully about her depression and the treatment by the father, and her mother immediately terminated her treatment, saying they wanted someone who was going to give their child "coping skills" and "executive function coaching" (one might say the first naming the strategy of the mother and the latter that of the father).

What we learn from this material about tweens is the effects of diving (or being thrust) into the liminal space of adolescence—what society is naming precocious—in part, because of the anxiety about their entry into it, as an anxiety that has become a part of discourse about both tweens and adult life. In fact, it's no surprise then that that contemporary co-ordinates of "mental health"—a robust discourse are targeting tweens and that they, sadly, are beginning to live up to the vulnerability attributed to them, diving into the pool of tweeness that has been created for them.

SIDE TWO: THE TWENTIES— TARRYING IN THE LIMINAL

Many young people come into psychoanalytic work with complaints around or about the pressure to passage, to transition, to mature, to grow up, and often with a sense of dread and danger of leaving one state of being or identity for another. For them, unlike the cohort of young people Jamieson described, it is the *exit* from childhood which stages an identity disruption resulting in trauma, anxiety, and symptom-formation. But for older adolescents it is the exit from adolescence into so-called adulthood that causes anxiety and trepidation. In Ireland, the senior cycle of education in secondary school culminates in a series of examinations called the Leaving Certificate, colloquially, "the leaving." At this point, for many young people there are opportunities for an experience of what Paul Stenner calls a "liminal hotspot," borrowing from the language of volcanic topology to think about the irruptions of psycho-social activity in response to disruption and passage (Stenner, Greco, and Motzkau, 2017). Indeed, many psychotherapists and psychoanalysts working with young people in Ireland testify to the signification of "the leaving" in symptom formation (see, for example, Walshe, 2017). In this way, what we can think of as the temporal logic of adolescence works together with the constitutedness of local, situated (and saturated) signifiers in order to produce symptoms which can be thought of as responses to what circulates in the Symbolic order. Or in Winnicott's astute observation, in adolescence "each individual is engaged *in* a living experience *and* a problem of existing" for which he added, the only remedy is the passage of time (Winnicott, 1961, p. 79, emphasis added).[2]

Alain Vanier points out that Lacan regarded adolescence as "primarily a social phenomenon of discourse," but noted that as such, the status of the speaking being in childhood, and we may add, in adolescence, is implicated in jouissance (Vanier, 2001, p. 579). The question is, which jouissance? In our time, neo-liberal ideology with its hand in the pocket of capitalism fuels the production of what Bauman calls liquid modernity, a kind of glorified state of liminal existence where perpetual movement and endless self-discovery are celebrated and glorified (Bauman, 2000). As such, the glorification of the liminal can operate so as to create the conditions for an interminable stay for the speaking being—in a strictly temporary transitional location—authenticated as that stay is under the promotion of a set of ideals of permanent liquidity at the level of identity (cf. Szakolczai, 2017; Verhaeghe, 2014). So in fact the liminal experience of adolescence itself undergoes a stretching and elaboration predicated upon the ideological value attached to deferral (of destiny, identity, status) on the one hand (transition, impermanence, and change taking on the properties of long-stay positions), and the business (*nay*, industry) of self-invention on the other (a thousand Instagram stories waiting to be posted, a million snapchats, a trillion tweets). Discussions about (so-called) extended adolescence often point up and mark out the idea that (a) there is nothing new in it—there being plenty of historical evidence to show how young people up to or beyond age twenty-five have in previous times (epochs) not been in any great hurry to move along to adulthood, or (b), socio-economic conditions have changed such that the opportunities for young people to grow up and move on are diminished (cf. Hill and Redding, 2021). Broadly speaking, sociological, psycho-social, and queer/deconstructionist treatments of adolescence and the idea of late-stage adolescence regard the phenomenon as a response to market conditions (see, for example, Owen,

2020), changes in educational opportunities, inflating property rental rates, and/or law. I have myself commented upon the relationship between law and the social bond in an essay examining the particularities associated with coming of age in twenty-first-century Ireland in light of changes to the Irish constitution making divorce, abortion, and marriage equality legal (Owens, 2020). What remains under-examined thus far however is the question of how the ideals produced under neo-liberalism's quest for endless self-invention and deferral of identity formation play out in adolescence at the level of the singular—in suffering and being, and moreover lead to what I am calling a tarrying in the liminal.[3]

During the past two decades, Lacanian (and other) psychoanalysts have been speaking and writing about the rise of "new symptoms" coordinated with changes in the social bond which orient the subject in relation to the Other. The most significant change is variously described as associated with the decline of the Name of the Father, a function akin to that of the ego ideal that Lacan had described as a symbolizing authority in the regulation of jouissance (Lacan, 2017). The promotion of competing ideals under neo-liberalism, ideals which foster the endless consumption of objects in the quest for identity production (which again can be endless), together with the effects of a deregulated jouissance reorganize the social bond, the ways in which the subject relates to the big Other, and the discourses of the symbolic order (which include the discourses of capitalism and neo-liberalism).[4] The (so-called) new symptoms associated with the social bond under (neo-liberalist) capitalism can therefore be thought of as short-cuts to jouissance often involving the body and the imaginary relationship with the small other. In fact, the lack in jouissance is especially pertinent in late adolescence where the push to adulthood and a more fixed identity presses upon the adolescent (and the adolescent's body) keenly; the body and the body's surfaces offering one after another failed solution in the form of endless opportunities and possibilities for "make-overs."[5] Tarrying in the liminal then, as a response to (ideological) changes in the social bond offers a better option for some speaking beings who find refuge in the shapeless, undefinable, legitimately deferred identity of the adolescent. Questions about sex and death, identity and independence, separation and attachment therefore (re-)emerge foregrounded almost as phobic constructions when it seems that the time has finally come to cut free of the liminal; in so far as they do, and in so far as they are articulated in the course of a psychoanalysis, a reconnection with the Symbolic may be established allowing for that adolescent to leave the liminal (and its discontents) behind.

BUT WHAT I REALLY WANT TO KNOW IS . . . SHOULD I STAY OR SHOULD I GO?

An eighteen-year-old adolescent came to see me alone, because she could. Her mother made a phone call asking for an appointment two months before her eighteenth birthday but the girl refused to take an offered appointment until after she turned eighteen and could legally attend alone. Coming of age legally, she explained, was only of limited value since now she is legally an adult, her fears—of dying and of growing up (in that order)—can no longer be put out of her mind. Throughout her teens she enjoyed school, friendships, family; she was "head girl," an athlete, "popular," "good," and (she added ultimately) had managed to avoid deciding upon a sexual orientation. I asked her to tell me everything she could about her fear of dying. She told me that her maternal grandfather died when she was six years old, and although she didn't remember him all that well, she remembered how devastated her mother was when he died. So, the one who suffers when there is a death in the family is her mother. What will happen (to her mother) when this girl dies, or if she "grows up"?

The timing of her appointment is then a relevant rehearsal of her loss to her mother. The fate worse than death, actually, is to have to grow up. A tragic nostalgia is situated in the future anterior; leaving adolescence behind in order to enter the kingdom of adults, is also at the very same time to stage a loss, to rehearse her death as her mother's child. But it is also to mourn what has been a pleasingly liminal existence and the self-permitted stay on a decision about sexuality. For, this girl is a lesbian, and unhappily so. She had thought that by eighteen, she might have "straightened out."

How older adolescents in our time can imagine the loss they fantasize of bringing upon their parents, especially their "perfect parents," when they finally leave adolescence behind is woven into symptoms which speak to their repressed ambivalence around these perfect parents as well as to what leaving parents behind will do to them. As tarrying in the liminal usually means living longer and longer with parents, there are often resurgences of older unresolved intrusion and/or Oedipus complexes in the form of complaints of rivalry and envy between siblings, and expressions of the tensions of ambivalence with one or other parent, or both.[6] Older adolescents find their fathers gross, greedy, lazy, or useless, ineffective, absent. Mothers are found to be domineering, bossy, over-involved, annoying, anxious, depressed. Or, both parents are just disgusting. Long after most children and young adolescents have overheard, or even actively listened out for the sexual encounters of their parents, late-stage adolescents are incapable of retaining the necessary distance—psychical and geographical—which allows them to put their parents' (active) sex lives out of their minds.

One twenty-six-year-old female client is struggling to leave home; the pandemic serves to externally justify her dallying, her tarrying at home. The middle child of a family, her older brother died when she was fourteen, and her younger sister has moved out with her boyfriend and another two friends into a shared house. She is left home alone with her parents, late fifty-somethings who like to have a few drinks on the weekend, stay up very late, enjoy the TV with the volume turned up loud, and have noisy fun sex later. The girl cannot manage to get to sleep before them and is woken up by them later on with their trips to the bathroom following their sexual adventures. Speaking about her parents' sexual relationship catches her in the grip of a horrified jouissance. Her dreams are full of torrid sex scenes which she is called upon to witness. The sessions are filled with what was unspeakable before; why must she be the one who has to see and hear what should remain invisible and inaudible. But nothing is said at home about all of these things which keep her awake and disturbed. And nothing was ever said at home about the circumstances of her brother's untimely death. If her tarrying in the liminal, staying too long—thanks to the pandemic—engages her in the painstaking unpicking of the inhibition she fomented following the family symptom of not speaking about the real, then her exit will be the result of a working-through first of the real of her brother's death, second of the real of the sexual relationship. It is striking how Lacan's insights in his *Note on the Child* of 1969 can also be useful in working with late-stage adolescents. Lacan's "Note," a type of letter (addressed to Jenny Aubry) contained two clinical insights in the form of principles. The first principle, Lacan maintained, was that the child's symptom answers to what is symptomatic in the family structure—a situation that Lacan described as the fundamental fact of the analytic experience (Lacan, 1969). In this regard, as he put it, the symptom represents the truth of the parental "sexual couple."

A twenty-two-year-old client in her final year of college is living with her parents and two younger sisters. She has struggled with anxiety and low self-esteem since her late teens. An intense relationship with a boy who suffered with very poor mental health between the ages of sixteen and eighteen left her with a sense of having lost her last teenage years, and, since her role in that relationship had been primarily a caring one, when the boy broke off the relationship with her after two years, she was bereft of her role and of the sense of self she had derived in that role. She described her parents as "hands-off," allowing her a huge deal of independence, not getting over-involved, "ideal" really. But, not really. As the work evolved, she spoke of having wanted her parents involved, of having wanted for them to intervene, to authorize an ending of that agonizing relationship. Gradually speaking about her parents as individuals, and as a couple, she saw two people who didn't take care of themselves, binge-eating, defensive, self-destructive. She came to see how her "independence" served like a pay-off, all the independence she wanted in exchange for not bothering them, or questioning the paradoxes of their jouissance. Her weighing up of the costs and tally of her independence mobilized a pushing towards "doing things by myself like an adult" on the one hand, and a pulling away back toward a needing to be looked after.

Navigating a departure from the liminal sometimes involves a *sinthomic* production. A Norwegian client started a three-year-long therapy with me when she was twenty-three.[7] She came with disordered eating and a jouissance conditioned on her inability to say no to herself as the urge to binge-eat overcame her regularly. Her mother and two older sisters had all had gastric band surgery to stop them from over-eating. She left Norway to try to separate from her family as living with them made her very unhappy and stuck in an endless (dis)comfort-eating cycle since with two out of the three women who had the surgery, it had failed to ultimately put a stop to it. When she was growing up, her mother would stuff her and her sisters, they couldn't leave the table until they were completely full; every celebration, any happy moment whatsoever was an opportunity for cake, and sweets. But she knew that her mother was unhappy, eating and drinking herself to sleep, that her sisters were overweight, depressed, lonely, and a bit strange. This girl has tried to do things differently. First the geographical separation, bringing about a liminal suffering; neither feeling at home when back there—she has changed too much—nor feeling at home when she is in Ireland—she is still too Norwegian, too much her mother's daughter. Three years of pushing all of this and more into words, finding strange new connections in her speech; she found it possible to tolerate the discomfort of a gap between the urge to fill it with food—her mother's symptom—and the sense of loss or emptiness of living differently, alone. Following a visit home in the second year of the work with me she showed me that she had done something interesting on her return. She'd had a tattoo on her upper arm; four words from the Norwegian national anthem, the closest in English we can get to a translation could be: "weathered, aged, over the water."

This was the bit of her that was, and is always Norwegian, an evocation of the motherland, reminding her of her mother and her sisters, and the place she grew up in; and there is more. The tattoo is inked in a beautiful script, none other than her own mother's handwriting. She'd had her mother write out the words and the tattoo artist copy them. In this way she carries her mother's hand-written message on her skin, but the message is of her choosing. For they are the necessary precise words that allow her to love her mother from afar, from "over the water"; as such it is an act that finally marks the end of a liminal phase in which she was held captive by her mother's desire and her mother's jouissance.

FINAL COMMENTS

Approaching adolescence from "both sides now," we came to our discussion of "the Tweenies" and "the Twenties" from both sides of the Atlantic. We were keen to consider the liminal singularities of the young people's lives that we hear about in our practices. They are, in Turner's famous phrase about liminality, the ones who live "betwixt and between," but they are also the ones who are redefining what lies betwixt and between, subjected as they (and we) all are to the prevailing discourses in our times which posit reinvention, becoming, and change as totemic objects of jouissance. Whether diving into the liminal as fugue from the constraints of childhood or tarrying there to compensate for a lack in jouissance imaginarized as a condition of adulthood, for younger as well as older adolescents it is often their bodies which suffer the ravages of symptoms in the oral dimension, the attacks to the skin, the devastations of the starved and purged. In so far as these ravages may be explained to a psychoanalyst, we believe that a subjectivizing of being may be reorganized.

REFERENCES

Alonzo, R., Hussain, J., Stranges, S., and Anderson, K. K. (2021). Interplay between social media use, sleep quality, and mental health in youth: A systematic review. *Sleep Medicine Reviews*, *56*, 101414.

Appleby, L., Richards, N., Ibrahim, S., Turnbull, P., Rodway, C., and Kapur, N. (2021). Suicide in England in the COVID-19 pandemic: Early observational data from real time surveillance. *The Lancet Regional Health-Europe*, *4*, 100110.

Aries, P. (1965). *Centuries of Childhood: A Social History of Family Life*. New York: Random House.

Bailen, N. H., Green, L. M., and Thompson, R. J. (2019). Understanding emotion in adolescents: A review of emotional frequency, intensity, instability, and clarity. *Emotion Review*, *11*(1), 63–73.

Bauman, Z. (2000). *Liquid Modernity*. Cambridge: Polity Press.

Caron, C. (2021). "8-Year-Olds in Despair: The Mental Health Crisis Is Getting Younger." *The New York Times*, 28 June 2021, https://www.nytimes.com/2021/06/28/well/mind/mental-health-kids-suicide.html.

Cottone, J. G. (2021). Why 25 could be the new 18. *Psychology Today*. https://www.psychologytoday.com/us/blog/the-cube/202107/why-25-could-be-the-new-18.

Cuddy, E., and Currie, J. (2020). Treatment of mental illness in American adolescents varies widely within and across areas. *Proceedings of the National Academy of Sciences*, *117*(39), 24039–46.

Curtin, S. C. (2020). State suicide rates among adolescents and young adults aged 10–24: United States, 2000–2018. National Vital Statistics Reports, vol. 69, no. 11. Hyattsville, MD: National Center for Health Statistics.

Curtin, S. C., Hedegaard, H., and Ahmad, F. B. (2021). Provisional numbers and rates of suicide by month and demographic characteristics: United States, 2020. April 9, 2021. Vital Statistics Rapid Release; no 16. Hyattsville, MD: National Center for Health Statistics.

Danniger, S. and Rouse, C. E. (2008). *The Price of Independence: the economics of early adulthood*. New York: Russell Sage Foundation.

Freud, S. (1905). Three Essays on the Theory of Sexuality. *S. E. VII*, pp. 123–246.

Freud, S. (1917). Mourning and Melancholia. *S. E. XIV*, pp. 237–43.

Ghandour, R. M., Sherman, L. J., Vladutiu, C. J., Ali, M. M., Lynch, S. E., Bitsko, R. H., and Blumberg, S. J. (2019). Prevalence and treatment of depression, anxiety, and conduct problems in US children. *The Journal of pediatrics*, *206*, 256–67.

Hall, C. (1987). "Tween Power: Youth's Middle Tier Comes of Age." *Marketing and Media Decisions*, pp. 56–62.

Hickok, H. (2021). "Under Pressure: How Social Media, Drugs, and the Changing Landscape of Sexuality Are Challenging Younger Generations' Mental Health." In *Everyday Health*, 1 Sept. 2021, https://www.everydayhealth.com/emotional-health/under-pressure/.

Hill, N. E., and Redding, A. (2021). *The End of Adolescence: The Lost art of delaying adulthood*. Cambridge: Harvard University Press.

Keles, B., McCrae, N., and Grealish, A. (2020). A systematic review: the influence of social media on depression, anxiety and psychological distress in adolescents. *International Journal of Adolescence and Youth*, *25*(1), 79–93.

Kluger, J. (2021, March 4). Teen Mental Health has suffered during the COVID-19 pandemic. In *Time*. From https://time.com/5943896/covid-19-teen-mental-health/.

Lacan, J. (1969). Note on the Child. (Trans.). R. Grigg. *Analysis*, *2*, 7–8. 1990.

Lacan, J. (1978). Discourse of Jacques Lacan at the University of Milan on May 12, 1972. In *Lacan in Italia, 1953–1978*, pp. 32–55. https://www.scribd.com/document/151026214/Milan-Discourse-Lacan Trans. Jack W. Stone.

Lacan, J. (2007). *The Other Side of Psychoanalysis. The Seminar of Jacques Lacan. Book XVII*. Trans. R. Grigg. New York: Norton & Co.

Lacan, J. (2017). *Formations of the Unconscious. The Seminar of Jacques Lacan. Book V*. Trans. R. Grigg. New York: Norton & Co.

Lacan, J. (2020). *The Object Relation. The Seminar of Jacques Lacan Book IV*. Trans. A. Price. London: Polity Press.

Lissak, G. (2018). Adverse physiological and psychological effects of screen time on children and adolescents: Literature review and case study. *Environmental research*, *164*, pp. 149–57.

McGowan, T. (2013) *Enjoying What we don't Have*. Nebraska: University of Nebraska Press.

Mendo-Lázaro, S., León-del-Barco, B., Polo-del-Río, M. I., Yuste-Tosina, R., and López-Ramos, V. M. (2019). The role of parental acceptance–rejection in emotional instability during adolescence. *International Journal of Environmental Research and Public Health, 16*(7), 1194.

Mitchell, J. (1966). *Joni Mitchell: Live at the Second Fret 1966* (2014, All Access Records, AACD0120).

Owen, G. (2020). *A Queer History of Adolescence: Developmental Pasts, Relational Futures*. Georgia: University of Georgia Press.

Owens, C. (2020). The Torso is Missing: Coming of Age in 21st Century Ireland. In *Psychoanalysis, Culture & Society, 25,* 376–93.

Protecting Youth Mental Health: The U.S. Surgeon General's Advisory. Office of the Surgeon General. Published online December 6, 2021.

Rusch, A., Rodriguez-Quintana, N., Choi, S. Y., Lane, A., Smith, M., Koschmann, E., and Smith, S. N. (2021). *School professional needs to support student mental health during the COVID-19 pandemic*. Front. Educ. 6:663871. doi: 10.3389/feduc.2021.663871.

Sawyer, S. M., Azzopardi, P. S., Wickremarathne, D., and Patton, G. C. (2018). The Age of Adolescence. In *The Lancet, Child and Adolescent Health, 2*(3), 223–28.

Schrobsdorff, S. (2016, November 7). Teen Depression and Anxiety: Why the Kids Are Not Alright. *Time* (188), 19.

Stainton Rogers, R., and Stainton Rogers, W. (1992). *Stories of Childhood: Shifting Agendas of Child Concern*. New York & London: Harvester Wheatsheaf.

Stenner, P., Greco, M., and Motzkau, J. (2017). Introduction to the Special Issue on Liminal Hotspots. In *Theory and Psychology, 27*(2), 141–46.

Strenger, C. (2005). *The Designed Self.* New Jersey: The Analytic Press.

Svolos, T. (2017). *Twenty-First Century Psychoanalysis*. London: Karnac.

Swales, S., and Owens, C. (2020). *Psychoanalysing Ambivalence with Freud and Lacan: on and off the couch*. London: Routledge.

Swanbrow Becker, M. (2021). "Educators Are Key in Protecting Student Mental Health during the COVID-19 Pandemic." Brookings, Brookings, 24 Feb. 2021, https://www.brookings.edu/blog/brown-center-chalkboard/2021/02/24/educators-are-key-in-protecting-student-mental-health-during-the-covid-19-pandemic/.

Szakolczai, A. (2017). Permanent (trickster) Liminality: The reasons of the heart and of the mind. In *Theory and Psychology, 27*(2), 231–48.

Tomšič, S. (2015). *The Capitalist Unconscious*. New York and London: Verso Press.

Twenge, J. M., Cooper, A. B., Joiner, T. E., Duffy, M. E., and Binau, S. G. (2019) Age, Period, and Cohort Trends in Mood Disorder: Indicators and Suicide-Related Outcomes in a Nationally Representative Dataset, 2005–2017. *Journal of abnormal psychology, 128*(3), 185.

Twenge, J. M., and Park, H. (2017). The Decline in Adult Activities among U.S. Adolescents, 1976–2016. In *Child Development, 90*(2), 638–54.

Vanier, A. (2001). Some Remarks on Adolescence with Particular Reference to Winnicott and Lacan. *The Psychoanalytic Quarterly, 7(3),* 579–97.

Verhaeghe, P. (2014). *What About Me?: the struggle for identity in a market-based society*. Trans. J. Hedley-Prôle. Melbourne & London: Scribe.

Walshe, M. (2017). Pushing the Envelope: A Skinful of Trauma. In Owens, C. and Farrelly Quinn, S. (Eds.). *Lacanian Psychoanalysis with Babies, Children, and Adolescents*. London: (Karnac) Routledge.

Winnicott, D. W. (1961). Adolescence: Struggling through the Doldrums. In Caldwell, L. and Taylor Robinson, H. (Eds.). (2016). *The Collected Works of D. W. Winnicott: Vol. 6, 1960–1963*. Oxford: Oxford University Press.

NOTES

1. This evidence can be considered as reliable across class, race, and ethnicity. The basis for the Twenge et al. study, for example, was from data drawn from the National Survey on Drug Use and Health, a nationally representative survey of US adolescents (51 percent female; 58 percent non-Hispanic White, 14 percent non-Hispanic Black, 19 percent Hispanic, 4 percent Asian or Pacific Islander, 5 percent multi-racial; Family Income ranging from 17 percent less than $20,000, 29 percent $20,000–49,000, 27 percent $50,000–74,000, and 27 percent $75,000 plus).

2. Adolescence as a liminal state of existence for which there is no cure but time as such calls up a sideways reference to Freud who was compelled to say the same thing about another liminal state of existence for which, likewise, there is no cure but time itself. That state is mourning (cf. Freud, 1917).

3. We can be reminded here of Carlo Strenger's work in *The Designed Self* from 2005 where he called attention to the (cultural) imperative at work in the shaping of Gen Xers' lives, arguing that identity-formation for this group could be seen as arrived at via what he dubbed "perpetual experiment" (Strenger, 2005, xxi, 1–24).

4. This change is directly linked to the ideological operations of capitalism that rely upon subjects conditioned to enjoy without limit, and to reinvent themselves constantly (McGowan, 2013; Svolos, 2017; Swales and Owens, 2020; Tomšič, 2015).

5. According to the British Association of Aesthetic Plastic Surgeons, 70 percent of eighteen–twenty-four-year-olds are interested in having procedures, and Botox use in the nineteen–thirty-four age group has increased by 87 percent between 2011 and 2016, with a further increase of 31 percent in 2017.

6. For example, a recent report from the EU agency Eurofound showed that the number of Irish people aged twenty-five–twenty-nine living with their parents grew at one of the highest rates in Europe between 2007 and 2017.

7. With the massive increase in employment opportunities for highly skilled technology workers in Dublin (and in Ireland more broadly) over the past fifteen years or so, my practice often includes clients from other European countries. In addition, an increasing demographic in my practice is that of younger adolescents—the children of non-Irish Europeans—born and raised in Ireland.

Chapter 5

Childhood and Adolescence

The Familiar Strangeness of Virtuality

Liora Stavchansky

PANDEMIC SOCIAL CONTEXT

At the beginning of 2020, when the suspension of activities and social distancing due to the pandemic (SARS-CoV-2) was announced as an international strategy, what we might call *the virtual bond* appeared more strongly and visibly. Although in a way, humanity was already moving toward this territory, generations before the 1970s (just to set a limit) were confronted with the imminent presence of the internet.[1]

This transition announced but not expected, far from correcting existing inequalities, reproduced them. Moreover, these differences have also shown the contingency of human life in nature. The human being is not necessary in an ecosystem, s/he is a foreigner—as *a subject,* a *speaking being*—in a habitat whose priority is harmony; s/he knows that their place is imbalance itself. It was Freud, in his text *Das Unbehagen in der Kultur* (Freud, 1930) (*Civilization and its Discontents*), who addressed this hypothesis, developing the conception of a psyche that works in conflict, in such a way that nature presents itself as complicated in its turn. In other words, for psychoanalysis it is strategic—epistemologically and clinically speaking—to assume the conflictive and destabilized nature of the human being rather than to approach it from the point of view of harmony or unity.

Based on this description of the pandemic context, I had the idea that people's faces have become more present in this social distancing. These faces once were familiar, but now they show the presence of the familiar becoming strange (*unheimlich*). In this sense, childhood, and adolescence—as discursive signifying figures—question and confront what is perhaps already out of fashion: the adult. Because for children and adolescents, virtuality has never been alien. My aim, then, is to examine the consequences of the pandemic not from adulthood but in reverse: from childhood and adolescence, to interrogate adulthood and shed some light on it via estrangement (*Das Unheimlich*).

It is possible to think of the *virtual bond* for children and adolescents as a relational variant. However, for some adults, this bond has become an atypical form of social relation, since it shows the face where nothing ends up being enough. This bond reveals the *boredom* of a *post-capitalist* era, in which the jouissance of the Other is found in the very network of the internet. I suggest: My plan here is not to question the advances of the scientific revolution, but to underline how the desire of the techno-scientist is inhabited by an excess of jouissance that simultaneously is concealed by pleasure itself. Correlative to this desire of offering infinite pleasure through technology and scientific solutions, we find boredom. Adolescence and childhood reveal to us a crucial human experience: boredom. Knowing how to deal with boredom is a question of the utmost importance for our time.

Childhood and adolescence point to foreign experiences that question the adult's know-how: how to accommodate and what to do in the face of death, sexuality, and boredom? Because, just like a virus, childhood and adolescence are the representation of the most familiar *foreigner*, because they have been "made" by capitalist pedagogy, pitying them as depositaries of *that* which is primary (infantile), but also situating them in the place of *aliens*, *strangers*, *evil-wilders*. In the face of this, there is nothing left to do but to share the dazzle of a *non-knowledge* equivalent to that of sexuality and death. *Childhood*, *sexuality*, and *death* are enigmas whose invitation is to create, to produce, taking advantage of the mythical potential of invention.

It is impossible to think of ourselves now as we did more than a few years ago since these *foreign figures* of youth and childhood are nothing more than irruptions of the real. It is, therefore, necessary to put ethical and biopolitical signifiers in tension, problematize social ties, and redefine new ways of thinking about the position of childhood, adolescence, and humanity as a whole.

Children and Adolescents: Potential Post-Capitalist Foreigners

The uncanny, "that class of the frightening which leads back to what is known of old and long familiar" (Freud, 1919, p. 220) reveals something—it is the familiarity with which we all live, at the same time it makes visible the anguish of *that* which returns as unpleasant: the time of boredom. Boredom as closeness to death. The foreigner is dangerous, his foreignness is a residue that threatens to cease *to be so*. It becomes unbearable when his condition begins to be reversed, founding another temporality in which the foreign begins to make us uncomfortable, due to the familiarity that, from the recognition of *what was*, makes us tremble. By losing its foreignness, it shows itself to be familiarly foreign. This foreigner is the one that does not end up being totally known, s/he is the difference that remains latent, an unfolding to a gap.

There is a time that is based on this gap, a time of emptying, of questioning the certainties and ideals under which culture tries to palliate (discomfort) in the face of the familiarly foreign. Racism, for example, is a structured response that distances itself from *that which* is foreign, a cause of anguish. On this level, childhood and adolescence function as radical foreignness. This happens when the adultness—as another sort of function—tries to get rid of childhood and youth with educational operators and behavioral technologies, which result in colonizing racism.

In this way, the foreigner has no history, s/he is *rootless*, and in order to link herself/himself (with the native), s/he acquires a language, subtracting something from his foreignness to perpetuate it. That is to say, the familiar only operate as long as the model of purification allows it, and this is how technological rationalities always have an impact on the body, as a way of not escaping what we know today as development.

In this sense, the *child* is a paradigm, a *child-rationality*. As Leandro De Lajonquière says "a childhood only exists as a loss, unknown, repressed, which is why it never ceases to be unwritten, to be uninscribed, to insist, to pulsate in 'us.' It insists as a temporal difference—an enigma—making us strangers to the present, foreigners in relation to 'ourselves'" (De Lajonquière, 2011, p. 219). The *child*, the *child* paradigm, is assembled from an indeterminate number of discourses that structure it as a *child-body*, as *child-rationality*, and also as a series of *child-illnesses*, in order to subsequently assemble a woman or a man.

The infantile as unconscious pulsates in order not to know itself, showing that real of which development itself cannot give an account. This approach by Freud refers to the non-knowledge that sexuality and death keep for themselves (Freud, 1905). In this respect, Lajonquière adds: "When an old being meets a child, he looks at himself in it as if it were a mirror" (De Lajonquière, 2011, pp. 219–20).

When an *old man* stands before a child, perhaps his desire is to capture *that* which is lost as his own, through the act of love and full fatherly-maternal love, for children are the blueprint of humanity, they will rule the world of tomorrow, and "we must be good enough to them. However, if we insist on declaring our love so much, it is because we find the love-hate amalgam intolerable. By cutting the Möbius strip we separate one from the other and thus fabricate one of the versions of the Child-object of (com)passion" (De

Lajonquière, 2011, p. 226). In this sense, the adult pretends to want to suffer with the child *that* which from his childhood insists on subsisting as lost.

Passion beckons, giving rise to conditions of full enjoyment on the part of educators, religious, or parents, to access the *child*'s body in an attempt to recover that lost trait of childhood itself. It is here that the lines between pure-love and pure-hate touch upon each other: "For its part, pure-hate breathes the dark reverse side of the version of The-Child, giving rise to the figures of the Evil-Wild and the Alien, cultivated by pedagogical and cultural deliberations of apocalyptic bias, condemned in advance to all kinds of failure [. . .] but also thrown to the very extermination" (De Lajonquière, 2011, p. 226).

It is in this encounter that the pedagogue who seeks to teach is trapped by this longing, since, in imparting knowledge, childhood itself and children show him the elusiveness of this knowledge, precisely that which sexuality and death announce as impossible, and which books limit themselves to transmitting.

The sexuality of the so-called "adult" is nothing more than the return of *that* inscribed *thing* that insists on not being written over and over again, in the babbling of fleshiness. Thus, s/he pities the child, as if childhood were that hell unrecognized by each of those who call themselves "adults." The adult pities instead of sharing. To share un-knowledge, since little is known about what is called "childhood," but much is intuited. This is how poetry, cinema, stories, legends, and myths are *the* other face of shared childhood, which produces differential ways of inhabiting the body and the world.

Childhood has been made up by capitalist pedagogy just like adolescence, but from a two-faced position—as we already mentioned–: pitying the child and the adolescent as depositaries of the infantile, or placing them in the position of the *alien*. There is a third option: to situate them as depositaries of the not-known—not-knowing about sexuality and death. Faced with these enigmas: *childhood*, *sexuality*, and *death*, the invitation is to create, taking advantage of the mythical potential of invention and dreaming.

But how not to fall into a romanticisation of childhood? The answer lies in the Freudian *polymorphic perverse*, therein lies the coexistence of death and sexuality in a creative dance that has no utilitarian purpose. The child places himself in the world as an explorer of hostile terrain. It would be absurd to place oneself in the place of the pure-good concerning the conceptions of childhood since compassion or outright rejection, when it comes to educating a child, functions as elements of the adult's death wish.

The adult ascribes to the infant a lack of understanding of certain words and discursive constructions. The reason for this failure is neither conscious nor evolutionary. Childhood occupies a subjective position that operates in the cultural framework. The *infant* only makes gestures, cries, and this is something that often distresses the adult, who does not know or does not remember what s/he knows about these gestures. Let us not forget that "infant" meant in Latin "unable to speak"; it comes from in- "not" + fant- "speaking" (from the verb fari). Unlike the *infant*, the child speaks, is a citizen of words, a *politei*, an inhabitant of the city. The child, dazzled by the sounds that already articulate words, enjoys and plays with them, twists them, mashes them, crushes them. It is through this mashing of words that the child can realize that they function as a pure veil covering the noises, gestures, these onomatopoeias that inhabit him as an *infant.*

The child operates an irreverent truth because through speech, s/he speaks of the impossibility of forgetting that dwells in their words; that which is impossible to forget and which makes littoral with the real. Thus, the infant experience traces the passage from *infant* to child, since the *infant* speaks with the body, making his gesture signify, inflaming the body, turning it into a sound machine. The child, on the other hand, makes the Other his drum, his wall, his place of echo, a decoder of sounds and gestures.

The Other is a place, a passage from *infant* to child that leads to the vertigo of virtuality, precipitating the journey, since it goes from the condition of the *infant* to adolescence. A passage that is organized through a register of non-voice towards another, where the voice itself is confused with echolalia. Thus, it can be affirmed that adolescence, as an experience linked to the speed of modern life, is presented as a halt of transitions, in function of the reduction to the imperative of the *here* and *now* of action. This abrupt temporal transition only takes place in rituals that have the function of locating, not only temporally, but of that which is impossible to say, implying an *event*, in this case, the *event of adolescence.*

The *event* announces itself as an inability to produce a knot with experience. It possesses a "between the lines" that belongs neither to content nor to form, and makes a sort of littoral—a blurry frontier—between that which escapes words and that which makes them possible. It is the irreducible separation between the *event*, which fractures the temporal chronology of *experience* situated as the effect of that fracture.

Event: Experience and Boredom

The disassociation between *event* and *experience* is anchored on the crossroads between acceleration and temporal arrest. What introduces difference and makes transitions possible is precisely the encounter between *event* and *experience*. In order to make this transition, a cut that presupposes a calm wait is required. Faced with the nullity of transitions of a continuum without stopping, there remains then the sensation of emptiness, linked to an attempt to capture a space that, from the outset, no longer has a place. This placelessness can be thought of as the logical time of adolescence, a point of transition and latency characterized by *event-sequences* that are organized as *experiences.* The stay of passage is, then, lived as an *experience* of pure gain, as an *accumulation of experience*, on pain of having crossed the field of *event-sequences.*

In this sense, the adolescent is a foreigner of time that may or may not become familiar, making the reference to the ominous resonate, that which, as a familiar stranger, falls under the effects of repression and returns via the suspension and emptying of time—a transition, a passage from one place to another, a promise of arrival. Adolescence represents a passage—made up, in turn, of small passages—from one place to another, but the arrival is not without reference to the point of departure, which orients the destination to which it is directed.

This frontier-space that is condensed in adolescence allows us to think about that point where neither childhood nor adulthood are definitive stays. Adolescence operates as a *hinge* movement where time and its topology dialogue profusely from the territories of waiting, transition, and boredom.

Adolescence represents that transition, in which boredom keeps for itself the problem of despair, which is nothing other than a capitalist temporality insisting on placing ideals, making adolescence escape from those frontiers. The adolescent is transition in the tedium of the same, showing the juncture of the experience that fragments the *event* of boredom.

Byung-Chul Han says: "It is not an uneventful time in which profound boredom first arises. The historical time of the revolution, which is rich in events, but has fallen out of the condition of duration and repetition, is particularly susceptible to boredom" (Han, 2017b, pp. 168–69).

One could add to this approach of the Korean philosopher that the moment in which the *experience* of the time of history and revolution are left *out* as alien registers, boredom is intensified to a great extent as a condition of the epoch in which the threat, but also the seductive invitation, is the *loss of time*: "The real lack of time does not happen because we lose it, but because 'time loses us.' Time itself empties itself. It does not generate any gravitation that connects and brings together. Boredom, after all, refers to the *emptiness of time*" (Han, 2015, p. 116).

The repetition of despair organizes a time of its own, emptied of the alienness of the time of history, an arrest that is the basis of boredom. The desire not to waste time unleashes, in desperation, a paradoxical paralysis that has in the figure of boredom one of its main elements: *time loses us,* in its connections and its suspended meetings. However, in the current era, boredom is avoided via the *virtual link* as a prosthesis. Even if such a prosthesis works to network the social, so to speak, it doesn't solve the problem of time.

There is a creation of a time that is always being *online* and *connected* at work. Nevertheless, form the logic of absolute boredom, "time is no longer fulfilling. The freedom of the acting subject by itself does not produce any temporal gravitation" (Han, 2017b, p. 169). Han will tell us, concluding this reflection on time and boredom, that "will only be genuinely broken if the *vita activa* incorporates the *vita contemplativa* into its critical pole and once again serves the latter" (Han, 2017b, p. 177).

The predominance of the imperative "act now!" paradoxically establishes the levels of profound boredom. The frenetic speed of time that incites us to do it, to not stop doing it, is what intrinsically promotes a profound boredom that, as an echo of the emptying of time, leaves the subject suspended at the limits of the *event* and *experience*, but without the recourse to waiting and, therefore, with the difficulty of the transition, of the passage from one time to another.

Thinking about adolescence in terms of the above cannot be achieved without appealing to a particularity, which does not necessarily have to do with the status of development. This invariably leads us to reflect on that passage that Freud linked to latency, insofar as it occurs at a time known as *puberty*. Adolescence is not a *leaving behind of* childhood, or a radical erasure of childhood, since, in this particular time of the subject, these two spaces echo from their coincidences and points of separation.

The longing for the time in which the distance between desire and satisfaction was presented as a circuit of direct action, organizes the times of other destinations of drive that can be found in the logical time of adolescence. Temporality functions as a resource that organizes and introduces cuts in that tendency towards the pure demand for discharge that characterizes drive. This is another name for the "principle of reality."

The foreignness of adolescence differs, in this sense, from the foreignness of childhood. So-called "apathy" functions as a resource in which the youth subverts her/his relationship toward others. Apathy as a disorder is transformed into its opposite by means of sublimation: the foreigner (who is the adolescent) tries to make a place for herself/himself.

Adolescents affirm their radical strangeness and represent themselves for the others through self-destruction, the annihilation of the other, creativity, or the poetic-tragic that includes all these solutions. These displays are their singular *pathos* of rebelliousness and detachment from the world, the way they affirm their radical strangeness, and how they represent themselves for the others. "The so-called apathy of children and young people is the return in the real of the anonymity of adult desire" affirms De Lajonquière (2011, p. 218). But the anonymity of what desire? Of the desire for death. What is unknown, in this understanding, is placed at a distance through representation, a label on which will fall the contempt and distance of adult's passion for fullness, an adult that always *knows:* ADHD, addict, problem child . . . in short: alien, foreigner, evil-wild. For this reason, it is possible to say that *adolescence is another name for the uneasiness of the language*.

For the adult and for scientific narratives, the adolescent appears as a radical anomaly. However, in the face of this anonymity—or boredom—the potency of the youth is highlighted: the *event* itself, not only in its intersections with *experience* but at the point at which, following Badiou, an *event* is nothing but a rupture in the ordinary order of things. Following the approaches of the French philosopher, the *event*, moreover, is not "something that is the fruit of a natural evolution, but of a rupture" (Badiou, 2004, p. 32), it functions as a supplement to continuity, it is discontinuous; that is to say, it is established as a supplement to the repetition of what there is.

Irruption and rupture, as inherent elements of the *event*, are also part of adolescence, of this *rebirth* into the world of words, with the cost of pain and surprise that this transition from an adolescent to an adult position implies. Perhaps that is why today there are more teenagers in their forties than there are under-age adults. To put it another way, adolescence has been perpetuated in the longing for adults who become their children's children. This reversal is perceptible in some families. These new configurations have become more noticeable and they stand for the ominous past where the familiar itself returns, something in the familiar that does not cease to be inscribed. In this sense, adolescence is not only a rupture but a *plus*. Adolescence bursts as unexpected, an event that appears beyond the principle of pleasure.

Event: A Time for Virus and Network Dominance

I referred to the link between childhood, adolescence, and virtuality. Let me approach this now from the point of view of the problematic of late capitalism and the modalities of social relation. Technology now is proposed as the foundation of unusual forms of life, given, among other things, by the demand for hyper-connection in *real-time* and the segregation implicit in this. Those demands range from being up to date all the time to being informed, even if one does not know what to do with the accumulation of information. For example, staying ahead of a time on what is not yet announced produces, as we have already seen above with Byung-Chul Han, the paralysis that characterizes this being *ready for action* all the time, an action that, paradoxically, never arrives. This is precisely the mechanism of boredom.

As José Barrionuevo states, we are inscribed in a time belonging to late capitalism, a time "characterised by the stimulation of consumption, the overvaluation of the image and the importance of the immediacy produced by the mass media that allow us to witness instantly, obscenely and crudely, images of something that is happening thousands of kilometers away, as phenomena of globalisation" (Barrionuevo, 2011, p. 22).

This project of the "free" subject, from which late capitalism draws its inspiration, faithfully coincides with the project of the information age, since the latter is premised on "[t]he promise of the Information Age is the unleashing of unprecedented productive capacity by the power of the mind" (Castells, 2010, p. 395), something that Pierre Lévy had already contemplated when he said that "a general movement of virtualisation affects not only information and communication, but also bodies, economic functioning, collective frameworks of sensibility, or the exercise of intelligence" (Lévy, 1999, p.13).

Here, we could read *virtuality* almost in its etymological meaning: virtual is the potential. In this case, the potential of the network. *Virtuality* is the power stored in something to which one could aspire. In this understanding, the network is *virtual* because it has the power *to* and the power *of*. Power *to* perform different tasks at the same time. Power *to* use the network for different purposes. Yes, the power *to* can function as a means to an end—and, in this case, it would be the end of any internet user—so the power *to* is the end that one wishes to achieve through the network. And while the internet could be used for many individual ends, the end, par excellence, is to standardize the behavior of individuals collectively, beyond the isolated and atomized behavior of each individual. The network's power *to* serves as a means to reach the power *of*. Likewise, the power *of* prefigures the behavior of the subjects; in this way, the power *to* becomes a transitory end, a circular end.

The social project is that of freedom, but the technological-virtual project of our time is that of transparency. However, the discourse of transparency has also been poured implicitly on individuals, properly speaking in the use of the internet and social networks. Byung-Chul Han has reflected on this Dictatorship of Transparency, considering that "the omnipresent demand for transparency" has increased "until it has become a fetish" (Han, 2015, p. 11) by totalizing it. Everything must be seen, but not just any old way, in *high definition*, both discursively and visually. Hence transparency becomes pornographic, that is, "unmediated contact between the image and the eye. Things prove transparent when they abandon their singularity" (Han, 2015, p. 12).

In a second moment, Han will also say, concerning transparency, that "unbounded freedom and communication are switching over into total control and surveillance" (Han, 2017a, p. 8). Therefore, virtual transparency, taken to its ultimate consequences, leaves the user without the possibility of transmitting any experience, by emptying of meaning any kind of repeated and trivial exposition of one's own experiences, and also, virtual transparency turns on the subject in the form of total surveillance. A digital panopticon that acts and gains strength from the same freedom with which the subject moves through the network of networks.

Every link visited, every page opened, every image posted or word written becomes data. The important thing is not that every action on the internet can be *quantified,* but rather that, by working with data, the aim is to have control over the measurement of any behavior of the subjects. This *quantophrenia*, this madness of quantification that users themselves feed, is the Collective Intelligence that Lévy talks about: "What is collective intelligence? It is an intelligence distributed everywhere, constantly valorised" (Lévy, 2004, p. 19).

Collective intelligence is the accelerated and sustained production of data by users. However, Lévy seems to think in a utopian way, considering that this intelligence implies the recognition and mutual enrichment of people. If the internet achieves anything, it is to block any possibility of recognition between users. Without *experience,* there is no bond, and when the transparency of the network and the contents published by people are emptied of their particular significance in order to become a homogenous generation, recognition does not occur, there is only pornographic exposure of images and words.

One of the great differences that appear today with social distancing, in virtual meetings, in the use of the internet, in *online* work, is that humanity has shown a different way of bonding—the *virtual bond.* The image, the use of digital platforms, the presence of *others* on screens, as well as the use of words when we speak—in a mediated interaction, constructs a device that is adverse to the face-to-face experience.

This idea has taken us by surprise because of its effects. Roberto Esposito opens his *Immunitas* text by describing this point:

> The news headlines on any given day in recent years, perhaps even on the same page, are likely to report a series of apparently unrelated events. What do phenomena such as the battle against a new resurgence of an epidemic, opposition to an extradition request for a foreign head of state accused of violating human rights, the strengthening of barriers in the fight against illegal immigration, and strategies for neutralizing the latest computer virus have in common? Nothing, as long as they are interpreted within their separate domains of medicine, law, social politics, and information technology. (Esposito, 2011, p. 1)

If we subtract the date of publication, we could certainly think that it was last year. And as Esposito indicates, these phenomena are not related within their fields of knowledge, but if we make a broader reading, it is feasible to find connections, not only with the effects of meaning but as evidence of *these* new transversal discursive *links*; *virtual links.*

VIRTUAL BOND: CHILDHOOD, ADOLESCENCE, AND VIRUSES

To conclude this reflection on *the virtual bond*, modern time, adolescence, and technologies, it is inevitable to address the question of the *current* time, *to* which is added (to the virtual) the figure of the virus, and not precisely a computer virus, but the SARS-CoV-2 virus as an event that has highlighted inequality, an event that has highlighted inequalities in our psychical economies as much as in our monetary economies. The drastic effects of the pandemic have led to a reorganization of the conditions of our daily lives. We have confined everyday life to the communication space par excellence—in which the majority of the population is inscribed—recurring to isolation, to social distance, to meticulous hygiene. This is our new space: the web and its sites, social networks, and virtual platforms. These spaces are the ones that "facilitate" the link between the members of the population, given that they are presented as hygienic and effective. It is paradoxical that time-emptying spaces are now vital resources for the population to remain, as far as possible, healthy and alive, as well as still being enrolled in the field of therapeutic societies.

I will comment next on how the virus (of deadly effectiveness) has impacted the scope of our ways of conceiving life. In this connection, the Italian philosopher Emanuele Coccia tells us:

> The last two pages of *Metamorphosis*, written long before the current pandemic, are devoted to viruses. I outline the idea that the virus is the way the future exists in the present. The virus, in fact, is a pure force of metamorphosis that circulates from life to life without limiting itself to the boundaries of a body. Free, anarchic, almost immaterial, not belonging to any individual, it has the capacity to transform all living beings and allows them to reach their singular form. Think that part of our DNA, probably around 8%, is of viral origin! Viruses are a force of novelty, modification, transformation, they have a potential for invention that has played an essential role in evolution. They are proof that we are nothing more than genetic identities of multispecies bricolage. (Coccia, 2020, p. 25)

What the virus represents in one's lifestyle is similar to what Freud referred to regarding the narcissistic wounds suffered by humanity since the discoveries of Copernicus, Darwin, and himself. The earth is not the centre of the universe, man is not the direct descendant of God, and "the ego is not master in its own house" (Freud, 1917, p. 143). This virus confirms that we are natives of a spectrum much wider than the *human condition*. The certainties of science, beliefs, social ties and shelter (that cavern in which we take refuge from that familiar stranger: the virus, the network) stumble. The virus invents, recreates, transforms, and places us in front of what Coccia refers to: "we are nothing more than genetic identities of multi-species bricolage." The virus, according to the philosopher, reaffirms what Deleuze and Guattari already said: "We form a rhizome with our viruses, or rather our viruses cause us to form a rhizome with other animals" (Deleuze and Guatari, 1987, p. 10). This radical familiarity with viruses is what currently confronts us with death.

However, and despite the invitation to stop and think about the need to include other forms of life in our *becoming life*, there is a radical resistance to think. To think ourselves beyond the discursive networks of non-stop, of acceleration, of production, of resisting and continuing in the time of late capitalism. By means of education, *psi* therapeutic practices, *home office*, are all withdrawn into the cult of the *new way* of life that, prepared for decades, would keep us away from the world we have contributed to build. We live in a world that wants nothing to do with the uncanniness of the human, which is paradoxically and radically a viral remnant.

The virus is a destroyer that invents and manages to metamorphose the path that leads us to death. It is a reorganizer of the fields of life and death, which takes away from biopolitics and psychopolitics the supposed organisation of a total control of the variables that would determine the forms of life that *have to be*. The virus predominates over biopolitics, it throws overboard, from its acephalous quality, any attempt by statesmen to define its deadly levels and its times of propagation and contagion. The virus forces the world to (partially) stop. It has disorganized, and continues to destabilize the certainties that force us to think about the ways of doing in the world, among which psychoanalytic *doing* is included. It is essential to stop and listen to the subjectivity of the epoch precipitated by the pandemic.

What I have been proposing throughout this chapter, is to make this equation "adolescent = virus" as a strategic (psychoanalytical) interrogation for our times. Because, like the virus, the adolescent is the representation of the most familiar foreigner. Will it be possible to listen to them online? What games will we be able to invent and reinvent? Is not the institutional apparatus of health and mental health, at this moment, an example of subjection to these forms which, in the face of the uncertainty of the virus, question biopolitics about its conditions of possibility?

These questions are issues that arise as a result of the decentring of the presence of the human being and the installation of a *virtual bond,* which has emerged as that foreign and everyday presence that has now become familiar.

This alien figure, which can be thought as an irruption of the real, leaves us with a mark that prevents us from denying it; that is to say, it seals in our habitual way of doing things *as if nothing were happening* and *everything continues the same way*. It is impossible to think of ourselves now as we did more than a year ago. We could even affirm that it is, to a certain extent, necessary to problematize, not only childhood and adolescence, but also to continue, together with them, to interrogate other signifiers, such as the body, bioethics, biopolitics, and psychoanalysis itself. Or perhaps, to raise the stakes a little higher, to de-center these effects in the study of childhood, adolescence, and humanity.

REFERENCES

Badiou, A. (2004). *Circonstances, 2. Irak, foulard, Allemagne/France*. Léo Scheer.

Barrionuevo, J. (2011). *Adolescencia y juventud: Consideraciones desde el psicoanálisis*. Eudeba.

Bartalani, C. (2020). "Cuando no se puede decir." *First International Meeting of Relatives of Genocide Victims for Memory, Truth and Justice*. Ediciones AMP.

Castells, M. (2010). *The Information Age. Economy, Society, and Culture. Vol. III. End of Millennium*. Blackwell.

Coccia, E. (2020). "El virus es una fuerza anárquica." In F. García (Ed.), *Capitalism and pandemic* (p. 20). Filosofía Libre.

De Lajonquière, L. (2011). *Figuras de lo infantil*. New Vision.

Deleuze, G., and Guattari, F. (1987). *A Thousand Plateaus. Capitalism and Schizophrenia*. University of Minnesota Press.

Esposito, R. (2011). *Inmunitas*. Polity.

Freud, S. (1905). "Three Essays on Sexuality." In: *The Standard Edition of the Complete Psychological Works of Sigmund Freud, vol VII*. Vintage.

Freud, S. (1917). "A Difficulty in the Path of Psycho-Analysis." In: *The Standard Edition of the Complete Psychological Works of Sigmund Freud, Vol. XVII*. Vintage.

Freud, S. (1919). "The Uncanny" In: *The Standard Edition of the Complete Psychological Works of Sigmund Freud, Vol. XIX*. Vintage.

Freud, S. (1930). "Civilization and Its Discontents." In: *The Standard Edition of the Complete Psychological Works of Sigmund Freud, Vol. XXI*. Vintage.

Han, B. (2017a). *Psychopolitics*. Verso.

Han, B. (2017b). *The Scent of Time: A Philosophical Essay on the Art of Lingering*. Polity.

Han, B. (2015). *The Transparency Society*. Stanford.

Lévy, P. (1999). *¿Qué es lo virual?* Paidós.

Lévy, P. (2004). *Inteligencia Colectiva. Por una antropología del ciberespacio*. Pan-American Health Organization.

NOTE

1. Chapter translated from Spanish by Carlos Gómez Camarena.

PART II

Places

Chapter 6

"I Love You More"

Making Childing Visible— Children's Emotional Labor in Affluent Libidinal Economies

Anne-Marie Cummins

INTRODUCTION

This chapter is about a hidden subject, a non-subject—the emotional loads carried by children on behalf of their parents' happiness. It examines emotional work done by children in affluent and Westernized societies and the ways in which children have become somehow "responsible" for parental happiness. It will also explore a corresponding parental anxiety which exists in the face of precarity and ontological insecurity to produce "perfected" children and "perfect" childhoods. A case is made for recognition and instantiation of the concept of "childing" as a form of emotional labor in the libidinal economy of family life.

Whilst it is common in discussions of the politics of the family and the politics of mothering to notice the expansion of the activities which fall under the umbrella of "parenting," there is very little commentary on what this expansion in relationality and relational tasks means for children. One exception is Högberg who noted: "I would claim that child labor in contemporary Westernized cultures is of an emotional kind; it involves compensating for the structural weakness of the family, containing conflicting emotions and taking responsibility to hold the family together" (2010, p. 249). Högberg draws attention to something behind the routine idealization of children's "sacred" place in the generational order and suggests they are being asked to do something productive and difficult on behalf of their families. In this, she goes well beyond the by now commonplace observation first made by Zelitzer (1994) that children are economically useless but emotionally priceless and hints at the emotional burdens laid at the feet of the sacred child.

A great deal of the time and effort of parenting in Westernized and predominantly white cultures is taken up with the production of and a pre-occupation with super-saturated childhoods oriented towards the reproduction of class privilege via education. Such highly invested-in (and increasingly, via reproductive technologies, expensively acquired) child-products are well placed to take advantage of opportunities in a global economy (Katz, 2008). However, another large portion of the work of parenting is an attempt to provide particular types of "quality" in parent-child relationships—whether calls for "quality time" or a call for so-called positive parenting. There is a common-sense certainty that what is required are particular types and frequencies of "positive" parental emotion-display and the suppression of other, "negative" emotions. Warmth, affection, happiness, pride, and joy are in. Anxiety, anger, distress, and discouragement are out. Quite aside from the bizarre division of emotional exchanges into "good" or "bad," we ought to note that these preoccupations make up much of the work of socially sanctioned normative parenting. Even if such ideals are not achieved, the model they are based on maintains its cultural hegemony. Questions that follow from these developments include: What are children now required to do in return? What forms of child-subjectivity are being shaped in this climate? What kinds of child subjects are needed to fulfill these parental demands?

The argument that is made here is that this kind of parenting (super-saturated, "positive" and performative) calls forth *childing*—a main feature of which is the requirement from children for frequent demonstrations of satisfaction, gratitude, pleasure, and reassurance of their own happiness. Childing is the emotional work children are routinely expected do to do to show to anxious parents that they are indeed "perfected" child-products whose emotional and growth needs have been met, and whose parents have supplied near-perfect childhoods. It is also argued that this comes with a cost to children—especially those who fail to deliver on their emotional targets. That there is not even a recognized term for this type of relationality is richly instructive. How this state of affairs arrived and some of the consequences for children are now sketched.

VERTICAL AND HORIZONTAL LIBIDINAL ECONOMIES

Firstly, some attention can be drawn to the *vertical libidinal economies* between adults and children, parents and children and what children now "mean" in the current generational order. The term "vertical" here indicates an unequal or hierarchical relationship between generations and the flow of libido *between* generations is discussed.

In what Lancey (2002) has called neontocracies (as opposed to gerontocracies) children are cast by adults as cherubs, simultaneously idealized and disempowered. Children occupy the sacred space once allotted to religion. To put it another way, they are the new opium of the people. They are positioned as happiness providers and natural anti-depressants. British author and psychoanalyst Adam Phillips has noted

> Children, I think, suffer—in a way that adults don't always realize—under the pressure their parents put on them to be happy, which is the pressure not to make their parents unhappy, or more unhappy than they already are . . . we are more dependent on our children than they are on us; and we are dependent, in brief, on their happiness. (Phillips, 2010, p. 90)

No longer is having children a contribution to the "common weal": no longer is it a social duty or a necessity—it is a personal and private choice undertaken in the expectation of existential fulfillment. But this is freighted by something else, something full of anxiety and desire. There is an anxious need to "get it right" which exists alongside a fetishistic attachment to the prevailing construction of childhood as sacred and children as the ultimate objects of fulfillment. Like commodities, and commodity fetishism, the image of the child enthralls, distracts and impels desire. As a social construction with numerous dimensions childhood is ever-ready and available as a receptacle for anxiety and projection. We might even say that, along with ideas about innocence and purity, this is the aspect of childhood which has been most stable.

Katz (2008) talks about childhood as "spectacle," as a site for commodification and accumulation. But what lends these processes extra psychic energy is adult anxiety. Anxiety over the future is routinely channeled or projected into the production of perfecting children and then finding ways to securitize their everyday lives and futures. Highly invested in children, groomed for competitive advantage are—at least in parental fantasy—securitized against this uncertain future. The quest for perfection and complete control, not realizable anywhere else in ontologically insecure times, re-surfaces in relation to children, whose value and social good we can all apparently agree on. Anxiety is the raw material of spectacle and there is much to be anxious about. Relays of adult anxiety about the political, environmental, and geo-political future become diverted into a spectacular absorption with childhood and attempts to tightly control children's experiences. Anxieties get displaced onto children as "projects" to be completed as near perfectly as possible. With the right planning and input, the psychic profit and loss sheet for each child shows a credit, and although that credit will rarely yield a financial return on investment it will likely yield a moral, narcissistic, or anxiety-reduction return. The processes described above work at the very practical level of material social practices but also "in the realm of the imaginary, of appearances, representation and crisis" (Katz, 2008, p. 7).

In Western societies, while paid child labor in the fields and factories and children's capacities to make direct financial contributions to family life has (mostly) ended, child labor as such has not so much ended as been transformed. There is an un-named and invisible emotional economy in which children's work now is to "be happy" and make parents fulfilled. Where once they functioned as an index of wealth and economic survival, now they are asked to function as an index of emotional wealth and as an emotional survival aid. Child labor now takes this much more indirect form of emotional labor which, if successful, sustains and stabilizes parents as parents, and also as economically productive subjects. What we might call children's emotional services are crucial to parental well-being and functionality. This is an emotional contribution with an economic dimension. However, this occult commodification of parent-child relationships, much like the concept of childing, is hard to see, hard to name, and runs against a certain fundamentalism whereby childhood belongs to the sphere of the sacred rather than the profane world of commercialization, profit, and loss. To even name it draws vulgar attention to mechanisms of pricing, investment, accumulation, and profit as they work in an intimate sphere. Worse, it is to suggest that this semi-conscious profit and loss sheet operates in relation to the value of children as emotionally rewarding subjects. If all goes well, they fulfill their parents' intimacy needs alongside demonstrating their worth as privately produced, super-saturated "investments" whose high commodity-value marks out the success of parental strategies of what Lareau, back in 2003, called "concerted cultivation."

In such vertical libidinal economies there is some recognition of the flow of affective desire downwards through the generations, but little attention given to the demands placed on the desired objects—children—and expectations upwards of reciprocity or mutuality. Parents' avowed desire is that children be as happy as possible in their own right, but as we have seen, this comes with an unvoiced wish that insists children demonstrate this by virtue of their contentment, happiness and, if possible, high levels of achievement. They are asked to generate parental happiness and self-esteem and to provide intense, sustained emotional recognition and reward. Inevitably, some children will be good "value for money" in this respect, others, as we will see later, will not.

Secondly, we need to consider the effects of *horizontal libidinal economies* set up by what Giddens (1991) calls pure relationship in both the formation of parental couples and in the desire to become a parent. By "horizontal," what is meant here is non-hierarchical relationships or equalized relationships between parents, as opposed to the vertical relationships between generations.

Amongst adults, the key dynamics of pure relationship are mutual self-disclosure and appreciation of each other's unique capacities to love and be lovable. Pure relationships however are by definition unstable and contingent, that is, they are entered into for their own sake only and only for as long as they remain satisfying to both parties. This has consequences not only for children's and adults' emotional well-being, but also for how children come to be positioned as supplementary or substitute sources of meaning and connection in the search for pure relationship. The shadow of pure relationship falls on children in ways which are rarely discussed.

One obvious shadow is what happens when a partner wishes to withdraw from the relationship. It can sometimes mean that investment in (adult) personal happiness is partly financed by inroads into children's emotional capital.

> In withdrawing from promises to each other, in pursuing their own individual destinies, the partners also withdrew from an implicit contract with their children, whose stake in the partnership had not been a voluntary choice. The partners' quest for self-fulfillment was purchased by discounting the longer-term interests of their kids (sic), by withdrawing some of the investment from their children, in order to invest in themselves. (Offer, 2006, p. 340)

Another shadow is that beyond the parental couple itself, a modified form of pure relationship comes to define adult-child relationships. As pure relationship became the currency for adults, the emotional work of the children of these unions changed accordingly. As Beck (1992, p. 118) put it "the child is the source of the last remaining, irrevocable, inexchangeable, primary relationship. Partners come and go. The child stays. Everything that is desired, but not realizable in the relationship is directed to the child." Under this pressure, parent-child relationships come to be freighted with the work of intimacy, self-fulfillment, and recognition. What was once straightforwardly relationally horizontal slips into something more vertical.

Often, what is being asked for as a barometer of "good" relationship is disclosing intimacy. To be clear, disclosing intimacy in this context is not to be understood in the sexual way but in terms of an intimacy of the self, meaning "close association, privileged knowledge, deep knowing and understanding and some form of love" (Jamieson, 1998, p. 13). One of the common ways of demonstrating this intimacy in family life is through what is known as "quality time." Parents in fact spend less time with their children than they did in the 1960s, but attempt to compensate by the pursuit of "quality time," something mutually rewarding, full of smiles, fun, emotional intensity, and high levels of closeness. More than this, disclosing intimacy is not just the domain of mothers, as might be expected. In 2008 Dermott coined the phrase "intimate fathering" to describe the way fathers were now likely to describe relationships with their children as "close." Good and valued relationships with children were attributed to the high levels of disclosure and "communication"—meaning the amount of talking, listening, and understanding which fathers felt themselves to do.

Behind the richness of routine quality-time and disclosing intimacy however lies something more anxious: for time-pressed parents, quality time acts as an emotional insurance policy. A re-assurance is being sought that the time spent away from their children has not somehow deprived or harmed them and can be off-set or mended. For children there is a subtle or not so subtle demand to make parents feel good, to have a good time, to be pleased and grateful and show themselves to be rewarding child-subjects. It is not surprising that in a climate of social anxiety about childhood, many parents experience intimacy and quality time with their children as reassuring evidence of "getting it right." Being privy to a child's wishes, fears and fantasies, detailed knowledge of and sympathy with the child's inner and outer worlds, are read as confirmatory of virtuous parenting. How this might feel to children, at least some of the time, is discussed in the following section on the emotional tasks of childing.

PARENTING CALLS FORTH CHILDING: THE EMOTIONAL LABORS OF CHILDREN IN AFFLUENT LIBIDINAL ECONOMIES

The concept of emotional labor as defined by Hochschild's 1983 book *The Managed Heart* is now almost forty years old. It describes, amongst other things, the ways in which emotion work as a requirement of paid, often female labor, takes its toll causing stress and burnout. Hochschild emphasizes the human cost of emotional labor. Emotional display is required in many lines of work, but this is known to be hard work since feigning emotion over a long period of time is exhausting. The resort to deep as opposed to surface acting, that is, fusing the authentic and the acted self can result in feelings of inauthenticity and emotional dissonance. It is not hard to see how emotion work is transformed into its opposite—not a source of human bonding and satisfaction but of alienation and eventual emotional burn-out. Like symbolic violence, emotional labor, whilst not classically oppressive, is a mark of one's subordination.

The concept of emotional labor has been widely deployed and over the last three decades there have been many empirical studies of parents, and especially women's, emotional labor, both at home and at work. Most recently,

Lin and others (2021) have discussed the way in which techniques of positive parenting, as well as promoting particular forms of emotional regulation, as part of the developmental project of creating emotionally rounded, competent and therefore "successful" child subjects, frequently leads to stress and burn-out amongst parents. Stress and burn-out amongst children is not mentioned. The authors of this article note that intensive parenting is taking on more and more job-like or work-like features where there are externally imposed prescriptions and standards, expectations from external bodies about "results" (having a school-ready child for instance) and greater external monitoring, control and sanction by statutory health and welfare services.

Assuming this reading of parenting as a job contains some truth about parents, why not apply it to children's relational work too? If parenting is a kind of job, and potentially a source of emotional labor, then so too is its relational twin, childing. One objection which could be raised to this and which will be addressed here is that children are clearly not employees in the sense described by Hochschild: they are not economically productive and so in theoretically precise terms they do not perform any labor, let alone emotional labor. If anything, it might be argued, they are the boss-class so, perhaps it would be better to opt for the term "emotion-work" and to say that, insofar as children provide any services in the family, these best fit the term "emotion-work," a term which is typically used to describe the business of keeping marriages, friendships, and other private relationships on track. However, while these arguments may have merit, the point being made in this paper is that there is more to be gained than lost in hanging on to the term "emotional labor" in relation to children and childing. The phrase can be used as an heuristic device to help make visible an otherwise invisible economics of sentiment and the operation of mechanisms of pricing, value, investment, accumulation, commodification and profit as they work in the intimate sphere of adult-child relationships. Moreover, we can also enquire about the function of denial or scotomization of the existence of childing as emotional labor. Psychosocially speaking, does *not* naming it serve any defensive purpose?

What follows is an attempt to make visible two of the clusters or typical formations of childing called forth by parenting in affluent libidinal economies. The first is a cluster of dynamics linked to the positioning of children as emotionally rewarding *projects* who fulfill their parents' intimacy needs. The second is what follows from positioning children as *products*—privately produced, super-saturated investments whose high future commodity-value marks out the success of parental strategies of concerted cultivation (Lareau 2003).

First, the pressure on children of parental desires that they be emotionally rewarding *projects*. Such a desire could only emerge in a neontocracy where children are in themselves prized objects and sources of happiness. In these libidinal economies, children are routinely looked to in order that they might provide emotional reassurance to parents via their evident happiness that mom and dad are "getting it right." There is a subtle demand for the performance of happiness and love (unhappiness is intolerable, hatred even more so) and for children to give, every day, shows of gratification, thanks, and assurances of their own happiness including the affirmation of love. "I love you," "No, I love you more": whichever way round the sequence comes, parent to child, child to parent, this shows how much each of the parties is under pressure to excessively please the other. Childing therefore becomes the emotional work children are routinely expected to do to show to anxious parents that they are indeed "perfected" child-products whose emotional and growth needs have been met, and whose parents have supplied near-faultless childhoods.

The desire that children be emotionally rewarding projects could also only emerge in a culture where children, by their very existence, are anticipated to compensate for the structural weaknesses in what are often contingent, conditional, and impermanent parental relationships. Here, children's "job," in times when often both parents work, is to figuratively speaking, guard the hearth fires. Once, this was the job of women, now it is more likely to be the child who is the "angel of the house," as the Victorians used to put it. Part of the task is hypervigilance in relation to the affiliation between parents. As Högberg (2010, p. 250) put it, "There was a time when parents endured and stayed together for the sake of the children, today, it seems to me, the children have to endure conflicts and mediate between their parents." Additionally, many of the practical problems which occur in family life concern complicated childcare arrangements where children may perceive themselves as causing problems and conflicts between their parents. In other words, children have to become watchful guardians of the adult relationship on whose "success" they depend. This, along with being emotionally rewarding child-subjects, is a burden which most children of previous generations did not have to bear.

A second group of emotional burdens of childing comes from parental desires to produce high-investment child *products* whose success (or not) can be used to "read-off" the extent to which parents have successfully created a "perfect" child who has had a perfected or fairy-tale childhood. In a culture of winners and losers raising a "successful" child, a winner, requires a degree of obsessionality and rule-following at a granular level and over long periods of time in regard to child-rearing practices and structures. This can be as ordinary and economically low-cost as subscribing to so-called Positive Parenting or any number of parenting "tribes" with a go-to manual, or, as financially intensive as enrichment programs, private schools and elite sports coaching. The aim will be to micro-calibrate the landscape of childhood, minimize risk (however conceived) and promote measurable outcomes or results which, at least in fantasy, optimize children's potential.

What kind of childing is called forth by this kind of parenting? The economically useless child can't demonstrate their worth through the production of chopped wood or a plowed field. Their sense of value and utility must therefore depend on praise and validation from parents. Likewise, the task of parenting is no longer to prepare children for traditional ways of life but to "cultivate" them. Parents' sense of value and utility will therefore depend on receipt of children's validation of their parenting. Validation from other parents or professionals is good but from your own children is best. Under such circumstances, parents and children get caught up in sets of mutually validating emotional dynamics which celebrate the limitless potential of children's talent and the corresponding virtue of parents in developing this "talent." These dynamics of mutually intense recognition are in some ways compensatory for the emptying out of functions from the modern family but they also mirror observations about the instrumentalization of subjectivity and personal involvement typical of managers and employees in creative knowledge work (Ekman, 2013). In such work, a fantasmatic dynamic is sustained through relational intensity and operates via the twin dynamics of grandiosity and "authenticity." Everyone is special. Everyone specializes in grandiose mirroring. For all its pleasures, there is something both exhausting and alienating in this dynamic. My suggestion is that something very similar happens in families where children are intensively cultivated and where disappointment and limit are difficult to accept. For children, the job is to succeed, to be seen to succeed, and to not mind the instrumentalization of subjectivity which lies behind their success.

We should not be fooled though by the appearances of authenticity described above. Something collusive and narcissistic is afoot wherein the child, product of and participant in grandiose mirroring, is simultaneously constituted as a perfectly alienated consumer of parental investment. In thinking of childhood as "spectacle" (Katz, 2008), we are put in touch with Debord's idea of capital accumulated to the point that it becomes mere image where what was once directly lived becomes empty representation. What childing entails in these circumstances is a simultaneously fulness and emptiness. Back in 1980, Kovel's work on the narcissistic family noted the paradox of parenting practices being simultaneously impinging and over-involved, and, at the same time remote, inauthentic and "as if." The child is the object of parental desire and self-esteem, but is not treated authentically as an "other" in his/her own right. By offering the child a sense of his own importance, says Kovel, the parents make it difficult for the child to acknowledge his or her disappointment in their shortcomings. One might add to this the burden of not *being* disappointing and protecting parents from so-called negative emotions.

The inverse of positive parenting, in the sense understood by the positive parenting movement, is positive childing—warmth, affection, happiness, pride and joy are in. Anxiety, anger, distress, and discouragement are out. Such relationships succeeds at an obvious level, but fail in a deeper sense. In fact, when parent-child relationships fail in this deeper sense, the main element which resists failure is "the quality of adornment" (Kovel, 1980, p. 94). At least the heavily invested-in child product can make the parents proud, even if the relationship is weak. This echoes what Katz wishes to say about spectacle concerning children to whom there is "value-added" via strategies of accumulation "The thing itself and having it are reduced to appearance . . . the image exceeds the object" (Katz, 2008, p. 8).

SOME COSTS TO CHILDREN

At no era in history has it been routine for children's proclaimed or suspected unhappiness to be so unbearable to parents. We want to fix them; their unhappiness is an intolerable rebuke. It is argued here that there are high and often unacknowledged costs to children of failing to deliver on emotional targets: or being a disappointing return on parental investment. Whatever their official status as sacred objects they are still expected to be emotionally rewarding *projects,* and emotionally rewarding high-investment *products*. What happens to the emotionally unrewarding or unhappy child, or to the disappointing child who fail to accumulate in value and to "optimize" their potential is that they must be written-off or fixed. It is no secret that right across Westernized and affluent cultures categories of childhood "disorder" have proliferated, that diagnoses of so-called "disorders" in children abound. The medicalization or criminalization of childhood have become the predominant forms of governmentality in children's lives. We might speculate failing to deliver on one's emotional targets might be behind the proliferation of autism, Asperger's, depression and bi-polarity "diagnoses" much as the rise in ADHD/ADD diagnoses coincides with the growth of standardized testing. Such diagnoses have led to an increasing number of medicated children across all classes "reflecting parental anxiety over perceived imperfections and the need to meet school and other institution's benchmarks of achievement and standards of normal behavior" (Katz, 2008, p. 12). At an empirical level, these are of course issues for further research. The case is being made here is that the unacknowledged demand for childing is behind the fact that more and more children—from all social groups—are falling into the categories of being emotionally unrewarding projects and emotionally unrewarding products.

Less dramatically, there are the everyday costs of being needed so much and children's attempts to resist this. Stress and burnout are commonly identified costs of the emotional labor performed by adults and by parents. Much research into emotional labor shows that there are problems with the cumulative intensities of compliance with emotional display rules which result in burn-out. How might this look with children? One answer comes when we think about what Sennett (1977) has called destructive *gemeinschaft*, the incitement to mutual self-disclosure and its link to what was earlier referred to as the demand for disclosing intimacy. This amounts to pressure, keenly felt by many teenagers, for a one-sided disclosure which they often experience as a coercive form of being known and "understood." It is an especial grief to many parents when they go from "hero" to "beg-friend" in the eyes of their teenage children (BBC News, 2018). To quote Sennett, whose analysis of destructive *gemeinschaft* takes in both horizonal and vertical relations in the family

> The fact of what the rules are objectively gets lost easily in a much more subtle but stronger process of asserting the self, guilt over that assertion, and triumph over the child in which the child is only a means to the parents' need for legitimation. . . . These are precisely the means by which a confused sense of object relations is instilled into a growing human being; that is, the means by which a narcissistic character disorder is built. (Sennett, 1977, p. 196)

It is possible to disagree with the claim that destructive *gemeinschaft* causes narcissistic character disorder whilst accepting the observation that its extraction is a triumph. One thing to repeat here about emotional labor—and by connection, childing—is its alienating character and that it is ultimately a sign of one's subordination.

NARCISSISM AND/OR OBSESSIONALITY?

There is one final comment to add about children's emotional labor in affluent libidinal economies which is to begin thinking of these developments not only through the usual lens of narcissism and a culture of narcissism (Lasch, 1979, Kovel, 1980) but also as richly illustrative of a type of obsessionality which may say something about the times we live in.

This is what Gherovici and Webster (2014) hint at when they refer to the obsessional factory of child-rearing programs and advice which are drawn on by some of their female patients presenting with obsessional structures. The contention being made in this paper is that these obsessional structures also apply to current parenting practices—and, by correspondence, to the childing they call forth. The obsession that collectively grips the project of parenting is to make a perfect world where unruly desire never makes an appearance because everything is under control. In fantasy, the parent is made perfect in relation to the child who can demand everything, and be granted it, but who actually, for preference, desires nothing of the parent. This is a type of libidinal economy where parents seem to want an Other, but one who does not authentically want or need. Just as, according to Lacan, the obsessional wants a Master who does not desire, so too the obsessional factory of parenting requires children who demand but who do not desire. It has already been noted that with their frequent absences in the world of work and the demand that the child "keep the home-fires burning," that parents need children who in a way do not need parents. Gherovici and Webster's observation about obsessional structures in relation to perfected parenting enriches our understanding of what is at stake, psychically. To quote at some length:

> In this type of parenting there is an obsession with limits which are solved through obsessional structures for children which preclude desire. . . . Parents seem more and more terrified of displaying their desire to their children and do everything to reduce their children's desires to satisfiable demands. . . . It is not childhood navigated as a series of wants, losses, difficult desires, and separations. It is a childhood in which these are to be controlled and covered over as much as possible. (Gherovici and Webster, 2014, no page)

The ideal child is in this instance one who makes no real demands and whose authentic hatreds are to be avoided at all costs. Assuming this to be true, or at least a plausible hypothesis, it follows that the predicaments of childhood in affluent libidinal economies include not just the ongoing performance of happiness but also a request for the internal deadening of a full range of childish desires and needs. This, and other implications of taking seriously the notion of childing, are in need of further thought, scholarship, and empirical research.

REFERENCES

BBC News. (2018). https://www.bbc.co.uk/news/stories-43331415. Accessed October 25, 2021.

Beck, U. (1992). *Risk society: Towards a new modernity.* Sage.

Dermott, E. (2008). *Intimate Fatherhood: a sociological analysis.* Routledge.

Ekman, S. (2013). Fantasies about work as limitless potential: how managers and employees seduce each other through dynamics of mutual recognition. *Human Relations, 66(9),* 1160–81.

Gherovici, P. and Webster, J. (2014). Observations from Working with Female Obsessionals. *European Journal of Psychoanalysis, (2)* 2014, https://www.journal-psychoanalysis.eu/observations-from-working-with-female-obsessionals/. Accessed March 31, 2021.

Giddens, A. (1991). *Modernity and Self-identity: Self and Society in the Late Modern Age.* Polity.

Hochschild, A. R. (1983). *The Managed Heart: Commercialization of human feeling.* University of California Press.

Högberg, B. (2010). Rethinking Childhood: The quest for participation and its implication for group relations. *Organizational and Social Dynamics, 10(2),* 238–62.

Jamieson, L. (1998). Intimacy Transformed: A critical look at the pure relationship. *Sociology, 33(3),* 477–94.

Katz, C. (2008). Cultural Geographies lecture: "Childhood as spectacle: relays of anxiety and the reconfiguration of the child." *Cultural Geographies, 15(1),* 5–17.

Kovel, J. (1980). *Narcissism and the Family.* Telos. http://journal.telospress.com/content/1980/44/88.short. Accessed March 31, 2021.

Lancy, D. (2002). *The Anthropology of Childhood: Cherubs, chattels, changelings.* Cambridge University Press.

Lareau, A. (2003). *Unequal Childhoods: Class, race and family life.* University of California Press.

Lasch, C. (1979). *The Culture of Narcissism: American life in an age of diminishing expectations.* Norton.

Lin, G-X., Hansotte, L., Meeussen, L., et al. (2021). Parenting with a Smile: Display rules, regulatory effort and parental burnout. *Journal of Social and Personal Relationships, 38(9),* 2701–21.

Offer, A. (2006). *The Challenge of Affluence: self-control and well-being in the United States and Britain since 1950.* Oxford University Press.

Phillips, A. (2010). *On Balance.* Penguin Books.

Sennett, R, (1977). Destructive Gemeinschaft. In N. Birnbaum, *Beyond the crisis,* Oxford University Press.

Zelitzer, V. (1994). *Pricing the Priceless Child: the changing social value of children.* Princeton University Press.

Chapter 7

The Precarity of Children's Mental Wellness in Aotearoa New Zealand

Kaye P. Cederman

The New Zealand government's "Child and Youth Wellbeing" initiative (2019) posits a utopian ideal: "Our vision for the Child and Youth Wellbeing Strategy is a bold one—that New Zealand be the best place in the world for children and young people" (NZ Government, 2019, p. 3). The term "the best place for children" suggests a single category of "children" exists in this country, when clearly, and the document fully recognizes this, there are vast differences in children's lives dependent upon hierarchies of race, class, ability, gender, and socioeconomics. For example, the 2021 research survey *Whakatika* (Amend, Fix, Rectify), explores the extent and impact of racism faced by Māori in Aotearoa, showing that 96 percent of Māori experience racism every day. "Racism is alive and well. It is intentional it is calculated; it is precise at ensuring the power and control of colonial structures remain in place" (Survey respondent, 51, wahine (woman), 2021, p. 9). As Tinirau (2021) asserts in his commentary on Whakatika:

> Racism deeply impacts a person's health—both physical and mental—as well as their *wairua* (the spirit of a person). . . . The harms of racism include grief and anger. Racism damages connections and compromises ability to pass on Māori ways of knowing and being to future generations. (Tinirau, 2021, p. 1)

Indeed, the boldness of the Government's utopic appeal suggests that a present-day truth concerning child and youth wellness and illness is being neutralized through governmental restraint and regulation. In his critique of the appearance of neutrality that pervades the machinery of institutions, Foucault (1984) had argued for the relinquishment of utopian schemes (p. 6). Consequently, a utopian future can be read as being generated by, and generating, methods of regulation, punishment, supervision, and restraint. This is "the machinery by which the power relations give rise to a possible corpus of knowledge, and knowledge extends and reinforces the effects of this power" (Foucault, 1984, p. 177).

The Child and Youth Wellbeing Strategy (2019) is a detailed set of new knowledges, governmental services and systems that have arisen from extensive consultation (10,000 New Zealanders, including children and young people) to discover what "all children and young people want and need for good wellbeing and what we can do to help" (2019, p. 3). There are also recent Ministry of Health documents such as *Kia Mānawanui Aotearoa* (To Be Proud) Long-term pathway to mental wellbeing (2021), and *Te Whakamaua:* Māori Health Action Plan 2020–2025 (*Te Whakamaua* To Fix Attention On), These have progressive implications for the mental health of Māori and Pasifika children but colonial power structures and regulations which have long acceded to the voices of a dominant Pākehā constituency means even this relatively progressive and inclusive social democratic government treads warily around issues of Māori and Pasifika policy or equality.

Despite this, there is recognition in the Wellbeing Strategy (2019) that the disparity between the NZ Government's utopic vision of wellbeing and actual mental health statistics amplifies the message that hierarchies of race and class have generated an epoch of illbeing. This is about more than the chronic difficulty of accessing mental health services, lack of equity, the long waiting lists, and shortage of trained professionals. To cite *Koi Tū* (Sharp, Pointed), The Centre for Informed Futures at the University of Auckland, this is "a silent pandemic of mental morbidity."

> The last decade has seen a rapid and concerning rise in youth psychological distress and suicide rates. Nationally [in Aotearoa], poor mental health for youth is persistently inequitable and worsening. Impacts of COVID-19 on youth mental health is likely to be extensive and enduring. Protection and promotion of mental wellbeing for youth is now a matter of urgency. (Koi Tū, 2020)

The contention is that child and youth mental health problems are now at crisis point. A portion of the blame for this spike is laid at the door of the pandemic COVID-19, the subsequent two-year lockdown and online teaching and learning. The Koi Tū (2020) research specifically asks why the rate of mental health problems has risen so quickly; and what aspects of young people's lives today are behind this. "In seeking answers we should examine both proximal issues such as the digital milieu, and more removed issues such as early life experience, trauma, educational structures, changing parenting, family and social contexts" (2020, p. 3). This means considering how pre-existing conditions in this country are intersecting with the digital milieu.

DISPLACING THE FAMILIAR

Waves of children have migrated with their parents to this isolated Pacific country or been born shortly after arduous sea voyages. Māori arriving first over 700 years ago; European settlers landing ashore in the 1800s, followed thereafter by an ongoing flow of refugees and immigrants from all parts of the world. Young Māori *tamariki* (children) and *rangatahi* (youth) were integral to *whanau, hapu* and *iwi* (families, communities, and tribes) as they were forcibly displaced by British armies, Pākehā traders and settlers; a colonizing imperial force delivering transformative change with, for example, guns, the English language, European sanitation and culture, Christianity, technology, and racist practices and attitudes, alongside the loss of Māori lives, lands, and language. The letters from the first European immigrants (such as my Great-Grandmother Wilhelmina who sailed from Germany on the *Shakespeare*, a "bride ship," in 1852) also report their anguish, shock, and fear, as well as intense loneliness for families and homelands and a meaninglessness accompanying "the displacement of the familiar" (Belich, 1996, p. 293).

Migration, racism, and colonization still form a relevant backdrop to contemporary children's lives but have been transformed by changes occurring over the last fifty years as Aotearoa has gone through extreme cultural, economic, and ideological change. Globalization, communications technology, economic growth, and competitiveness now situate subjects amidst a social, ecological, and psychic environment that is increasingly altered. Kelsey (1999) argues that this global trend compounds the alienation, apathy and withdrawal of people, families, and communities of the poor and disaffected. It also reflects debate over the unsustainable social costs engendered by free market theories, including how pro-active government policies have shattered urban and rural communities with no regard for the effects on people's lives. For Kelsey

> The urban poor—Māori and Pacific islands people, the elderly, women alone, single parents, young unemployed, working-class families, new immigrants, the mentally ill, among others—were trapped in enclaves of unemployment, homelessness and poverty. (Kelsey, 1999, p. 368)

Kelsey describes New Zealand as now clearly polarized along lines of race, gender, age, and economic class. She cites one in five New Zealanders and one-third of the country's children as living in poverty, more than twice as many as in 1988. In 1999, "Māori families were two and a half times (and Pacific Islands families three and a half times) more likely to live in poverty than Pākehā families" (p. 368).

Such narratives of psycho-social impoverishment, alienation, illness, and anxiety surround the political economy and provide a backdrop to how children's mental illness is now experienced. These narratives also inevitably position the individual amidst the corporate, consumerist, "identity mania" constituting what Baudrillard calls "neo-individualism" (Baudrillard, 1994, p. 104). All the while, various psycho-social agencies urge people to meet norms of being "free-choosing," autonomous, happy, and fulfilled, in accord with other consumerist liberal democracies.

SYMPTOMS

As a child and adolescent psychoanalyst, the first questions I ask myself when meeting new child patients and their families are always about the symptoms, meaning the unique efforts each child makes to manage their suffering. To whom or what do the symptoms refer? What are their meanings and functions? To whom do they relate? What might they tell us about how this family handles jouissance? If symptoms are the way in which a child copes with something problematic in their life, then they also shine a light on where the problem and possibly the solution might be found.

Koi Tū (2020) highlights symptoms in Aotearoa such as suicidality and depression based on socioeconomic inequities, including gender, within cohorts of youth.

> The gender inequities in youth mental health highlighted in the Youth19 findings are not new. Between 2000 and 2019 the Youth 2000 findings reveal female youth consistently have rates of depression symptomatology and suicidality that are almost double the rates reported by their male peers . . . 2019 survey findings show the gender inequity in depression has increased among Pasifika youth with a sharp increase in female rates to 37 percent compared to 15 percent for males. (Menzies, Gluckman, and Poulton, 2020, p. 4)

Sharp of UNICEF New Zealand pinpoints "ADHD, anxiety, autism, bipolar disorder, conduct disorder, depression, eating disorders, intellectual disability" (Sharp, 2021). Indeed, significant clinical literature, like Benvenuto (2014), reminds us that children's symptoms have a distinctive contemporary bias. The most ubiquitous reflect disorders of depression, post-traumatic stress, and neurological "information processing" difficulties/disorders, self-harm and cutting, suicidal thoughts, addictions, loneliness and sexual/gender anxiety and distress.

We know from Freud that "A symptom is a sign of, and a substitute for, an instinctual satisfaction which has remained in abeyance; it is a consequence of the process of repression" (Freud, S. 1926, p. 91). From a Lacanian perspective the symptom is more of a response by the subject to the Real; a trauma that has emerged for the child. It is another found in an uncanny dimension where the death drive is working, and language is overwhelming the subject.

Kristeva (1996) argues that Freud's text *Beyond the Pleasure Principle* (1920) reveals that Freud's conviction that the pleasure principle dominated psychic life was augmented by his belief that the purest drive was the death drive. Kristeva (1996) finds it helpful to consider Freud's claim that "while Eros means the creation of bonds, Thanatos, the death drive, signifies the disintegration of bonds and the ceasing of circulation, communication, and social relationships" (Kristeva, 1996, p. 79). She claims that the disintegration of bonds constitutes a "melancholic-depressive composite" because both melancholia and depression are stamped by "a divestment of social bonds and the ceasing of all relationships [and] a devaluation of language" (p. 80). In Kristeva's words: "No, we're not interested in your society, your activities, or your language. We are different from that; we do not exist; we are dead" (p. 80).

If we wonder to whom contemporary symptoms refer in their meanings and functions, and their social and familial context, there is a quality about them that seems to resist being solely quantified in any geographical, socio-cultural, ethnic, or racial terms. This urges consideration of how children's symptoms in Aotearoa today reflect the intersection of socio-cultural inequities and immersion in the newly digital and psycho-technological way of life.

HOMO DIGITAR

Understanding Aotearoa's self-determination through the lens of this technological revolution can be categorized in Baudrillard's terms as "a frenzied proliferation of signs of the real and of 'difference': 'reality' and 'difference'" (Baudrillard, 1981, p. 86). Aotearoa, like other Western nations, now experiences models of consumption, production, progress, and development, which prolifically hyper realize such models of reality in their own image. In this view, the spread of digital technology is a new form of cultural imperialism. Traditional experiences of Māori asserting *rangatiratanga* (leadership, chieftainship, self-determination) and attempts to remake European and American reality so that it is meaningful to Māori, Pākehā, Asian, and Pasifika subjects in Aotearoa are now confronted and transformed by the hyperreal and global nature of mass consumer society and techno-scientific change.

With the technological proliferation of hyperreality in the interests of the marketplace, choice and commodification precede and supersede the reality of former ways of life for children and families. Children's lives like other aspects of "hyper" culture, must now be understood as primarily facilitating a pragmatic and commodified function. In Baudrillard's terms, the relation between such reality and its representation is deeply problematic because of the currency of the simulated production of cultural and emotional phenomena. It is as if reality has changed so drastically that we are now confronted by what it is to be a child on social media sites and platforms, the virtual communities and networks. This is childhood as simulation in the present rather than "real" childhoods—as a relation of past/present—with its anchoring in some originary moment. Critical engagement with the manner of this transformation includes recognizing how the technological wizardry of the media and advertising anticipates and programmes, or operationalizes, the binaries constituting modem children's lives, and manipulates the linearity of cause-effect relationships. One's overarching sense is that the industry of hyperrealized childhoods, impacting upon young bodies, symptoms, and psyches, reflects a totalitarian system whose slick profusion and dominance entirely over-rides what it is telling us about (Baudrillard, 1981, p. 11).

Soler (2014) provides further insight into the symptoms of childhood suffering as socio-cultural inequities are intersected within the digital milieu. She describes the present socio-cultural sphere where families strive for "some sham surplus jouissance, without any transcendence, and the ineptitude of scraping a living within the balance of producer-consumer" (p. 191). The only social bonds are between the consumer and the product. This environment leads to "an increasing fragmentation and an instability of social bonds, and leaves individuals always more exposed to insecurity and loneliness" (p. 191). She is touching on the very foundations of symbolic capital, the knowledge that adults are responsible for their children's social bonding, psychical development and sexuation; in other words, the values that support humanity. As Soler puts it, such knowledge "offer[s] the support in organizing [their] innermost defenses" (p. 192). The human values that do exist are not part of the globalized marketplace but are fragmented, local and individual (Soler, 2014, pp. 97–98).

She further implies that the death drive is tensional with current marketing technologies, and that such sublimation can threaten the subject's ability to focus on what is important in forming crucial family and societal relationships. In short, the psyche itself is jeopardized by the transmission of normative and pathologizing symbolic material.

LIKE CRACK FOR HER

Far from being immersed in a social bond that supports and values humanity, children in Aotearoa are now being trained collectively to be well-organized and competent consumers. Alongside this, each family structure is distracted by machines that light up when touched, problem-solve, boost memory, make connections, simulate sex, keep babies alive, find mates, and comfort the elderly. Is the infant or child stupefied or hyper-stimulated when she sees the car dashboard flash, when she texts Nānā on the iPhone, takes photos and sends them to Instagram, slides the iPad screen to make the puppy bark, and speaks *te reo* (Māori language) to Dad on Skype? Semuels lends insight into "a new approach to children's TV," with the program CoComelons from Moonbug Entertainment.

> The toddler's face is glowing green from the tablet in her hands, which shows a cartoon boy singing a nursery rhyme and dancing with dinosaurs. The toddler doesn't know what dinosaurs are or what the lyrics mean, but she's so entranced that she doesn't blink when her mother calls her name. "It's literally like crack for her," says her mom. (Semuels, 2022, p. 77)

Semuels argues that CoComelons' runaway popularity owes a lot to the pandemic, which put children in front of screens far longer (and with the legitimating function of education). Since then, the show has generated "a live tour, a Spotify podcast, and just about every form of merchandise you can imagine, from bubble machines to throw pillows" (p. 77). "Data is literally at the heart of everything we do" says Moonbug's head of creative. Semuels claims that for CoComelon executives,

> The show tries to model good behavior so that kids and parents alike can see how a loving family would behave in an ideal world (p. 79). Not only is CoComelon, like everything on the web designed to be addictive, it grooms children to "start depending on screens for stimulation and soothing . . . what we really want is for kids to be able to amuse and soothe themselves . . . the show's success gets kids attached to an entity whose primary interest is selling them stuff." (Semuels, 2022, p. 79)

Children and parents are now at the interface of digital machines that harvest information. This means that machines are on intimate terms with us, or on terms denoting, what Weatherill more accurately calls "electronic intimacy and transparency" (2004, p. 103). As Semuel's critique of CoComelon suggests, machines now entrance, soothe and stimulate as well as nudge, comfort, delight, frighten, arouse, measure, and speak.

The posthuman perspective, according to Hayles (1999), includes a blend of embodiment, technology, and culture, with an emphasis on valuing information more than the "natural" aspects of our human embodiment, and where the liberal humanist subjectivity of today is understood as a mere evolutionary blip. By reading Hayles with an eye on the child, the posthuman child's body would be seen as the first of many prostheses that a girl or boy would handle and control. The child is therefore seen as being assembled in such a way as to be "seamlessly articulated with intelligent machines" (p. 5). She stresses that the scarce commodity in this realm is human attention and argues that technology will counteract this by freeing up attention for only the most important tasks (Hayles, 1999, p. 287).

Yes, devices do provide instant information, connection, concepts and much more but at what social and psychical cost? How can the processes of cultural identification, subject formation, of parents' mediation, attachment and desire, and a child's identifications within family dynamics compete with the hand-held, or wrist-carried, flickering signification? As we know subject formation demands hours of intense human attention: loving, watching, listening, waiting, and responding—between parents/caregivers, and their child. The process demands an immersion in the myriad of socio-cultural experiences of sound, speech, gaze, language, human interaction, and movement related to desires, demands, and needs. Can the subtlety, nuance, and complexity of familial interactions and experiences of the "we" compete with psycho-technology, the highly enticing visual messages of technology?

TRANSITIONAL SPACES

We've all seen that tiny, wide-awake infant sitting in their carrycot while their parent or caregiver sits in front of them looking only at their mobile phone for long periods of time. What are the culminative effects of this kind of neglect? For Stiegler (2011) the key question that the capitalist industrial economy poses for the theory of the unconscious, and for the theory that desire is founded upon repression, is the question of the effects of technology on this desire.

> Each child's encounter with the form and function of technology generates "a drive-based regression founded on the destruction of libidinal energy insofar as it binds the drives through the intermediary of pharmaka that weave the symbolic, from Winnicott's transitional and pre-verbal object to the signifier that founds the thought of Lacan (Stiegler, 2011, p. 160).

Stiegler (2010) claims that marketing technologies have distorted adult and child relationships, so that adults have become less responsible for their children. Parents and grandparents are infantilized in a reversion of values "that confuses all normal references, dynamites traditional hierarchies, destroys culture and education . . . this becoming adult, develops from infancy through a relationship of identification with parents who educate the child" (p. 4). He characterizes Freud's concept of primary identification as being practically indelible and that it is in operation throughout the first five years of life. It is a condition of access to the superego through which the adult transmits to the child being educated the ability to internalize. The familiar name of which is "the law": in identifying with the adult, the child identifies with what the adult identified with while they themselves were being educated, and this is repeated from generation to generation: this repeated identification is thus what both distinguishes and links the generations (2010, p. 4).

When a young child's attention or their parents' attention is constantly diverted by technology the process of identification is undermined. There are also changes in the synaptic organization of young brains to the detriment of "deep attention" so that children are more susceptible to attention problems and hyperactivity (2010, p. 18). The key point is that identification and deep attention underpin the adult transmission of knowledge, which is crucial to each child's subject formation. "In this sense, adults' primary responsibility is the transmission of the reality principle as a formalized and encoded accumulation of intergenerational experience" (Stiegler, 2010, p. 8).

As the psycho-technologies assume control of the child's developing attention and distract their parents, transitional spaces and transitional objects become problematic. These spaces are pivotal to all systems of care and nurturing; a transitional space is primarily about caring. According to Stiegler, "to play with a child is to take care of the child, opening the paths by which transitional spaces are created, paths that stimulate . . . everything that forms the symbolic order and the "dream language of myths" (Stiegler, 2010, p. 4). Such care is destroyed in the current milieu, because a child's undivided attention is crucial to transmission of the symbolic realm from adult to child. "This lost care is also the reciprocal recognition of ancestors by their descendants, which is also vital to the formation of proper attention" (2010, p. 15). He quotes Winnicott:

> Transitional objects and transitional phenomena belong to the realm of illusion which is at the basis of initiation of experience. This early stage in development is made possible by the mother's special capacity for adapting to the needs of her infant, thus allowing the infant the illusion that what he or she creates really exists. (Winnicott [1953, p. 97] as quoted in Stiegler [2010, p. 14])

Stiegler expresses the assault to the social bond and symptom, our senses, our memories, and our humanity as children's lives become increasingly immersed in digital technology. His claim is that these influential changes in community and family life powerfully affect each child's psyche. The loss of traditional parental attention, roles and skills problems with primary identification and transitional phenomena also clearly resonate with present-day symptoms such as childhood despair and sublimation, depression, feeding and other bodily problems reflecting the current epidemic of self-harm, "cutting," suicide, addictions and sexual/gender anxiety.

THREAT OR THERAPY

Ironically, alongside this technological immersion there is an increasing reliance on digital milieu to respond to and relieve the mental distress of parents and children. "Screen time: threat or therapy for teen mental health? Where do you stand?" features an image of Fleming, from the University of Wellington's Health Faculty (2022). The image presents the idea of researching "scalable ways to improve mental health" through digital tools (2022, p. 3). In the foreground, Fleming stands holding her phone, while several students—they look like medical students—gaze intently at their devices in the background. The message implies that digital tools themselves are unproblematic; if only they are "leveraged" correctly; "at a time when youth mental health is an urgent issue in New Zealand, how can we leverage digital platforms so that they are helpful, not harmful for young people?" (2022, p. 3).

Understanding that the solution to children's mental health problems is to be found in digital platforms must have Silicon Valley rubbing its hands in glee. Morozov (2013, p. 1) argues that such thinking is a pervasive and dangerous ideology that he calls "solutionism": "an intellectual pathology that recognizes problems as problems based on just one criterion: whether they are 'solvable' with a nice and clean technological solution at our disposal" (Morozov, 2013, p. 1). In this view, child mental health is currently a "problem" because we have, or are developing, the tools to deal with it—and not because we've taken all the philosophical pros and cons into account. In his view, genuine problems "might require long and protracted institutional responses, not just quick technological fixes" (Morozov, 2013, p. 1).

> Silicon Valley, oddly, likes to wear its "solutionism" on its sleeve. "In the future," says Eric Schmidt, Google's executive chairman, "people will spend less time trying to get technology to work. . . . If we get this right, I believe we can fix all the world's problems." (Morozov, 2013, p. 1)

All the world's problems? Following Morozov, perhaps Silicon Valley not only generates the symptoms exacerbating the precarity of children's mental health, but also devising how those very symptoms can be fixed by technology? We know that some children are now provided with immersion in digital technology as a form of cognitive behavior therapy; Starship Children's Hospital in Auckland uses virtual reality headsets to relieve the anxiety of sick children and guide them through some procedures. Perhaps today's specific symptoms, which are so difficult to quantify in traditional terms, are a symbolic, almost last-ditch appeal to reconnect children's lives with those things that are life-enhancing over technologies that generate banality? Are we distracted by emphasis on the uncanny symptoms, chronic difficulty of accessing services, the long waiting lists, the lack of trained professionals, when this is merely creating a demand based on lack? While Silicon Valley tries to get the technology in place to sell solutions?

KNOWING ME, KNOWING YOU (AH-HA)

I have outlined how the digital environment is implicated in "solving" the specific symptoms of mental illbeing, while also impacting on children's psychic and collective individuation. Instead of learning about self and other—"Who am I?"—in traditional ways, through culture, parents, family, friends and community, children attempt to singularize themselves through products suggested by the market which exploits this. "Narcissizing to excess and in vain, they experience their failure, at which point they finally lose their image: they no longer love themselves and prove to be less and less capable of love" (Stiegler, 2014, pp. 60–61).

Following Silicon Valley's "solutionism" and after seeing the Swedish band Abba being hyper realized as digital avatars replicating their former youthful selves, it is easy to imagine the Metaverse devising child avatars for experiencing real spaces and opportunities to "play" in "healthy" environments; perhaps even virtual play-based early childhood centers or the French *Maison Verte* (Green House) or the child clinic of psychoanalysis? But can virtual reality really simulate the real world of a child's relationships, body, mind, and senses? A place where children experience the meaningful "we" of social bonds and learn about personal, embodied attributes such as love, spontaneity, and freedom.

As a child and adolescent psychotherapist, the breakdown which is now occurring in the symbolic and in relationships is antithetical to Lacanian psychoanalysis which stresses the importance of understanding that the child is immersed in a whole symbolic realm of language long before its birth and that the child clinic must take the parents' lives into account when working with a child (Mannoni, 1987, p. vii).

There is no digital tool to replicate the space of child psychoanalysis, which is primarily a place of subtlety, nuance, a repertoire of human relationship and response. For example, consider a situation where a child's questions are not replied to directly through Zoom or a device but are referred to the child in person with "what do you think?," using as few words as possible. Such "conversation" includes the adult looking, listening, and carefully observing the child's "gestures, expressions, mimicry, sayings, lapses, mistakes, as well as spontaneous drawings" (Dolto, 2013, p. 112).

Could avatars possibly replicate the analytic dimension, where, as Mathelin explains, analysts remain "alive and creative, ready to . . . be surprised, educated, unsettled" (Mathelin, 1999, p. 17). Theory is a mere accompaniment to each uniquely distinctive encounter with parents and children; and the analyst should be humble, unprejudiced, flexible, accessible, "open to the other and to the unconscious. If theory guides us, it is only so we may better listen to our analysands . . . each child has his own theory, and it is from him that we get it" (Mathelin, 1999, pp. 17–18). What is exceptional is how such clinical work is based on the transference and the complete experience. Can Silicon Valley make connections with the language of the body, which is a vital aspect of "the unsayable?" (Rogers, 2006, p. 202). Rogers involves speech, silences, play, art, dreams, and bodily silence; to listen to a child so that they can say more and say, "the unsayable." The child "knows where to lead me and she can be responsible for the havoc, suffering and choices of her own unconscious life" (Rogers, 2006, p. 202).

CONCLUSION

> Our lane is just a humble and narrow part of the road, although we often carry on as if that whole road belongs to us. We Pākeha struggle to realise we're often in the middle of the road blocking the natural flow for others. . . . There's a great deal of good work to do in our lane. We can have a full-time job challenging ourselves and helping each other deal with our racism and colonial ignorance. (Delahunty, 2022, p. 1)

My claim is that the specific symptoms and profusion of children's mental illness in Aotearoa reflect a desolate otherness that has come about through disturbed social relationships including cultural alienation, the breakdown of traditional families and communities, racism, unemployment, homelessness, and poverty overlaid by immersion in the digital environment. "Disturbed" in this context includes recognition of how the simulated childhoods of advertising, social media, TikTok, Facebook, etc. persistently disseminate "children's activities" such as "happy normal family life," "play," and "adventure" in a variety of forms, effectively masking the loss of previously embodied, relational, culture-based, Māori, Pākeha, Pasifika, and Asian experiences. The smells, sights, feelings, and sounds of prior forms of childhood are now hyper realized to be bought and sold. Trees, rivers, bush, and sea that marked prior sites of play are now the realm of eco-tourism, loggers, or property investors. The guile and violence of children's play is governed by health and safety regulations and structured into supervised sport, video gaming, and Apps that simulate war. The survival of childhood itself is subject to change by shifts in family size that are intensely constrained and shaped by technology, social media and hyperreality.

The fragmentation of children's psychic reality is characterized by hierarchies that have replaced the symbolic social bond; these are digitized hierarchies controlled by entertainment, social media, communications, and information technology. We have become lost in a world of technical efficiency, spectacle, banality, and totalitarianism. Huge advertising budgets shape desires, needs and wants as our bodies, minds and emotional states are directed into "desiring," "needing," and "wanting" the objects of consumerism. As Kristeva tells us, mental illness is becoming more common as countries experience

> A fragmentation of the social fabric that offers no way out from (and may even intensify) the fragmentation of psychic identity that depressed people experience in their own lives. . . . [In this milieu], culture is a precious, yet highly volatile resource. (1996, p. 80)

The Māori language term for "precarious" is *pāhekeheke*, literally "to be slippery, uncertain, unstable." What is uncertain from my perspective is how Pākeha psychoanalysts can best respond to the symptoms and fragmented reality of our work with children in Aotearoa today. My concern is that this is indeed pāhekeheke, as clinical work, children, families, and communities become more and more subject to the "crack" of global technology. We must remember too that Pākeha work should include self-examination as a culture committed to the rejection of all forms of racism as "colonization is an ongoing project that we must name to reject" (Delahunty, 2022, p. 1).

I concur with Kristeva that culture, although highly volatile, is a guiding light for how to proceed. And as Morozov (2013), tells us that very genuine problems call for extensive institutional responses rather than quick technological fixes. Humans have always found the means to solve problems but what will it take for Aotearoa to confront the contemporary symptoms of children's mental illness within an environment of total digital immersion?

Can we do what it takes to design and support our cultural diversity through community, child and family initiatives, ideas and places which emphasize and prioritize the balancing acts of psychoanalytic enquiry, equality, equity, relationship, and mental wellbeing?

A recent institutional response is to possibly align child and adolescent psychotherapy more in keeping with expanding the social capital of all children and families, seen in the New Zealand Association of Child and Adolescent Psychotherapy's engagement with *Ngā Rerengao te Tiriti,* 2016 (Community Organisations Engaging with the Treaty of Waitangi). This has certainly been a long time coming but it is to support Pākehā to foster a closer engagement with our founding document, the Treaty of Waitangi. The goals are to build relationships between people, organizations and a *Kaupapa* Māori way of working, based on the collective vision, inspiration and purpose of Māori communities and an understanding of the Treaty.

Another initiative is spelt out by the NZ Government's Budget 2022:

> To deliver . . . better mental wellbeing services and support with 195,000 primary- and intermediate-aged children set to benefit from the continuation and expansion of the *Mana Ake* (Stronger for Tomorrow) services . . . help children learn skills of mental wellbeing such as coping with changes or challenges, managing their emotions, building positive relationships, or overcoming grief and loss. (Mana Ake, 2022, p. 1)

It is evident that the future vision of Aotearoa as "the best place in the world for children and young people" is utopian. Too many precious children, youth, their families, and communities are presently grappling with mental illness. Addressing the precarity of children's mental wellbeing means proceeding critically with mental health resources, cross-cultural governmental and Kaupapa Māori initiatives which challenge the problems exacerbating mental illness—including systemic racism. It is also vital to undertake initiatives critically appraising Silicon Valley as "a cause of" and "a solution to" child and youth mental illness. These will be long and protracted journeys; ongoing, and involving consultation between all communities, as well as personal and professional relational work.

REFERENCES

Baudrillard, J. (1981). *Simulation and Simulacra.* Sheila Faria Glaser (Trans.). The University of Michigan Press.

Baudrillard, J. (1994). *The Illusion of the End.* Chris Turner (Trans.). Stanford University Press.

Belich, J. (1996). *Making Peoples.* Allen Lane. The Penguin Press.

Benvenuto, B. (2014). "Childhood and Today's Discontent." In *Child Analysis, Journal of the Centre for Freudian Analysis and Research*, 25, 62–77.
Delahunty, C. (2022). Staying in our lane. *E-Tangata*, July 3. https://e-tangata.co.nz/reflections/staying-in-our-lane/.
Dolto, F. (2013). *Psychoanalysis and Paediatrics*. F. Hivernel and F. Sinclair (Trans.). Karnac Books.
Fleming, T. (2022). Are Digital Platforms Helpful or Harmful for Teenage Mental Health? https://www.stuff.co.nz/technology/digital-living/127992891/are digital-platforms-helpful-or-harmful-for-teenage-mental-health.
Foucault, M. (1984). *Nietzsche, genealogy, history*. P. Rabinow (ed). The Foucault Reader. Pantheon Books.
Freud, S. (1953–1974). "Inhibitions, Symptoms and Anxiety," *The Standard Edition of the Complete Psychological Works of Sigmund Freud.* Ed. J. Strachey. 24 vols. Hogarth Press.
Hayles, N. K. (1999). *How we became posthuman*. University of Chicago Press.
Irigaray, L. (2002). *To Speak is Never Neutral*. Continuum, 79–80.
Kelsey, J. (1999). *Reclaiming the Future: New Zealand and the Global Economy*. Bridget Williams Books.
Kia Manawanui. (2021). Long-term pathway to mental wellbeing. https://www.health.govt.nz/system/files/documents/publications/web3-kia-manawanui-aotearoa-v9_0.pdf.
Koi Tū. (2021). The Centre for Informed Futures. University of Auckland. https://informedfutures.org/wp-content/uploads/Koi-Tu.
Kristeva, J. (1996). *Julia Kristeva Interviews*. R. M. Guberman (ed). Colombia University Press.
Krotosky, A. (2022). The Digital Human. BBC4. https://www.bbc.co.uk/programmes/b01n7094.
Mana Ake. (2022). https://manaake.health.nz.
Mannoni, M. (1987). *The Child, his Illness and the Others*. Marefield.
Mathelin, C. (1999). *Lacanian Psychoanalysis with Children*. Other Press.
Menzies, R., Gluckman, P., and Poulton, R. (2020). *Youth Mental Health in Aotearoa New Zealand: Greater Urgency Required.* https://informedfutures.org/wp-content/uploads/Youth-Mental-Health-in-Aotearoa-NZ.pdf.
Morozov, E. (2013). The Perils of Perfection. *New York Times*. https://www.nytimes.com/2013/03/03/opinion/sunday/the-perils-of-perfection.html.
New Zealand Government. (2019). *Child & Youth Wellbeing Strategy/Annual Report*, 4. https://www.childyouthwellbeing.govt.nz/resources/child-and-youth-wellbeing-strategy-annual-report-20192020#prime-minister-foreword.
Ngā Rerenga O Te Tiriti. (2016). Treaty Resource Centre. https://trc.org.nz/sites/trc.org.nz/files/Application/Nga-Rerenga-o-Te-Tiriti.pdf.
Reid, P., Cormack, D., and Paine, S-J. (2019). Colonial histories, racism and health—The experience of Māori and Indigenous peoples. In *Public Health*, 172, 119–24.
Rogers, A. (2006). *The Unsayable*. Ballantine Books.
Semuels, A. (2022). "Cuckoo for CoComelon." *Time*. Vol. 199, NOS, 11–12.

Sharp, M. (2021). *Poor Mental Health in Children and Young People Cannot Be Ignored.* UNICEF, Aotearoa, New Zealand.

Soler, C. (2014). *Lacan—The Unconscious Reinvented.* Karnac Books Ltd.

Stiegler, B. (2007). "Technoscience of reproduction." *Parallax 13*(4), 29–45.

Stiegler, B. (2010). *Taking Care of Youth and the Generations.* S. Barker (Trans.). Stanford University Press.

Stiegler, B. (2011). "Pharmacology of Desire: Drive-based Capitalism and Libidinal Dis-Economy. In: *New Foundations.* D. Ross (Trans.). Number 72. Lawrence & Wishart.

Stiegler, B. (2014). *Symbolic Misery: Volume 1, The Hyper-industrial Epoch.* B. Norman (Trans). Polity Press.

Te Aka Māori Dictionary Te Murumara. https://maoridictionary.co.nz.

Tinirau, R. (2021). Survey reveals Māori grief and anger at daily experiences of racism. https://www.nzherald.co.nz/kahu/survey-reveals-maori-grief-and-anger-at-daily-.

Virilo, P. (1991). *Lost Dimension.* Daniel Moshenberg (Trans.). Semiotext(e).

Weatherill, R. (2004). *Our Last Great Illusion.* Imprint Academic.

Whakatika Survey (2021). https://teatawhai.maori.nz/resources/whakatika-report/.

Chapter 8

Storying

Re-Writing History of Children and Families in Migration

Elizabeth Quintero

Listening to stories of children and families who have migration experiences reveals important information. Through stories we make emergent meaning slowly over time, and our brains and hearts have "license" to work together to make sense of experiences. Stories may be the ultimate methodology to document authentic experience, to re-write history of children and families in migration, and to create action. Children and families have experienced traumas of dislocation during migration for decades.

This chapter discusses dissociated places and experiences across varied childhoods during several of the global refugee crises in recent decades. I have had opportunity to listen to and learn from children and families through stories for years in a variety of situations that directly relate to migration in current troubled times. This work, viewed through the lenses of children and youth, interrogates migration situations with respect to post-colonial discourses of listening to, learning from, and taking action supporting children and youth. In analysis of research about storying over past projects (Quintero, Callaway-Cole, and Taha-Resnick, 2021; Quintero, 2015; Quintero and Rummel, 2014) colleagues and I have listened to and learned from stories of family history, culture, language, and disruption of traditional child development theory. We see an urgency for listening to children's stories and experiences.

STORIES WITH MIGRATING FAMILIES AND CHILDREN

Stories are inclusive of history and language, cultural priorities, myths, folktales, and imaginative elaboration. Barad (2014) interweaves stories within different times, and she explains,

> This paper starts out in the middle by going forward to the past—not in order to recount what once was, but by way of re-turning, turning it over and over again, tasting the rich soil from which ideas spring, and opening up again to the uncountable gifts given that still give, to proceed to the place from which we never left/leave. (p. 168)

This resonates with my stance about children's storying. We can turn stories over and over again and find new ideas and uncountable gifts. I explain different contexts of children and families, over several decades, to make the point that children's stories about their experiences are vivid, complex, and brave. Throughout the examples, the strengths of children and youth who have experienced migration are highlighted.

I have learned over the years that children are the experts at combining factual reality and a version of fantasy that they contrive as they try to make sense of their worlds (Really, is there a monster under my bed? Really, is Santa Clause black or white or a woman?). Stories are important for all children, and especially displaced children, as they attempt to sort out the harsh realities of migration and things they imagine in dramatic experiences of their journeys. They see horror, and also shards of love that they might put together in a mosaic in their imaginations (a smile, a hug, a hot meal). The stories that children create can be absolutely necessary for day-to-day survival. I have also learned that for children and their families, nothing is better than learning together, intergenerationally. I have learned we can support and promote this learning without abandoning educational standards or traditional objectives.

From the beginning of my career, I had worked in early education programs with parents of young children who were often struggling with economics, work (with and without legal documentation), language issues, and difficulties with "codes of power" (Delpit, 1988). Some parents had had some years of formal education, and many had had no formal education at all. Yet, I never met a parent who was not passionate about supporting the learning of her or his children. Also, I never met a parent who was not generous to share knowledge from lived experience with all of us. When the children, the parents, and their cultures and lives were valued, great leaps in learning, literacy, and biliteracy occurred.

The stories I have learned from intergenerational, bilingual family literacy projects, go back to the late 1980s working on the El Paso border and then in the 1990s working with families and children from Laos, Vietnam (mostly Hmong), and Somalia who had recently migrated to northern Minnesota from refugee camps in Asia and Africa. Both intergenerational family literacy groups were organized according to a model designed to provide participatory, critical literacy and biliteracy opportunities for families and young children studying together.

Intergenerational, Bilingual Family Literacy Programs were and are complex, and they differ according to participants' needs and strengths. Yet, I maintain these programs offer more than traditional parent education programs and more than many student tutorial programs. These experiences convinced me that children, their parents, and their educational guides can provide leadership in critical, participatory literacy programs (and other programs) focusing on story. In terms of literacies and languages, we have known for decades that children who have an opportunity to learn in their native language, while learning a second language, reach full cognitive development in two languages (Garcia-Sierra, Ramírez-Esparza, and Kuhl, 2016; Cognitive Neuroscience Society, 2013). Students and their families who speak languages other than English can, and should, continue to nurture their home languages while their English acquisition (or that of a different target language) is in progress (Anzaldúa, 1999; Cognitive Neuroscience Society, 2013; de la luz Reyes, 2011). The languages and literacies in all learning environments enrich each other; they do not prohibit the learners becoming fluent and literate in English. More recent studies suggest that bilinguals surpass monolinguals in tasks of memory and memory flexibility (Blom, Kuntay, Messer, Verhagen, and Lescman, 2014; Brito and Barr, 2014). Luk and Bialystok (2013) found that bilingualism is multi-faceted. Hoff (2018) found that bilingual children's competencies reflect the quantity and quality of their exposure to each language. This, in hindsight, is more evidence of the advantage of learning situations with multilingual and intergenerational students together. We saw this over and over again.

Stories from El Paso, Texas

For many reasons, in the El Paso project we did not ask who was a recent immigrant, who was documented or not, or who actually lived on which side of the river. Parents of kindergarten students and all their children of varying ages (in eight schools) participated in classes once a week after school. One class meeting, we were "schooled" by a five-year-old who was an expert at combining factual reality and a version of fantasy as he made sense of his world. And we listened. In a class with six families (one parent from each family) and their children, the experienced teacher was leading an oral language discussion at the beginning of class focusing on Community Helpers. She was expert at involving both children and parents and accepting parts of the discussion in either, or both, English and Spanish. I entered to observe as participants were giving examples of what a community helper does. Vicente,[1] age five, sat with his mother and raised his hand. When the teacher acknowledged him to speak, he spoke eloquently about having a "Ghostbuster" in his house. Vicente's mother calmly smiled as he began to tell the tale. Other parents and children listened intently.

The teacher was surprised that Vicente wasn't talking about firefighters, doctors, nurses, sanitation workers, as some of the examples she had used in her introduction. After a few seconds, she used her authority to refocus the conversation by saying that she didn't think a Ghostbuster was a real community helper. Vicente didn't skip a beat. He politely disagreed and explained that he shared a room with his baby sister who was afraid of the dark. He explained that he always told her that she would be protected in the dark by the Ghostbuster and then she would fall asleep. Just as the teacher started to say, "But a ghostbuster isn't real . . . " I jumped in and quickly asked the assistant teacher to carry on with the group discussion because I had something to talk with the teacher about urgently. I went with her in the hallway and apologized sincerely for interrupting her teaching, but said it was really important.

I reminded her of our discussions about the pretend/reality fuzzy line in children's thinking at this age, and said Vicente was showing us his creative action in support of his sister. I said also I noticed how proud Vicente was to tell his story and how proud his mother was too. I reminded her of our definition of literacy[2] and asked her if she would please re-enter the class, the discussion, and continue as if a Ghostbuster could be a community helper. I said I'd talk with her in more detail at our meeting after the class.

I felt bad, knowing I'd violated her lead in the class. She was flustered but kept her composure. She didn't resign. She continued to be a strong and important part of the project. Most importantly, I was careful to see Vicente and his mother as they left the building after class, and I told them I really liked his story about the Ghostbuster. Then Vicente showed me the picture and language experience story he and his mother had drawn and written together. This was a vivid example of a child telling his story of action (Quintero et al., 2021).

Vicente was determined to tell his story that his family clearly supported to his teacher and the literacy class. The need for caring adults to support displaced children's stories as authentic and palliative is urgent. We adults don't always understand the ways children compose their stories. Those of us who have not experienced horrific migration journeys cannot be experts on the facts of the stories nor the shards of light and hope in the mosaics created in children's imaginations. It is our job to listen, support the storytellers and trust their imaginative and factual styles as they process their experiences.

Stories from Duluth, Minnesota

In the early 1990s, a group of Head Start Educators, an Adult Basic Education teacher, and a group of teacher education students working with me decided to collaborate with some of the mothers who had recently settled in our community. The mothers were multilingual as a result of living in refugee camps in Thailand for many years; they offered to be our co-teachers and co-researchers. So, the second project, Poj Niam Thiab Meyuam (Mother/Child School) began for Hmong women and their infants, toddlers, and preschoolers.

The Poj Niam Thiab Meyuam project was implemented in a similar format as the El Paso Project FIEL. And it is important to relate that both projects continued with adaptations according to community needs for many years after the pilot projects. The collaboration of children, families, educators, and student teachers tied together the multiple histories, very different journeys, and incredible strengths of the learners and the other educators who worked together tirelessly.

Like participants in the El Paso project, the children in the Minnesota project spoke in two languages—Hmong and English (and later when Somali families joined—Somali and English). With their parents joining them, children often sang and "showed off" their English with a storybook reading in one breath, and then turned to their mothers to elaborate on the description begun about polar bears, for example, in Hmong in a private conversation. Pae, age four, on one occasion turned to one of the teachers and asked in English, "If polar bear fights brown bear who wins?" He showed us all that his imagination was helping him make sense of his world, and he showed his bilingual skills as he integrated the two languages in his action to communicate with his mother.

In 1995, Hmong families in the family literacy classes initiated the action of creating books, in Hmong and English, with stories of family histories documenting political strife, war, migration, and generations of family solidarity. They made audio tapes of the stories in Hmong and English for each family to take home and share. They were adamant that their children have access to Hmong history and oral and written language (Quintero et al., 2021).

The young children in the family classes were excited and confident using two languages, and their parents smiled and nodded as the communication evolved, even though the parents were often not as proficient in the different languages as their children. Nevertheless, in separate meetings when planning the bilingual book creations of family histories, the parents acknowledged that it would be very difficult for their young children to maintain their understanding of, and proficiency in, oral and written Hmong language. They were adamant about supporting the children's bilingual abilities and knowledge of family and cultural history. So, the books they collaboratively created included contributions by members of all families (elders and children). The parent/teacher group raised enough funding to support a translator/editor and duplication of books for every family to take home.

STORIES FROM THE UNITED KINGDOM

A different context of teachers supporting children and families in different ways came from our work in the United Kingdom, always listening to stories. During a variety of Study Abroad Programs in which most participants were masters level education students particularly interested in children and youth experiencing migration, we heard stories. We sought information, experience, and transformational perspectives about issues of refugee and migrating families. Our work combined critical theory, post-structuralist theory, and qualitative methods. This combination of theoretical frameworks and qualitative methods promoted educational research connecting their own lives, experiences, and stories to their study. And, as the two intergenerational bilingual family literacy projects discussed previously had recently occurred, I related many of the stories from those projects to the students in Study Abroad Programs in the United Kingdom.

We addressed the challenges and the nature of collaboration among families, schools, and communities for the purpose of supporting all children's success in educational settings. Emphasis was placed on family history and culture, models of parent involvement, forms of communicating with parents, parent education, working with families in crisis, and identifying resources for families. At the time, despite on-going in-country and international contention, the United Kingdom was an active center of collaboration among advocacy groups supporting refugee parents, educational programs, and community agencies. Professionals in many agencies (both government sponsored and private) worked to meet daily challenges of supporting families in their desire and need to maintain their cultural roots while learning the skills and ways of life for successful living in a modern, but unfamiliar, society. Students and I visited schools, early childhood programs, community centers, and government programs of the Refugee Council UK in various neighborhoods. We had opportunities to interview family members and children from a variety of situations to inform our work.

In this ongoing work, I visited a Primary School in northeast London. Numbers of first- and second-generation newcomers lived in the community and brought their children to the school. The school's population was 3 percent White (mostly Eastern European immigrants), and 97 percent were from predominantly Asian and Black communities. Almost all the children were bilingual or learning English as a new language in addition to their home languages (Quintero, 2015, p. 153).

The teacher leader who had worked with children here relayed many stories about the children and families who were first- and second-generation immigrants to the UK. I spent time with him and a group of children in reception (first year in primary school) in the school. I listened and saw examples of stories and action initiated by the children. I saw children using fact and fantasy (and the help of their friends) for making sense of their world.

The teacher retold stories of the boys he'd come to know, respect, and learn from. He had worked in the school for several years, and had long relationships with the children, their families, and the community which reflected different histories, strengths, and challenges. Inspired by the children and their fantasy and pretend play, he initiated qualitative research with a group of boys for his master's thesis. His research was in part focused on the question of whether violence seen and used in pretend stories and symbolic play of children should be prohibited even if the situation was monitored and there were rules about not hurting other students. This educator was confident about the altruism of the boys (after participating with and observing them), their care for their friends, and their intelligent strategies for using fantastical stories for meaning making.

This educator's ideas were controversial even among his trusted colleagues. His research uncovered complicated findings. He shared an example of children's difficult experiences in life (trauma of migration, lack of safety in a new neighborhood/country, etc.) appearing with a mix of fact and fantasy. The teacher explained:

> One morning, Don seemed quiet and withdrawn from his friends. I joined the group on the carpet and asked what was wrong, Ali told me that Don's house had been burgled. I asked Don if he wanted to talk about this if this was upsetting him. He began retelling how he had been woken up by his Mum screaming and how he had had seen the burglars.
>
> "In my house we were all asleep and the downstairs alarm went, and my Mum said there's a burglar in the house and my sister screamed and was crying . . . "
>
> At this point Ali put his arm around Don and augmented Don's story: "Yeah, then you did a flip and got your laser guns and killed them," Ali explained how Don had then somersaulted over the stairs, had taken out his swords and killed the burglars. Then Ali, in his role as "assistant narrator," said, "hundreds more came up the stairs, but Don was too strong for them all and he used his Power Ranger skills to kill them all. We got some more guns and lizards and we kept shooting and there were so many burglars. We got all our guns and swords

> and fighted [sic] them and there was blood and we killed them all and a big momma came in a car with the police, and they came and helped us." (Quintero, 2015, p. 163)

The educator explained what happened next.

> Don's appearance instantly changed. He joined Ali, all smiles, on the carpet to act out his slaying of the burglars through a range of staged rolls, dives, and pretend fight scenes. After this short play, he sat back down with me, told me he felt better, and I told him that his Mum loved him and wouldn't let anyone hurt him. (Quintero, 2015, p.163)

Ali was consoling his friend and both boys used fantastical games they had played many times to describe a pretend situation (now with a real-life situation) with possibilities to protect against assault. The teacher educator respected the fantasy, and of course, reminded the child of the unquestioned reality that his mother loved him and wouldn't let anyone hurt him.

STORIES FROM SOUTHERN CALIFORNIA

Considering children and youth in southern California, a teacher education student was tutoring students who had been in migration and were then in high school. Fernanda, the education student, was a Latina from East Los Angeles. In her research journal she explained her work with learners having experienced migration from the local community. She had participated in a variety of settings from infant and toddler programs to tutoring support programs in middle school and high school. Fernanda, a third generation Californian, appreciated and used both the Spanish language of her ancestors in Mexico and the English language of her school, state, and country.

An excerpt from her journal documented a conversation between her and a high school student. The incident pushes our understanding of family circumstances and migration contexts across generations and across roles of interaction. She wrote:

> A tenth grader approached me asking about my own living situation. "Maestra, usted vive sola?" (Teacher, do you live alone?) she asked. I said I had a roommate, then I had to explain what a roommate was, and that yes, I take care of my personal things. She asked if I missed my family, but specifically she asked if I missed my mother. At the moment this wasn't awkward; later I made the connection.
>
> A while later that day she shared with me that she had lived in Mexico while her mother lived and worked in California. In Mexico, this high school student

> had had to go to school, work, and maintain a home for her eight younger siblings. Three years ago, her mother brought her here to California, and here she is. She is a straight "A" student speaking English very well, soaking in academic information, and was well on her way to college and to being a success story.
>
> But . . . now, she is being taken out of my program. Worse than that, she is being taken out of school as a whole. Her mother is moving her to Las Vegas with no plans to enroll her in school. (Martinez, 2013)

A few years later, in 2019, in a different community in southern California, I met Akila at her elementary school through a tutoring program supporting students who had arrived in the United States as asylum-seekers. Akila had migrated from Syria six years previously; she and her family had suffered through unimaginably traumatic experiences. She cried uncontrollably when her parents brought her to kindergarten in California. She was unable to stop crying and screaming, so she was unable to stay at school. The school sent a tutor to her home regularly for the first year to gradually ease her acclimation to her new home, community, and language. I wondered if the services had been available to address her deep trauma more thoroughly, could she have acclimated more smoothly and quickly to her new community and school?

When I met her, Akila was in fourth grade using English as her third language. She glowed with intellect, curiosity, and personality. While she has become beloved in her school and was voted by her peers as the "good citizen" of her class, she was sometimes perceived by teachers as "tricky." This was because sometimes she was more interested in literacy and telling stories about her own life and family's history than assignments given her in "early reader" texts. Her passionate spirit and personal history weren't always recognized. This was, and is, a complex educational situation in which school staff has a lack of access to professional development about students' histories and ways to connect their lives to appropriate instruction.

In addition, while Akila is happy with her stable home and school life in her community, broader inequities in the school district are real. Through the personal stories of the children and their families, we have learned that financially challenged families in the city are at risk because of inadequate health care, inadequate access to fresh and nutritious food (even though Akila reported that her mother is the "best cook" of the family's halal food). Furthermore, the part of the city where she lives is devoid of streetlights and public transportation. We have first-hand documentation that investment and attention to neighborhoods such as hers is urgent.

Theory, Methods, and Justice

Barad (2007) reminds us:

> Justice, which entails acknowledgment, recognition, and loving attention, is not a state that can be achieved once and for all. There are no solutions; there is only the ongoing practice of being open and alive to each meeting, each intra-action, so that we might use our ability to respond, our responsibility, to help awaken, to breathe life into ever new possibilities for living justly. (pp. x-xi)

Our responsibility "to breathe life into ever new possibilities for living justly" as Barad expresses has challenged us sorely. My research relating to migrating children, youth, and families has been reconceptualized of postmodern and narrative theoretical influences as an inclusive framework umbrella (Barad, 2014; Dahlberg et al., 2013; Freire, 1985; Hérnandez-Ávila and Anzaldúa, 2010; Nelson, 2009; Parnell, 2012; Parnell and Iorio, 2016). I am attuned to daily life realities affecting learners who are immigrants and those who are currently migrating through uncertain global landscapes. My focus has been on the use of stories, both positive and negative, among faculty, community activists, children, and adult student teachers. As the stories have been shared, they've generated theoretical questions about the confluence of frameworks of study, pedagogical work regarding story, and justice.

Moss's (2019) theoretical stance illustrates a perspective of poststructuralism and focuses on collaboration with co-researchers. Moss (2019) explains, "postfoundationalism relativizes, because there can be no one objectively right answer in a social world of multiple perspectives—but this should not be confused with anything goes. . . . For we must take responsibility for this process and for our choices" (p. 38). Dahlberg and others (2013) note the importance of lived experiences and stress that in order to avoid silencing some learners' voices we must listen to stories that may be different from our own. Collaborators and I have found "third spaces" (Bhabha, 2004) in childhood and youth learning by listening to the power of stories with and through integrated curriculum (Quintero et al., 2021). These spaces encourage opportunities to use families' home languages while addressing target languages and to include varied family histories in curriculum. Moss maintains that "both politics and ethics are first practice" (2019, p. 55).

Our work has been strengthened by the research of Nelson (2009) who provided alternatives to traditional developmental theory during the first five years of life. She stressed that children are "components of an integrated system" (p. 186) and she maintained, "stories bear directly on the problems of different minds, different selves, and different times that are central to the child's emerging understanding of the world" (p. 172). For some educators this work guided a reconceptualization of the status quo developmental theories that did not resonate with communities we work with. In fact, the social understanding between the self and others ties Nelson's work to the theorical work of Anzaldúa whose theory is described as "an overarching theory of consciousness . . . all dimensions of life, both inner—mental, emotional, instinctive, imaginal, spiritual, bodily realms—and outer—social, political, lived experiences" (Hérnandez-Ávila and Anzaldúa, 2010, p. 177). Both theorists documented personal history and meaning making within the contexts of self, family history, and lived experience. Such complex intersections of meaning cry out for story as a framework. Both Nelson and Anzaldúa's stances are strongly related to using the stories of children and youth who have experienced migration around the world.

Theory and Methods Using Story

These theoretical influences that open up inclusion of lived experiences of migrating people challenge us to rethink theoretical and pedagogical methodology. Scholars are currently suggesting Testimonio as a way to bridge story and research methodology with inclusive self-designed nuances. These approaches support migrating people's stories being listened to, documented, and learned from as trajectories for action. Testimonio as a research methodology has been described as "a narrative practice popularized in Latin American social movements in which an individual recounts a lived experience that is intended to be representative of a collective struggle" (Mangual Figueroa and Barrales, 2021, p. 1).

For example, Mangual Figueroa and Barrales (2021) present qualitative research based on the framework of Rigoberta Menchu's writing. They elaborate on Testimonio explaining that storytelling—and counter storytelling, in particular—can help to change negative mainstream views of racially minoritized groups. This has led to collective formations in academia, such as the Chicana Feminist group, who view testimonio as influencing "a narrative format as redemption—as takers of the stories, as readers of the narratives, and as creators of the analysis" (Mangual Figueroa and Barrales [2021], p. 526). And they maintain Testimonio is a methodology that is paramount to justice.

> By creating opportunities for students and professors of color to tell and record their own stories, this qualitative approach illustrates that racially minoritized individuals can and do hold valuable forms of knowledge, thereby shifting the epistemological terrain of social science research. (Reyes et al., 2012, *45*, 526)

Mangual Figueroa and Barrales (2021) are explicit in their methodology to honor children and youth's first-person narratives and give attention to language as data and to the ideological significance of the words to denote identity in their work. This attention to authenticity, identity, respect, and inclusion can be strongly supported through story.

Callaway-Cole (2019), researching stories of migration with Latina women and families, used foundational work of Fierros and Delgado Bernal (2016) that focused on Chicana/Latina feminist theory and methodology that is relational and honors participants as co-constructors of knowledge and healing connecting everyday lived experiences with research. Delgado Bernal began using oral histories from her family storytelling and Chicana feminist methodologies in the 1990s. She disrupted epistemological boundaries to show how possibilities for conducting research and reconceptualizing teaching learning could be inclusive of participants lived experience. She argued that these interventions could challenge normative ways of conducting research and teaching to envision a more inclusive future (2020).

Over a decade ago, Saavedra (2011), Latina, feminist scholar and language arts teacher of children and youth, began using testimonies. She collaborated with young students using a methodology that reflected their histories, languages, and possibilities. Saavedra (2011) wrote in a professional language arts journal:

> This was not about teaching to Latina/os and other minorities as groups. . . . This was about centering the experiencias (experiences) and cuerpos (bodies) of all students in facets of the curricula. In this article, I want to introduce the Latin American genre known as testimonio. . . . As a way to expand our current understandings of language arts, especially as it is applied to immigrant, border crossers, and transnational students. (p. 261)

I recall, as I advocate for new theories for listening to youth and children's stories, that even Foucault (2001) said,

> I call a theorist someone who constructs a general system, either deductive or analytical, and applies it to different fields in a uniform way. I'm an experimenter in the sense that I write in order to change myself and in order not to think the same thing as before. (pp. 239–40)

This thinking regarding theory, methodology, and story points to another "experimenter" currently. Author Dave Eggers collaborates with and believes the best about children and students of all ages—especially those who've had challenges of growing up with migration and all the uncertainty that brings (Laity, 2018). Through the complex course of meeting students who have migration histories, getting to know them and earning their trust, he has touched upon a new slant of methodology that builds upon what has been previously discussed (as above) in Latinx literature as Testimonio.

Eggers's collaborative writing in *What is the What* (2006) with Deng Valentino, tells a complicated story of Deng's migration, and also tackles the complications of documenting and sharing the story. The novel's subtitle,

"The Autobiography of Valentino Achak Deng," refers to a Sudanese refugee who explains in the preface that "over the course of many years, I told my story orally to the author. He then concocted this novel, approximating my voice and using the basic events of my life as the foundation" (Preface, n.p.).

Even though several scholars have called this work collaboration by Deng and Eggers a form of testimonio, the telling of the stories can be complex. A book reviewer explained that because of gaps in Deng's childhood memories, Eggers used his own research and experiences in Sudan to give context and cohesiveness to the story. His additions forced Eggers to label the book "fiction." The reviewer goes on to say that the book should be given the respect of other non-fiction books such as *The Lost Boys of Sudan* and considered an accurate text about the complicated history of Africa's war-torn nations (Prose, 2006).

The reviewer explains reasons for her pushing back against the label of Deng's story as fiction. She says that the phrase, the *Lost Boys of Sudan,* has instant name recognition for many Americans who may not remember how and why the boys in Sudan were lost. The horrific story began during the second Sudanese civil war, from 1983 to 2005, and displaced tens of thousands of children. The children wandered through war zones and resettlement camps. Many boys were killed, and many were tortured, and experienced incalculable trauma. Prose (2006) points out that by reading this collaborative work of stories by youth who experienced the reality, there is no doubt of the impact of the story and the witness it brings.

I agree, and considering authenticity, children and youth are experts at telling important historical stories in ways that often combine fact and fantasy. Whatever name might be given an inclusive methodology that supports children and youth who have struggled with migration, I see promise in these collaborations. Acknowledging the wisdom of folk tales from Asia and Africa, and myths from ancient Greeks, legends from American Indians, Celts, and Byzantine cultures, and other ancient cultures all around the world right up to Joseph Campbell's *The Hero with a Thousand Faces* (2008), we see documentation of myth, art, and anthropology in the form of story as informative. This documentation is often intergenerational and almost always collaborative. I maintain that a category of Testimonio reflecting a collaboration of children and youth with designated trusted collaborators could bring sorely needed stories of human experiences in difficult times.

INTERNATIONAL RESEARCH SUPPORTING MIGRATING CHILDREN AND YOUTH

Recent international research of migration documents journeys and obstacles that migrating children and youth face. A UNICEF study (Hovil et al., 2021) urges us to reimagine migration responses worldwide. While the study documents children migrating in the Horn of Africa, the identification of specific messages and recommendations relates to work with migrating children everywhere. They (Hovil et al., 2021) acknowledge that migration is increasingly complex. Families and children migrate within their countries and move across borders to flee violence and war, to seek employment, to reunite family, and for a mix of other reasons. The authors warn, "Migration always entails some risk, but some states' restriction of legal pathways for regular migration and stronger border controls have made these movements more dangerous for migrants worldwide" (Hovil et al., 2021, p. 3).

The authors maintain that there is a lack understanding about the impacts of migration on children and young people. More information is needed before it is possible to design responsive policy and programming. Risks of unsafe migration for all who choose to move, including children, must be explored. The authors stress that we give primacy to children and youth's own experiences in order to build an accurate picture of migration informed by those who live it (Hovil et al., 2021).

The research report offers findings, organized around three key messages. First, the complexity of children and young people's migration journeys needs to be better understood for appropriate policy and program responses. This especially relates to the premise that children and youth be listened to as they describe their experiences through story so their histories of migration may be rewritten more accurately. It is important that children and young people define their own migration narrative. Second, the research reports that children and youth see themselves as primary agents of their migration story, and can articulate their perspectives, experiences, and their needs and aspirations. And third, there is evidence that children's safety and well-being on migration journeys represents critical challenges that need investment and attention. The authors report that children and youth see themselves as primary agents of their migration story, and can articulate their perspectives, experiences, and their needs and aspirations (Hovil et al., 2021). The researchers offer recommendations that are not often seen in current policies and demand that mechanisms be developed to end migrant child detention, separation of children from parents, and returns policies that risk violations of child rights.

STORY MOVING READERS AND WRITERS TO ACTION

As we reconsider ways to support children, youth, and families, we acknowledge what the American Association of Pediatrics names the "torture" and "child abuse" (Soboroff, 2020) inflicted upon children separated from their parents in detention centers around the United States during the past years. In 2017 we began to see children in ICE detention centers in the United States drawing poignant pictures and writing stories about themselves in cold "cages" and covering themselves with "aluminum foil" blankets. We realized the horrific meaning-making terrified children were experiencing.

Poet Aida Salazar's (2020), *Land of the Cranes*, is a poetic account told by a fictional nine-year-old girl, Betita, writing from a detention center in the United States. Salazar wrote the book, for youth to adult audiences, to protest immigrant roundups. She created the stories based on her own family's past experiences that reflect the horrific situation that persists to this day. Salazar (2020) ends her book in a letter to the reader in her own voice. She says,

> Thank you for taking the journey with Betita. May you, like her, search to find light in your darkest hour, or as her Papi says, "find sweetness in your struggle." May you see that as a child, like Betita, you have the power to write, to draw, to speak up against and shut down the forces that seek to make migrants criminals. (p. 245)

Also, Salazar (2020) effectively combines poetry, literature, while acknowledging factual truths at the end of her Acknowledgements for *Land of the Cranes* (p. 247), by offering, "My most heartbroken love for the seven children" (she documents their names),

> who lost their young lives while in immigration custody and to the unnamed migrant children who have also died while incarcerated or while crossing the border, to those separated from their parents to those who have been or remain incarcerated and endure(d) the brutality of that experience. You matter, and I am so sorry. (Salazar, 2020, p. 247)

Salazar is a passionate, trusted collaborator for children's and youth's stories that we hear, authentically. We must encourage all people with power to acknowledge and respect Salazar's plea (2020) to her young readers, "May you see that as a child, like Betita, you have the power to write, to draw, to speak up against and shut down the forces that seek to make migrants criminals" (p. 245).

REFERENCES

Anzaldúa, G. (1999). *Borderlands/LaFrontera.* Aunt Lute Books.

Barad, K. (2007). *Meeting the universe halfway: Quantum physics and the entanglement of matter and meaning*. Duke University Press.

Barad, K. (2014). Diffracting diffraction: Cutting together-apart. *Parallax, 20*(3), 168–87. http://doi.org/10.1080/13534645.2014.927623.

Bhabha, H. K. (2004). *The location of culture*. Routledge.

Blom, E., Küntay, A. C., Messer, M., Verhagen, J., and Leseman, P. (2014). The benefits of being bilingual: Working memory in bilingual Turkish-Dutch children. *Journal of Experimental Child Psychology, 128*, 105–19. https://doi.org/10.1016/j.jecp.2014.06.007.

Brito, N., and Barr, R. (2014). Flexible memory retrieval in bilingual 6-month-old infants. *Developmental Psychobiology, 56*, 11561163. htttps://doi.org/10.1002/dev.21188.

Callaway-Cole, L. (2019). *Testimonios of strength and cariño: Mexican-American families resisting Trump era politics*. [Unpublished doctoral dissertation] California State University Channel Islands.

Campbell, J. (2008). The hero with a thousand faces (The collected works of Joseph Campbell) New World Library; Third edition.

Cognitive Neuroscience Society. (2013). *Decoding how babies learn language: Q&A with Patricia Kuhl.* www.cogneurosociety.org/cns-2014-blog-coverage/.

Dahlberg, G., Moss, P., and Pence, A. (2013). *Beyond quality in early childhood education and care: Languages of evaluation.* Routledge.

de la Luz Reyes, M. (2011). *Words were all we had: Becoming biliterate against the odds*. Teachers College Press.

Delgado Bernal, D. (2020, Spring). Disrupting epistemological boundaries: Reflections on feminista methodological and pedagogical interventions. *Aztlán: A Journal of Chicano Studies 45*(1), 155–69.

Delpit, L. D. (1988). The silenced dialogue: Power and pedagogy in educating other people's children. *Harvard Educational Review*; *58*(3), 280–98. doi.org/10.17763/haer.58.3.c43481778r528qw4.

Eggers, D. (2006). *What is the what: The autobiography of Valentino Achak Deng.* McSweeney's.

Fierros, C. O., and Delgado Bernal, D. (2016). Vamos a platicar: The contours of pláticas as Chicana/Latina feminist methodology. *Chicana/Latina Studies*, *15*(2), 98–121. Retrieved from journal.malcs.org.

Foucault (2001). *Madness and civilization.* Routledge.

Freire, P. (1985). *The politics of education: Culture, power, and liberation.* Bergin & Garvey.

Garcia-Sierra, A., Ramírez-Esparza, N., and Kuhl, P. (2016). Relationships between quantity of language input and brain responses in bilingual and monolingual infants. *International Journal of Psychophysiology, 110*(2016), 1–17. https://doi.org/10.1016/j.ijpsycho.2016.10.004.

Hérnandez-Ávila, A., and Anzaldúa, G. (2010). Interview. In A. C. Elenes (Ed.), *Transforming borders: Chicana/o popular culture and pedagogy*. Lexington Books.
Hoff, E. (2018). Lessons from the study of input effects on bilingual development. *International Journal of Bilingualism, 24*, 62–78. doi.org/10.1177/1367006918768370.
Hovil, L., Gill, M., Genovese, I., Bueno, O., Kaplan, J., and Subrahmanian, R. (2021). *Reimagining Migration Responses: Learning from children and young people who move in the Horn of Africa*, UNICEF Office of Research—Innocenti, Florence.
Laity, P. (2018, June 22). Dave Eggers: "I always picture Trump hiding under a table." *The Guardian.* www.theguardian.com/books/2018/jun/22/dave-eggers-interview-circle-lifters.
Luk, G., and Bialystok, E. (2013). Bilingualism is not a categorical variable: Interaction between language proficiency and usage. *Journal of Cognitive Psychology, 25*, 605–21. http://doi.org/10.1080/20445911.2013.795574.
Mangual Figueroa, A., and Barrales, W. (2021). Testimonio and Counter storytelling by Immigrant-Origin Children and Youth: Insights That Amplify Immigrant Subjectivities. *Societies* 2021, *11*, 38. https://doi.org/ 10.3390/soc11020038.
Martinez, F. (2013). *Research Journal*. Unpublished manuscript.
Moss, P. (2019). *Alternative narratives in early childhood: An introduction for students and practitioners.* Routledge.
Nelson, K. (2009). *Young minds in social worlds: Experience, meaning, and memory*. Harvard University Press.
Parnell, W. (2012). Experiences of teacher reflection: Reggio inspired practices in the studio. *Journal of Early Childhood Research*, 10(2), 117–33. https://doi.org/10.1177/1476718X11407982.
Parnell, W., and Iorio, J. (2016). *Disrupting early childhood education research: Imagining new possibilities.* Routledge.
Prose, F. (2006, December 24). *The Lost Boy. www.nytimes.com/2006/12/24/books/review/Prose.t.html.*
Quintero, E. P. (2015). *Storying learning in early childhood: When children lead participatory curriculum design, implementation, and assessment.* Peter Lang.
Quintero, E. P., and Rummel, M. K. (2014). *Storying, a path to our future: Artful thinking, learning, teaching, and research.* Peter Lang.
Quintero, E. P., Callaway-Cole, L., and Taha-Resnick, A. (2021). *Making space for storied leadership in higher education: Learning with migrant and refugee populations in early childhood and teacher education contexts*. Springer. https://www.doi.org/10.1007/978–981–16–4157–2.
Reyes, K., and Curry Rodríguez, J. E. (2012). Testimonio: Origins, Terms, and Resources. *Equity Excell. Educ.* 2012, *45*, 525–38.
Saavedra, C. M. (2011). Language and Literacy in the Borderlands: Acting upon the World through "Testimonios." *Language Arts*, *88*(4), 261–69. http://www.jstor.org/stable/41804262.
Salazar, A, (2020). *Land of the cranes.* Scholastic Press.
Soboroff, J. (2020). *Separated: Inside an American tragedy*. HarperCollins.

NOTES

1. All names changed to protect privacy.

2. We defined literacy as: a process of constructing and critically using language (oral and written) as a means of expression, interpretation and/or transformation of our lives and the lives of those around us.

Chapter 9

States of Nowhere-Ness in Children and Adolescents

Ionas Sapountzis

Many articles in the psychoanalytic literature have focused on the difficulties of working with withdrawn and disengaged patients, patients who seem cut off from the world and who have ceased to process their experiences. Psychoanalysts have used terms such as "psychic deadness" (Eigen, 1996), "non-experience" (Ogden, 1989a), "foreclosure" (McDougall, 1984), and "psychic retreat" (Steiner, 1993) to describe adult patients whose withdrawal or "retreat" from contact is not temporary or transient but represents an entrenched and stable feature and their way of being in the world.

In the child and adolescent psychoanalytic literature there have also been, over the years, several references to cases of children who seem very withdrawn and difficult to engage. Spitz (1946) reported that infants who faced prolonged separation from their mothers displayed significant emotional symptoms such as grief, anger, and apathy. He called this emotional state "anaclitic depression" and pointed out that if the separation lasted longer than five months, the infants' state of depression was likely to deteriorate dramatically and to affect every aspect of their functioning. Winnicott (1952) also made references to the profound effect a sudden and prolonged separation from the mother can have on infants. Although Winnicott did not base his observations on infants who were hospitalized as Spitz did, he noted that young children who find their separation from their mother to be unbearable can become immobilized by terror and can display a kind of withdrawal that to Winnicott was akin to "psychotic depression" (p. 222). Tustin (1972) also wrote about the emotional state of young children when there is a breakdown in their communication with their mother early in their life and the holding environment ceases to be. When that happens, the absence of the mother leaves a "black hole" (p. 26) in the infant's psyche that feels overwhelming and terrifying. Alvarez (1992, 2012) expanded Tustin's work by focusing on children whose withdrawal and emotional disengagement are exacerbated by severe cognitive deficits. For these children, lack of contact and breakdowns in communication may not be experienced as assaults or ruptures. Instead, they may add to the absence that already exists and to the emptiness they experience. But with the exceptions of Alvarez, Tustin, and Spitz, who focused on children who seemed to be disconnected from the world and themselves, most analysts describe cases of children and adults who have not given up even though they are very withdrawn. Whatever their level of regression and disengagement, these individuals still carry the hope of being found (Winnicott, 1963) and still desire to maintain contact with others.

Durban (2017) recently articulated a different kind of withdrawal, one that is not caused by cognitive deficits, abandonment in infancy or persecutory experiences, but by repeated losses early in a child's life and the psychic absences these losses generate in the child. He described the case of a little boy, Fhadi, whose profound losses at a very early age had obliterated his sense of safety in the world. The little boy had retreated to a "state of nowhere-ness," a state in which internal and external links had ceased to exist and he seemed unaware of what was happening around him. He went on in life in a state of "being without" (p. 182) the links he needed, and without any sense of desire or signs of agency.

States of nowhere-ness, however, can also be experienced by children and adolescents who have not sustained the profound losses Fhadi had, and are not as disengaged as he was. They can be experienced by children who are facing profound deficits that make it challenging to go on and by children who—unlike Fhadi—are aware of the nowhere-ness they find themselves in. They can be experienced by children who are drowning in the inner turmoil and negativity that engulf their lives like a psychic envelope (Anzieu, 1990). They can also be experienced by children who find little in the gaze of others and have to go on without the validating presence they need or, by children who are deeply threatened by what they see in that gaze and try to cope by not seeing and not thinking. Even though these children are not as disconnected from themselves and others, their multiple failures and the failures they experience in others can leave them without the internal and external links they need and feeling nowhere as subjects. One can of course argue that these are children in persecutory states, but these states are so pervasive and so devoid of supportive presences that the children end up *feeling without* and with nothing to hold onto. Their capacity to act and react and their seeming awareness of time and space (Ekstein, 1983) can mask the psychic nowhere-ness within, the absence these children experience as they go on without the links they need, and without the ability to contain their emotions and understand their reactions.

STATES OF NOWHERE-NESS FROM A PROFOUND LOSS

In Durban's (2017) deeply evocative paper, little Fhadi is a five-year-old Lebanese boy whose symptom presentation had led to an earlier diagnosis of autism spectrum disorder but whose history and the unimaginable losses he had experienced in the first two years of his life, and his responsiveness to the treatment Durban provided, suggested that he was not a child on the spectrum. In fact, his presentation resembled the cases of anaclitic depression that Spitz (1946) had described more than fifty years before in children who had withdrawn to a state of non-responsiveness and sought and expected nothing from their caregivers. Fhadi's mother had committed suicide before Fhadi turned one, and he was left in the care of his grandmother and aunt. Both of these women were grieving for their own respective losses, the grandmother for the loss of her other son, and the aunt for the loss of her husband. Both women died within a year after the death of Fhadi's mother—the grandmother from natural causes, and the aunt after being kidnapped and murdered by an opposing militia—leaving Fhadi without any maternal figure from the age of two. Two years later, Fhadi's father, an officer in the Southern Lebanon Christian militia, fled with Fhadi and his older sister to Israel to avoid reprisals from the advancing Hezbollah fighters, resulting in another loss and the family becoming literally homeless.

Durban (2017) makes a distinction between the state of nowhere-ness, in which all internal links have ceased to exist, and the state of homelessness, in which some links still exist. The latter refers not so much to the physical loss of home as to the psychological loss of a holding place, the sense that one has no one to turn to who can make him or her feel "at home with the other" (p. 183). For Durban, the state of homelessness refers to the temporary or prolonged loss of containment, whereas the state of nowhere-ness refers to the destruction of that possibility and thus to the destruction of any expectation by a child of ever being taken in by the other. Present in the experience of homelessness is an awareness of what is missing and a wish or longing, however frail, for a repair or restoration, whereas in a state of nowhere-ness any painful memory and any glimmer of hope have ceased to exist.

The state of nowhere-ness Durban (2017) describes bears some similarity to the state of hopelessness that people who have experienced profound setbacks in their lives can find themselves in. Much like the experience of homelessness, the experience of hopelessness implies an awareness of what is missing, of the hope that cannot be entertained and must be resigned from. By contrast, the lives of children in states of nowhere-ness are characterized by a devastation that feels complete and leaves no room for entertaining even a faint idea of what is missing. Children in such states experience themselves as "largely invisible" and live in a "chronic state of helplessly 'being without,' with nowhere to go, and no-one home" (p. 182).

Fhadi seemed to exist *without* having any expectations of ever finding what he was missing. He avoided eye contact and did not respond when spoken to. He appeared to derive experiences from the sensations he generated through his repetitive and seemingly mindless acts. He walked around carrying a piece of wood in one hand, which he bit periodically, and a dirty washcloth that had belonged to his grandmother in the other. The two objects—one soft and one hard (Tustin, 1986)—conveyed how barren his life was and how little he had been left with. They alluded to the losses he had experienced and the profound emptiness he had felt ever since and conveyed how he went on in life with the ever-present feeling of "being without." But Fhadi's symptoms and body language, the emotions he evoked and the orphan-hood he communicated with his presence, also suggested that even though he did not seem to have any hopes and expectations, contact was a faint possibility if one persisted in seeking him, as Durban did. Fhadi existed not in a state of retreat, for such a state implies some agency, some sense of threat one needs to protect oneself from, but in a state of vacancy that was created by the profound losses he had sustained that had wiped out any sense of safety in him. Yet, although he seemed not to be conscious of any wishes or expectations, his wishes, to paraphrase Grotstein (2000), were not unconscious of him, and he responded to Durban when the possibility of contact became a reality for him and he felt his interest and determination to reclaim him (Alvarez, 1992).

STATES OF NOWHERE-NESS AND SEVERE DEFICITS

In her groundbreaking work with children who have retreated from contact, Tustin (1972, 1990) argued that children who encounter discontinuities or breakdowns in their relationships with their mother retreat to a state of non-engagement and non-processing out of a need to forget the experience of the rupture that has happened and, more importantly, out of a need to block the memory of a mother who was not responsive. According to Tustin, children who have experienced a breakdown in their relationship with others need to "obliterate" the memory of the trauma by "blanking out not-me objects" (1972, p. 171). Such acts of obliteration are examples of "negative hallucination" (p. 171) as they signify a state of being in which a child hallucinates that he or she does not need an Other and has no memory of the Other. Little

Fhadi existed in such a state of negative hallucination as he went on in life without the sensation or memory of an internal presence or of ever locating that presence in his life. He just seemed to exist disconnected from anyone and seemingly indifferent to anything around him.

Ogden's (1989b) concept of the autistic contiguous position and Alvarez's (2012) writings on children who are not withdrawn but "undrawn" (p. 13) or never drawn also seem to overlap significantly with the state of nowhere-ness Durban describes in his paper. The autistic contiguous position Ogden proposed is also a state of being that is devoid of a sense of agency, of "I-ness" (p. 53), and experiences are registered almost exclusively through the sensations one creates through one's acts. Using Tustin's ideas about hard and soft objects, Ogden argued that individuals in the autistic-contiguous position experience the boundaries of their existence through the sensations these objects generate for them. Their experiences arise from "relationships of sensory contiguity" (p. 53), with the sensory surface providing these children with the sense of boundedness and rhythmicity they need to go on. These sensory experiences—one soft and one hard—correspond to the "autistic shapes" and the "autistic objects" Tustin (1986, p. 280) has drawn attention to in her work. The former, according to Ogden, contribute to a basic sense of self-cohesion through the soft sensations they generate, while the latter contribute to a sense of a boundary and protection through their sensations of hardness and edged-ness.

Unlike Tustin and Ogden, who wrote about children and adults who seek to preserve or establish some continuity through the experiences of "object-ness" and "thingness" (Ogden 1989b, p. 55) they find in soft and hard objects, Alvarez (2012) centered her clinical observations on children who do not even seek such sensations or have little interest in them. These are children who exist in seemingly "affectless states" (p. 12) and show no interest towards anything or anyone. Although many of these children seek to generate sensations through mindless and repetitive acts, most seem resigned to the profound absence they experience within and the absence or resignation they elicit in others. The level of functioning of these children points, as Alvarez observed, to mental conditions where thoughts and experiences remain not "dismantled but unmantled; not projected but as yet never introjected; not dissociated but as yet unassociated" (1992, p. 95).

Although Fhadi also existed in a state in which he expected nothing, the nothingness he experienced stemmed from the traumatizing losses he had been subjected to. He had lost whatever little maternal attention he had experienced early in his life and was left with a terrifying sense of absence that, in Tustin's words, he had to "obliterate" (1972, p. 171). Robbie, Cynthia, and David, the children Alvarez (1992, 2012) described in her work, had never internalized such a maternal presence and found themselves experiencing not an absence that followed the loss of a maternal figure but an absence that was ongoing and left them without the "live company" (Alvarez, 1992) they needed. These were children for whom internal links had not been destroyed and were not avoided, but instead had never been made. Yet, despite the difference in terms of what had contributed to the destruction of the internal links in these children and to the absences they experienced in their lives as well as to the lack of agency they conveyed, they were all children who lived in a state devoid of thoughts and expectations and went on in life as if disconnected from the rest of the world. They simply existed in space and went on in life in a state of *being without*, without an understanding of themselves and others and without experiencing themselves as present in life.

THE NOWHERE-NESS OF NEGATIVE STATES

The state of nowhere-ness Durban and to a lesser extent Alvarez speak of can be extended to children who also find themselves *being without*, even though the absences that mark their lives do not stem from a terrifying loss or a severe cognitive deficit. It can be extended to children whose negative experiences define every aspect of themselves and their lives, like children who have been subjected to severe trauma (Bleiberg, 2001) or experienced profound neglect that has affected their cognitive development (Music, 2009). It can also be extended to children who are acutely aware of their own limitations and feel unable to organize the flow of emotions they experience and the flow of demands they are being faced with. To Durban, children who are aware of what is being missed are in a state that is not as dire as the state of nowhere-ness. They are in a state of homelessness that suggests not only a level of awareness of what is missing but also some capacity to tolerate, even at a very rudimentary level, the pain of what is being missed and what they do not have.

One can argue, however, that the homelessness many children experience is not simply the homelessness that stems from an awareness of what was and is no more and the links that have ceased to exist that have left them with no one to turn to, but also from an awareness, however ill-formed, of what cannot be found. The sensation of something that is absent, of a containing presence that cannot be found, along with the sensation or fear of who one cannot be, can lead a child or adolescent to a state in which he or she feels nowhere as a subject. Eng and Han (2018) recently pointed to a different manifestation of psychic nowhere-ness, one that is not caused by severe trauma or profound neglect, but by the ongoing absence, many Asian American adolescents experience who have left their families at a young age to attend boarding schools and to pursue college degrees in English-speaking countries. Despite their cosmopolitan manners and seeming ease with the world, these adolescents find themselves psychically dislocated between "everywhere and nowhere" (p. 128) filled with an absence that has become a background presence (Grotstein, 2004) in their lives.

The categorical distinction Durban (2017) makes between states of nowhere-ness and homelessness overlooks, in my view, the nowhere-ness of children who feel nowhere within and children who cannot hold on to themselves and who experience their relationships with others as collapsing or as nonexistent. States of homelessness and nowhere-ness may not necessarily exist on a continuum from least to most severe, from a state in which one is aware of what one is missing to a state in which that awareness is obliterated and one finds oneself with nothing to hold onto and hope for. Rather, I would like to argue, they can coexist especially if the awareness or, pervasive sensation, of what is no more leaves a child feeling at a loss and unable to hold on to himself or herself. The nowhere-ness children feel can also stem from the very homelessness they experience, from the absence of someone who can make them feel held when they are faced with catastrophic events that are deeply threatening to them. Unlike Fhadi, for whom the unbearable had happened very early in his life to be formulated as a thought he could evacuate, children who face catastrophes at a later age, at an age when thoughts and a sense of self and others have had a chance to be formed, are left in the wake of an absence that can evoke, to quote Bion (1957/1967), a "dread of imminent annihilation" (p. 43). Seeking to rid themselves of experiences that feel unbearable to them, these children also risk ridding themselves of their own minds and as a result finding themselves nowhere, as subjects to face sensations and feelings that feel unmanageable and terrifying.

The state of nowhere-ness of children who are experiencing their internal and external world as collapsing was conveyed very poignantly in a drawing that was made by a young girl who had become almost nonverbal after the death of her mother. The girl sat motionless on her seat and did not respond to my initial attempts to engage with her in the session. When she was presented with a line and asked if she wanted to make something out of it, she proceeded to make an elaborate drawing of geometric shapes falling, as if tumbling to the ground. She spent more than half an hour doing the drawing, seemingly out of a wish to keep my inquisitiveness at bay, but most likely because she was expressing for the first time, even though she probably was not aware of it, the collapse she had felt inside, an experience she could only present in the abstract.

Over the next two sessions she made other abstract drawings, drawings that seemed to primarily serve the purpose of filling the page. These drawings, which she did in silence, also conveyed the emptiness she felt inside, an emptiness she had no words for. The young girl responded to my invitation a few weeks later to make something out of the squiggly lines I presented to her. The game of squiggles (Winnicott, 1971a), which quickly became a game in which I was presenting her with squiggly lines and sometimes simple dots and she was making the drawings, was played mostly in silence. She would nod when I named what she had made and would listen to my associations to what she just made, but only spoke when I could not identify what she had made.

The game went on for several months, during which her drawings evolved from the formless and abstract shapes she had made at the beginning to vague expressions about the emptiness she felt and then to the loss she had experienced. They evolved from the cascading shapes she made to drawings of clouds, empty prairies, and tiny figures in space and later, to drawings of unopened letters, black holes, and hands reaching into space. A few months after her first drawing, she began to use colors in her drawings and to fill them with objects and people engaged in activities they enjoyed. At that point she had begun to talk about activities she liked, her pets and her school and several months later, about her desire to join a play in school.

This young girl's case suggested that she was in a state of homelessness as the loss of her mother had left her feeling that she had no one to turn to. The hole she felt within, a black hole she drew more than once in her squiggles, pointed to the paralyzing sense of absence her mother's passing had created in her. Her capacity to locate the absence and to symbolize it in the drawings she made, a capacity she was able to access in the course of the treatment, does not negate how lost or broken she felt in the months following the loss of her mother and the psychic nowhere-ness she experienced as a result.

Bion (1962/1967) and Winnicott (1974/1989) have written about the internal disintegration that unfolds when children find little or no containment for their acts or experience their caretakers as being overwhelmed by their behaviors and unable to understand their emotional state. Children who experience their parents as unable to respond to emotional states that feel overwhelming end up, according to Bion, experiencing their emotions and sensations as feared objects that need to be avoided. More importantly, they end up introjecting the absence they encounter in their parents' responses as well as the intolerance or confusion with which their acts were met. Children who internalize the experienced absence may find themselves in a state of "no K" (O'Shaughnessy, 1988, p. 182), a state in which they seek to not know and to not make links. If that state is ongoing, if existing in a state of "no K" becomes their primary mode of being in the world, "self and object become increasingly bizarrely confused" (O'Shaughnessy, 1981, p. 95), leaving them unable to make sense of emotions and experiences that feel inchoate and fragmenting. What could be a thought, or the emergence of a thought, becomes an absence, and more importantly, an absence of the possibility of a thought and of what might be found.

In his influential paper, *Fear of Breakdown*, Winnicott (1974) focused not on the "nameless dread" (Bion, 1962/1967, p. 116) children experience when their need for containment is not met, but on the fear that lingers after an experienced rupture. Winnicott, of course, wrote about children who have a sense—if not an awareness—of what has happened and are fearful that what happened before might happen again. These are also children who can entertain, however consciously, not only a fear but also a wish (Ogden, 2014), the wish that what happened in the past and the failure that was experienced will turn out to not be so in the future. But that level of awareness does not negate the psychic nowhere-ness that can emerge from the experience of *being without*, an experience that can be so traumatizing as to leave a child experiencing the past in the present and also in what the child anticipates to happen in the future. The awareness of what happened and the awareness of what is feared and what is hoped does not negate the "primitive agony" (Winnicott, 1974/1989, p. 81) children experience when they find themselves *being without* the mother's understanding and facilitating presence. It is an agony that in Winnicott's view can bring the child to an "unintegrated state" (p. 81) that can evoke the sensations of "falling" and collapse.

The frightening prospect of *being without* may have accounted for the frequent outbursts of a little boy who would come for his sessions in a state of rage and would take almost half the session to quiet down and to tolerate my presence. His hollering and his aggressive attempts would noticeably decrease when I focused on the "whatness" (Alvarez, 2012, p. 2) of his behavior, on how upset and angry he felt. Sometimes I had to repeat that statement more than once as the little boy would fling himself face down onto a pile of pillows that were on the floor and would dissolve into angry sobbing. He did, however, listen when I stated that I will not be asking him any questions since he seemed so upset and when I told him how difficult it was for me to see him so upset and how much I did wish I could say something to make him feel better. He would accept the extra pillows or the blanket that I would give him a minute later to make himself more comfortable, and he did listen, and by that time he was almost silent, when I would share with him a thought I had about him after our last session or a thought I had about something he had made or said. The little boy would typically get up at that point to look for the materials he had used in his previous sessions to show me another idea he had or to draw a plan of something that would be better than what he had made last time. He would then proceed over the remaining half of the session to put together what he had just told me or had drawn for me, and I felt that it was very important for him to show me what he could do and how he could improve on what he had made last time by balancing all the different-sized blocks he could find on the shelves. His elaborate structures gave a good sense of his capacity to plan, to persevere and to imagine, and he would leave the room feeling calm and seemingly very satisfied with himself and with what he had made. The following week, he would appear again in a state of rage and acted as if the playroom was the last place on Earth he wanted to be.

The treatment was interrupted a few months later, when the father got a job at another city and the family had to relocate. Sometime later, I learned that the boy's mother had killed herself and that he and his siblings were left in the care of their paternal grandmother. Looking back at the little boy's insistence on balancing blocks of all sizes in ever more complex constructions, I cannot help but wonder about all the balancing he had to do on the cusp of a catastrophic collapse that was looming in the future and about the present and future breakdown his unconscious was conscious of. The little boy, one can argue, was not in a state of nowhere-ness as he was still holding on, however tenuously, to the possibility of a different outcome, of his mother being able to balance her cascading emotions in her life. He could feel his mother's deterioration and he had to rid himself of these thoughts, leaving himself in a state of "no K" to face all alone a pending tragedy that was feared but could not be imagined.

Like Winnicott and Bion, Green (1986) also reflected on what happens to a child's development and emotional well-being when the child experiences his or her mother to be unavailable or nonresponsive. The mother's emotional unavailability leaves the child experiencing an absence that cannot be understood and cannot be named. It leaves a child in the negative (Green, 1986, 1999, 2005), always preoccupied, whether consciously or unconsciously, by what is missing and what the child does not have. What is critical, according to Green (1999), is not just the level of trauma and the kind of disillusionment the child experiences, but also the level of "psychic reduction" (p. 11) that takes place when children are faced with the unthinkable and the internal disorganization such experiences can cause. When that reduction involves a withdrawal from the desire for an object, it results in a state of "disobjectalization" (p. 12), a state that is akin to the "no K" state O'Shaughnessy (1988, p. 182) described, in which individuals feel emptied of thoughts and are filled with sensations that cannot be expressed with words. Bion described a similar process of "denudation" (1962, p. 97) that occurs when individuals seek safety in not knowing and not owning which, if left unaddressed, can degenerate to "nullity" to a state of being where one feels, like little Fhadi did, nowhere as a presence.

Such internal states, notes Levine (2013), can often only be conveyed through their non-representability, through the patient's "unrepresented chaos or void" (p. 59). It is through the lack or absence they evoke in the other, like the absence of sympathy that the rageful boy evoked with his acts, that one can begin to get a sense of the dread that is being experienced, of the catastrophe that has been registered and also the absence that is feared. Unlike the angry boy who conveyed through his rageful acts the absence he felt and feared, the little girl who had lost her mother conveyed the absence she experienced through her silence and through the absence she evoked in others.

The literature is filled with cases of children and adolescents who disinvest themselves from any expectations and find themselves feeling empty inside. Avoiding contact with others, avoiding noticing and reflecting on experiences enables these children and adolescents to ward off the fear of what they might find and what might happen again. Children who come from highly conflictual environments that leave them feeling deeply disorganized inside as well as children with underlying neurological conditions that contribute to impulsive or seemingly incomprehensible acts elicit responses from others that are negative if not punitive (Laezer, 2015; Salomonsson, 2004, 2011; Sapountzis, 2020). The provocative and seemingly incomprehensible acts many of these children engage in enable them, Bleiberg (2001) observed, to create their environment and in so doing, to create a sense of predictability that counters the helplessness they feel and the incoherence or fragmentation they experience. These acts also offer clues about internal states that cannot be communicated with words. They offer clues to the psychic reduction that has taken place and to the psychic scaffolding that has not happened, leaving these children in a state of *being without*, without the presences they need and without feeling themselves present in life.

There is a risk, when reflecting on the experiences of children who struggle and who seem lost and non-responsive, to focus on their symptoms and diagnoses and miss the void within, the emptiness that they feel inside. That risk is heightened, I feel, with children and adolescents who seem not only to expect nothing from others, but also to want nothing from them. The experienced void alludes to a different tragedy, to the collapse of "being" (Winnicott, 1971b, p. 82) and to the illusory sense of safety that can be found in the not, in the negation of one's expectations and wishes.

The case of an adolescent male who was very self-conscious about his neurological condition and the physical deformities it had caused was, on the surface, that of a young man in retreat (Steiner, 1993), who found safety in distancing himself from anything that made him feel exposed and seen. He was a young man who could not tolerate his own gaze and refused to step out of his house for fear of what he would find and what others would see in him. The young man's desperate act of psychic self-mutilation left him further entrenched in a reality where, to paraphrase Green (1999, p. 5), only the negative was real. The young man who could not tolerate who he felt he was and who he was convinced he would remain sought refuge in the "nullity" (Bion,

1962, p. 97) he created, in the nothingness he retreated to and the nothingness he found. The distance may not be that great from the intentional nothingness of the individuals Green describes and the young man displayed to the pervasive and reflexive nothingness Fhadi conveyed through his acts and to the nothingness that is experienced by children with severe cognitive deficits. Whatever the differences in how these individuals present themselves and are experienced by others, they all seem to have internalized the experience of feeling *without,* without a sense of self and others and without the hope and desire of finding and of being found (Winnicott, 1963/1965).

FROM NOWHERE-NESS TO SOMEWHERE-NESS AND SOMETHING-NESS

The cases presented in the literature consistently indicate that the journey from a state of not-processing to one where internal states can be tolerated and thinking can begin to emerge, involves perseverance by a facilitating other and faith in what can be found. It also involves the determination to find meaning in the child's acts and to amplify the child's timid initiatives and to make some-thing out of the seeming no-thing.

Durban (2017) felt the need to speak in his own maternal language, Hebrew, to Fhadi, even though the little boy could only understand a few words in that language. He felt the urgency to reach the little boy, to speak to those parts of Fhadi's inner world that had been left uncontained and unattended. Mostly, he felt the need to speak to Fhadi from within, in the language and melody of his own childhood (Beebe and Lachmann, 2002). Alvarez (2012) moved her face in front of Robbie's line of vision and called his name to demand his attention and to draw his gaze. She felt the need to speak to him loudly, with "more emotional urgency" (p. 22). It is an urgency that is needed for something to emerge and become the beginning of something else. Salomonsson (2007, 2011) felt the need to speak to the distress infants experienced by focusing not on what they understood at the lexical level, but what was taken in at the emotional level, at the tone and affect his statements conveyed, "the musical content of the intervention" (p. 609) as he put it. With the silent girl who had lost her mother, I felt the need to accept her silence and to give her the space she needed to present herself without speaking about herself. With the angry little boy, I felt the need to acknowledge how distraught he felt and how upsetting that was to me, and to then share the thoughts I had about him over the week, the thoughts he had evoked in me and left me with, and also, the thoughts I was having at that moment.

What I feel analysts convey through their different manners of engaging with their young clients is the urgent desire to reach these children and also, the willingness to continuously examine their own reactions and to reflect on how their young clients are responding to them. The desire to reach these children and to find something meaningful in them and with them can be transformative experiences for children who have felt the absence of the Other in their lives and find themselves disintegrating inside. Reaching children and adolescents who seem to actively seek the absences that mark their lives and for whom *being without* brings a temporary relief from the sense of *feeling without*, may be harder to achieve, but one needs to persevere and insist on what can be created and what can be found.

Alvarez (1999) gives a brief account of the treatment by "Miss N" of Cindy, a four-year old girl who seemed to have "no apparent desire for anything" (p. 99). The little girl would walk aimlessly around the room without noticing anything. But Miss N was very attentive to any flicker of a response from Cindy and was quick to give meaning and to "amplify" (p. 100) the slightest sign of initiative, however brief or seemingly inconsequential that seemed to be. "I think you want to say something" (p. 100), Miss N would say when Cindy opened her mouth, even though it was not clear that Cindy had intended to say anything. When Cindy absentmindedly touched some plasticine, Miss N. noted that perhaps Cindy wanted to make a mark. Much like Fhadi, who responded to Durban's persistence in instilling meaning in the room, Cindy responded to Miss N's attention and determination to create a meaningful exchange with her. She no longer moved aimlessly in the room and became more responsive to Miss N. A few months later, she noticed that Miss N was using a different word than she was using to refer to the same object, a recognition of an other's perspective that is a major step in a child's development. Salomonsson (2007) showed the same insistence and the same faith in what can emerge when he spoke to infants who were experiencing a variety of symptoms about the distress they felt as they expressed it in the "here and now" (p. 129) of the session. He displayed a similar level of sensitivity and attentiveness, a similar desire to understand them and to express to them what he thought was going on in them.

Common in these cases, however, is not simply the therapists' desire to seek and find and the faith in what could be found. Common also is the parents' commitment to the treatment so that something can begin to emerge. Fhadi was in a state of nowhere-ness, but his father made sure that he would not be left there and insisted that Durban would be his son's therapist. Robbie, the young boy who featured in several of Alvarez's papers, was also in a state of disconnectedness, but his parents made sure he stayed in treatment and continued to be in treatment for years. This is also true in the cases of David, John, and Peter that Tustin (1972, 1986) presented in her books. And it was true in the case of the silent girl whose grandmother insisted that she stay in treatment despite the lack of any observable changes during the first months.

Children who experience nothing, find nothing, or expect nothing, and children who seek nothing to preserve something are all, despite differences in etiology and developmental histories, children who have to go on while *being without* the internal and external links they need. The parents of the children Salomonsson, Alvarez, Durban, and Tustin describe, like many other parents who recognize the significant difficulties their children experience and seek treatment for them, made sure that their children would not remain in that state of *being without*, but that they would be given the opportunity to be found so that something could emerge for them. They made sure that they would find a "home in others" (Durban, 2017, p. 183), a holding place that would enable them to *seek* and over time to make meaning (Slade, 1994), like the little girl did with her drawings, and that they would not remain in a state of nowhere-ness. It seems that it always comes down to that. The nowhere-ness children feel can evolve into a state of somewhere-ness once there is a facilitating Other, one who is determined to not let the state of absence or emptiness be and instead, seeks to find what "is there, waiting to be found" (Winnicott, 1963, p. 181).

REFERENCES

Alvarez, A. (1992). *Live company: Psychoanalytic psychotherapy with autistic, borderline, deprived and abused children.* Routledge.

Alvarez, A. (2012). *The thinking heart: Three levels of psychoanalytic therapy with disturbed children.* Routledge.

Anzieu, D. (1990). *Psychic envelopes.* Karnac.

Beebe, B., and Lachmann, F. (2002). *Infant research and adult treatment: Co-constructing interactions.* Analytic Press.

Bion, W. R. (1962). *Learning from experience.* Basic Books.

Bion, W. R. (1963). *Elements of psychoanalysis.* Heinemann.

Bion, W. R. (1967). Attacks on linking. In W. Bion, *Second thoughts: Selected papers on psycho-analysis* (pp. 93–109). Jason Aronson. (Original work published 1957.)

Bion, W. R. (1967). A theory of thinking. In W. Bion, *Second thoughts: Selected papers on psycho-analysis* (pp. 110–19). Jason Aronson. (Original work published 1962.)

Bleiberg, E. (2001). *Treating personality disorders in children and adolescents: A relational approach.* Guilford.

Durban, J. (2017). Home, homelessness and no-whereness in early infancy. *Journal of Child Psychotherapy, 43*(2), 175–91. doi.org/10.1080/0075417X.2017.1327550.

Eigen, M. (1996). *Psychic deadness.* Jason Aronson.

Ekstein, R. (1983). *Children of time and space, action and impulse*. Jason Aronson.

Eng, D. L., and Han, S. (2018). *Racial melancholia, racial dissociation: On the social and psychic lives of Asian Americans*. Duke University Press.

Green, A. (1986). The dead mother. In A. Green, *On private madness* (pp. 142–73). Karnac.

Green, A. (1999). An introduction to the Negative in psychoanalysis. In A. Green, *The work of the negative* (pp. 1–13). Free Association Books.

Green, A. (2005). The work of the Negative. In A. Green, *Key ideas for a contemporary psychoanalysis: Misrecognition and recognition of the unconscious* (pp. 212–26). Routledge.

Grotstein, J. S. (2000). The myth of the labyrinth. In J. S. Grotstein, *Who is the dreamer who dreams the dream? A study of psychic presences* (pp. 189–218). The Analytic Press.

Grotstein, J. S. (2004). "The light militia of the lower sky." The deeper nature of dreaming and phantasying. *Psychoanalytic Dialogues*, *14*(1), 99–118. doi.org/10.1080/10481881409348776.

Laezer, K. L. (2015). Effectiveness of psychoanalytic psychotherapy and behavioral therapy treatment in children with attention deficit hyperactivity disorder and oppositional defiant disorder. *Journal of Infant, Child and Adolescent Psychotherapy*, *14*(2), 111–28. https://doi.org/10.1080/15289168.2015.1014991.

Levine, H. B. (2013). The colourless canvas: Representation, therapeutic action, and the creation of the mind. In H. B. Levine, G. S. Reed, and D. Scarfone (Eds.), *Unrepresented states and the construction of meaning. Clinical and theoretical contributions* (pp. 42–71). Karnac.

McDougall, J. (1984). The disaffected patient: Reflections on affect and pathology. *Psychoanalytic Quarterly*, *53*, 386–409.

Music, G. (2009). Neglecting neglect; some thoughts about children who have lacked good input and are "undrawn" and "unenjoyed." *Journal of Child Psychotherapy*, *35*(2), 142–56. https://doi.org/10.1080/00754170902996064.

Ogden, T. H. (1989a), *The primitive edge of experience*. Jason Aronson.

Ogden, T. H. (1989b). The autistic-contiguous position. In T. Ogden, *The primitive edge of experience* (pp. 47–81). Jason Aronson.

Ogden, T. H. (2014). Fear of breakdown and the unlived life. *The International Journal of Psychoanalysis*, *95*, 205–23. https://doi.org/10.1111/1745–8315.12148.

O'Shaughnessy, E. (1981). W. R. Bion's theory of thinking and new techniques in child analysis. *Journal of Child Psychotherapy*, *7*(2), 181–89.

O'Shaughnessy, E. (1988). W. R. Bion's theory of thinking and new techniques in child analysis. In E. Bott-Spillius (Ed.), *Melanie Klein today: Developments in theory and practice, Volume I: Mainly theory* (pp. 181–94). Routledge.

Reed, G. S. (2013). An empty mirror: Reflections on nonrepresentation. In H. B. Levine, G. S. Reed, and D. Scarfone (Eds.), *Unrepresented states and the construction of meaning. Clinical and theoretical contributions* (pp. 18–41). Karnac.

Salomonsson, B. (2004). Some psychoanalytic viewpoints on neuropsychiatric disorders in children. *International Journal of Psychoanalysis*, *85*, 117–36. doi.org/10.1516/002075704322798978.

Salomonsson, B. (2007). "Talk to me baby, tell me what's the matter now": Semiotic and developmental perspectives on communication in psychoanalytic infant treatment. *International Journal of Psychoanalysis, 88*, 127–46. https://doi.org/10.1516/04P3-FUER-0U41-LLN8.

Salomonsson, B. (2011). Psychoanalytic conceptualizations of the internal object in an ADHD child. *Journal of Infant, Child and Adolescent Psychotherapy, 10*(1), 87–102. doi.org/10.1080/15289168.2011.575711.

Sapountzis, I. (2020). From Jackson Pollock to psychic blades: Climbing the semiotic ladder in working with children with ADHD. *Psychoanalytic Psychology, 37*(4), 305–12. doi.org/10.1037/pap0000296.

Slade, A. (1994). Making meaning and making believe: Their role in the clinical process. In A. Slade and D. Palmer Wolf (Eds.), *Children at play: Clinical developmental approaches to meaning and representation* (pp. 81–107). Oxford University Press.

Spitz, R. A. (1946). Anaclitic depression; an inquiry into the genesis of psychiatric conditions in early childhood. *The Psychoanalytic Study of the Child, 2*(1), 313–42. doi.org/10.1037/h0045987.

Steiner, J. (1993). *Psychic retreats. Pathological organizations in psychotic, neurotic and borderline patients.* Routledge.

Tustin, F. (1972). *Autism and childhood psychosis.* Hogarth Press.

Tustin, F. (1986). *Autistic barriers in neurotic patients.* Yale University Press.

Tustin, F. (1990). *The protective shell in children and adults.* H. Karnac Books.

Winnicott, D. W (1958). Psychoses and child care. In *Through pediatrics to psychoanalysis* (pp. 219–28). Basic Books. (Originally published 1952).

Winnicott, D. W. (1965). Communicating and not communicating leading to a study of certain opposites. In D. W. Winnicott, *The maturational processes and the facilitating environment* (pp. 179–92). International Universities Press. (Original published 1963.)

Winnicott, D. W. (1971a). *Therapeutic Consultations in Child Psychiatry*, Hogarth Press.

Winnicott, D. W. (1971b). Creativity and its origins. In D. W. Winnicott, *Playing and reality* (pp. 65–85). Routledge.

Winnicott, D. W. (1989). Fear of breakdown. In C. Winnicott, R. Shepherd, and M. Davis (Eds.), *D. W. Winnicott: Psycho-analytic explorations* (pp. 87–95). Harvard University Press. (Original published 1974.)

Chapter 10

Inconspicuous Precarity

The Impossibility of the Inherently Creative Child

Katherine Martin

As portrayed in aspects of cultural materials like marketing, literature, and published philosophies on education, inherent childhood creativity is revered as a natural attribute, and situated as an emblem of modern Anglo-American youth identity. This concept, flush with the romantic ideals of bourgeois childhood, gained momentum in the mid-nineteenth century, and spread as an assumed fundamental trait for Western children by the early twentieth century. Concurrently, in the late nineteenth century experts in medicine and those in the budding field of psychoanalysis put forth a framework delineating typical pediatric development. The milestones established were circulated through parenting books, manuals, and other available publications, for consumption by parents, nurses, and a growing body of youth-focused professionals in the United States and Europe. The expanding mass of white, middle-class parents found themselves measuring their children's physical and mental progress, as attention became fixated on children's personalities, use of leisure time, and creativity.

Adults' obsession with what they believed to be *inherent* childhood creativity, alongside a rigid framework of linear development, constructed a limiting binary for youth and a contradictory identity trap. In this chapter I bring attention to both concepts to provide background on these naturalized assumptions of modern childhood. How can children embody both idealizations: the malleable, imaginative individual brimming with creative ideas, and the linearly developing every-child following regimented routine and clearly defined expectations? Acknowledging that creativity is a complex and shifting concept responsive to cultural nuances makes it alarmingly restrictive, and susceptible for use as a marker of social hierarchy or as a broad sociological homogenizer, just as other individual character traits were used in the late nineteenth and early twentieth centuries. This is especially true when the former is overlooked, and instead the concept of childhood creativity is assumed as a supposedly ingrained and identifiable trait when considering historically marginalized groups. So I ask, most pressingly, where do children identified outside of those typically associated with inherent creativity (i.e., white, middle-class boys) fit into this schema, and how do we shift our thinking to include these children in history, as opposed to just the *idea* of these children as an abstraction?

To interrogate this dualism, in this chapter I examine Marie Paneth's account of the Branch Street children from her 1944 book *Branch Street: A Sociological Study* and employ Judith Butler's (2009) concept of precarious lives, and precarity in consideration of Paneth's theories and methods. I highlight the precarious spaces experienced by the children due to their socioeconomic status and war-torn living conditions, and look critically at their reinforced position of precarity, solidified by their place outside of the inherently creative child trope, as Paneth emphasized the use of arts-based rehabilitation methods with these young people. I argue that through their resistance to both idealized developmental confines, the Branch Street children force us to acknowledge that this contradictory identity trap was impossible to fulfill, and instead set them up to exist within a tension of should-be and constantly-lacking. Keeping Butler's scholarship, specifically regarding the relationality of precariousness, in mind could help remind those in authoritative positions over youth that this vulnerability of the creative identity affects both adults and children (Millar, 2017). In order to help emancipate children from this impossible selfhood, it is imperative to recognize inconspicuous places of childhood precarity, problematize the under-examined concept of the creative child, and to reimagine rigid limitations imposed by a universal, normative framework of development and the concept of the romanticized, imaginative youth.

STANDARDIZATION OF LINEAR CHILD DEVELOPMENT

In the late nineteenth century, the consensus that children were simply mini adults began to fade, and the concept that the child was instead a separate and special category from adults became more widely accepted. This reconceptualization helped spark the professional medical and scientific study of children's bodies and minds (Hulbert, 2003). In response to the years of medical theories formulated on the basis of adult bodies, then transposed onto youth, physicians and psychologists clamored to study children in the burgeoning field of pediatric medicine. The practice of observing actual children for medical and scientific purposes became more common, as children became noted as "specimens" (Hulbert, 2003, p. 70) in need of intensified research. Parallel to the work of medical professionals, progressive reformers involved with philanthropic organizations took the initiative to survey large groups of children and mothers, and started keeping detailed records providing statistics to aid both private and federal programs in understanding the needs of children and families (Lindenmeyer, 1997).

Through the use of scientific practices like observation and experimentation, new to this crop of youth-focused medical professionals, and the information gleaned from reformers' surveys, in the early twentieth century a framework for how a child should grow and develop was defined, and standardized milestones of pediatric development were established (Smuts, 2008). Experts like Holt and Gesell developed growth charts, which noted things like ideal height and weight measurements by age and proper behavioral patterns, and the psychologist Binet created the standardized IQ test, which influenced standardized testing and child classification, impacting agendas such as compulsory schooling laws, hygiene education, and nutrition assistance programs (Fass, 2016). For the first time, children in the early twentieth century were expected to meet certain physical and mental development marks as demanded by medical professionals, progressive educators, and federal authority figures. European and American mothers were suddenly expected to measure and carefully record the growth of their young to compare them to the experts' charts and guidelines. Mothers whose children did not measure up were to follow child-rearing experts' advice, and work to fix issues that were surely due to their parenting errors. These new standards were portrayed as key to raising a healthy, promising child, as the rise in science and medical knowledge was touted as objective, thus disseminating truthful and untenable instructions (Sealander, 2003). These authoritarian childrearing guidelines provided a linear path from infancy to adulthood, and emphasized conformity, regardless of the realities of race, class, gender, or geographical location.

However, many of the systemized and regimented medical research processes were based on information gleaned from white middle class children. This was reflective of early twentieth century race and class issues which centered the white male as the top species, such as in the theory of eugenics, and set the stage for medical professionals and federal programs to use insight gathered to define a standardized framework for the "proper" development of children stemming from a small, exclusionary base sample. These clear and rigid guidelines defined which children exemplified ideal childhoods, those that were white, male, and middle class, and which fell outside of this exclusionary space, those that were anything else.

CONSTRUCTION OF THE INHERENTLY CREATIVE CHILD

The creative child figure is an easy one to imagine, especially in modern Western culture. Existing literature, originating from the mid-nineteenth century forward, emphasizes a universalist assumption that all children are inherently creative, and easily and often engage in some form of art making. Much of this idea stemmed from the arena of progressive education in America, and psychoanalysis in Britain and the United States. As scholar Camilla Nelson posits, in the mid-nineteenth century the child's creative development was considered to be "a process of potential unfolding within destiny," and "aligned the destinies of the individual and the nation" (Nelson, 2014, p. 32). The image of this particular child can be seen emblazoned across toy packaging, art material companies' marketing campaigns, and within the pages of family-oriented magazines. To nail down this ideal, most modern Euro-American child rearing guidebooks since the early twentieth century emphasize the importance of imagination, quiet play and a distinct children's creative culture (Cross, 1997).

But what or who, I implore, is this inherently creative child? What does this do to influence our assumptions pertaining to children and youth? As easy as the creative child figure is for us to imagine, it proves to be much more difficult to define. Camilla Nelson quotes Sawyer highlighting, "to explain creativity, we first need to agree on what it is, and this turns out to be surprisingly difficult" (Nelson, 2014, p. 47). As noted, the physical and cognitive growth and development of a child was charted and defined in the early twentieth century there is a clear path from point A to point B. While the concept of the child as inherently creative is considered a given within most disciplines, when examined it does not have the same clear framework as other patterns of development. In fact, the concept of creativity itself is not easily or concretely defined, with Merriam-Webster defining it as "the ability to create," and "the quality of being creative" (Merriam-Webster.com), and Oxford Languages explaining it as "the use of the imagination or original ideas, especially in the production of an artistic work" (Oxford Languages/Google). Additionally, through her extensive research, Nelson argues that even though the term creativity is recently found most everywhere, it is a modern concept "making its first appearance as an English noun in 1875" (Nelson, 2010, p. 1). If there is no solid, long-running working definition of creativity, how is creativity assumed as such a static, idealized childhood norm?

The concept of creativity is shrouded in complexity, inextricably bound to ideas like imagination, originality, and genius. There are science-based scholars, such as KyungHee Kim, who emphasize creativity can be empirically measured through standardized tests like the *Torrance Tests of Creative Thinking*, then improved upon by practicing the use of creativity (Kim, 2011), psychologists who believe creativity is all about how the practices of creativity are categorized, as children employ low level creativity, or "little-c" (Beghetto and Beghetto, 2009), and scholars who focus on the requirement of particular materials and environments to enhance the creative process (Glaveanu, 2012; Cropley, 2016). Even though these conversations differ, they all still assume that children are born with "everyday creativity, which can be found in nearly all people" (Beghetto and Kaufman, 2009, p. 1).

The ease with which the creative child is accepted as a naturally occurring entity is one of recent history. Not long ago children were considered unable to employ creativity, as they were seen as the opposite of rational and unable to function at a "high level"—key traits necessary to experience the pang of creative spark for the production of works of art (Glaveanu, 2011). It wasn't until early in the twentieth century that children were underscored as creative beings. Reflecting a modernized protectionist view of children, as white, middle-class youth's familial and societal roles changed, they no longer spent time working for wages, and instead were encouraged to participate in healthy play and activities which would help shape proper personalities and values. Much early discussion of the child as creative took place in progressive educational spaces. For example, in the 1930s, child experts like psychologist Lev Vygotsky and progressive education reformer John Dewey insisted that children should be encouraged to use "imagination" and "creative process," as well as appreciate art making practices in everyday life (Ayman-Nolley, 1992). This, combined with more attention to visual culture and art appreciation in the primary school classroom, helped solidify the concept that productive creativity and art making should have a prominent space within the world of children.

The construction of this creative child figure, steeped in romantic ideologies of childhood, is dangerous if left unexamined. Although the creative child figure is difficult to define clearly, there are still some assumptions which make it possible to define who are not historically included within the category of the inherently creative child. This concept of inherent creativity, which permeated childhood development, education, play and consumer culture, revered alongside the rigid, normalized framework of linear development, reinforced white, middle-class partiality, constructed a limiting binary for youth, and a contradictory identity trap. I do not argue, however, that these concepts are always or necessarily pitted against each other, or mutually exclusive, but rather two distinct paths that children were expected to simultaneously fulfill. With this in mind, I ask where children that are outside of white, middle-class culture fit into these idealizations? Even more importantly, do they, or do they need to, at all?

PRECARITY AND PRECARIOUS SPACES

> "The House" is a condemned house in the street. All the houses in Branch Street are condemned. It is a condemned street. That does not alter the fact that a little more than a hundred children live in Branch Street. (Paneth, 1944, p. 7)

Judith Butler tells us that "'precarity' designates that politically induced condition in which certain populations suffer from failing social and economic networks of support and become differentially exposed to injury, violence, and death. Such populations are at heightened risk of disease, poverty, starvation, displacement, and of exposure to violence without protection. Precarity also characterizes that politically induced condition of maximized vulnerability and exposure for populations exposed to arbitrary state violence . . . against which states do not offer adequate protection" (Butler, 2009, p. 2). Her scholarship gives us theoretical tools necessary to examine particularly marginalized populations, especially those that are considered at-risk due to social, state and political neglect or violence. The use of precarity and precarious lives indeed helps to make obvious dangerous and tenuous positions children hold that are often overlooked on the pages of historical narratives, and where and how certain childhoods fit into a larger childhood schema rigid with white, middle-class normativity.

Employing Butler's theories, I argue the children of Marie Paneth's 1944 book, *Branch Street: A Sociological Study*, both encounter precarity, as well as embody precarious lives. These physical and mental realities encompassed their lived experiences, and were conscientiously documented by Paneth. For example, Paneth recorded that the children inhabited and played in a poverty stricken, bombed-out area of war-torn London, which Paneth repeatedly referred to as a "slum" (Paneth, 1944, p. 9). The children of Branch Street face all which Butler puts forward as constituting a precarious life: a population suffering from a politically induced condition and state induced violence, living within heightened risk for poverty, starvation and death, and politically induced maximized vulnerability. The youth of Branch Street were inextricably tied to precarity through the tangible danger of their living conditions, and the impossibility for any hope for a future due to both physical and systemic violence and oppression. Their lives were reinforced as simultaneously inconspicuous and obtrusive, as they navigated mostly ignored yet highly regulated spaces with little systemic or state support.

Most notably, Paneth's descriptions drive home that the Branch Street children were a population dealing with substandard living circumstances from politically induced conditions and state induced violence. For example, the central location for Paneth's work with the children was a condemned house-turned-shelter-turned-play center. According to Paneth, this play center existed on a street composed entirely of condemned homes, damaged by war. There is little protectional oversight from the state or officials, as, "It is a street into which the police do not attempt to go" (Paneth, p. 7). Due to equity-oriented issues like lack of access to goods and services, as well as other age-related limitations being a child creates, this environment forced them to band together to navigate everyday corporeal challenges like warmth, shelter, and nutrition. Their living conditions situated these children within the promise of real bodily harm, caused by the state induced violence, and coinciding socio-economic instability of poverty. Paneth explains that the existing challenges prevented the children from common childhood experiences like regular attendance in school, intact homes in which to grow and develop, and protected living and play places.

Circling back to Butler's theory, in conjunction with issues regarding their immediate environment, the Branch Street children lived amongst heightened risks due to, and resulting in, poverty, starvation and death. Paneth describes the children's family situations as dismal, often alluding to unsavory sexual practices, unhealthy drinking habits, abuse, and abandonment. She condemns the total lack of parental care through statements like, "These people have not yet learned to feed themselves and their children" (Paneth, p. 37), and throughout the book teeters between pity and indignation for, and disgust at both the youth themselves and the children's parents. Paneth often describes the children as "not in good health" (Paneth, p. 37), and recounts that their bodies were afflicted with wounds and scabies. Only few and far between does Paneth mention broader systemic challenges like poverty, working or deceased parents, and unsanitary living conditions as contributing to the families' socioeconomic statuses.

However, rather than placing blame solely on the youth or their mothers, Paneth does make clear that due to politics of war and class status, these children were offered little to no state protection forcing them into a lived reality of constant vulnerability. She describes their continued exposure to fallout from war, as well as susceptibility to long term damage caused by both their environment and social landscape. Since their homes did not offer "enough room to keep themselves clean" or "room where they could wash their bodies or clothes" (Paneth, p. 38), and "of the 400 children tested only 3" were of satisfactory nutrition (Paneth, p. 36), Paneth expressed disappointment that these children employed petty crimes such as breaking-and-entering and theft to stay alive. This heightened their precarity and vulnerability through the added layer of potential punishment from authority figures and the justice system, and, according to Paneth, brought into focus the impossibility of improved lives and productive futures.

From the beginning of the book, and only intensifying throughout, Paneth's descriptions make clear the Branch Street children existed outside of any kind of ideal developmental norms. She emphasized that they were unhealthy, unkempt, unkind, and completely void of positive attributes. Since the Branch Street children are excluded from the framework of linear development due to their precarious lives, how do we situate them within constructions of childhood which often hinge on physical and mental observance of these standards, especially in consideration of the creative child ideal?

Resistance to the Creative Child Figure

Paneth crafted *Branch Street* as an autobiographical account of her time working at a repurposed shelter-turned-youth-center in an undisclosed area of London in the early 1940s. Her narrative focused on the children that populated Branch Street, and detailed their interactions with her, adult reform workers, the public, and each other. She wrote in great detail about her dedication to rehabilitate the young people of Branch Street through the use of art, play, and skill-building, yet often stressed how inexperienced or ill-equipped they were. She noted that "the level of their painting was very low indeed," and that "they had little choice of ideas, they were rigid and thin in the way they expressed them and far below their age in ability" (Paneth, p. 90). Despite her insistence in using art as a method of saving these youth, Paneth's discussion of the children's artwork is surprisingly harsh, directly stating, "To look through the bundle is a sad experience" (Paneth, p. 90). For a trait like creativity that was supposedly ingrained in all children, Paneth focuses much attention on the Branch Street children's *lack* of creative ability, and general artistic ineptitude.

Although Paneth believed the children would be saved by her work with them, and rehabilitated through the power of art making, play, and handicrafts like sewing, throughout her account the children did not respond favorably. For example, Paneth's assumption that the children yearned to paint and draw is met with strong opposition by the youth, exhibited through disobedience, violence, and extreme acts of vandalism. She noted that the children had "a queer urge to break, to spoil and to besmirch" (Paneth, p. 60), and described chaotic evenings where children "started using the painting material as projectiles with which to shoot at the rest of us" (Paneth, p. 11), or "upset all the water jars" (Paneth, p. 12) during wild refuse battles. Regardless of Paneth's assumption that all children were inherently creative, and that art-making and craft work would be a successful method of rehabilitation, the Branch Street children generally did not comply.

Examining this text highlights just how crucial implementing Butler's theories of precarity and precarious lives are to better contextualize marginalized youth in both their social and lived spaces. Paneth's reliance on the "mysticism" (Tomlinson and Holme, 1934) of the inherently creative child trope only served to reinforce the Branch Street children's marginalization and precarity, forcing them deeper into stigmatization and alienation. The Branch Street children were often defiant and chose not to participate in adult-directed activities, thus earning them nicknames like "young hooligans" (Paneth, p. 61) and "criminals of the future generation" (Paneth, p. 120). By resisting performing tasks, especially those of art and handicraft focus, are the Branch Street children refusing to produce what they considered menial child's work, or protesting against the idea of reforming their identity, or maybe both? Were these young people aware that the do-gooder adults who came to save them already saw them as excluded from redemption? If we look from Butler's perspective, could we argue the children are, consciously or unconsciously, trying to work against remaining within the vulnerable and/or disposable label?

Most intriguingly, Paneth concludes *Branch Street* with the lament that even after months of reform-oriented service at the Branch Street play center, the children were still destined for certain doom. She describes her efforts as failed because the youths did not seize the opportunity to improve themselves and enjoy the moralistic activities for betterment that she provided. She emphasizes that the children were products of their environment, and that they would be unable to break free of their low status due to the inevitability of intergenerational transmission of immoral behavior, like drinking, swearing, and questionable sexual practices. Just a few pages from the end she notes, "And I do not see much hope for my gang. What we could do for them was only patchwork and the result is most doubtful" (Paneth, p. 125). Paneth resolves to walk away from these youths as lost causes, and as fated to repeat their intergenerational cycles. Acknowledging this, I argue their resistance to the idealized construction of the creative child figure was effective. Although the children did not necessarily elevate their socio-economic status, which was quite the lofty goal of Paneth's to begin with, in the end they did fight and earn an identity they could claim as their own, serving to problematize assumptions of their victimhood.

Emancipation from an Impossible Contradiction

Due to both their circumstantial precarity and chosen resistance, the Branch Street children do not fit within typical, normalized or idealized childhood spaces. To disrupt a problematic dialogue this historic narrative presents, how can we reimagine and address the space these children inhabit? Acknowledging Butler's theory of precarity allows us to look past seeing the Branch Street children as trying to fit into typical and normalized childhood spaces and instead recognize them as claiming another. In short, resistance discourse asks us to recognize the act of resistance as power and agency. Here the children "engage in daily acts that undermine power" (Rosales and Langhout, 2019, p. 3), harnessing resistance as their source of power and control within confined adult-managed arenas. Even though the youth continue to come back to the play center, as opposed to boycotting it all together, to normalize the concept that "actions that undermine power are resistance" (Rosales and Langhout, p. 3), is to see beyond limiting binaries produced by this historic narrative. I argue that through the children's resistance to both idealizations of childhood, they legitimize their lives and claim their place outside of these impossible norms. The Branch Street children resisted the adult authority figures' concepts of rehabilitation, thus bucking modern tropes of childhood which often assume children need to fulfill certain expectations for "optimal growth" (Hulbert, p. 158), and follow adult-directed guidance to attain it. Instead of condemning young people who do not follow a linear path of either being saved through reform or doomed due to resistance, how do we celebrate this claiming of identity and emancipate the Branch Street children, and others of their precarious ilk. I ask this particularly acknowledging that they ran, and youth continue to run, up against impenetrable borders like standardized and linear developmental frameworks, and the homogenized concept of the inherently creative child figure.

Here it seems imperative to consider how I am using the term impossible, as I draw attention to the impossibility of the inherently creative child figure in the title, and throughout. Merriam-Webster defines "impossible" as "incapable of being or occurring," or something "felt to be incapable of being done, attained, or fulfilled" (Merriam-Webster.com). Boundaries created by culturally constructed frameworks, like the linearly developing or creative child, which make attainment of popularly idealized childhoods almost impossible, remain oppressive if left unexamined and unchallenged. Scholarship which pushes back against naturalized child figure tropes, like the creative child and the linearly developing child, to bring to light under-examined lives of marginalized youth is imperative for a more inclusive, and deeper understanding of childhood both past and present. By recognizing that children assert their own agendas when faced with adult-directed tasks and reading across the grain for parallel narratives in both historic and contemporary texts to locate and reposition fringe youth while interrogating assumed concepts would help liberate them from impossible spaces and perpetual exclusion. Butler wants us to look at precarity beyond labor and political instability, two issues which concerned Paneth, and instead see precarity and precariousness as an ontological concern within the reality of social structures, capitalism, and modern politics (Millar, 2017).

Acknowledging that youth bring their own individual and collective selves to tasks and relationships is critical for a child-centered approach to examining and understanding marginalized communities. Repositioning ourselves again and again as we critically think about children and their actions, especially when considering interactions between adult authority figures and youth, is necessary to keep from ascribing particular and inappropriate identities onto them. Paneth presents a fundamental problem when she assumes these children living in their precarious environment needed her to save them by using art-based activities, then dooms them to continued woe because they resisted her methods. While Paneth details the serious everyday challenges that the Branch Street children face, she does not offer any reflective consideration to their behavior aside from what she sees at face value. This is where alternative readings can be of service. Instead of passively accepting these children as a "most rude, unruly and exceptionally difficult group" (Paneth, p. 9), we can readjust to appreciate them as engaged in their individual and collective identities in relation to outside forces. just as scholar Lexie Scherer argues, we need to celebrate that "the children came to the activity with their own agendas," "these agendas were involved with identity work," and reframe "resistance as agency" (Scherer, 2016, p. 14). These children did not exist within a vacuum, and the complexities of their childhood experiences need to be acknowledged as both imposing and imposed upon. For example, scholar Karen Wells discusses children as "agents who are constrained by the social structures that they are situated within but who do not passively succumb to these structures; they are agents or actors and they make society as much as society makes them" (Wells, 2017, p. 2). While childhood "agency" is contested, and admittedly a bit of a tired concept within many academic discourses, it is something significant to consider regarding the actions of the Branch Street youth *not* participating in so-called rehabilitative activities.

Instead of continuing to perpetuate problematic readings of childhood, like improperly labeling and stigmatizing children as "troubled children" (Doroshow, 2019, p. 2) or as Paneth posited, as "hooligans," because they do not fit into white, middle-class ideals, scholarship decentering hegemonic colonial ideals as the natural is imperative. For example, while its focus is contemporary children, Carla Shalaby's 2017 book *Troublemakers: Lessons in Freedom from Young Children at School* unapologetically aims to confront structural, social and cultural barriers marginalized children face. Shalaby calls out obstacles for often ignored youth, such as children of color, children with difference, or any child excluded from white, middle-class spaces. In her work, Shalaby plays with loaded childhood ideals like innocence, creativity, education, and family to help bring attention to the violence of these oppressive concepts. For example, do we understand the child that cannot, or just doesn't want to, act as a producer in institutional or mediated settings? What do we do with children who are not considered as having inherently creative identities due to race, class, gender, or socioeconomic status? While her book highlights present-day urban children, it reinvigorates and problematizes long-standing issues considering the construction of ideal childhood spaces-impossible to attain for those historically excluded.

In addition to recognizing children's personal and collective agency, reading across the grain for more than one narrative in both historical work and contemporary texts can help bring precarious childhoods into the light, not as impossible, but rather as parallel. More scholarship which considers children as complex figures, and who may not fit into naturalized childhood identities provided by socio-cultural structures, like creativity or developmental norms, is critical to emancipate youth from these rigid boundaries. For example, I assert, alongside scholars like Cropley (2016) and Ogata (2013), that creativity has a history, and is a socio-cultural construction (i.e., not natural). Looking through this lens helps us make space for children like the Branch Street children, for, as Camilla Nelson argues, the concept of childhood creativity was/is constructed through specific moments in history, as opposed to the common assumption that it is ahistorical and a natural attribute of all children (Nelson, 2014). Adopting this idea more widely offers a more grounded perspective regarding the concept of childhood creativity, and breaks it down to something malleable and relative, as opposed to inherent and/or divine.

Using a child centered lens makes space available to examine the hegemonic nature of conceptual constructions, like both the creative, and linearly developing child figure. Looking at children's lived experiences, especially with an intersectional lens (the combination of categories like gender, race, age, class, etc. to examine power structures), is incredibly useful for dismantling dangerous categorical confines and tropes, like the construction of the creative child. Although these complicated perspectives are not always easy to find when considering historical narratives, making the task of locating fringe youth even more important. Re-politicizing this neutralized and assumed childhood space would bring necessary attention to the limitations created by it. More scholarship examining specific cultural assumptions, like inherent childhood creativity or the need for reform for fringe youth, within historical and contemporary texts is key here. Locating and repositioning marginalized children while acknowledging the complexity of their individual experiences and recognizing the naturalized violence done through normalization of middle-class white children as the basis for comparison will demand radical upheaval and rejection of historic structures.

By carefully examining both the standardization of linear child development and the normalization of inherent childhood creativity as cultural constructions, it allows us to interrogate some problematic assumptions about childhood. By acknowledging that both linear developmental frameworks and the concept of inherent creativity are based in white, male, middle class privilege we can more openly see how they serve as exclusionary boundaries for certain populations of youth. Bringing awareness to these spaces of exclusion and gaps in existing academic research, as well as broader scale print media, helps support an intervention upon hegemonic and narrow-minded scholarship which assumes these privileged concepts are axis points of childhood experience. Thoughtful analysis of historic narratives of childhood can inform contemporary issues by calling out the impossibility of the inherently creative child figure, and bringing to light ongoing dangerous assumptions about childhood made therein. This could serve to open up spaces for children embodying precarious lives to enter the conversation not as other, but as also, and help emancipate these young people from the confines of impossibility.

REFERENCES

Ayman-Nolley, S. (1992). Vygotsky's perspective on the development of imagination and creativity. *Creativity Research Journal*, *5*(1), 77–85.

Beghetto, R. A., and Kaufman, J. C. (2009). Beyond Big and Little: The Four C Model of Creativity. *Review of General Psychology*, *13*(1), 1–12.

Butler, J. (2009). Performativity, Precarity and Sexual Policies. Revista de antropología iberoamericana, *4*(3) ASOC ANTROPÓLOGOS IBEROAMERICANOS EN RED, 321–36.

Cropley, A. (2016). The Myths of Heaven-Sent Creativity: Toward a Perhaps Less Democratic But More Down-to-Earth Understanding. *Creativity Research Journal*, *28*(3), 238–46.

Cross, G. (1997). *Kids' Stuff: Toys and the Changing World of American Childhood.* Harvard University Press.

Doroshow, D. B. (2019). *Emotionally disturbed; a history of caring for America's troubled children.* The University of Chicago Press.

Fass, P. (2016). *The End of American Childhood: A History of Parenting From Life on the Frontier to the Managed Child. Princeton University Press.*

Glaveanu, V. (2011). Children and creativity: A most (un)likely pair? *Thinking Skills and Creativity, 6(2)*, 122–31.

Glaveanu, V. (2012). What Can Be Done with an Egg? Creativity, Material Objects, and the Theory of Affordances. *Journal of Creative Behavior, 46*(3), 192–208.

Hulbert, A. (2003). *Raising America: Experts, Parents, and a Century of Advice About Children.* Alfred A. Knopf.

Kim, KyungHee. (2011). The Creativity Crisis: The Decrease in Creative Thinking Scores on the Torrance Tests of Creative Thinking. *Creative Research Journal, 23*(4), 285–95.

Lindenmeyer, K. (1997). *A Right to Childhood: the U.S. Children's Bureau and Child Welfare, 1912–1946. University of Illinois Press.*

Millar, K. (2017). Toward a critical politics of precarity. *Sociology Compass, 11*.

Nelson, C. (2010). The Invention of Creativity: The emergence of a discourse. *Cultural Studies Review, 16(2).*

Nelson, C. (2014). The Creative Child: Constructing Creativity Through Early Childhood Education in Modern America. *Knowledge Cultures*, *2*(3), 29–50.

Ogata, A. (2013). *Designing the Creative Child: Playthings and Places in Midcentury America*. University of Minnesota Press.

Oxford Languages—Google Online. Retrieved from www.google.com/search?q=define+creativity&oq=define+&aqs=chrome.0.69i59j69i57j69i59l2j0i433i512l2j0i131i433j0i433i512l3.1560j0j7&sourceid=chrome&ie=UTF-8.

Paneth, M. (1944). *Branch Street: A Sociological Study*. George Allen & Unwin LTD.

Rosales, C., and Langhout, R. (2019). Just Because We Don't See It, Doesn't Mean It's Not There: Everyday Resistance in Psychology. *Soc Personal Psychol Compass*.

Scherer, L. (2016). Children's Engagements with Visual Methods Through Qualitative Research in the Primary School as "Art That Didn't Work." *Sociological Research Online*, *21*(1).

Sealander, J. (2003). *The Failed Century of the Child: Governing America's Young in the Twentieth Century. Cambridge University Press.*

Shalaby, Carla. (2017). *Troublemakers: Lessons in Freedom from Young Children at School*. The New Press.

Smuts, A. (2008). *Science in the Service of Children 1893–1935.* Yale University Press.

Tomlinson, and Holme, C. G. (1934). *Picture making by children*. The Studio, limited.

Wells, K. (2017). *Childhood Studies: Making Young Subjects*. Polity Press.

PART III

Identities

Chapter 11

The Weaponization of Childhood in Mussolini's Ethiopian Laboratory and Its Revenants in Present Day Italy

Paula Salvio

Throughout the second Italo-Ethiopian war (1935–1936), ordinary Italian households tracked the progress of Italian troops marching into Ethiopia by following updates on the popular radio show "Radio-voyage in the Empire." Children posted pins on linoleum maps that were fastened to their living room walls to mark the advance of the Italian army into the city of Adigrat and the town of Adowa. Board games, such as *The Conquest of Abyssinia,* came tucked in children's cereal boxes and rendered Italy's brutal invasion of Ethiopia a children's game (Carlo Erba S. A., 1936). This particular board game, designed in 1936 by the Carlo Erba baby food manufacturer, instructed children to "march" from the city of Asmara in Eritrea, the starting point for the Italian military campaign, to the capital city of Addis Ababa. Bombings and fighting forces were drawn on the board to turn the invasion into entertainment while inculcating in children an unquestioning loyalty to the fascist state of Italy.

This chapter opens the archive of another form of material culture that circulated throughout Italy during the second Italo-Ethiopian War—Italian colonial postcards.[1] The postcards, designed by Aurelio Bertiglia, are part of the everyday material culture that circulated in fascist Italy and contributed to constructing the narrative used to legitimize Italy's imperialist invasion of Ethiopia.[2] These postcards are important today in shedding light on facets of Italian fascist imaginaries, revealing how the invasion of Ethiopia was presented to the Italian public and providing examples of the weaponization of childhood and childhood innocence. The postcards, because they still circulate in Italy, particularly at flea markets and in souvenir shops, also suggest the return of fascist ideology and imaginaries today as revenants of that invasion, an invasion that Italy has relegated to the margins of history.

Aurelio Bertiglia (1891–1973) had a strong reputation as a propaganda artist in Germany, which is one reason Mussolini selected him to drum up public support for the Italian invasion. Bertiglia's images depict Italian soldiers as a welcomed and liberating presence in Ethiopia. Similar to the board game *The Conquest of Abyssinia,* postcards frame the Italian invasion of Ethiopia as child's play. Each of Bertiglia's postcards depicts Italian soldiers and Ethiopians as children. But the child depicted in the postcards is no monolithic version of childhood, and the childhood innocence portrayed has very different meanings and purposes.

The figures resemble cherubs, which in Judeo-Christian iconography serve the will of God, perform divine duties in the earthly realm, and are exemplars of world order. Thus the child figures depicting Italian soldiers in Bertiglia's post cards can be read as performing divine fascist duties for Mussolini. Furthermore, these cherubic children transform the brutality of the invasion into an innocent and purifying project. Bertiglia's Ethiopian children, however, are not depicted as cherub-like. They are rendered with racialized facial features that resonate with the picaninny, an anti-black caricature that circulated in the United States and British Empire in the nineteenth and early twentieth centuries. Bertiglia's Ethiopian children have bulging eyes, red lips, and wide mouths, and they are often portrayed kneeling in gratitude or submission. These are children whose "innocence" or primitive status requires adult supervision, education, and discipline.

Focusing on Bertiglia's postcards, this chapter first provides a historical context for the second Italo-Ethiopian war and places in relief key racial aspects of the imaginary of Mussolini's fascism. Second, it considers Bertiglia's weaponizing of childhood innocence in terms of differing versions of childhood and innocence; in terms of its relationship to the idealized fascist citizen/soldier; and in terms of an exclusionary social practice that works according to a racialized logic and determines which children are worthy of state protection (Garlen, 2019; Bernstein, 2010, 2011; Faulkner, 2011, 2014). Third, the chapter connects the disavowed fascist invasion of Ethiopia to present-day Italian policies pertaining to migration and restricted citizenship. I argue that the racial violence directed at Ethiopians, as well as at Libyans, Somalis, and Eritreans during the invasion, reverberates today in the lives of second-generation Afro-Italians, who continue to face racial violence in the afterlife of Italy's fascist past. The invasion of Ethiopia has become entangled with Italy's current racial laws against migrants from Africa, as well as with

Figure 11.1 Children in uniforms painting a map of Ethiopia, Eritrea colonial postcard (Aurelio Bertiglia, colonial postcard, 1936).

Source: Image courtesy of the Wolfsonian Institute, Florida International University.

Italy's restricted citizenship laws that withhold citizenship from children born in Italy to parents not born in Italy.[3]

ESTABLISHING ETHIOPIA AS A HUMAN LABORATORY

Between 1935 and 1939, Italy conducted a brutal invasion into Ethiopia. Mussolini, in part, viewed the invasion as payback for Italy's defeat in the first Italo-Ethiopian war in 1895–1896. But he also saw this invasion as a project to reclaim Italy's imperial past. Ethiopia became the site of a laboratory for the cultivation of the fascist soldier/male. There, Italians would be refashioned into disciplined, virile soldiers through a curriculum grounded in the same values instituted in Italian public schools and fascist mass organizations.

In 1935 Mussolini defied the 1925 Geneva Protocol's ban on the use of chemical weapons by shipping 617 tons of mustard gas to Ethiopia to be used indiscriminately on the civilian population. Mustard gassing was a particularly horrific weapon that with conventional weapons led to a quarter-million Ethiopian deaths by 1938, 17,800 of them were women and children (Ben-Ghiat, 2017). Despite Italian brutalities, Ethiopians resisted, provoking Italians to use industrial killing tactics, such as aerial gas bombings, open-grave executions, decapitations, castrations, and the burning and razing of civilian quarters and Red Cross camps, war crimes not often associated with Mussolini.[4] When the League of Nations condemned Italy's invasion into Ethiopia and placed sanctions on Italy, Mussolini lashed out at the League and portrayed his country as a "virtuous victim," who he claimed was simply trying to "bring civilization to backwards lands, build roads and schools and diffuse the hygiene and progress of our time" (Ben-Ghiat, 2001, p. 126).

A master rhetorician, Mussolini's rant against the League of Nations garnered support from Italian intellectuals and prompted even more Italians to commit to fascism. Italian intellectuals began to embrace Mussolini's vision of Ethiopia as the site of an exceptional social experiment, a laboratory for human reclamation—*bonifica umana.* Intellectuals such as Luigi Pirandello and Giovanni Gentile supported Mussolini in establishing the battlefield in Ethiopia as a lab where the "not-so-fully born" Italian soldier would become the fascist soldier conceived of as white, Aryan, and Christian.

By the summer of 1938, Mussolini was enforcing the racial laws in Italy that excluded Jews from almost every sector of Italian public life, which had devastating consequences for those in Italy who were deemed unfit or dangerous (Ben-Ghiat, 2001, p. 200). On August 5, 1938, the periodical *La Difesa della Razza* (*In Defense of the Race*), published articles contrasting the superiority of Italy's Roman cultural heritage to the assumed primitive character of African cultures (Pankhurst, 2007). "The racist ideas embodied in this publication were important," argues historian Richard Pankhurst (2007), "in that they influenced—and reflected—Italian government policy and thinking throughout the occupation of Ethiopia.This was particularly the case in relation to urban segregation, discriminatory education and health policies, and, above all, attitudes to establish miscegenation and half-castes (para. 16)."[5] If, as historian Ruth Ben-Ghiat (2017) argues, the Ethiopian war brought the dictatorship a new level of popular support in Italy, at the same time it provoked anxieties about social chaos, ethnic confusion, and miscegenation.

Fascist anxieties about miscegenation, stitched into *The Manifesto of Race* and the 1938 Racial Laws, demanded rigid borders between races. They also prompted a particular psychic armoring that can be understood in terms of Klaus Theweleit's classic work on the fascist body and fascist soldier. Drawing on Deleuze and Guattari, Theweleit contrasts molecular masses, which are fluid, multiple, and always changing, with molar masses, which channel the flow of desire into rigid, hierarchical, organizational structures or totality formations that are overseen by the fascist leader (1987b, pp. 3, 75). The Italian racial laws that governed Italy and Ethiopia can be understood as a response to the fear of engulfment by the "foreign" Other and fear of dissolution of identity when confronted by the Other or any degree of difference that threatened the unified "we." Ethiopia then, became a human laboratory where the not fully born Italian soldier could learn to be a soldier/male who according to Theweleit's analysis is an ascetic subject who produces not bliss, but death (1987a, p. 216). He battles against "everything that constitutes enjoyment and pleasure" (1987b, p. 7). According to this psychoanalytic model, Bertiglia's representations of Italian soldiers as cherubic children can be understood as a rendering of the fascist soldier's male ego as tenuous and "not yet fully born" (1987b, p. 213). The fascist soldier, not yet fully born, does not identify with the father as in the Oedipal model but with punishment, military drills, beatings, and combat. Theweleit maintains that:

> The punishments of parents, teachers, masters, the punishment hierarchies of young boys and of the military, remind them constantly of the existence of their periphery (showing them their boundaries), until they "grow" a functioning and controlling body armor, and a body capable of seamless fusion into larger formations with armorlike peripheries. If my assumptions are correct, the armor of these men may be seen as constituting their ego. . . . Drill and torture, it seems, are to be seen as the extremes of more general forms of bodily perception. (1987b, p. 164)

The postcards designed by Bertiglia reveal the wider colonial imaginaries at play in Italy under Mussolini. Illuminating Mussolini's fascist project to turn Ethiopia into a laboratory of human reclamation and to make "Italy Great Again" by reclaiming Africa as the Romans had done, the postcards present the invasion and ensuing violence as a civilizing mission that could garner support from the Italian populace. But they also reveal the psychic work of reclaiming the soldier male from the not fully formed child. That work involves pain, suffering, and violence as well as the weaponization of childhood and childhood innocence.

Weaponizing Childhood and Childhood Innocence

Within the imaginary of Mussolini's fascism, the white, Catholic, Italian child stood as a symbol or stand-in for the Italian people and was envisioned as a future citizen soldier of Mussolini's fascist state. In the case of Bertiglia's postcards, the Italian child represents Italian fascist aspirations and the triumph over the weaker or pernicious natives, who were described in the diary of an Italian nurse who served in Ethiopia as "children [who] must be treated gently, but firmly corrected. It is appropriate whenever entering into conversation with them to always keep calm" (Hawkins and Sweet, 2015, p. 176).

Figure 11.2 Italian soldiers "feeding" weak and hungry natives (Aurelio Bertiglia, colonial postcard, 1936).
Source: Image courtesy of the Wolfsonian Institute, Florida International University.

The Italian invasion of Ethiopia was consistently presented as one of liberation, as depicted in the postcard in Figure 11.2 (Bertiglia, 1936b), in which Italian soldiers feed and liberate the weak natives who look on bewildered. The entry in the Italian nurse's diary resonates with Tyler Stovall's analysis of the history of equating children and colonial natives with savages who must be civilized through education (2021, p. 54). Stovall turns to the work of Elisabeth Wessling to underscore the ways in which the child-savage trope

> often became a reality for colonial administrators: As an outgrowth of the child-savage trope, colonial regimes in the overseas territories were often patterned after parent-child and teacher-child relationships in the metropolis. Raising children and ruling natives were structured as kindred practices. (Stovall, 2021, p. 55)

The use of Bertiglia's cherubic images of Italian soldiers to "sell" Italy's invasion of Ethiopia conveys, as Eden K. McLean argues in her study of fascist education, the assumed racial immaturity of Ethiopians and the necessity for Italian foreign oversight (2018, p. 156). Bertiglia's racialized depictions of Ethiopian children resonates, as stated earlier, to images of the picaninny, a black child who was typically depicted outdoors and often inviting violence.[6] Characteristics of picaninnies often included very dark or jet-black skin and exaggerated eyes and mouths. Robin Bernstein notes that:

> When threatened, picaninny characters might ignore danger or quake in exaggerated fear; when attacked, they might laugh or yelp, but in either case, they never experience or express pain or sustain wounds in any remotely realistic way . . . it is this absence of pain that unifies the construction of the pickaninny across differences. The pickaninny may be animalistic or adorable, ragged or neat, frightened or happy, American or British, but the figure is always juvenile, always of color, and always resistant if not immune to pain. (2011, p. 35)

In each of the postcards presented in this chapter, the Ethiopian children appear as incapable of feeling pain—whether it be the pain of hunger, slavery, or colonial penetration. "At stake in pain," argues Bernstein, "was not only justification for violence, but also eligibility for citizenship and humanity. Visible pain established individuals' and groups' subjectivity—and therefore . . . their worth as citizens" (2011, p. 50). The Ethiopian subject, who would never be eligible for Italian citizenship, was cast as possessing nothing more than black insensateness.

A careful analysis of the postcards offers a glimpse into how childhood innocence functions in fascist imaginaries. On a general level the invasion of Ethiopia and by extension a variety of fascist projects, were rendered harmless, innocent, pure, and salutary for the agents and targets of such projects. On closer view, the Italian soldier was specifically rendered as playful, innocent of evil intentions, and helpful. This is not the innocence of childhood in need of education or discipline. Instead it is the child as redeemer, the child as pure goodness, the child who according to Matthew (18:3) we must become to enter the kingdom of heaven. The Ethiopian child figure, as I've noted, emerges as if not savage then as in need of discipline, training, salvation, and rescue. They are happy idiots bereft of wisdom and unable to survive or lead civilized lives on their own. We can see, then, how childhood innocence is weaponized in different ways in this propaganda but still serves to disguise the horror of fascist projects, specifically the invasion of Ethiopia.

There is, however, another way to read the childlike figures depicted in the postcards.

The assumption of childhood innocence has long been challenged by scholars working in the fields of the curriculum theory (Farley, 2018; O'Loughlin and Johnson, 2010; Silin 1992; Boldt, 2002, Garlen 2019; Salvio, 2020), literary theory and philosophy (Bond-Stockton, 2007; Faulkner, 2011; Bernstein, 2011). Innocence, derived from the Latin meaning "not harming" suggests that someone who is innocent will not harm themselves or others. In her study of innocence and American childhood, Robin Bernstein argues that once innocence became entangled with childhood, the connection became and continues to be raced. Such entanglement often excludes non-white children from innocence and in turn from childhood. Bernstein emphasizes that "popular culture suggested that if they weren't innocent, then they weren't children. If they weren't white, they weren't innocent" (2010, para. 9).

The scholarship of political philosopher Joanne Faulkner resonates with Bernstein's understanding of race and childhood innocence. Faulkner argues that the child who is rendered innocent "both remembers and forgets *for* the community: first, by representing to the community a past it feels is lost; and, second, by representing an unconscious into which adult cares can be invested and expunged" (2011, pp. 127–28). In Faulkner's studies of innocence, she maintains that children are a direct target of eugenic theory and practice: what ought a culture protect and cultivate? What ought a culture limit and contain? Which children are worthy of protection? (2014). Which children, asks Faulkner, are socially desired? She asks "who must, in turn, be protected from those children seen to fall short of innocence?" (2014, para. 2).

The image of children in figure 11.3 captures the idea of the innocent child both forgetting and remembering for the community. In this postcard, Italy appears not only to successfully liberate Ethiopians from slavery, but to also avenge its defeat at Adwa in 1896, thus rewriting a past defeat, and in the words of Klaus Theweleit, "getting the war lost back—re-winning that lost THING: As long as we have lost, the war will not be over" (1993, p. 283). For Theweleit, innocence is defined as "without knowledge of defeat." To become innocent again Theweleit argues:

Figure 11.3 ***Genti del Tigrai Tacazze*** **(The People of Tigrai) (Aurelio Bertiglia, colonial postcard, 1936).**

Source: Image courtesy of the Wolfsonian Institute, Florida International University.

> the soldier has to kill again . . . that's one of the giggling rules of male logic. Women give birth to something *different* from themselves. . . . Men are *re-born* by killing. They always stand up, re-erect out of something that dies around them. . . . *War* ranks high among the male ways of giving birth. (1993, p. 284)

Theweleit maintains that a lost war turns the fascist soldier into a sort of woman. He will not regain his control, virility, and position on top unless he gets a replay—a replay in which he wins. It is no wonder that Mussolini had high hopes that the second Italo-invasion of Ethiopia would re-masculanize Italy. Such an interpretation offers yet another way to understand the deployment of childhood in Bertiglia's postcards. The Italian child-soldier signifies the potential to be reborn as Mussolini's fascist ideal.

If we continue to scratch the surface of the postcard in figure 11.3 (Bertiglia, 1936c), we will find references to October 8, 1935, the day the Italian army entered Makalle, Abyssinia, and General Emilio de Bono declared that slavery was abolished in Abyssinia; Italian rule would be beneficent, not violent. In the postcard we see Ethiopians, dressed in traditional clothing, released from slavery by Italian soldiers. The wide-eyed Ethiopian girl on the left, characterized as a picaninny with her woolly hair, watches with a sense of surprise and gratitude as an Italian soldier kneels before an enslaved Ethiopian to remove the shackles from his ankles. The Ethiopian slave's head is bald and shiny, two recurring features of the portrayal of picanninnies in Bertiglia's postcards. The baldness perhaps suggests the lack of virility and potency. Attached to the stone wall is a notice in Italian and Amharic signed by General De Bono, abolishing slavery in Tigray. Roughly, it reads: "People of Tigray; Boys; listen; you know that wherever the Italian flag is raised there is freedom, therefore, in your country, slavery under any form, is abolished." The postcard cultivates a false memory that disavows Italy's violent colonial history, uses images of childhood innocence, coded in cherubic figures and picaninny caricatures, to erase the brutalities inflicted by Italy in 1935; and obscures the racial violence that continued to ensue after Italy "freed" Ethiopia from slavery. In fact, just like the French and British elsewhere, the Italians proceeded to forcibly induct "suitable slaves" into the Italian army.

Faulkner goes on to argue that the myth of childhood innocence also serves as a fetish, a way to obscure reality by leaving purported social, political, and historical truths unchallenged and uncomplicated. This consequently produces a form of "false memory" that disavows a violent colonial past (Faulkner, 2011, pp. 128–29). In this way, the myth of childhood innocence works to conceal the ways in which the complex social, economic, and political relationships that build an empire are produced. In the context of the Italo-Ethiopian war, the Ethiopian children subjected to an Italian colonial education were rendered abject—dirty and morally monstrous. Pankhurst notes that "under Italian occupation, two distinct educational systems were put into place in Ethiopia: one for Italians or members of the dominant race, and the other for subject peoples" (1972, p. 375). The philosophy of fascist education for natives of Ethiopia maintained that "the school must be a political instrument for the peaceful penetration and moral conquest of the native population" (Pankhurst, 1972, p. 366). Implicit in this aim is a belief in the moral and intellectual inferiority of Ethiopian children as well as their need to be civilized through a curriculum that emphasized hygiene to protect Italians living and or serving in Ethiopia from miscegenation.

Ethiopian children, considered dangerous, ignorant, and dirty, concerned Mussolini precisely because of their capacity to infect the Italian colonialist agenda. The Ethiopian child stood on the other side of "innocence," that is, on the other side of not having the capacity to harm oneself or others. In this sense, childhood innocence was used as a weapon of war by fascist Italy through a process that deprived Ethiopian children of the opportunity to be, in Faulkner's words, innocent. "To be a child deprived of the opportunity to be innocent," argues Faulkner, "is a more radical experience of vulnerability that involves the withdrawal of the community's concern . . . Childhood innocence is thus purchased by a forgetting, or oblivion, of the social relationships and distinctions through which security is produced for some by the rest" (2011, pp. 128–29). In other words, security for the Italian, Catholic, fascist child living in Ethiopia came at the expense of the Ethiopian child.[7] Ethiopian children living under Italian occupation can be understood as figuratively invested with threats associated with the fascist *unconscious*: crimes of rape and assault; fear of interbreeding and race mixing; and according to Theweleit's account of the fantasies of fascist men, a hatred and dread of women accompanied by a dread of dissolution, of being swallowed, engulfed, annihilated.

Following Faulkner, I want to underscore that the difference between conscious and unconscious knowledge is critical to the ways in which a society understands or grants children agency. Is the child regarded as a capable, promising proto-citizen (citizens in progress) deserving of substantive rights—public education, family formation, healthcare, and the right to transfer economic benefits from one generation to the next? Or is the child stripped of legal status, excluded by sovereign power from the protections afforded by the juridical order? The innocence afforded to white, Catholic, Italian children living in Ethiopia and Catholic, white middle-class children in Italy meant that they had to be protected from the moral contagion of inferior races. "Children deprived of the privilege that would confer innocence upon them," argues Faulkner, "unsettle the parameters of our self-understanding" (2011, p. 6). This doctrine of innocence, as Julie C. Garlen (2019) argues in her studies of childhood as an exclusionary social practice, has operated and continues to operate to maintain white supremacy in Italy today.[8] In the following section, the concept of childhood innocence, maintained through a "rhetoric of protection," is placed in relief as we examine another of Bertiglia's propaganda postcards. This postcard represents Italy's bombing of Red Cross hospitals in Ethiopia as well as Italy's claim that, despite killing civilians in the hospitals, Italy's status as Aryan rendered them innocent of war crimes committed against "savage Africans."

Propaganda As Gentle Penetration

While Italy's use of mustard gas has been extensively documented, its systematic bombardment of hospitals that were operated by Red Cross Societies from Sweden, Austria, Britain, Egypt, and Switzerland is imperfectly erased from the historical record. Pankhurst has documented at least twenty-two cases of Italian aerial targeting of Red Cross facilities throughout the war.[9] This assault, argued Mussolini, was a defensive act because, he argued, Ethiopians were using the field hospitals as protective shields. In another colonial postcard drawn by Bertiglia, he depicts Italian soldiers stabbing/penetrating Ethiopian child soldiers with bayonets.

The Ethiopian children portrayed in this post card are dressed partly in Red Cross uniforms and partly in military uniforms (see http://www.historyrevealed.eu/africa-new/ethiopia-eritrea/european-pop-culture.html?start=10). One Ethiopian child carries a Red Cross umbrella decorated with Ethiopian motifs. There are red crosses drawn on the rumps of the Ethiopian children. The Italian soldier to the right uses his bayonet to penetrate the anus of an Ethiopian child soldier who has fallen to his knees. By the side of the fallen soldier is a box of British made dumdum bullets marked with a Red Cross emblem. The bullets, prohibited by the 1899 Hague Declaration, signals Italy's rage at the League of Nations for supporting Ethiopia's use of these weapons (Gordon and Perugini, 2020, p. 6). On one hand, this postcard accuses the Red Cross of serving as a protective shield for Ethiopians and accuses the League of Nations of supporting the Ethiopian government in its battle against Italy. On the other hand, the postcard captures the violent fascist project of using propaganda, in the words of Andrea Festa, as "as a political instrument for the peaceful penetration and moral conquest of the native population" (Pankhurst, 1972, p. 364). Despite the violent imagery, there is no blood in this scene, and the soldiers are once again children who are simply playing a game. The Ethiopian children are rendered as barefoot picaninny caricatures who feel no pain as they are anally penetrated with the bayonets of cherubic Italian soldiers.

Colonial penetration, however, is always violent. This postcard represents fascist propaganda as a practice of racial conquest of Ethiopians, and symbolizes Italy's unconscious anxieties about miscegenation, social chaos, and ethnic confusion. The Italian soldiers depicted in this postcard represent the Italian imperial call to civilize the Ethiopian natives by force of arms if necessary, for their violation of the principle of distinction (i.e., distinguishing between combatants and civilians).

The use of childhood innocence as a weapon of war represented in this postcard demonstrates specific ways in which Bertiglia's propaganda concealed the violence that fascism relied on to build its empire and penetrate the psyches of a native population that was viewed as morally and intellectually inferior (Pankhurst, 1972, p. 366). This propaganda also conceals the homoeroticism and homosexual panic implicit in versions of the fascist pedagogical project and in the fascist fascination with the male anatomy and terror of femininity.

FACETTA NERA (*LITTLE BLACK FACE*)

In 1935 Renato Micheli wrote the lyrics to *Facetta Nera* (*Little Black Face*). Music was composed by Mario Ruccione. The song, written to celebrate the

Figure 11.4 Ethiopian female and Italian soldiers singing *Faccetta Nera* (Aurelio Bertiglia, colonial postcard, 1936).

Source: Image courtesy of the Wolfsonian Institute, Florida International University.

advance of Italian troops into Ethiopia, quickly became a popular marching song. "Little blackface" was the name given to the female Abyssinian slave who awaited Italian soldiers to liberate her and take her to Rome. Written before the promulgation of racial laws in 1938, the song was enormously popular in Italy. Despite its popularity, Mussolini censored the song in 1938. He believed *faccetta nera*, as Afro-Italian writer Igiaba Scego explains, was "too half-breed in nature: it sang the praises of the union between the 'races' that was inconceivable in his imperial Italy, which would soon after pass the race laws that deprived Jews and Africans of rights and life" (2016, para. 10). Eventually the song was rewritten with lyrics that offered a more racially "hygienic" scenario.

The song continues to represent, in the words of Scego, "the purest quintessence of Fascism" (2016, para. 6). Informing Italian fascism are fantasies surrounding miscegenation, the belief, as Charles Burdett argues, "that there is a border that defines what is and what is not '*sangue giusto*' (just blood), and that any mixing between Italians and Ethiopians will lead to the degeneration of the members of the occupying power" (Burdett et al., 2019, p. 58).

Bertiglia's postcard (1936e) portrays an Ethiopian female child surrounded by Italian male soldiers who are reading the lyrics of *faccetta nera* from music sheets. The Ethiopian child looks on with a sense of disbelief as she is serenaded by the chorus of soldiers who promise both liberation and love. The simplistic portrayal of Italian soldiers singing *Faccetta Nera* imperfectly erases the racial violence unleashed on any resistance to Italian rule and the contradictions of the workings of the biopolitical project of the Italian regime. Despite Italian laws against intermarriage and cohabitation between Italians and Ethiopians, these laws were commonly broken, thus violating the principle of Italian nationality law and *jus sanguinis*, which determined who did and did not have access to Italian citizenship. This law continues today.

The postcard of children singing an apparently simple song such as *Faccetta Nera* speaks directly to Faulkner's claim that childhood innocence is used to disavow the complex and violent histories that afford innocence to a privileged few. *Faccetta Nera* continues to be sung in Italy, particularly among neo-fascists who aim to attack anti-racist activists. Most recently, while Italo-Somali political activist Maryan Ismail was speaking at a rally, an older man, in a fit of rage, began to sing *Faccetta Nera* in her face. This attack was, writes Scego, "more or less like using the N-word. Because of its role in Italian fascist history, *Faccetta Nera* cannot be considered a song with neutral significance" (2016, para. 4).

The Afro-Italian Scego recalls children singing this song to humiliate her when she left school at the end of the day. The song is popular as a ringtone on cell phones, as evident in the documentary *Videocracy*, directed by Swedish-Italian Erik Gandini about the impact Italian television has on Italian culture and politics. The song was sung by Giacomo Sceglie on Italy's *The Voice* in 2017 and received over 10,000 likes (Paolacci, 2017). The song is seductive, notes Scego. Even to an anti-fascist, the oom-pah-pah beat is captivating. Scego refers to a memorable scene in Dagmawi Yimer's docufilm, *Va'pensiero*:

> A group of mothers sing(ing) the song to Mohamed Ba, the Senegalese cultural mediator and actor. He is shaken up and discouraged. He tries to explain to them that *Faccetta Nerra* is a song from the twenty-year reign of Mussolini, but the women ignore him . . . they feel some sort of forbidden pleasure in singing it. (2016, para. 7)

Scego points to a central paradox embodied in this song, which perennially sparks controversy. The paradox revolves around the color black, "nera." Facism, notes Scego, saw itself as white and European. The paradox is that this song of liberation:

> Sang the glories of a "carnal" union with the Black subjects it intended to subjugate . . . a popular ditty that conceals a clear reference to sexual violence behind a fantasy of liberation . . . a Black woman, in the regime's view, simply could not be an Italian. That would imply rights of citizenship that Italian fascism was far from extending to the conquered Africans. Rights of citizenship that, by a treacherous twist of historical irony, seem equally elusive in the present. (2016, para. 20)

The tenacious purchase that Italian colonial racial fantasies continue to have on the laws governing citizenship in Italy today call for critical scrutiny, particularly as an imperialist, fascist nostalgia among sectors of contemporary right-wing Italians surges and rights of citizenship continues to be withheld from Afro-Italians.

CONCLUDING REMARKS

Viewed within the field of childhood studies and curriculum theory, Bertiglia's postcards serve as a record of how fascism used depictions of childhood and childhood innocence as weapons of war. Theweleit teaches us that for the not fully born fascist soldier, innocence is understood as "without knowledge of defeat" (1987b, p. 191). At the same time, for the not fully born fascist soldier, the site of war is, Theweleit argues, "first and foremost his own body; a body poised to penetrate other bodies and mangle them in its embrace" (1987b, p. 191). Etched into Bertiglia's apparently innocent postcards are themes of racial violence that imperfectly erase a history of Italian death production in Ethiopia that has been relegated to the margins of history. The narrative fragments etched into Bertiglia's propaganda used images of childhood innocence to establish Mussolini's production of death as nothing more than a children's game. The rich archives of Italian fascist material that include seemingly trivial objects such as postcards, children's games, toys, and domestic knickknacks. These objects offer curriculum theory substantial insights into the ways in which innocence became the exclusive province of the Italian, fascist, white, Catholic child, while relegating African children to spaces devoid of innocence and casting them as persons incapable of feeling pain or deserving citizenship.

REFERENCES

Baudendistel, R. (2006). *Between bombs and good intentions: The International Committee of the Red Cross (ICRC) and the Italo-Ethiopian War, 1935–1936*. Berghahn Books.

Ben-Ghiat, R. (2001). *Fascist modernities: Italy, 1922–1945*. University of California Press.

Ben-Ghiat, R. (2015). *Italian fascism's empire cinema*. Indiana University Press.

Ben-Ghiat, R. (2017, January 27). *Making Italy great again*. Slate. slate.com/news-and-politics/2017/01/mussolinis-racial-policies-in-east-africa-revealed-italian-fascists-ambitions-to-redesign-the-social-order.html.

Bernstein, R. (2011). *Racial innocence: Performing American childhood from slavery to civil rights*. New York University Press.

Bernstein R. (2010, April 29). *The invention of childhood innocence*. The Harvard Gazette. news.harvard.edu/gazette/story/2010/04/the-invention-of-childhood-innocence/.

Bertiglia, A. (ca. 1936a). *Children in uniforms painting a map of Ethiopia, Eritrea, and Somalia green, white, and red* [illustrated postcard]. The Wolfsonian-FIU (Digital Catalog),The Wolfsonian FIU Library Collection, Miami Beach, USA. digital.wolfsonian.org/WOLF089301/00001.

Bertiglia, A. (ca. 1936b). *Italian colonial troops distributing food to Ethiopian children* [illustrated postcard]. The Wolfsonian-FIU (Digital Catalog), The Wolfsonian FIU Library Collection, Miami Beach, USA. digital.wolfsonian.org/WOLF042914/00001.

Bertiglia, A. (ca. 1936c). *Genti del Tigrai Tacazzé* [illustrated postcard]. The Wolfsonian-FIU (Digital Catalog),The Wolfsonian FIU Library Collection, Miami Beach, USA. digital.wolfsonian.org/WOLF044694/00001.

Bertiglia, A. (ca. 1936d). [Illustrated postcard of Ethiopian children wearing Red Cross emblems, chased by Italian children with bayonets]. Collection unknown. Retrieved March 13, 2022, from ic.pics.livejournal.com/glebwiktorow/50724117/5400883/5400883_600.jpg.

Bertiglia, A. (ca. 1936e). *An Ethiopian girl and Italian boys in colonial military uniform singing* [illustrated postcard]. The Wolfsonian-FIU (Digital Catalog), The

Wolfsonian FIU Library Collection, Miami Beach, USA. digital.wolfsonian.org/WOLF091478/00001.

Boldt, G. M. (2002). Toward a reconceptualization of gender and power in an elementary classroom. *Current Issues in Comparative Education. Teachers College, Columbia University, 5*(1), 7–23.

Bond-Stockton, C. B. (2007). *The queer child: Or growing sideways in the twentieth century*. Duke University Press.

Burdett, C., Ferrini, A., and Giuliani, G. (2019). Roundtable on visuality, race and nationhood in Italy. *Journal of Visual Culture, 8*(18), 53–80.

Carlo Erba, S. A. (1936). *La Conquista Dell'Abissinia* [children's board game]. The Wolfsonian-FIU (Digital Catalog), The Wolfsonian FIU Library Collection (ETHI).digital.wolfsonian.org/WOLF061899/00001.

Carroll, R. (2001, June 25). *Italy's bloody secret.* The Guardian. www.theguardian.com/education/2001/jun/25/artsandhumanities.highereducation.

Diel, L. (1936). *"Behold our new empire"—Mussolini* [illustrated book]. The Wolfsonian-FIU (Digital Catalog), The Wolfsonian FIU Library Collection, Miami Beach, USA. digital.wolfsonian.org/WOLF091481/00001.

Duschinsky, R. (2013). Childhood innocence: Essence, education, and performativity. *Textual Practice, 27*(5), 763–781. DOI: 10.1080/0950236X.2012.751441.

Farley, L. (2018). *Childhood beyond pathology: A psychoanalytic study of development and diagnosis*. SUNY Press.

Faulkner, J. (2011). *The importance of being innocent: Why we worry about children.* Cambridge University Press.

Faulkner, J. (2014, April 29). *Childhood innocence.* Encyc: Eugenics Archive. eugenicsarchive.ca/discover/encyclopedia/535eec8b7095aa0000000236.

Garlen, J. (2019). Interrogating innocence: Childhood as exclusionary social practice. *Childhood, 26*(1), 54–67.

Gasperini, O. (1938). *Rural Radio Corporation, Radio Journey in the Empire. The Reclamation of Land and of People, N. 16. Radio Programs, N. 91–92* [poster]. The Wilsonian-FIU (Digital Catalog), The Wolfsonian FIU Library Collection, Miami Beach, USA. digital.wolfsonian.org/WOLF027134/00001.

Gordon, N., and Perugini, N. (2020). *Human shields: A history of people in the line of fire*. Cambridge University Press.

Hawkins, S., and Sweet, H. (Eds.). (2015). *Colonial caring: A history of colonial and post-colonial nursing*. Manchester University Press.

McLean, E. (2018). *Mussolini's children: Race and elementary education in fascist Italy*. University of Nebraska Press.

O'Loughlin, M. and Johnson, R. (Eds.). (2010). *Imagining children otherwise: Theoretical and critical perspectives on childhood subjectivity.* Peter Lang Publishing.

Pankhurst, R. (1972). Education in Ethiopia during the Italian Fascist Occupation (1936–1941). *The International Journal of African Historical Studies, 5*(3), 361–96.

Pankhurst, R. (2007). *History of the Italian Fascist Magazine "La Difesa della Razza."* Marxists.org. www.marxists.org/archive/pankhurst-richard/2007/03/x01.htm.

Paolacci, S. (2017, February 11). *Faccetta Nera a The Voice Italia* [Video]. Youtube. www.youtube.com/watch?v=QBLxiRldcmg.

Salvio, P. M. (2020). Palimpsestic pedagogies: Mapping fascist violence against children from Mussolini's dictatorship to present day Italy. *Journal of Curriculum Inquiry, 50*(4), 291–308.

Scego, I. (2016, April). *The true story of "Faccetta Nera."* Words without Borders. www.wordswithoutborders.org/article/april-2016-women-write-war-the-true-story-faccetta-negra-igiaba-scego.

Silin, J. (1992). *Sex, death, and the education of children: Our passion for ignorance in the age of AIDS.* (1992). State University of New York Press.

Stovall, T. (2021). *White freedom: The racial history of an idea.* Princeton University Press.

Theweleit, K. (1987a). *Male Fantasies Volume 1: Women, Floods, Bodies, History.* University of Minneapolis Press.

Theweleit, K. (1987b) *Male Fantasies: Volume 2: Male Bodies: Psychoanalyzing the White Terror*. University of Minneapolis Press.

Theweleit, K. (1993). The bomb's womb and the genders of war: War goes on preventing women from becoming the mothers of invention. In M. Cooke and A. Woollacott (Eds.), *Gendering War Talk* (pp. 283–334). Princeton University Press.

The Wolfsonian-FIU. (2021, January 11). *Curator's Choice: Imperialism and everyday life* [video]. Youtube. www.youtube.com/watch?v=0MbU76GMIT8.

NOTES

1. The first Italo-Ethiopian war took place 1895–1896. This war was provoked by the disputed Treaty of Wuchale, which the Italians maintained established Ethiopia as an Italian protectorate. A full-scale war broke out in 1895, with Italian troops from Italian Eritrea securing initial success until Ethiopian troops counterattacked Italian positions.

2. Mussolini abided by the Augustan model of ritual, policy, public display, and colonization, and his belief in his own destiny as a successor to the Roman emperors.

3. For an extensive analysis of the ordinary objects coming unto Italian homes during the invasion of Ethiopia, including radio shows, children's board games, and household maps, all used to sell the colonization of East Africa to Italians, see David Rifkind's presentation on imperialism and everyday life (The Wolfsonian-FIU, 2021).

4. In fact, no Italian war criminal was tried for war crimes committed during World War II. Of more than 1,200 Italians sought for war crimes in Africa and the Balkans, not one has faced justice (Carroll, 2001).

5. For a discussion of this publication in the context of public pedagogy, see Salvio, 2020.

6. The word, which dates back to the seventeenth century, described any child of African descent. By the time Bertiglia was producing his post cards, the term was used pejoratively in reference to black children in the United States, Britain, and to aboriginal children of the Americas, Australia, and New Zealand (Bernstein, 2010).

7. As well as the Jewish child under Mussolini's fascism.

8. Also see Duschinsky, 2013.

9. See also Baudendistel, 2006.

Chapter 12

Necrophobia as a Nihilistic Preoccupation in Paternal Fantasies of Maturation Gone Awry

Louis Rothschild

Freud's self-analysis (1900) reveals evidence of trauma disrupting the intersubjective space between father and son. Oft cited examples include the dysregulated words from Freud's father Jakob that Sigmund would amount to nothing following his childhood offense of urinating in his parent's bedroom. That utterance haunted Freud's mind as a life-long self-reproach (cf., Bonomi, 2015).[1] Yet, father Jakob's identification with an aggressor (cf., Ferenczi, 1933/1980) is only one defensive side of this traumatized matrix. The other being a withdrawal illustrated in Jakob informing his son that an anti-Jewish[2] man had knocked Jakob's new fur hat off in the street during the Sabbath, and that he had done nothing to defend himself (Freud, 1900). A binary algorithm that being passive and vulnerable amounts to nothing while something may be gained through aggression haunts this dyad. Of interest is the dissociation of vulnerability to aggression shown in Freud's assertion that he saw his father as weak, and sought surrogate identifications from Moses to Hannibal's father as fuel for a lifelong motivational press felt by most of his inner circle (Shengold, 1993). Links may be made between Jakob's passive and aggressive style, and Sigmund's declaration that he was ready to kill a man who made an anti-Jewish remark on a train (Freud, 1961 in Gilman, 1993). Furthermore, an intergenerational wound running toward Jakob's grandchildren may be gleaned in Freud's apparent dissociative response of indifference regarding his own son's serving in World War I (Rozmarin, 2020). To that end, Freud's work has been considered to center around identifications with aggression (Rozmarin, 2020), and his colleague Sandor Ferenczi's treatment of aggression has been considered a deconstruction of the disembodied or dissociated aspects of Freud's system (Bonomi, 2018).

MAN ENOUGH

This chapter considers childhood precarity as mentalized by 21st century fathers, who, like Freud, have incorporated a traditional masculinity that normalizes dissociation and indifference, but in regard to raising sons, seek to situate the disembodied in a manner that resonates with Ferenczi. Of concern is how a father moves from indifference to feeling, and how counter-dependent individuation may be amplified or reduced by a father's psychology. Herein, indifference is considered part of an overdetermined and traumatic relational representation of fathers and sons found in a father's mind, which in this case is haunted by the nightmare that a son may amount to nothing.

Placing emphasis on dissociation as a normative and violent socio-cultural phenomena called masculinity is an additive act of inclusion (cf., Layton, 2020). Doing so complicates matters through the recognition that a cultural lens need be as central as is a family systems lens that focuses thought on such matters as Freud *also* suffering due to being represented as a replacement for his deceased brother (Anisfeld and Richards, 2000). This focus on cultural or hegemonic violence creates a revisionist dream for contemporary fathers, whereby Jakob Freud's heart could remain open in a manner befitting a feminist caretaker that could in fact grieve a dead son and situate anti-Jewish sentiment. The extent that this dream is idealistic points to the challenge to reconstitute masculinity in effort to render greater intersubjective sensitivity between fathers and sons in a manner that might diminish chronic social and cultural violence.

Two recent monographs written as letters from fathers to teenage sons (Black, 2020; Coates, 2015) reveal a dire press to break out of a dehumanized or "doer/done to" (Benjamin, 2018) frame of dissociative indifference in order to cultivate loving bonds between fathers and sons. Central to each is an awareness that dehumanization is a common factor fueling self-reproach in neoliberal consumer society that threatens the well-being of a rich and diverse world in which breakdown is common, and recovery is extraordinary. The fathers in these books are lovingly preoccupied with separation, and to that end, the real and imagined dangers their sons face. Each author seeks to situate the toxic masculinity that is part and parcel of a traumatized mentation that in addition to other external, environmental threats, endangers their respective childs' lives. Each father assumes and writes to a son's life-affirming understanding as an addressed subject, and this may be read as a wounded plea or life affirming enactment in response to a darkness in which bravado is found in rape, pillaging, and murder. One monograph, *Between the world and me* by Ta-Nehisi Coates (2015) is the work of an urban, Black journalist and comic book writer. The other, *A better man: A (Mostly Serious) Letter to my son* by Michael Ian Black (2020) is penned by a suburban white, culturally Jewish man who first made his way as a comedian. Taken together alongside some of their other writing and my own personal reflections, the two works allow for an intersectional analysis and deconstruction of masculinity. In each work, fear motivates a need to express loving concern regarding circumnavigating threats to creative movement with and beyond broken containers. Each writer favors a conception of gender lightly held (Harris, 2005) in contrast to an anxious conception of gender as a solid state that generates reactive violence (Corbett, 2016).

Coates and Black each write to challenge the status quo regarding manhood in a manner reminiscent of Nietzsche's (1882/1974) madman screaming that men killed god or poet Lawrence Ferlinghetti's (2007) idea of a creative writer as a nonviolent barbarian. In this, they also harmonize with Erich Fromm's (1964) expansion of the meaning of necrophilia to include a love of the mechanical over the organic. In light of Fromm, I consider the fear expressed by each author to be a *necrophobia* defined as the traumatic experience of perceiving that one is dwelling in a perverse age in which terror appears endless and the lines between the organic and mechanical are blurred (cf., Knafo and Lo Bosco, 2017). Hegemonic masculinity dictates that experiencing necrophobia is not a productive discontent, but is a sign of a personal sickness or failure. One exacerbating aspect of this discontent is a tendency toward a shame based silence that insidiously dictates that one hide fear in order to be seen as masculine. Hiding itself may be expressed through the perpetuation of violence that reinforces identifications that one is not afraid. Through privilege, fear may be disproportionately denied. That these authors express such fear on the page as opposed to in the private confines of a psychotherapy consulting room works toward legitimizing fear, vulnerability, and grief as part of a masculinity suitable for raising children. This is the sort of exposure needed to treat the necrophilia that gives rise to necrophobia. It is significant that each author identifies as a cis man, and as a members of social groups that have known persecution.

LEARNING TO FLY WITH BROKEN WINGS

The inhabited vulnerability that accompanies sitting with psychotherapy patients may have factored into feeling horror while listening to Ta-Nehishi Coates read his then recent publication *Between the world and me* (2015) on

National Public Radio after leaving my office for an errand. My car remained in park with the radio playing. Stopping me were lines from page eighty-two: "You are all we have, and you come to us endangered. I think we would like to kill you ourselves before seeing you killed by the streets that America made." Not far from my mind was my then in press paper (Rothschild, 2016) on the threats of abandonment and sacrifice to children in neoliberal culture. However, that writing was about psychological death; Coates was addressing the physical body, childhood precarity, and murder. Coates writes to his son about how his childhood fears of either being hit by his father's belt or being shot by a classmate in the street were now fears that he embodied about his own son. Of inhabiting this worry as a father, he writes to his son, "in this I was unoriginal" (p. 14). In addition to reading Freud, having myself been beaten by a classmate, and in also having a son, Coates's intergenerational concern resonates as a terrorized and terrified witnessing of the insidious danger of a violent disembodiment (cf., Grand, 2000) that is a component if not the center of what has come to be called toxic masculinity (hooks, 2004) and is located across socio-cultural contexts.

The contextual threat of bullets in *Between the world and me* marks a specific location whose coordinates are in part comprised in an intersection of race, class, and gender (Crenshaw, 1989) leaving me aware of privilege in temporality and geography. As a Jew born in the mid-twentieth century United States, I live knowing that all of my grandparents were also born in this country and were young adults at the outbreak of World War II. Auschwitz was across an ocean, and, for me, in another time. Coates shares a literal fear of being a target of violence in the street with Jakob and Sigmund Freud that did not mark my childhood. I write this knowing that rates of anti-Jewish violence increased in the United States following the election of Donald Trump (Dreier, 2020), and that the bully who left me with two black eyes while a middle school student was anti-Jewish and racist in his expressed pleasure about his family having owned Nazi memorabilia and slaves. In this I am reminded that a tendency to favor violence over yielding has been linked to the manner in which political rhetoric conceives of vulnerability as a productive or cancerous aspect of masculinity (cf., Lakoff, 2016). Looking backward in time, a few years after the Civil War ended in the United States, I see a German-speaking teenager traveling alone down the Mississippi River, the patriarch of my family who had left the Austrian satellite town of Nordstetten located in the Rhineland of present-day Germany. At that time, racist literature depicted Jews, Africans, and Native Americans as equally dangerous to the so-called White race (cf., Gilman, 1993). The ease in which Jews as a religious group are racialized in order to naturalize violence reveals that unstable ground on which race stands, and the reason that it has been a historically useful concept for imperialism. Then, 352 Jews lived in Nordstetten, and by 1910 that number would be 39 (Sauer, 1989). A century earlier, Jews had paid a special protection tax to the Austrian emperor, and a Code Noir was written in Paris to align slave policies in Louisiana with other Caribbean colonies while simultaneously naturalizing and essentializing race. Interestingly, in addition to naturalizing justifications for the enslavement of Black folk, the Code Noir or Black Code officially banned Jews from Louisiana. However, one hundred years before my relative set foot there on his way to Mississippi, two Jewish merchants had already established a business in New Orleans (Berry, 2018). As with manumitting a slave in word for good service and in deed because of kinship (Berry, 2018), loopholes exist, and privilege has never been equally distributed (cf., Altman, 2020). The decline of the Jewish population in Nordstetten was part of a vast precursor of insecurity as Europe marched toward war. Coates' writing to his son about the potential of being shot by a policeman speaks to a particular vulnerability of being faced with institutionalized violence known to Freud, and potentially felt by any reader of Thomas Mann's (1969) *Magic Mountain* in which a helpless protagonist loses his life to the outbreak of World War I. Despite having been shaken by bullying and made aware of history regarding membership in a minority religion, I was also aware that Hitler was dead, and of a white male privilege that as a kid, afforded a feeling of overall safety in the street. Illusion or not, on most days I do not pause before moving my car into drive. However, privilege like any defense does not guarantee safety, and I am not original in experiencing Coates's apt description of Whiteness as an illusion of invulnerability and protection as something that may be shaken and shattered (Benjamin, 2018, p. 222).

The format of *Between the world and me* intentionally follows the structure of James Baldwin's (1963/1992) civil rights era letter to his fifteen-year-old nephew concerning the traumatic effects of racism and the challenge of integration that calls for a social change. Violence remains, and Coates's letter to his fifteen-year-old son begins with the reflection on the thought of "what it means to lose my body" (p. 5). Coates states that he writes to his son because people of color are beaten and killed by uniformed officers. He adds that this is old, that racism breaks bodies, and that the Social Sciences and Humanities reveal this history of race as a naturalized construct exploiting variation to organize the social (cf., Haslam, Rothschild, and Ernst, 2002). Coates further adds that he has fear in never believing that "it will be okay" (p. 10).

Coates's work quickly became a lightning rod for multiple critics. The author's pessimistic fear has been wondered about as possibly arising from a metaphysical assumption that without a theistic ground, that the entire world bends towards injustice (Steinmetz-Jenkins, 2017). With a different emphasis on injustice, racial and carceral scholar Michelle Alexander's (2015) review applauds Coates for following in Baldwin's footsteps, and praises each book for an absence of code switching that might be found in works addressed to a White audience. Following the publication of Coates (2017) writing on the Obama administration and the rise of Donald Trump, philosophical activist Cornel West (2017) berated Coates as a neoliberal for a failure to link his critique of racial violence to other social variables such as sexuality and to the imperialism and predatory capitalism of the United States. Debate between Coates and West became heated to the point that Coates deleted his Twitter account (Lartey, 2017). In consideration of the manner in which masculinity is implicated in predatory imperialism, West's critique is aligned with Coates's deconstruction of masculinity in a manner made difficult by Coates's tendency to situate race as being of greater significance than gender. Intersectionality is not simple, and that complexity may well be the point, as complexity may facilitate humility.

In his letter, Coates uses the trope *dreamers* to describe those affluent enough to live in a manner oft referred to as the American Dream thus having the privilege to maintain denial of their own flaws in a manner consistent with an identification with an aggressive positionality that becomes a "habit and addiction" (p. 150). Coates's more recent work in comic books illuminates his neoliberal dilemmas concerning the addictive quality of aggression. The Captain America (Coates, 2019; Coates and Kirk, 2021) comics penned by Coates are an important complement to his letter as the comics contain a portrait of Coates's gendered purview. Coates describes this world from the perspective of one who wishes to believe in the American Dream, that Captain America believes in the dream, and that the desire to believe terrifies Coates (Coates, 2018). In his aggression, Captain America feels that his violence delivers justice. To consider Captain America in the context of Coates's work is to wonder if the superhero is dreaming in a manner dissociated from his own vulnerability. As an artist, the ability to stay with fear as opposed to disavowing risk is felt in his work as Coates wonders to his son, how to "erect a democracy independent of cannibalism" (2015, p. 105).

Penned three years before the actual violent insurrection at the nation's capital, Coates illustrates his deadly nightmares that include right wing violence on the national mall in a divided United States (Coates, 2019). In the comics, Coates re-works present-day terror into the Captain American story. There, Captain America and terrorists with a leader named Red Skull, face off in a version of the present. In this storyline, White supremacist terrorists have conquered the United States, are subsequently defeated, and manage to then frame Captain America for murder. Writing Captain America in 2021 (Coates and Leonard, 2021), terrorist leader Red Skull is shown as an internet presence complaining that man has become a caretaker and offers ten rules for life to become strong through escaping what is called "the feminist trap." The issue ends with Captain America being told that the terrorists are trying to do more than kill people, that they are trying to kill an idea. The issue led conservative psychologist Jordan Peterson to wonder on Twitter (Ferme and Vary, 2021): Had a version of Peterson's ideas been linked to the villain Red Skull? As depicted in Coates's art, Peterson (2018) has built a following through his dichotomized naturalization of discontinuity as masculine and relationality as feminine while suggesting that postmodern philosophy has exacerbated fatherlessness through critiques of domination. In regard to Peterson finding himself in the comics, Coates appears to be laboring to situate the dangerous allure of a neoliberal promise trading in nationalist tropes within hegemonic masculinity in a manner consistent with Yates's (2015) psycho-social formulation that psychic alienation and fragmentation underly the chaotic center of unregulated financial mismanagement while neoliberal ideology generates idealistic discourses of order, harmony, and prosperity that deny violence and trauma.

The enticement to cultivate a masculinity that proclaims prosperity beyond doubt is also found in Coates's letter as he writes to his son that in Black manhood is a secret wish for totalizing security (p. 283). Yet, Coates and Peterson differ in regard to the valence of such a wish that is consistent with the difference between necrophilia and necrophobia. For Peterson, security is the absence of threat. For Coates, security entails facilitating a vulnerability that can acknowledge working with a threat. I credit Coates for addressing such conflicted vulnerability in a fashion that resonates with Frantz Fanon's (1967) thought that the ego defense of withdrawal is not available to Black men who fear that to love is to risk the trauma of abandonment. Linking Coates with Fanon's idea is an awareness that it is traumatic reactivity that separates a relationally sensitive assertiveness from aggressive acts that shatter relations (cf., Benjamin, 1988).

In my consulting room, the press to exhibit a relentless capacity in attempt to avoid the relational contact that can signal abandonment is not unique to Blacks or men. This is to say that reactive violence rooted in dissociation and trauma is a problem that resides beyond any particular racial or gendered identification. Yet, there is something specific to being identified as Black and as a man in the 21st century United States (cf., Philogène, 2004). One explanation for the amplification in precarity when targeted racial identity is combined with masculine identity is that hegemonic Whiteness embodies an institutionalized aggression that projects the excess of a fantasized and totalizing masculine idealization of security onto Black males (Adams, 2019). These projections render perceptions of Black masculinity as being harder, stronger, and more prone to violence while simultaneously devaluing Black fathers as flawed for embodying these very traits (Adams, 2019). Like sexist projections, racist projections aim to disavow insecurity through a perverted sense of privilege for those identified as White and men. Simultaneously, these representations reinforce for Blacks (and others such as women) the secret if not unconscious sense of failure and wish for its opposite that Coates and Fanon describe. Being a recipient of scapegoating projections affords a unique context from which to perceive cultural violence that can facilitate additional defensive scapegoating, a breaking of cyclical violence, or a messy admixture of toxicity and nourishment (cf., Eigen, 1999). With a security that facilitates a non-defensive response to vulnerability, alliance building is possible (Sevitch, 2002). Making matters difficult for alliance building, an exclusive focus on racial or gendered identities may weaponize perceived in-group homogeneity to camouflage structural factors such as inequalities in housing and schooling furthering the effects of alienation (cf., Archangelo and O'Loughlin, 2021). Further, the present-day institutional violence of social inequity and racialized projections found in the United States co-exist in a historicity in which Black men face risk factors unknown to Whites due to centuries of disavowal reaching back to slavery and the failures of reconstruction (Vaughans, 2014). In a manner that gives merit to West's critique, Coates fails to explicitly link his wish for security to his albeit uncertain belief that some have '"safety' [quotes original] in schools, portfolios, and skyscrapers" (p. 85). Intersectional analysis reveals that the safety Coates fantasizes about is at best only defensively available to a few at the top of a complex social hierarchy. Through an intersectional focus, it is possible to consider the effects of racial violence while simultaneously voicing that others are also targeted recipients for physical violence and prejudiced projections. As with Coates's expressed fear regarding Captain America's beliefs, his use of quotes around the word safety suggest an awareness that precarity extends beyond racial categorization. Illuminating this common ground aims to open up possibilities for alliance building between alienated subjects of all groups who know othering from Palestinian refugees to Native American and White citizens in the United States who share experiences of dislocation in traumatic intergenerational histories such as the Nakba, Trail of Tears, and Dust Bowl era migration.

A TRAIN TO CRY

Writing In the *New York Times*, Michael Ian Black (2018a; 2018b) considers the disavowal of vulnerability within traditional masculinity to be a multigenerational problem. Black considers that this problem underpins the psychology of the mostly male perpetrators of school shootings who, caught in a dissociative split, have psychically disintegrated. Black's thesis is that once vulnerability is equated with emasculation, there is nothing for males to avow in order to navigate the waters of identity development. As noted above,

Freud knew this split, and his inability to situate traditional masculinity as a defense is itself a testament to the remarkable challenge to render gender a soft assembly (cf., Harris, 2005). Black's Op Eds were published prior to his (Black, 2020) book which has been considered a primer, penned by a snarky comedian who at times exceeds his grasp in addressing his cis straight white son in a patriarchal world (Greene, 2020). Published five years following Coates's *Between the world and me*, Black's *A better man: A (mostly serious) letter to my son* appears with similarities to its predecessor especially as the title informs that the work is a letter from a father to a son. In learning of this newer book, I thought that someone had found a need to write a version for the suburban, White, somewhat liberal, cargo-pant wearing set that may not be drawn to Coates much less Baldwin. Such a thought represents a siloed fragmentation of the lingering impact of segregation that is challenged by Coates and others. Coates (2015) writes to his son while reflecting on his time as a student at Howard University where he wrestled with the essentialist thought that Black culture in the United States did not have an award winning ghetto writer like the Jewish Saul Bellow. Coates adds in his letter that he broke through such segregated thinking, and came to see that Saul Bellow could be everyone's. Such a sentiment is also found in Jewish philosopher Emil Fackenheim's (1968) writing that as a White man, he needs Baldwin in order to situate a shared social world. Further, working toward a new humanism concerning the dis-alienation of Black men identified as "the other" [quotes original] Fanon writes that he is "deprived of the possibility of being a man" by witnessing anti-Jewish prejudice (1967, pp. 88–89). Herein is a cosmopolitan humanism pointing to the danger of fragmented isolation regarding prejudice, violence, and vulnerability that speaks to a need of these books to work together.

Black begins his book writing that the impetus for it occurred in 2012, three years before Coates's letter was published, when the Sandy Hook school shooting occurred. Black's son was attending school a few miles away from the site of that shooting, and he writes to his now older son that words like lockdown did not exist when previous generations considered schooling. He adds in comedic style that he does not know how to explain mass murder to a child that has only known the death of a hamster. Each of these books grapples with how to situate the threat of mass murder to these particular children's lives across vastly different cultural contexts. To that end, Black's work represents an opening in concert with Coates's wonder of what will happen when vulnerability becomes real for the privileged. I wish that Black had referenced Coates in his book, as Black like Coates is sounding an alarm to his son that identification with an aggressive sense of invulnerability is a social problem. These letters regarding young boys and social dangers represent an opportunity for shared identification and alliance building as the threat of bullets moves across racial and class lines and into buildings that had previously been considered zones of safety.

Linguistics matter, and Coates (2015) writes that "being named Black is being at the bottom" (p. 55). In autobiographical fashion, a White man named Black (2020) writes that his parents divorced in childhood, that he never had a bed in his fathers' home where he was only welcome on weekends. His mother had left to partner with another woman, and Black describes knowing dislocation from an early age. Connecting to his present, Black writes about the privileged anxiety of working with fear as the comedy industry is no longer a bastion for White males. He considers this a good problem, worth working with, and simultaneously confesses that he changed his father's German Jewish name of Schwartz to its English translation black in attempt to placate fear of standing out. To this name change, Black adds, "that is what two thousand years of paranoia will do to you" (p. 236). Referring to traditional masculinity as a masquerade, Black shares that he cultivated an entire comedic personality on withdrawal. As noted above, Fanon defines withdrawal as privilege. However, as an index of dissociation used to facilitate laughter, the aloof mask of Black's stated withdrawal like Freud's professed indifference regarding his son's military service resonates with Coates's secret wish for total security as each seeks to disavow fear and pain. The school-yard wish that names will never hurt me is just that, a wish.

Disavowal of vulnerability is born as a response to fractured love (Bass, 2000), so associating to vulnerability in a loving fashion becomes an act of resistance. Black writes to his son that as a boy, a classmate threatened him with a switchblade, and called him a kike. He was punched in the face, and subsequently could not open his mouth. Like Coates, he writes of being afraid about the safety of his body. Drawing on scholars such a Michael Thompson (e.g., Kindlon and Thompson, 2000) and bell hooks (2004) Black considers that the unspoken truth of masculinity is that fear is not confined to women. Black writes: "We raise boys to go to war; we go to war because of the way we raise boys" (p. 135). In his letter, Black expresses concern in seeing that his daughter continues to foster an integrated relationship with her feelings while his son has become detached. His writing makes a plea for emotional re-integration and hopes that his son's generation might shatter traditional masculinity while finding the good in being playful, competitive, and willing to test limits. Similarly, Coates writes of learning to love differently through encounters with diversity, and that he wishes that he could be even softer with his son, so that his son will also continue to grow through nurturing encounters in order to be able to ethically respect every human being as singular yet wounded.

Enacted across racial and gendered lines (Solnit, 2014), reactive violence in response to perceived or disavowed abandonment underscores the need of a psychological security that can forgo the defensive reactivity that Judith Butler (1992) has named *Penis Size Envy* for the wish of being chronically strong and steady amidst the relentless doubting that fuels the devaluing of psychological and social roles marked feminine (cf., Kupers, 1993; Rothschild, 2003). Indeed, within envy is a contempt of lack that attempts to deny the benefits of cultivating a security that embodies a flexible curiosity in experiences of uncertainty and variation (Diamond, 1998; Ducat, 2004). As reactivity and withdrawal manifest differently among and within individuals, a focus on variability within and between social groupings such as fathers, is inherently critical of binaries. Black/White and man/woman support asymmetrical splitting thereby reinforcing reified social representations that idealize the impersonal and normalize a way of being that works against alliances and life itself (cf., Benjamin, 1988; Waling, 2019; Iacoviello et al., 2021).

TOWARDS A CONCLUSION

The denial of vulnerability reinforces an atomized isolation whose reactive battle cry may be heard in the phrase, "You have to succeed no matter what" (Palacios, 2014, p. 227). Such sentiment and denial fits as a key index of a predator-prey model of life that trades in the psychotic anxieties of split-off groups (Eigen, 2009). One is lead to experience an impenetrable diaphragm of distrust between oneself and the world (Williams, 2010). What is a father to do? Working toward increased trust are ideas that citizens may unite in institutional commitments across and through mutual respect of cultural differences (Appiah, 1997). Such respect aims to secure a base for the un-defended openness found in the fragility and fallibility of dreaming and desire. Simultaneously, neoliberal marketing technologies threaten to reduce children to valuations of purchasing power, rendering subjectivity a lost artifact to mechanical civilization (Cederman, 2017; Stiegler, 2011; Voela and Rothschild, 2019).

As a boy, my brother and I had been playing football in the street over several days with two Black boys who we invited into our home. It was hot, we wanted soda. After crossing our threshold, they attempted to pay for their drinks. We refused their money, and all returned to the street. Through that confused and confusing transaction we lost some dear companions that day as they never again crossed the neighborhood defining street to enter our White neighborhood to play. Was it our refusal to accept a few coins? Had the professed indifference to coins, combined with the luxury of food surplus and perceived comfort (in what appeared to me a modest home), led my new friends to identify as too vulnerable? Had they been "protectively" punished by their caregivers for entering our home? Or scolded for crossing into our neighborhood? These questions reveal a loss that haunts me, and I dedicate this chapter to their memories, and to the work of embodied witnessing that aims to foster alliances and to inoculate and prevent such trauma.

REFERENCES

Abraham, N., and Torok, M. (2005). *The Wolf Man's magic word: A Cryptonymy*. University of Minnesota Press.

Adams, C. J. (2019). Black Fatherhood in a Time of Fluidity. *Psychoanalytic Perspectives*, *16*(3), 326–39.

Alexander, M. (2015, August 17). Review of the book *Between the world and me*, by T-N. Coates. *The New York Times*. www.nytimes.com/2015/08/17/books/review/ta-nehisi-coates-between-the-world-and-me.html.

Allswang, B. (1985). *Anti-Judaism, anti-Semitism, and anti-Zionism: A theoretical and empirical analysis of the anti-Jewish phenomenon throughout its history to the present.* Unpublished doctoral dissertation, Loyola University of Chicago.

Altman, N. (2020). *White privilege: Psychoanalytic perspectives*. Routledge.

Anisfeld, L., and Richards, A. D. (2000). The replacement child: Variations on a theme in history and psychoanalysis. *Psychoanalytic study of the child*, *55*, 301–18.

Appiah, K. A. (1997). Cosmopolitan Patriots. *Critical Inquiry*, *23*(3), 617–69.

Archangelo, A., and O'Loughlin, M. (2021). Exploring Racial Formation in Children: Thoughts from an Encounter with Black Children in Brazil. *Journal of Infant, Child, and Adolescent Psychotherapy*, *20*(3), 215–29.

Baldwin, J. (1963/1992). *The fire next time.* Vintage Books.

Bass, A. (2000). *Difference and disavowal: The trauma of eros*. Stanford University Press.

Benjamin, J. (1988). T*he bonds of love: Psychoanalysis, feminism, and the problem of domination.* Pantheon Books.

Benjamin, J. (2018). *Beyond doer and done to: Recognition theory, intersubjectivity and the third.* Routledge.

Berry, J. (2018). *City of a million dreams: A history of New Orleans at year 300*. The University of North Carolina Press.

Black, M. I. (2018a). The boys are not all right. *The New York Times*. Retrieved March 21, 2021, from www.nytimes.com/2018/02/21/opinion/boys-violence-shootings-guns.html?referringSource=articleShare.

Black, M. I. (2018b). The downsides (and upsides?) of aggressive masculinity. *The New York Times*. Retrieved March 21, 2021, from www.nytimes.com/2018/02/28/opinion/aggressive-masculinity-boys.html?referringSource=articleShare.

Black, M. I. (2020). *A better man: A (mostly serious) letter to my son.* Algonquin Books of Chapel Hill.

Bonomi, C. (2015). *The Cut and the building of Psychoanalysis, Volume 1: Sigmund Freud and Emma Eckstein.* Routledge.

Bonomi, C. (2018). *The Cut and the building of Psychoanalysis, Volume II: Sigmund Freud and Sandor Ferenczi.* Routledge.

Butler, J. (1992). The lesbian phallus and the Morphological Imaginary. *Differences: A journal of feminist cultural studies*, *4*, 133–71.

Cederman, K. (2017). Left to their own devices? Child psychoanalysis and the psycho-technologies of consumer capitalism. In C. Owens and S. F. Quinn (Eds.), *Lacanian psychoanalysis with babies, children and adolescents: Further notes on the child* (pp. 251–64). Routledge.

Coates, T-N. (2015). *Between the world and me*. Spiegel & Grau.

Coates, T-N. (2017). *We were eight years in power: An American Tragedy.* One World.

Coates, T-N. (2018, February 28). Why I'm Writing Captain America and why it scares the hell out of me. *Atlantic*. www.theatlantic.com/entertainment/archive/2018/02/we-who-love-america/553991/.

Coates, Ta-Nehisi (2019). *Captain America, 1*. Marvel Worldwide.

Coates, T-N., and Leonard, K. (2021). *Captain America: All die young*, 28. Marvel Worldwide.

Corbett, K. (2016). *A murder over a girl: Justice, gender, and junior high*. Henry Holt and Company.

Crenshaw, K. (1989). Demarginalizing the Intersection of Race and Sex: A Black Feminist Critique of Antidiscrimination Doctrine, Feminist Theory and Antiracist Politics. *University of Chicago Legal Forum,* 1989 (1). http://chicagounbound.uchicago.edu/uclf/vol1989/iss1/8.

Diamond, M. J. (1998). Fathers with sons: Psychoanalytic perspectives on "Good Enough" fathering throughout the lifecycle. *Gender and Psychoanalysis*, *3*, 243–99.

Dreier, P. (2020, January 17). Why anti-semitism is on the rise in the United States. *Dissent*. www.dissentmagazine.org/online_articles/anti-semitism-rise-trump.

Ducat, S. (2004). *The Wimp Factor: Gender Gaps, Holy Wars, and the Politics of Anxious Masculinity*. Beacon Press.

Eigen, M. (1999). *Toxic nourishment.* Karnac Books.

Eigen, M. (2009). *Flames from the Unconscious: Trauma, Madness, and Faith.* Karnac Books.

Emery, E. (2002). The ghost in the mother: Strange attractions and impossible mourning. *The Psychoanalytic Review*, *89*(2), 169–94.

Fackenheim, E. L. (1968). *Quest for past and future: Essays in Jewish Theology*. Beacon Press.

Fanon, F. (1967). *Black skin, white masks.* C. L. Markmann (Trans.). Grove Press.

Ferenczi, S. (1980). Confusion of tongues between adults and the child. In M. Balint (Ed.), E. Mosbacher (Trans.), *Final contributions to the problems and methods of psycho-analysis*, pp. 156–74. Brunner/Mazel. (Original work published 1933.)

Ferlinghetti, L. (2007). *Poetry as insurgent art*. New Directions Publishing.

Ferme, A., and Vary, A. (2021, April 06). Jordan Peterson Says He Inspired the Villain in Ta-Nehisi Coates's "Captain America" Comic. *Variety.* variety.com/2021/digital/news/jordan-peterson-red-skull-ideologies-ta-nehisi-coates-captain-america-1234945126/.

Flannery, E. H. (1965). *The anguish of the Jews: Twenty-three centuries of anti-Semitism.* Macmillan.

Freud, S. (1900). *The Interpretation of Dreams. S. E., 4*: ix–627. Hogarth Press.
Freud, S. (1961). In E. Freud, (Ed.), T. Stern and J. Stern (Trans.): *Letters of Sigmund Freud 1873–1939*. Hogarth Press.
Fromm, E. (1964). *The heart of man: Its genius for good and evil*. Harper & Row.
Gilman, S. (1993). *Freud, Race, and Gender.* Princeton University Press.
Grand, S. (2000). *The reproduction of evil: A clinical and cultural perspective.* The Analytic Press.
Greene, J. (2020, September 15). Michael Ian Black has some wisdom for his son (and maybe for yours) [Review of the book *A better man: A (mostly serious) letter to my son,* by M. I. Black]. *The New York Times.* https://www.nytimes.com/2020/09/15/books/review/michael-ian-black-a-better-man.html?referringSource=articleShare.
Harris, A. (2005). *Gender as a soft assembly.* The Analytic Press.
Harris, A. (2019) Melancholic Fathers: Tantalizing and dangerous objects. *Psychoanalytic Perspectives, 16*(3), 340–52.
Haslam, N., Rothschild, L., and Ernst, D. (2002). Are essentialist beliefs associated with prejudice? *British Journal of Social Psychology, 41*, 87–100.
hooks, b. (2004). *The will to change: Men, masculinity, and love*. Washington Square Press.
Iacoviello, V., Valsecchi, G., Berent, J., Borinca, I., and Falomir-Pichastor, J. M. (2021). Is Traditional Masculinity Still Valued? Men's Perceptions of How Different Reference Groups Value Traditional Masculinity Norms. *The Journal of Men's Studies,* 1–21.
Kindlon, D., and Thompson, M. (2000). *Raising Cain: Protecting the emotional life of boys.* Ballantine Books.
Knafo, D., and Lo Bosco, R. (2017). *The age of perversion: Desire and technology in psychoanalysis and culture*. Routledge.
Kupers, T. A. (1993). *Revisioning Men's Lives: Gender, Intimacy, and Power*. The Guilford Press.
Lakoff, G. (2016). *Moral politics: How liberals and conservatives think*. University of Chicago Press.
Lartey, J. (2017, December 20). Ta-Nehisi Coates quits Twitter after public row with Cornel West. *The Guardian*. www.theguardian.com/books/2017/dec/20/ta-nehisi-coates-quits-twitter-after-public-row-with-cornel-west.
Layton, L. (2020). M. Leavy-Sperounis (Ed.): *Toward a social psychoanalysis: Culture, character, and normative unconscious processes.* Routledge.
Mann, T. (1969). *The Magic Mountain.* H. T. Lowe-Porter (Trans.). Vintage Books.
Nietzsche, F. (1974). *The gay science* (W. Kaufmann Trans.). Vintage Books. (Original work published 1882.)
Palacios, M (2014). Between fantasy and melancholia: Lack, otherness, and violence. In L. Auestad (Ed.), *Nationalism and the body politic: Psychoanalysis and the rise of ethnocentrism and xenophobia* (pp. 225–46). Karnac Books.
Peterson, J. B. (2018). *Twelve rules for life: An antidote to chaos.* Penguin Random House.

Philogène, G. (Ed.). (2004). *Racial identity in context: The legacy of Kenneth B. Clark.* American Psychological Association.

Rothschild, L. (2003). Penis. In: M. Kimmel and A. Aronson (Eds.), *Men and masculinities: A social, cultural, and historical encyclopedia,* 597–99. ABC-Clio.

Rothschild, L. (2016). Coercive elements and the threat of child sacrifice: *The Lego Movie*. In: R. Garrett, T. Jensen, and A. Voela (Eds.), *We Need to Talk About Family: Essays on Neoliberalism, The Family and Popular Culture*, 353–69. Cambridge Scholars Publishing.

Rozmarin, E. (2020). Fathers Don't Cry: On Gender, Kinship, and the Death Drive. *Studies in Gender and Sexuality, 21*(1), 38–47.

Sauer, P. (1989). The Jewish communities in Wuerttemberg and Hohenzollern. Stuttgart: W. Kohlhammer Publishing House Stuttgart. In, Bernstein, C. B., The *Rothschilds of Nordstetten: Their history and genealogy.* (Original work published 1966.)

Sevitch, B. (2002). W. E. B. Du Bois and Jews: A Lifetime of Opposing Anti-Semitism. *The Journal of African American History*, *87*, 323–37.

Shengold, L. (1993). *The boy will come to nothing: Freud's ego ideal and Freud as ego ideal.* Yale University Press.

Solnit, R. (2014). *Men explain things to me*. Haymarket Books.

Steinmetz-Jenkins, D. (2017, October 22). Is atheism the reason for Ta-Nehisi Coates's pessimism on race relations? *The Guardian.* www.theguardian.com/commentisfree/2017/oct/22/atheism-ta-nehisi-coates-pessimism-race-relations.

Stiegler, B. (2011). Pharmacology of Desire: Drive-based Capitalism and Libidinal Dis-Economy. D. Ross (Trans.). *New Formations: A Journal of Culture/Theory/Politics, 72*, 150–61. Lawrence & Wishart.

Vaughans, K. C. (2014). Disavowed fragments of the intergenerational transmission of trauma from slavery among African Americans. In K. C. Vaughans and W. Speilberg (Eds.), The *psychology of black boys and adolescents*, volume 2, 563–75. Praeger.

Voela, A., and Rothschild, L. (2019). Creative failure: Stiegler, psychoanalysis and the promise of a life worth living. *New Formations: A Journal of Culture/Theory/Politics*, *95*, 54–69.

Volkan, V. D. (in press). Finding the truth in individual and large-group psychology. In S. Akhtar (Eds.), *Truth Developmental, Cultural, and Clinical Realms*, 203–26. Phoenix Publishing.

Waling, A. (2019). Rethinking Masculinity Studies: Feminism, Masculinity, and Poststructural Accounts of Agency and Emotional Reflexivity. *The Journal of Men's Studies*, *27*(1), 89–107.

West, C. (2017, December 17). Ta-Nehisi Coates is the neoliberal face of the black freedom struggle. *The Guardian.* www.theguardian.com/commentisfree/2017/dec/17/ta-nehisi-coates-neoliberal-black-struggle-cornel-west.

Williams, M. H. (2010). *Bion's Dream: A Reading of the Autobiographies.* Karnac Books.

Yates, C. (2015). *The play of political culture, emotion and identity.* Palgrave Macmillan.

NOTES

1. Linking the impact of a dysregulated parent on a child's mind are considerations that what is felt as radioactive (Harris, 2019) or indigestible (Abraham and Torok, 2005; Emery, 2002) becomes a trauma clot (Eigen, 1999) fueling chronic alienation or self-reproach.

2. Anti-Jewish is used instead of the racialized and essentialist misnomer antisemitic (cf., Flannery, 1965). After finding Anti-Judaism used in a paper (Volkan, in press), some additional research revealed that the term antisemitism originated in nineteenth century Germany in order to racialize Jews (Allswang, 1985). Continued usage of the term perpetuates this prejudicial mythology.

Chapter 13

Re-Finding Lost Boys

Lessons from Literature and the Clinic

Marilyn Charles

Literature affords a means for piecing together fragments of experience into hypotheses about the making and meanings of a human life. As an essential form structuring all human experience, stories provide a vehicle for exploring the complexities of life, self, and relationships, and for passing along what we have learned to future generations (Charles, 2015). Literature offers models of the social world, a means of "telling the world to yourself" (Walker, Byatt and Norfolk, 2006, p. 340) through an embodied experience, in which universal themes can be recognized within the cultural and historical contexts in which they are embedded. Through kinesthetic imagery and the evocation of affect, fiction invites a simulation of social interaction (Mar and Oatley, 2008), *expressive enactments* (Sikora, Kuiken, and Miall, 2011) that illuminate not only the world and our lives but also our ethics and principles (Freeland, 1997). From the safety of the displacement, we are able to "become" another character, obtaining a sense of what it might be like to inhabit an alternative reality.

In turn, psychoanalysis can be seen as an evolving method through which the search for meaning might open up channels for further development that had been foreclosed or otherwise hampered. From Freud's archaeological dig to Lacan's (1978) recognition of some of the hazards of that digging, there has been a growing recognition of the possibilities that psychoanalysis holds, if we can step back from our attempts to "understand" and, instead, focus on providing a space in which the person might learn and grow. Bion (1977) warns against the hazard of knowing rather than learning. Taking seriously his admonitions against memory and desire, along with Lacan's warnings regarding becoming lost in the desire of the other, we see that we can spoil the space with our own investments, and are reminded to lean in with our interest and lean back with our intentions. We have learned a great deal from the literature on attachment and parent-child relationships that reminds us to have our eye on the person who is developing, trying to recognize and keep in mind their feelings, needs, interests, and desires. In that way, the consulting room becomes a space within which, as Bion (1990) puts it, the person might come to know themselves.

Conceptualizing the psychoanalytic space in this way has resulted in an evolution of thinking about the process, itself, in increasingly developmental terms. Bion's (1967a, 1977) particular mode of engagement took a stand for the not-knowing that is legitimately at the core of any encounter with another being, and his work on a theory of thinking meets current exploration of the metacognitive capacities so crucial to reflective functions. His admonition to abstain from memory or desire (Bion, 1967b) meets Lacan in the ethical imperative also undergirding Lévinas (1974), in which the call from someone's otherness must be met across that gap without trying to elide precisely what is unique and particular to them.

There is always the risk, in any form of caregiving, that whatever we are blind to will undermine the developmental efforts of the other. Psychoanalysis affirms our inevitable blindness, reminding us that the unconscious is alive and well in each of us, guiding our movements in ways we might be able to recognize but can never entirely anticipate or control. This recognition invites the analyst to provide a space in which knowledge might grow, to lean in with our care and attention such that possible meanings might be considered. Transference is ubiquitous, and enactments are a form of embodied exploration. We need repeated encounters, bumps, and collisions so that our own fantasies might be revealed sufficiently that we can catch glimpses of the person who is ambivalently trying to find and conceal themselves from view. Working at tolerating the bumps and bruises, and remaining open to what might be revealed, helps to provide the conditions under which learning might occur.

Recognizing ways in which development is impeded when parents are not sufficiently available to their children is crucial to this particular view of psychoanalysis. If we take seriously Winnicott's (1971) admonition to recognize the particularity of the child and their needs, we are in a better position to find ourselves in relation to the challenges faced by our patients. Lacan (1978) highlights our tendency to defer to the desire of the other. Development proceeds in relation to the person who meets our needs, holds our hand and, optimally, stands at the right distance and believes in us as we take our first independent steps, neither too close in nor too far away. The analyst must be willing to find the right distance through which to support the other person's development while also not standing in the way, to recognize the story being told of failed or thwarted development, and look for places where what has been foreclosed might be reopened and worked through. Laplanche (1995, 1997) reminds us that the shadows of our presumptions fall very hard, and most insidiously when we are aware not of them.

As psychoanalysis has broadened its scope, we can better see how the unconscious holds the patterns of meanings that inform and undergird an individual's life, mind, and ways of being (Charles, 2002a). Again, we find Bion and Lacan pointing in the same direction, in the particularity of the individual being Lacan (1974–1975) recognizes in his exegesis of the *sinthome,* and in the ubiquity of the dream space highlighted by the Bionian field theorists (Civitarese, 2006; Ferro, 2009). Recognizing the potency of these patterned meanings shows how the unconscious insists on the *form* of the meanings and their interrelatedness. This recognition opposes our tendency to simplify, concretize, and diminish the richness and profundity of the embodied meanings through which identity is formed. From this perspective, psychoanalysis, like all profound change, is fundamentally disruptive, even *catastrophic*, to use Bion's (1977) term. This disruption provides an alternate lens for investigating the nexus between subjectivity and the contexts in which it is evolving. Rather than positioning ourselves as interpreters of entrenched meanings, we can open up possibilities "by disrupting and disorganizing" congealed meanings so that the "functions become clearer, including its functions for us" (Parker, 2005, p. 177).

NARRATIVE AND IDENTITY DEVELOPMENT

Identity develops in the context of the family and cultures through which lived experience is translated. The foundations are built in the early interactions with caretakers through which we learn to make sense of self and experience, augmented by the process of narrativization through which a life story is built (Charles, 2014). Attentive parents mark the child's experience as worth orienting towards, inviting the child to be the subject of the conversation rather than merely the object of scrutiny, irritation, devotion, or blame. In Winnicott's (1971) terms, the baby looks into the mother's eyes and discovers themselves through whatever is reflected there.

The attachment literature chronicles the tragedy of the child who encounters empty, preoccupied eyes, but the eyes of adoration or disdain can also provide a misrecognition that derails development rather than affording the beginnings of a stable foundation. When the parents are not stable within themselves, the press towards moving on rather than coming to terms with difficult experiences leaves parents less available as resources for their children in the crucial function of identity development that *depends* on the child's ability to emerge as the focus of the parent's interest in a moment of need. In turn, the analyst needs to be sufficiently stable in her being that she can tolerate her own dysregulation and move towards the thinking in difficult moments that invites the analysand to do the same. Gallese's (2009) work on mirror neurons affirms the importance of modeling truth and integrity in our own negotiations with difficult moments.

The attachment literature highlights different ways in which children react to insufficient parenting. Some become more clinging, whereas others reactively detach in ways that impede their ability to find their way into the social matrix. I continue to be haunted by an image from a presentation by Stephen Suomi (2011), an attachment researcher, an image of an ape clinging to a tree, looking lost, alone, and terrified. I see that look in lost young men I encounter who have been unable to find their way into the social world. Without sufficient grounding to be able to be at home within oneself, it can be impossible to find a home in the world. At times, these young men find respite and rescue in a psychoanalysis that affords them the possibility of self-discovery within a matrix of recognition and care.

THE LOST BOY IN LITERATURE

Literature provides opportunities to *learn from our experience,* guided by the author's pen. We can find many instances in literature of the lost boy who becomes caught between the characterization that is evolving within the family versus his own needs and feelings as he experiences them. In *The Children's Book,* for example, A. S. Byatt (2009) considers the complexities of identity development through a mother and son who are so closely entangled that the son cannot find his own way into the world. By offering different vantage points, Byatt invites us to recognize Olive and Tom as individual beings who are profoundly dependent on one another but whose needs conflict tragically.

Psychoanalysis teaches us that latent meanings lurk beneath the surface presentation, inviting us to consider how our clinical minds might be informed by the pattern of the story we are offered. Bion's (1977) grid insists that meaning is found, not so much in the content of a story, but rather in the functions being performed (Charles, 2002b). From that framework, we can consider the story within a story. Byatt uses the genre of historical fiction to point to relational dilemmas that transcend space or time. In *The Children's Book*, "real and imaginary worlds collide and intermingle once again—in this case a comfortably middle-class Edwardian world" (Alfer and Edwards de Campo, 2010, p. 118).

The realm of fantasy is introduced most pointedly through Olive. This character draws on particulars from the life and work of Edith Nesbit, both in terms of the fantastic character of her stories and the nontraditional nature of her household and politics. Along with the fiction she creates for publication, Olive is writing a book for each of her own children, devising strange and magical countries "populated by half-beasts, people who could change their skins and sizes, sometimes by choice and sometimes by accident, so that you might find that you were a human child one moment, and a hedgehog the next" (Byatt, p. 80).

The stories that initially appear to be a gift to and way of being with her children are increasingly revealed to be narcissistic self-indulgences that Olive lives in and through. The lovely, stimulating environment in which her children are expected to flourish is largely empty of sustenance, relying, rather, on surface presentation for its power. Olive does not seem equal to the task of attending to any individual child's need that challenges her own well-being, and her husband, Humphrey, is similarly unavailable. Through these characters, we see the striking difference between the fantasy of parental love and care versus what may be demanded in real time, much less during a moment of crisis. We see their children each struggling against the bonds of a love that does not recognize them sufficiently as individual beings to allow them to grow.

The attachment literature shows that if early engagements build sufficient self-regulatory capacities, then the child is free to learn. If not, then that fundamental instability conditions all later learning and experience (see, for example, Fonagy et al., 2002). Disruptions become traumatic *because* they derail. In order to survive, the child learns to orient to the parent's needs and feelings rather than their own. Tom is represented as the favored child, who enjoys this position until his needs conflict with those of his parents. At that juncture, he is left to his own devices. Finding respite in the natural world, he increasingly becomes the feral child in relation to the fantasied Tom of the mother's tales.

Because the antecedents are more difficult to discover, inherited trauma is more likely to haunt us than trauma that is experienced directly. The untold story courses through us in the rhythms of affect-laden meanings. These embodied, enigmatic messages speak directly but cannot be translated because our parents and their ancestors had not been able to work through the trauma sufficiently to pass along the keys to those meanings. We see Olive haunted by her own history of death and deprivation, developing narratives that explore her traumatic past in the displacement, in this way attempting to relieve her distress. But distress that is displaced and avoided becomes a pitfall, a trap awaiting us at every turn, a hazard we see unfolding. When the ancestral history has been encrypted, development is foreclosed (Charles,

2019, Derrida, 1996). When the keys to the secret meanings are lost in an archive that has become impenetrable, the secrecy itself can be perversely satisfying. The satisfaction depends on an essential not-knowing in the dyad, resulting in an impossible enmeshment between parent and child. Unresolved, these types of secrets further alienate us from ourselves and from one another, as we see unfold so disastrously in the novel.

The parental failure to be sufficiently separate to recognize the child's legitimate needs undergirds the tragedy we encounter in Byatt's novel, as we see how disruption plays out in the characters and in their relationships with one another. Failure is experienced as shameful and, in *The Children's Book*, we see, not only failures in the parental roles but also to hold steady against external pressures. Social acceptance often comes at the price of self-denial, thereby tainting identity with the shame inherent in that denial. Shame breaks the interpersonal bond, making it difficult to encounter the type of repair that might be found through human connection. In Lévinas' (1974/1991) terms, the human "face summons me to my obligation and judges me" (in Lawton, 2005, p. 214). In the novel, the mother's failure to come to grips with her own history leaves her unable to recognize the needs and feelings of her children, leaving the children at odds with themselves, searching for a place in a world they have never truly been invited into.

In writing her tales, we see Olive hiding and displacing aspects of self as a way of not facing her own negative self-identity. From a Kleinian (1946) perspective, her stories provide a means for projecting her bad feelings outward, trying to keep them at a safe distance. We also see how this maneuver fails. Failing to integrate her own trauma leaves her unable to help her children to face theirs. We see her caught in a world of part-objects, where whatever cannot be tolerated in the self is projected outward into the characters inhabiting her tales. As we know all too well from clinical experience, the disowned bits inevitably persecute us from without, constant reminders of precisely what we are denying.

Initially beguiling as a character, Olive's fundamental flaws are increasingly revealed, particularly in her role as mother. What begins as a bond between Olive and each of her children seems to become a burden and even a source of bondage. Whereas Dorothy and Hedda divorce themselves from the fantasy world of their mother, Tom, the oldest and dearest child, becomes so entangled in his mother's fantasies that they ultimately destroy him.

In her fairy tales, we see ways in which Olive is trapped by her own history as a miner's daughter, and her failed mourning in relation to family members who were lost underground. In disavowing these lowly origins, there is little room to come to grips with some of the threads of her own story, which then become displaced into her children's stories. We can wonder, for example, to what extent Tom's lost shadow represents her own childhood, deliberately displaced in ways that haunt them both. This disavowal leaves the children "held hostage by the adults' various plottings [as] they struggle to assume authorship of their own lives" (Alfer and Edwards de Campos, p. 124).

Through her characters, Byatt entertains various positions a child might take in relation to an enchanting but unavailable mother. Tom, enthralled by his mother's invitation, seems to have a sense that the world she offers to him is his, "simply to take it in and know it. Underneath the earth, in an imaginary realm of rock tunnels and winding stairs, the shadowless seeker, with the trusted Company, never growing older, never changing their intent, travelled on towards the dark queen weaving her webs, and snares, and shrouds" (Byatt, p. 235). In contrast to the symbiotic bond entwining Olive and Tom, Dorothea rejects the world of words, the dark recess offered by their mother, spinning tales from the underground. Hedda, in turn, does not merely reject the mother's stories but insists on uncovering the family mysteries that have been shrouded by Olive's fantastic world of words.

We see Olive and Humphrey each turning a blind eye to the needs of the children when they conflict with their own desires. Their acts of betrayal obstruct the redemption potential inherent in the human encounter (Lévinas, 1969/1991). Rather, the denial of their children's suffering by Olive and Humphrey results in betrayals so profound that Dorothy is ravaged and alienated, and Tom cannot even survive when he is finally faced with the truth he had been avoiding.

Tom had previously caught terrible glimpses, beneath the façade of the doting mother who appears to love him above all else, of the narcissistic mother who indulges herself at his expense. Publicly and graphically, he discovers that the story that had appeared to be a private offering of love actually represents his erasure as a unique human being. The mother through whom he legitimately hoped to find himself was finding herself through him, making of her eyes an empty mirror. The roles had been reversed, leaving him unable to find himself sufficiently to truly leave home. What had seemed to have been a source of sustenance had actually left him gutted and alone.

The story of *Tom Underground* that had been their tie to one another in a private, seemingly idyllic, world becomes public in the form of a play (Byatt, 2009). Through Tom's eyes, we see Olive's utter ruthlessness. She "plundered the children's stories sometimes, for publishable situations, or people, or settings" (p. 81). Olive tries to pretend that she has not done violence to her son, even when she watches him receive his invitation and, seeing his name in the title, say, tonelessly, "I wasn't asked. Or told" (p. 521). So caught in the fantasy that drives her forward, she is blind to the pain she inflicts on her child.

Tom attends the theatrical performance of *Tom Underground* in a state of shock. "He was both not-thinking and not-believing. Something had been taken from him, certainly, but in these lights, against this backcloth, it was something fabricated and trivial, which it made no sense to mourn" (p. 524). He leaves the theatre and keeps walking until he reaches the sea, and lets it take him. "He didn't fight," writes Byatt (p. 533). His mother, all the while, tries to pretend that she has not done violence to her son. Her oblivion seals his fate. "It is very hot," she says when he disappears after the play, "I hope he enjoyed the play" (p. 524).

In this novel, through its call to recognize the universality of trauma, we see how literature can illuminate ways in which we are all implicated in what Caruth (1991) calls the "indirect referentiality of history" (p. 187), such that "history, like the trauma, is never simply one's own, that history is precisely the way we are implicated in each other's traumas" (p. 192). *The Children's Book* offers a rendering of history in which individual characters speak to us from the intersection of personal temperament, social role, and cultural and historical context, such that we can consider the various elements and their relationships to one another (Byatt, 2009). Through that perspective, we can consider how those elements manifest in our own spaces and times. It is always easier to cast the past aside as remote and alien rather than to personalize it sufficiently to learn its lessons, and yet, the displacement can also help us to face painful realities. Whatever is excluded from consideration becomes the phantom haunting at our heels (Charles, in press).

A CASE ILLUSTRATION

The impasse in *The Children's Book* is not worked through. In contrast, when men carry burdens similar to young Tom enter our consulting rooms, we have the opportunity to invite a different ending, one in which parent and child can each survive and, perhaps, find themselves and one another in the process. At the Austen Riggs Center, a private psychoanalytic hospital in western Massachusetts, we have the luxury of being afforded four times weekly psychotherapy along with the possibility of adjunctive family work. Such encounters help family members to face their troubles rather than becoming further mired in the pain and their defensive maneuvers. It is difficult for well-intentioned parents to face ways in which their child's needs have not been met. And yet, it is precisely in orienting to the child's experienced reality that healing might happen. In turn, the recognition of the legitimacy of each person's feelings and perspective invites the child into a more textured understanding of the parent.

These considerations invite us to try to orient to each individual's experience, so that we might empathically engage with them in their struggles. This stance is most crucial when we sit with those who find themselves situated outside of consensual culture, to try to hear the call of truth, and enter as empathically as we can into resonance with the person's experience. From that place, we are in a better position to find links between *their* words and experience, and our own, and to have a sense of where the difficulties arise *for them*. It is difficult to witness extreme suffering and yet, in such respectful engagement, the person who has become lost might begin to locate themselves in relation to the life story that could not previously be formulated. Identity forms within the context of consensual meanings built in respectful, intimate engagement with one another. When the family has been unable to integrate an individual into the family story, a psychoanalytic perspective can provide an arena in which what has been forced into the realm of concrete metaphor can be reflected upon and integrated into a story in which each person's perspective can be recognized as legitimate and meaningful.

I think, for example, of a young man in his late thirties who describes himself as Atlas, holding up the world. This is the position in which he finds himself in his family of origin, standing accused of being the source of whatever suffering prevails. "Paul" has been wounded by what feels like a forced exclusion from the world of human beings and finds himself driven ever further from the dangerous realm of feelings and embodied meanings. When I first met him, he had been so distanced by his suffering that he could only speak from the realm of ideation. Our work entailed traversing the gap between his precise meanings and my embodied sensibilities, often bumping quite jarringly against the disjunctions between the two. Over time, our growing ability to meet in the middle helped Paul to locate himself in relation to the relatively rigid code of ethics he had adopted, and the discomfortingly messy world of human feelings.

As Paul learned to accept his own humanity and the needs and limits of other family members as legitimate as well, he was slowly able to begin to find his own place within the social surround and also within his family. His family members, in turn, slowly learned to hear Paul's sincere and poignant attempts to engage, rather than becoming so defensively polarized by his idiosyncratic phrasings. My own challenge was to recognize the good intentions of family members and also ways in which each could become hurt and hurting, and to try to invite greater reflectivity through my speech rather than merely inciting greater reactivity. This work requires recurrently taking a stand for the importance of each person being able to get their bearings and find their way, in the process learning more about self and other, and recognizing that each person has their own gifts and perspective. Opening up to the other's perspective not only affords greater insight but also enlivens the whole.

When the family cannot tolerate the demands made by the child whose needs go unmet, the child must either capitulate to the family's limits or go rogue, attempting to safeguard the core of identity by remaining outside the bounds of consensual reality. This situation results in an impasse in which care can seem to press towards imminent annihilation. I saw such a moment occur in the work with Paul and his family. As his mother became increasingly empathic to her son's distress, she became increasingly distressed as well. Suddenly, she announced that she would not be taken in by the forces of darkness. Rather, she positioned herself firmly in her own story, in which the family history had been one of joy and gladness, leaving her son alone in his private hell. Paul is then positioned, once again, as the source of all badness within the family story. This place in which the mother becomes caught highlights Lacan's ideas regarding the Imaginary, profoundly personal universes each of us inhabits—apperceptive rather than perceptive—even when it seems to match with the experience of others (Lacan, 1974–1975). There is an ambivalent urge in each of us to sustain but also to break through the confines of the Imaginary—the transference relationship—into something authentic. Such engagement both demands and makes possible a different level of truth-telling. As we can see in the preceding example, that juncture can require that we face what feels like catastrophic change in the hope of healing the terrible rupture that occurs when transgenerational trauma has impeded knowing.

To oppose his own mother's preference for a romantic fantasy that covers over her son's distress, Paul insists on a bare truth that takes no account of people's feelings. Rather, he is motivated by a fierce desire to divest of the "upholstery" with which most people cover over the truths that feel too raw, too bare to disclose. His family tries to reach out to him, but their words become barriers to the closeness each both longs for and occludes. Much like Bion's (1977) exegesis of the relationship between the *Establishment* and the *New Idea,* Paul becomes the mystic who speaks truth in his particular haiku form, un-upholstered and seemingly obscure, yet cutting to the core as best he can. We see him trying desperately to find something real in relationship but obstructed in his efforts by his failure to take feelings into account. Notably, as his family therapists stand with him, insisting on the value of his speech, his parents, slowly, painfully, over time shifted from attending these "torture sessions" to "help their crazy son," to a more respectful engagement with ways in which his truths have been occluded by their fears.

In this repositioning, the parents meet the challenge posed by Lacan (1978) to see themselves being seen rather than positioning their son as the alien being. This type of movement is well depicted by Gadamer (1975) in his statement, "To seek one's own in the alien, to become at home in it, is the basic movement of spirit, whose being is only a return to itself from what is other" (p. 15). From such a vantage point, we are in a better position to be respectful of the truth-seeker's bumps and bruises and thereby to help them build a navigational map in relation to their own experience. Paul finds himself positioned as the excluded voice who speaks back to the family about the blindness that keeps them alienated from one another. Relegated to the position of primary knower of whatever is excluded from the family consciousness—Atlas holding up the world—Paul is left to constitute himself as *a* knower rather than *the* knower, a subject in his own right, leaving family members to move towards greater becoming as they face their own truths—and lies.

Those who do not fit within the family discourse are often left—or thrust—outside the gates. Their suffering makes a demand on us, marking the ethical imperative that Levinas (1974/1991) says is lodged in the human face. I link that call to the memory I have of Stephen Suomi's (2011) avoidantly-attached young apes, caught in the wilderness between the barred childhood home and the impossibility of finding a new one. Their reactively alienated attachment style left them unable to learn the skills or relational knowledge that might have facilitated the transition to a new home. I see that suffering in those, like Paul, who have been pushed outside the gates by family and social structure, left to suffer in a wilderness that seems endless and unendurable. Structurally, I see this dilemma in the terms that Lacan referred to as the psychotic position, through this language recognizing that the experience of being left outside shapes the individual in a process of abjection in relation to the social surround from which they are excluded (Vanheule, 2011).

Recognition of the force of abjection and marginalization in the etiology of what we have come to term *psychotic disorders*, individuals in northern Finland have developed what they term the *Open Dialogue Method* (Seikkula et al., 2006). Based on a humanistic, person-centered approach to human struggles, teams of health providers go into the home of families where an individual is suffering from a psychotic break and talk with the sufferer and family members about the problems they are encountering. In the process of listening, talking, formulating, and respectfully engaging with one another, the affective intensity within the family is attenuated and family members are invited to more effectively think about their dilemmas. If you think about what we know about mirror neurons (Gallese, 2009), it makes sense that such engagement helps to set a process in place whereby the alienated individual and other family members are provided models of reflective thought and effective problem solving.

In my work with individuals, like Paul, whose meanings are opposed within the family structure, being able to work with the family as a whole is an incredible gift, bringing into vivid relief the interpersonal dilemmas at play. That frame of reference in even one case helps us to take seriously and try to think and feel our way into speech that can otherwise sound odd, metaphoric, or even inconceivable. That type of experience can also help us recognize ways in which what seems inconceivable can be a function of our defenses against the suffering that is marked by such speech. In describing himself as Atlas, holding up the world, Paul marks his experience of alienation, while also recognizing the privilege afforded by this marginalized position. This phrasing aptly describes the position in which he finds himself in his family of origin, accused of being the source of whatever suffering prevails. Although his speech is unconventional, it is also quite precise and cogent, but lodges at that odd juncture of concrete metaphor that is often called psychotic.

Entering into the family dialogue, one discovers the good intentions and presumptions of care that cover over the defensive moves against engaging with the speech of the identified patient. Doublings and splitting of meanings are everywhere; Paul is accused of a lack of empathy at precisely the moment when he is showing, in his own way, an empathic recognition of the suffering of another family member. Family members seem unaware of his earnest efforts or the legitimacy of his pain. Rather, he is accused of caring only about himself while he sits isolated from the protective care of the family that laments his exclusion as though it were self-imposed. I find these meetings dizzying, often leaving them in need of reassurance from my co-therapist as to what has just transpired, walking away on unsteady feet, as though I had just stepped off a carnival ride.

That carnival-ride sensation also occurs at times in my sessions with Paul. In some moments, our conversations are engaged and animated. At times, however, a shift suddenly occurs and I become suspect, one of *them*—those well-intentioned caregivers whose utter blindness makes them dangerous. I struggle with the me-them, insisting that there is a *me* guiding my speech and behaviors, but that I am also willing to think about ways in which the *them* in me might color or inform my speech. My willingness to struggle provides some assurance, and yet, at times the stumbling is so jarring that I am thrust off balance. In one such moment, when Paul's fear had so denuded my speech of whatever meaning had been intended, I was taken aback, as though the wind had been knocked out of me. In trying to describe my experience of the moment, Paul named the Gravitron, the carnival ride in which one is thrust backward, spinning. We could both recognize that I was, for those moments, in the place where Paul spends much of his time, and how difficult it is to get one's bearings, much less think or engage with another person, from that place.

Paul's depiction of himself as Atlas seems apt, if one is willing to allow the possible meanings to accrue and resonate. Such recognition, however, requires a willingness to take one's own place on the Gravitron and to recognize how bits of refused meanings pile up and take their toll. In these efforts, it is useful to consider how these myths and metaphors might mark a place where one is stuck in the family, but that reflective consideration might also open up the possibility of a different ending or path. For Atlas, holding up the world, his family may, in some sense, need him to stand in this position, but perhaps the world will still exist even if he lets go of his burden? From this perspective of possibility, I make this suggestion to him. My reflections bring up for me the question of how we might use myth in more creative, generative ways, beyond the recognition of an entrenched pattern, perhaps by locating the myth within the constellation of the family dynamic in which it is embedded. In this way, we can better see how it *becomes* universal rather than necessarily *being* universal.

In these efforts, I find my way back into the realm of the reflective space through which meanings can be considered, played with, and amended. That ability to play within one's own mind, and also with others, affords us the flexibility needed to make our way in the world. Tom came to an impasse when his trauma was marked but there was insufficient parental attention to provide a lifeline to hold on to. Paul, in contrast, did have an attentive other on whom to rely while he tried to find his way into the social matrixes of past, present, and possible futures. At times, psychoanalysis provides the play space within which intrapersonal needs and feelings can be encountered, marked, and put into context. With these basic building blocks of metacognition in place, there is room to encounter and make sense of the others with whom might engage in the interpersonal learning so essential to socio-emotional development.

CONCLUSION

Psychoanalysis is not only a vehicle for self-discovery. It is also a means for better understanding the human condition, making it an important tool for psychosocial research. There is an ethical dilemma at the heart of such research, where various "goods" may be juxtaposed against one another within the context of both the legitimate variations of meanings across cultural difference and the hazard of what Castañeda (2006) calls the "epistemological and moral violence of knowledge writing, and representation" (p. 128). When we position ourselves as a knower rather than a fellow traveler, we run the risk of over-writing someone else's incipient self-knowledge.

From Fabian's (2012) perspective, the purpose of such research is to obtain knowledge "that changes the knower as well as the known" (p. 449). As we can see from the illustrations offered from both literature and the clinic, we can all be misled by "good intentions" that lead us astray because we are not open to the very learning needed to organize and refine our understanding. Through research that is open to new learning, there is development at the individual and group levels. In this way, turning our psychoanalytic lens reflectively on our lost children offers us, not just the possibility of saving one lost soul, but perhaps helping us all to develop greater wisdom through which to better shelter and shepherd our children as they grow.

REFERENCES

Alfer, A., and Edwards de Campos, A. J. (2010). *A. S. Byatt: Critical Storytelling.* Manchester: Manchester University Press.

Bion, W. R. (1967a). *Second Thoughts: Selected Papers on Psycho-Analysis.* New York: Jason Aronson.

Bion, W. R. (1967b). Notes on memory and desire. *Psychoanalytic Forum,* 2: 271–80.

Bion, W. R. (1977). *Seven Servants.* New York: Jason Aronson.

Bion, W. R. (1990). *Brazilian Lectures.* London, UK: Karnac.

Byatt, A. S. (2009). *The Children's Book.* London: Chatto & Windus.

Caruth, C. (1991). Unclaimed experience: Trauma and the possibility of history. *Yale French Studies,* 79: 181–92.

Castañeda, Q. E. (2006). Ethnography in the forest: An analysis of ethics in the morals of anthropology. *Cultural Anthropology,* 21(1): 121–45.

Charles, M. (2002a). *Patterns: Building Blocks of Experience.* Hillsdale, NJ: The analytic Press.

Charles, M. (2002b). Bion's grid: A tool for transformation. *Journal of the American Academy of Psychoanalysis*, 30(3): 429–45.

Charles, M. (2014). Trauma, Childhood, and Emotional Resilience. In N. Tracey (Ed.), *Transgenerational Trauma and the Aboriginal Preschool Child: Healing through Intervention*. Lanham, MD: Rowman & Littlefield, pp. 109–31.

Charles, M. (2015). *Psychoanalysis and Literature: The Stories We Live.* New York: Rowman & Littlefield.

Charles, M. (2019). The dream and the image: Creative transformations in psychoanalytic space. *American Journal of Psychoanalysis,* 79: 174–95.

Charles, M. (in press). *The Haunting of Hill House:* Psyche, Soma, and Destiny. *American Journal of Psychoanalysis.*

Civitarese, G. (2006). Dreams that mirror the session. *International Journal of Psychoanalysis,* 87(3): 703–23.

Derrida, J. (1996). *Archive Fever: A Freudian Impression.* E. Prenowitz (Trans.). Chicago: University of Chicago Press.

Fabian, J. (2012). Cultural anthropology and the question of knowledge. *Journal of the Royal Anthropological Institute,* 18: 439–53.

Ferro, A. (2009). Transformations in dreaming and characters in the psychoanalytic field. *International Journal of Psychoanalysis,* 90(2): 209–30.

Fonagy, P., Gergely, G., Jurist, E., and Target, M. (2002). *Affect Regulation, Mentalization and the Development of the Self.* New York: Other Press.

Freeland, Cynthia A. (1997). Art and moral knowledge. *Philosophical Topics,* 25: 11–36.

Gadamer, H.-G. (1975). *Truth and method.* New York: Continuum.

Gallese, V. (2009). Mirror neurons, embodied simulation, and the neural basis of social identification. *Psychoanalytic Dialogues,* 19: 519–36.

Klein, M. (1946). Notes on some schizoid mechanisms. In *Envy and Gratitude and Other Works, 1946–1963* (pp. 1–24). London: Hogarth Press, 1975.

Lacan, J. (1974–1975). *Seminar XXII: RSI* (C. Gallagher, Trans.). www.LacaninIreland.com.

Lacan, J. (1978). *The Four Fundamentals of Psycho-Analysis*, A. Sheridan (Trans.). New York: W. W. Norton, 1977.

Laplanche, J. (1995). Seduction, persecution, revelation. *International Journal of Psycho-Analysis,* 76: 663–82.

Laplanche, J. (1997). The theory of seduction and the problem of the other. *International Journal of Psycho-Analysis,* 78: 653–66.

Lawton, P. N. (2005). Love and justice: Lévinas' reading of Buber. In: *Lévinas and the Question of Religion*, C. E. Katz (Ed.), pp. 212–19. Urbana and Chicago: University of Illinois Press.

Lévinas, E. (1969/1991). *Totality and Infinity: An Essay on Exteriority,* A. Lingis (Trans.). Dordrecht: Kluwer.

Lévinas, E. (1974/1991). *Otherwise than Being or Beyond Essence,* A. Lingis (Trans.). New York: Springer.

Mar, R. A., and Oatley, K. (2008). The function of fiction is the abstraction and simulation of social experience. *Perspectives on Psychological Science,* 3: 173–92.

Parker, I. (2005). Lacanian discourse analysis in psychology: Seven theoretical elements. *Theory & Psychology,* 15(2): 163–82.

Seikkula, J., Aaltonen, J., Alakare, B., Haarakangas, K., Keränen, J., and Lehtinen, K. (2006). Five-year experience of first-episode nonaffective psychosis in open-dialogue approach: Treatment principles, follow-up outcomes, and two case studies. *Psychotherapy Research,* 16(2): 214–28.

Sikora, S., Kuiken, D., and Miall, D. S. (2011). Expressive reading: A phenomenological study of readers' experience of Coleridge's *The Rime of the Ancient Mariner. Psychology of Aesthetics, Creativity, and the Arts,* 5: 258–68.

Suomi, S. J. (2011). Risk, resilience, and gene-environment interplay in primates. *Journal of the Canadian Academy of Child and Adolescent Psychiatry*, 20(4): 289–97.

Vanheule, S. (2011). *The Subject of Psychosis: A Lacanian Perspective.* London: Palgrave MacMillan.

Walker, J., Byatt, A. S., and Norfolk, L. (2006). An interview with A. S. Byatt and Lawrence Norfolk. *Contemporary Literature,* 47(3): 319–42.

Winnicott, D. W. (1971). *Playing and Reality.* New York: Basic Books.

Chapter 14

Fractional Distillation

On Psychoanalysis' (Mis) Formulation of Autistic Children

Ben Morsa

There is much work yet to be done to offer affirming and humane treatment to autistic people. This chapter is an attempt to sketch some contours of what such an approach might look like, set in the history of the treatment of autistic people, with particular attention to the role psychoanalysis has, and could play. Autism exists in something of a professional silo in the discipline of psychology. Colleagues who consult with me, and graduate students I teach, express a sense of lack in training related to autism. Many describe autism as a separate specialization in the mental health field—more separate, and more special, than other areas of practice. This chapter will critique the categorical spectra of autism and autism professionals using the metaphor of a fractionating ("fracking") column. I hope to elucidate various breakdowns that impinge meaningful work with autistic people. I will critique prevailing notions of autism treatment generally with particular attention to my own clinical and theoretical specialization—psychoanalysis.

FRACTIONAL DISTILLATION

Imagine a bag of different colored marbles. Blue, green, red, yellow, orange, purple, the whole rainbow is in the bag. Perhaps you want to separate the green marbles out. It is as easy as finding all the green marbles and pulling them out of the bag—one at a time. But suppose you want to separate a mixture of liquids rather than a bag of marbles. This process is known as distillation. As the mixture boils, the differing boiling points of the component liquids allows for their separation and collection as each evaporates. The distillation apparatus collects the evaporated liquid (distillate) and condenses it. This separation (fractioning) is also a purifying process. Distillation drives the purity.

Fractional distillation salvages the crude oil via the fracking column by subjecting it to iterative cycles of intense heat and pressure. In the fractionating column, evaporation and condensation distill the mixture along lines of purity, siphoning off lower forms for lesser uses (paving, diesel, automobiles), and intensifying the distillation process to increase the purest fraction (rocket fuel). There are striking parallels to prevailing ethos of autism assessment and treatment. Below, I will explore these parallels by following autistic scholar and theorist, Yergeau (2018), and applying their critical inquiry to the work of Frances Tustin (1992/2021), a seminal psychoanalytic theorist of autism.

Both Applied Behavioral Analysis (ABA) and psychoanalysis share the common project of creating higher functioning [sic][1] autistics. They accomplish this by figuring autism (and autistic people) as a panoply of developmental deficits (and, sometimes, gifts) and endeavoring to remove or remediate a child's autism (as if the two were separable). This figures autistic people as lesser humans and turns therapy into a human-making project—the eponymous fractionating column of this paper. By identifying autistic people as fractional humans, and meticulously cataloging their deficits, these treatment approaches install themselves as neurotypical missionaries rescuing children from the sticky crude of autism by distilling their higher-functioning [sic] parts.

This distillation as intervention scaffolds human relationship through explicit, or implicit, education in the use of shared symbols. Here, the symbolic order is the highest order, set above the ostensibly primitive movements and communications of autistic children. This establishes a hierarchy of humanity where treatment aims to drive the autistic individual to higher levels of functioning (more friends, more eye contact, more metaphors, fewer stims, better grades, full-time employment, etc.). Treatment (distillation) drives the purity and leads to more, or less, productive members of society. The link to social survival ensures the necessity of autism treatment, much like capitalism ensures the necessity of fossil fuels. But it is hard to distill necessity from excess, especially when they are two sides of the same Other.

High functioning autism is a murky and problematic construction with a haunted history. Many associate high functioning autism as akin to, or synonymous with Aspergers, named for Hans Asperger. Accounts (Chzech, 2018) of the role he played in studying children he assigned his name raise complicated questions about the ethics of assigning individuals as higher and lower—questions of life and death. The psychoanalytic reader recognizes the ghost of splitting. High-functioning [sic] is generally thought to be a term that divides autistic community, but also, autistic individuals from themselves, as the push to become higher functioning frequently (always?) includes the mandate to be less autistic. Under the pathology paradigm of autism, more autism is lower functioning—what a drag.

I am positing a meaningful connection between behaviorism and psychoanalysis where both aim toward the goal of making the patient higher functioning and, by extension, less autistic. Many autistic people (and, increasingly, psychologists) use the term masking to describe a process where autistic people strive for "higher-functioning," sometimes through elective extinction of their autistic phenotype. But since Freud's hydraulic metaphors of the mind first powered the analytic imaginary, psychoanalysis has been keenly aware of how depleting, and therefore unsustainable, wearing a mask is. When psychoanalysis forgets this, we witness the return of the repressed.

Masking precedes meltdown, or burnout. I will describe these as the inevitable psychic and emotional exhaustion that besets an autistic person driving themselves to higher functioning. Camouflaging (another term for masking) correlates with higher levels of depression and anxiety (Hull et al., 2019). Masking (and the social survival it holds out as a carrot) can easily become a stick. Here, I feel, the therapist can be helpful, so long as they do not repeat, "stop hitting yourself" as the golden ticket to higher functioning.

These treatments require a form of manic denial because propelling an autistic person to higher levels of functioning historically involves rescuing [sic] them from their autism. This entails a denial of reality (the patient is autistic, after all) but also the existential depression of burnout, which trades the social model of disability for a capitalist model of resource extraction. Some argue (e.g., Wilkenfield and McCarthy, 2020), that therapies like ABA are unethical because they locate an inherent part of a person's being as the object of change and because they do so without considering the voice, or preferences, of the person subject to change. Masking is not only akin to the manic defense because it denies connection / relationship with autism (and the autistic person), and because of the depression that results, but also because it *denies* the voice of the autistic person.

DEMI-RHETORICITY: WHAT PARTIAL VOICES CARRY

Yergeau's *Authoring Autism* (2018) is a compelling review of theories and therapies of autism. They offer compelling critique of behaviorism and psychoanalysis. Yeargeau, who is themself, autistic, demonstrates how these theories necessarily figure autistic people as inhuman, even anti-human because of their constructed distance from the social and proximity to death. They begin with a claim that clinical theories are rife with "shitty narratives" about autism and autistic people. These narratives persist,

> because their rhetorical power derives from the figure of the autistic as unknowable, as utterly abject and isolated and tragic, as a figure whose actions are construed less like actions and more like neuronally willed middle fingers. (p. 3)

The narratives are sticky, like shit, and refer to something tragic and unpleasant—something to flush away. This unpleasantness is not only out of the individual's control ("neuronally willed") but is also oppositional ("middle finger") and simultaneously justifies the position that an autistic person is not agentic (the body drives the mind) and is antisocial (they oppose speech).

Yergeau (2018) notes popular and professional discourses define autistic people as ahretorical, lacking in capacity to tell their own stories in ways others will recognize. Or, more crudely, "these narratives are shittier than the shit they claim to represent . . . [because] in these constructions, our shit holds more power than we do" (p. 3). By examining these shitty narratives, Yergeau is also pushing back against those who give their shit more rhetorical power than their voice.

These shitty narratives endow autistics with demi-rhetoricity—a term Yergeau (2018) uses to denote the ways that autistic voices, intentions, and subjectivity are always viewed as partial. Autism is a syndrome without a singular etiological theory that captures the variegated etiology and functioning of the panoply of autistic figures, presented as an array of "fractioned and fractionable disorders" (p. 47). Yergeau is sensitive to the paradox that these therapies present to autistic people by overriding their voices with catalogs of deficits and promises of higher levels of functioning. Yet, this salvation is illusory and poses an existential threat for, "we can always make ourselves better if by 'made better' we mean do violence to ourselves and our cultures" (p. 49).

THE DISORDER OF UNSUSTAINABLE SPECTRA

Achieving this salvation requires an emancipating other who by brute force or persistent influence can carry the autistic person away from death (and into life), out of the auto- and into the coop-, from low to high, from sensation to the symbolic. Failure to cooperate with the (neurotypical) symbolic is the capital autistic crime. For, as Yergeau notes, the one theory that eternally returns about autism is that the autistic individual is asymbolic, unable to play, incapable of social pretense, and therefore, by nature, antisocial. The specter of the antisocial infuses the clinical imaginary of the autism spectrum

[sic]. Perhaps this is why autistic theories and therapies have such a spectral and panoptic feel to them—their incessant and lurid looky-loo quality, their totalizing frameworks of change. Is it surprising that autism awareness campaigns compare autism to cancer? They are on the lookout for death and death's acolytes, constantly categorizing its signifiers and founding its referents, defining what counts as life and living by contrasting it with the unknowable other that is autism.

Treatment necessitates a disciplinary process, which Yergeau (2018) likens to the tightening of a coil meant to "spring" autistic children "into symbolic action" (p. 53). The child undergoes the arduous work of disciplining themselves with the therapist's voice in mind, correcting their bodies in conformity with discourse—an application of the disciplinary power Foucault critiqued (1977/1995). Neurodevelopmental systems, psychogenic autistic objects, echolalia, genetic mutations, environmental pollution, vaccines, blue puzzle pieces, and theories of mind need not be in agreement with each other in order to function in tandem to describe autistics' lack of functioning, locate them as an object of concern, and justify intervention, for the greater good. Such disciplinary processes pose the question, can the therapist compel—through the force of reinforcement or the magnetism of the transference—the autistic child to see the value of being like everyone else?

Poststructural critique rests on the constitutive exclusion of being like everyone else. Foucault (1997/2003) emphasized that biopolitical regimes not only write knowledge onto the body but that in doing so they parcel out, to greater or lesser degree, the right to life. These disciplinary regimes—be they parent guides, applied behavioral analysis, or research papers touting the naturalness of neurotypical bodies—work together to condition autistic people to move their bodies just so. If they fail, then perhaps they are simply playing with their shit, a neuronally willed middle finger. Affect theorists like Sara Ahmed (2010) articulate the lifelessness of systems that mandate conformity and compliance and hurl assignations (willful, melancholy, obstructive, disruptive) to bodies that do not follow these mandates. Butler (1990), and others, have deconstructed the phallogocentrism of binaries—their tendency to reify structures of power, to produce parallel concepts of natural/unnatural, normal/abnormal, saint/monster- and the meaningful ways that linguistic binaries are much more than words and can seriously hurt you.

Following the paradoxical logic of autism theories, as the autistic person progresses to cure, they necessarily become less autistic, and (constructed as) less able to speak or advocate for alternate ways of being with autism. In *The Little Mermaid*[2] (Clements and Musker, 1989), Ariel visits Ursula with a wish to be "part of that world" of land-dwelling humans. When Ursula mentions payment, Ariel comes up short. Ursula reassures her, she can make payment by surrendering her voice. How is Ariel to woo her lover with no voice?

Ursula implores, “don’t underestimate the importance of *body language*.” Treatments that require autistic people to surrender their voice (and ways of being) often offer body language as a ticket to the top. Is it? I argue this promise rests on the manic denial of autism, one that fails to internalize the humility poststructuralism offers.

The next section reads the work of Frances Tustin (1992/2021), a central psychoanalytic theorist of autism. Drawing upon the specific theoretical tools of Yergeau, I aim to track the ways that the theory and therapy proffered by Tustin establishes a psychoanalytic fractionating column that risks meltdown by denying autistic voices.

HOME IS WHERE WE START FROM

The ontology of autism vexes clinicians and researchers alike. The question “What is autism?” remains opaque and contentious and, by extension, so does the authority to identify or diagnose it. Still, among psychoanalysts, Tustin has been granted the authority to speak to what autism *is*. For her, autism is a two-factor condition representing an admixture of constitutional proclivity in the child and contributing factors in the environment.

Specifically, Tustin (1992/2021) views autism as the result of an infant’s traumatic experience of separateness (from the breast, from the mother, from others, from the world). The child does not experience the loss of the breast as the loss of another, but rather, the loss of a part of its own body. Later, Tustin will warn of the threat autistic self-centeredness poses to society. Because, the autistic child is unable to negotiate the facts of separate life they resort to a number of pathological (or pathologized, my addition) mechanisms for protection—namely, autosensuousness (a sort of masturbatory fixatedness on one’s sensorium), autistic objects (asymbolic and anti-human, hard/rigid objects in both the material and the psychic sense), and confusional objects (those where relationship / identification with the object is confused / entangled). Unlike the neurotypical child, the autistic child is unable to achieve equanimity with separation because it is working with faulty tools that only serve to drive the autistic child away from the loving human herd.

Tustin (1992/2021) terms this a type of psychosis likening autistic children’s “traumatic psychological birth” to Bion’s (1962) psychological catastrophe. Bion’s “psychological catastrophe” is a visual, archaeological, and ballistic metaphor. Where Freud saw the unconscious more like a neat set of sedimented layers, Bion saw it more like the crater of a mortar blast—with different layers mixing and interweaving, like the debris of a warzone. Tustin (1992/2021) harnesses this metaphor to theorize autistic children’s development where, in her words, "later stages have been experienced precociously and out of phase, alongside current and earlier stages, in a confused and disordered fashion" (p. 107). Autistic developmental phases, in her neurotypical eyes, become "jumbled" and "telescoped" as a result of the autistic child's repetition compulsion—their constant repetition of the traumatic catastrophe of their separation from mother, and the faulty objects they resort to that, for Tustin, only make matters worse.

In this metapsychology, autistic development is a psychotic cascade where autism repetitively reinforces itself and resists social symbols. This "jumbled" and "precocious" autistic condition spawns autistic objects. Unlike the vaunted Winiccottian transitional object (1971), the phantasy associated with the autistic object (if there is any at all) is "crude" and "very close to bodily sensations" (p. 124). Use of these objects keeps the child in a crude, bodily place. The autistic object is a barrier, not a bridge—a paradoxical shell that is both necessary for survival and antithetical to aliveness, beauty, and civilized humanity because it robs the child of shared symbols. Without the capacity to create and share symbols, the child cannot access theory of mind, empathy, play, creativity, joint attention, language that is alive and enlivening and the capacity to self-soothe. For all her treacly tenderness toward the autistic condition, Tustin firmly locates herself in the catastrophic site of the pathology paradigm of autism.

Tustin (1992, 2021) lists several key characteristics of autistic objects. They are generally "hard" objects that protect the "soft" child from the experience of a "hard" world. Autistic objects are also unrealistic—meaning, "they are not used in terms of the function for which they were intended" (p. 124). She clarifies that a "realistic point of view" recognizes that autistic objects are used in ways that are "unrealistic and meaningless" while adding that the autistic child experiences them as, "absolutely essential" (p. 124). For me, these claims to reality are the site of the catastrophe of relational breakdown. Tustin has installed herself as the voice of the real and realism and from a patronizing, symbolic [sic], remove locates the autistic child as understandably, but pathetically, using hard objects to protect themselves from an overwhelming and intrusive world. But what if the autistic child has a point?

Before considering the point of view of the autistic child, I would like to address the way that Tustin cautions us from doing just that. For Tustin, adults' naive respect for autistic objects demonstrates, "their power to keep the autism going and to get others to collude with it" (p. 127). It is somewhat unclear whether the "their" refers to autistic objects' or autistic children's power. Analysts frequently struggle with they / them / their. Either way, it is a malevolent, controlling, infectious power against which parents and therapists must remain vigilant for it is born in a place where mother's (civilizing) love is refused—"autistic children . . . lack civilizing relationships with other human beings" (p. 128). If adults are not vigilant, they will become autistic objects themselves—drawn into sticky crude of autism.

Tustin's (1992/2021) writing is most revealing when she allows herself a musing about the link between autism and society. For example, "the autistic child (or the autistic child in all of us) is always trying to rubber-stamp the world in terms of rigid systems which seem to be 'me'" (p. 133). Later rhetorical flourishes link autism with bigotry," "fanaticism," "perversion," and "fetishistic objects" (p. 133, 138). These are all the pathological outgrowth of a person who is unable to wait, to use imagination in that period of waiting to cope, to symbolize what is lost and outside of the body, to build a bridge to reality and relationship, in other words, to live a life worth living. If this smells like a shitty projection, perhaps Tustin's characterizations of autism are a bit too on the nose.

The defining features of autistic objects—hardness, circularity, rigid use, and lifelessness also reveal Tustin's (1992/2021) technical and theoretical limitations. I would like to play an autistic game—pronomial ambiguity. The following is a quote from Tustin. When reading it, ask yourself, "what/who is the referent for the they/them in this statement?"

> As a result of the paucity of fantasy in them, they are used in an extremely canalized and repetitive fashion. They are static and do not have the open-ended qualities which would lead to the development of new networks of association. They are the result of, and result in, vicious circles of activity which become entrenched. It is inevitable that writing about them should become imbued with this circularity to some extent. (pp. 124–25)

The they/them above refers to autistic objects ("dominated by sensation") but could also reference autistic children. This is consistent with the incantatory descriptions of them Tustin offers across hundreds of pages. Alternately, they/them reflects a confusion between Tustin and her object (autistic object/autistic child).

Take this quote—"For the *child*, an autistic object is primarily a *sensation*. But the observer is aware of the object which provokes the *sensation*" (p. 128). Autistic children provoke sensations in us. So, do our own internal objects. The delicate dance of the two is what I feel is meant by the idea of a relational psychoanalysis—and countertransference. Some may find it overwhelming, even unbearable, to *be with* an autistic child and their autistic object(s). Many would object that the potential of *being with* such children (in any kind of psychoanalytic sense) is slim to nonexistent. It can be hard to be with the other acknowledging the gulf of separation between us.

Tustin's autistic object offers us delusory protection from this reality. For, "in times of extreme crisis, hard autistic objects are liable to seem to break under the strain and to let the child down" (p. 134). The powerful sensations of countertransference can lead to the tragic catastrophe of letting the child down. Tustin's writing suggests she is making use of autistic children as a kind of autistic object—perhaps in response to, "the frustration of unbearable disappointment" (p. 132) she projects into the child. "Another result is that the children themselves are vulnerable to being manipulated as autistic objects instead of being treated as human beings. The *echo-praxia* of some autistic children is an extreme example of this" (p. 132). And what of this analyst's echopraxia?

Reading these descriptions of accounts of clinical work with autistic children leaves much to be desired—play, empathy, creativity, the free web of associations. Tustin has painted herself into a corner where those things, the elements of psychoanalysis, are not possible in the analytic treatment of an autistic child. In the face of intense countertransference, she turns away from the child, so that she may theorize how to rescue it from itself and, by extension, all of society from them. For there is nothing prosocial about an "unrecovered" autistic child. By rescuing children from their autism, Tustin is doing (civilizing) work. And much like the missionary's recourse to refrain, Tustin engages in a kind of echopraxia of her own—the echopraxia of the pathology paradigm of autism. It is as if the treatment room holds two people, echoing off of themselves, as they struggle to establish connection, or, even, the desire for connection.

My use of the word missionary is intentional in my critique of this British author writing in the wane of British empire in the late twentieth century. Tustin's descriptions of the hazards of therapy with autistic children parallels the description of the primitive other in colonial discourse. She speaks about autistic capacities with appropriate reverence but is equally suspicious of them when they refuse the observation and influence of the civilizing therapist. Take for example, autistic children's drawings. Tustin likens these to "the cave paintings of primitive man" (p. 153), noting that, like cave paintings, they are infused with the magic of symbolic equation (art involves a doing to) and created with the intent to "control" or "dominate." These children do not make use of the civilizing function of the symbol, the ultimate psychoanalytic crime, Tustin warns one of the greatest dangers is that the therapist will sleep on an autistic child's tendency to ape the symbolic—to appear *as if* they know how to use symbols for communication and connection while all the while using these to control, dominate, and devastate much like the, "sympathetic magic in which a replica of a person is stuck with pins in order to annihilate that person" (p. 154). The sticky crude of autism is always there, ready to pull the child (and the unwitting therapist deceived by them) into the heart of darkness—the asymbolic and anti-human.

Tustin offers us sound advice for this dilemma when she cautions, "we do not interpret in terms of the *content* of the picture, but in terms of the child's *intentions*" (p. 154). Because she views autism as antithetical to development (of the child, and of society) Tustin figures autism asymbolically—that is, in a way that speaks more to a rupture between her and autism than to a meaningful psychoanalytic encounter with it. Despite the empathic and concerned content of her message, Tustin's intent is decidedly neuronormative—a kind of neurodevelopmental missionary who, at times, sees therapy as a rescue project for autistic children, which actively distrusts their voices, and compels them to deny the things that make them themselves all for the desire of the Other.

A poignant example of this is her remarks on hand flapping. Flapping hands have become a rallying point (a social symbol?) for autistic community. Generally, flapping hands is a stand in for the broad array of motoric stereotypies and repetitive behaviors autistic people exhibit. They may occur because of excitement, (over)stimulation, or upset and they are an object of scorn and remediation in many clinical circles. Autistic communities have reclaimed hand flapping as a natural (to autistics) way of being and expressing that being. Rather than reflecting a failure of psychic containment (as Tustin suggests), hand flapping is the mechanism by which autistics contain ourselves and each other. It is radical to move a body in non-normative ways. Try it sometime on an academic panel or in the walls of a psychoanalytic institute. And if repetition is the form of the action, it has the added bonus of getting analysts to (masturbatorily) speculate on how much like masturbation it is and what an unrepentant masturbator you are.

The reader may by now recognize the maneuver—Tustin encounters a phenomenon that she finds challenging because of its radical difference, she then creates a narrative of a lost child trapped in the horror of that difference, only to legitimize an unusual (for psychoanalysis) intervention. When discussing hand flapping, she advocates for more *active* approaches, "which take the form of holding the child's hands when he is flapping them or using them for his idiosyncratic stereotypies" (p. 176). She likens the child flapping hands to someone in a state of tantrum or ecstasy. The child is in a state of physical overwhelm without containment. Crude oil must be distilled to be productive—a hands on approach.

Tustin steps in, grabs hands, and begins her incantations. "I can hold it for you . . . There's no need to flap . . . There's no need to rub your hands together . . . Tustin is holding the upset . . . Tustin is holding the flap . . . Tustin is holding you together." The power of Christ compels you (Friedkin, 1973).[3] Properly *handled* [emphasis mine], [tantrum and ecstasy] can stimulate mental growth and development. If they are left to "flap" around in an uncontained way, pathological autistic maneuvers are exacerbated (pp.176–77). She adds that she repeats these and similar phrases, "over and over again." Whose ehcolalia is pathology? Tustin intrepidly works to contain the ecstatic overwhelm of the autistic child whose body will not be contained by the symbol. And like a true missionary, she cannot accomplish this without laying hands on the child.

Despite Tustin's apparent tendency to confuse her struggle to relate with the other with the other's obvious bad intentions, we can acknowledge her likely laudable intentions in offering a therapeutic alternative to behaviorism—which acknowledges no possibility of an autistic theory of mind. Does psychoanalysis not interrogate the very "possibility" of this for anyone? Perhaps she was confused by the similarities and caught up in the messy web of associations that permeate the symbolic. There is something at once tragic and poignant about reading the flapping hands passage. I am by no means in disagreement with the experience of overwhelm that comes with being autistic and the therapeutic potential of playing to contain this overwhelm. But playing, in the Winiccottian (1971) sense, requires two real people doing real things, which means an acknowledgment of each by the other as real and really playing. Hands restraining hands are not playing.

My link to *The Exorcist* above, is more than a playful nod to my alma mater. When the analyst swerves out of a relational space and into a position of power over a pathologized child, the treatment begins to look like an exorcism. In this instance, the analyst seeks to forcibly remove autism from the child or extinguish it through "containment." The relational tradition in psychoanalysis (e.g., Aron, 2001; Mitchell, 1988), and the post structural theorists I have discussed above challenge the notion of a knowing expert, acting with good intentions, by applying power to the mind/body of a marginalized person. Theories that criticize the shibboleths of modern epistemology often resist offering neat definitions—part of their project is to critique how authoritative definitions become problematic. As an alternative, relational theorists speak to ideas like co-construction and the relational field as the site of meaningful encounter between analyst and patient. This preserves some sense of mutuality between patient and analyst. Similarly, the post structural critics I cite are, perhaps, more cautious about offering definitions and prescriptions but, in their place, do outline guiding orientations and inquiry for further work. This chapter has advocated for the importance of this humility.

Tustin is onto something by wondering about the symbolic and containment in work with autistic children. But I disagree with her project, which, to me, appears to be caught up in mistrust of autistic being and expert definitions offered from the outside. Lacan's (1975/1991) critique of the analyst's ego seems relevant here. Deligny (2015) introduced a related concept—wanting. This brings us to the concluding section of this chapter, where I hope to gesture toward an alternative psychoanalytic model of work with autistic people, one that acknowledges the reality and legitimacy of their being as a true psychoanalytic relationship. It begs the question, is psychoanalytic therapy for autistic children possible if it does not require the analyst to lay hands on the child?

THE ARACHNEAN

Fernand Deligny founded a commune for nonverbal autistic children in the French mountainside during the 1980s. He was well versed in psychoanalysis and contemporary with Deleuze, Guattari, and Althusser. His collection of texts and photographs in *The Arachnean and Other Texts* (2015) counter the normative psychoanalytic project of creating subjects by drawing our attention to networks. His descriptions of networks have all the wonder of someone drawing your attention to a spiderweb. He does not offer a sharp definition of the network, in part, because he is critiquing the work of definition through language (as am I). Networks refer to organizations of (non) human relationship that are becoming, indeterminate, and most effective without outside intrusion. True to the theories of his contemporaries, Deligny privileges indeterminacy with words like *vague* ("a wave . . . movement of the water's surface") and *vaguer* ("to stray, to wander about at random" [p. 37]). His writing is not academic, in the sense of using deductive logic to establish an argument, but it is alive. It is alive and striving with a concept he describes as the network.

Deligny draws our attention to the network by demonstrating it in the form of his writing. Rather than define the network, he invites us to be with it. The network is indeterminate and becoming, perhaps like the rhizome (Deleuze and Guattari, 1987). What it lacks in definition, it makes up for by tracing the value of being-with that does not make demands of the other. Deligny's network at times seems to reference the drawings and movements of the autistic children, the mode of being of autism, and the potential realized in relationships where one party does not attempt to rescue/cure another. Like a spiderweb, the network is always being built, in ways humans cannot force, but can certainly destroy. I read this as a critique of expertise that applies itself to other bodies. Diagnosis, definition, and the deficit structures of autism risk overburdening the autistic child and, implicitly, something of the potential of the human relationship.

Deligny appears to walk a wandering and narrow path in his exposition of the network, where he attempts to write about his object while allowing it to be itself. Whether achievable or not, the intention matters, and his writing reflects sensitivity to overburdening relationship like "those beings who have difficulty tolerating the notion that things make themselves and prefer to believe that they make them with full knowledge of cause and effect" (p. 36). Before burdening autistic people with our expectations of their functioning, perhaps we could tolerate the notion that autistic people also make themselves.

The network is like a spiderweb, out of the direct control of humans, even as it connects with them, much like the way a spider uses a nook as the foundation of its web. Deligny is much less concerned with what humans can do to preserve the network (perhaps a sign of "wanting") and much more concerned with the ways that humans destroy networks (and networks' recurring persistence—you can dash a spiderweb, but more will come). He uses terms like wanting and the thought-out project to express concern about the ways that productivity, control, and "an excess of purpose" destroy networks—and harm the humans in them. The excess of purpose is a "drilling project" (p. 41) that leaves the network in tatters and drives its architect, the Arachnean, away. For, "networks are woven outside the abusive grip of society" (p. 41).

That abusive grip extends to children. Deligny's writing visits nature—spiderwebs, beaver dams—in its meditation on the possibilities within and without society's overburdening. Our ecology is overburdened. And, Deligny adds, the instinctual (the spider's spinning of its web) is devalued, in part, because it does not explain itself and defend its productivity. The network cannot be a thought-out project because the "thought out project demands to know what it is doing" (p. 45). It requires measurement, explication, recognition, and a return on investment. And if therapies aim to convert autistic children to neurotypicality, we might say that, at best, they only achieve, "an overburdening so constraining it passes for the network's way of being" (p. 42). If therapy succeeds in helping a child pass as (neurotypically) human, then it passes neurotypicality off as a true, and achievable, way of being—one that eclipses autistic being.

In this system, the newborn is like "a larva that has to be stuffed with acquired learning" which becomes "a matter of the ex-newborn becoming autonomous in learning to think (like everyone else)" (p. 49). This speaks to the tragic irony of making the autistic child like everyone else in the name of developing their autonomous functioning because the thought-out project involved deprives them of their autonomy and leads them to wander off the path. I suspect many will bristle at the suggestion that we let autistic children be (autistic) and Deligny saw this too. But he also saw what is lost when wanting pressures autistic children to function at higher levels in order to survive.

> There is always somewhere, who knows where, a High Court that watches over rights; where the flip side of the law, as it were, can be seen; if, under the pretext that, however "autistic" they may be, they indeed have the right to want, even if

> they haven't acquired the practice of the thought-out project, I inflict this right on them and condemn them to a likeness—an identity—that is all the more burdensome because it is fictitious. Certainly, they have a right to the higher level; but what can they do with this right, if not live the disarray of extravagating, which literally means to wander off the path. (p. 50)

The fractionating column may drive autistic children to higher levels of functioning, but it does so by transmuting them into something unrecognizable through a process which is unsustainable.

What alternatives exist? To answer this, we must allow ourselves to wander. We may also need to suspend the thought-out project of the symbolic. The network is never fully outside the symbolic. But the symbolic order, Deligny suggests, closes off potential connections or, we might say, the free web of associations. Or rather, it incompletely structures the network, much like the nook in which a spider builds its web. What if the analysis of autistic children could serve as such a nook, one that supports them weaving their web, a home for the Arachnean, rather than leaving it tattered by laying hands? We can learn something from Deligny's aim, "to limit [himself] to the ingenuity of innate action, to be awed by it, and not to try and clear up its mysteries" (p. 47). Here I am reminded of the innateness of flapping hands and open to the possibilities of what could happen if we allowed ourselves to be more awed by its mysteries.

At this late stage, our wandering returns to Yergeau (2018), and their proposition of autistic entelechies. They draw upon Aristotle's definition of entelechy, "a finality or cause that is possessed within and unto itself" to distinguish between normative entelechies, "with which . . . psychoanalysts . . . behold and thereby decompose the autistic" and autistic entelechies (p. 75). They define the latter as being, "noteworthy for their *perseveration and persistence* (emphasis mine) rather than their im/perfection" (p. 75). Yergeau (2018) seems to be calling attention to movement, indeterminacy, and striving which is not far off from Deligny's (2015) attention to wandering and instinct. Motion, striving, wandering. He reminds us these are verbs that do not require objects. Normative entelechies aim to nurture a seed into a plant but perhaps they also overstuff the larvae and thrash the Arachnean's web. Autistic entelechies are meaningful because of their very *movement* and only devalued in the thought-out projects of fractionating columns that objectify autistic people into neurotypicality. This reframing allows the analyst to move from a position of beholding (where they be holding) the child to draw them to higher levels of thinking like everyone else and to a position of awe, of radical being with, of movement and striving where the object need not be defined.

Perhaps the latter will ultimately be more sustainable because it does not view the autistic child as crude oil to be refined but embraces the sensations of flapping hands so that we may hear autistic voices—whether verbal or not. Perhaps this very chapter is not a symbol of codified expertise, but one of wandering with (wondering with) an autistic psychoanalyst. Can one be an autistic psychoanalyst? It may only require asking, what would it mean to wander in an analysis with an autistic child, free of the tattering laying of hands of the thought-out psychoanalytic project?

REFERENCES

Ahmed, S. (2010). *The promise of happiness*. Duke University Press. doi.org/10.1215/9780822392781.

American Psychiatric Association. (2013). *Diagnostic and statistical manual of mental disorders* (5th ed.). https://doi.org/10.1176/appi.books.9780890425596.

Aron, L. (2001). *A meeting of minds: Mutuality in psychoanalysis*. Routledge. /doi.org/10.4324/9780203767214.

Bion, W. R. (1962). *Learning from experience*. Karnac.

Butler, J. (1990). *Gender trouble*. Routledge. doi.org/10.4324/9780203824979.

Clements, R., and Musker, J. (Directors). (1989). *The little mermaid*. [Film]. Buena Vista Pictures.

Czech, H. (2018). Hans Asperger, national socialism, and "race hygiene" in Nazi-era Vienna. *Molecular Autism*, 1–43. https://doi.org/10.1186/s13229-018–0208–6.

Deleuze, G., and Guattari, F. (1987). *A thousand plateaus: Capitalism and schizophrenia* (B. Massumi, Trans.). University of Minnesota Press.

Deligny, F. (2015). *The arachnean and other texts* (D. S. Burke and C. Porter, Trans.). Univocal Publishing.

Foucault, M. (1995). *Discipline & punish: The birth of the prison* (A. Sheridan, Trans.). Random House. (Original work published 1977.)

Foucault, M. (2003). *Society must be defended: Lectures at the College De France 1975–1976* (D. Macey, Trans.). Picador. (Original work published 1997.)

Foucault, M. (2003). *Abnormal: Lectures at the Collège De France, 1974–1975* (G. Burchell, Trans.). Picador. (Original work published 1999.)

Friedkin, W. (Director). (1973). *The exorcist*. [Film]. Warner Bros.

Hull, L., Mandy, W., Lai, M-C., Baron-Cohen, S., Allison, C., Smith, P., and Petrides, K. V. (2019). Development and validation of the camouflaging autistic traits questionnaire (CAT-Q). *Journal of Autism and Developmental Disorders*. *49*(3), 819–33. https://doi.org/10.1007/s10803-018–3792–6.

Lacan, J. (1991). *The seminar of Jacques Lacan book 1: Freud's Papers on Technique 1953–1954*. (J. A. Miller Trans.). W. W. Norton & Company. (Original work published 1975.)

Mitchell, S. (1988). *Relational concepts in psychoanalysis: An integration*. Harvard University Press.

Tustin, F. (1992). *Autistic states in children*. Routledge. (2021)

Wilkenfeld, D. A., and McCarthy, A. M. (2020). Ethical concerns with applied behavior analysis for autism spectrum "disorder." *Kennedy Institute of Ethics Journal, 30*(1), 31–69. https://doi.org/10.1353/ken.2020.0000.

Winnicott, D. W. (1971). *Playing and reality*. Routledge.

Yergeau, M. (2018). *Authoring autism: On rhetoric and neurological queerness*. Duke University Press.

NOTES

1. Authors use the editorial convention [sic] to indicate that they recognize an error in the original source they are citing. I use [sic] to call into question the erroneous usage of terms like "high functioning autistic [sic]."

2. In the movie, Ariel, daughter of the, rather patriarchal, sea king, Triton, falls in love with a human man. Her father is of no help, so she turns to Ursula, the sea witch. Help comes as a bargain—in order to change form and fulfill her desire to be part of the human world, Ariel must surrender her voice.

3. In *The Exorcist*, a priest attempts to exorcise the demon possessing a young girl, Linda Blair. He frequently chants, "the power of Christ compels you."

Chapter 15

Negotiating Agency in the Formation of Subjectivity

The Child, the Parental Other, and the Sovereign Other

Michael O'Loughlin

My purpose in this chapter is to explore two types of events that expose children to peril.[1] The first refers to a challenge that all infants and children face, namely the complexity of taking in the symbolic system of the world through encounter with the parental Other. This encounter works tolerably well most of the time, but, as I will illustrate, occlusions, foreclosures, and misrecognitions—which may be unconscious on the part of the parent—can greatly complicate the construction of subjectivity and the development of the "going on being" that Donald Winnicott (1960a) noted as a marker in an infant of a sense of ease with the world. In extreme cases, as André Green noted, limitations on a child's capacity for self-definition, agency, and creativity may be so straitened that a child may be "forbidden to be" (1972, p. 152) and may fail to develop a capacity to think freely and give an account of themselves. The second type of precarity refers to children who experience misrecognition at the hands of sovereign authorities. A child may be placed in what Agamben (2005) calls a "state of exception" by virtue of their identity as a child who is indigenous, a refugee, orphaned by war or genocide, trafficked for child or sexual labor, a member of a caste, class, sexual, ethnic, racial, religious, or other out-group, or through growing up in a repressive or colonized society. Or, indeed, a child may grow up with parents or ancestors who have suffered such circumstances and may experience intergenerational sequelae of familial or collective suffering. Speaking of such affected groups,

Leonor Arfuch noted that the "radical disparity of the gaze" ensures that "the other does not attain the status of the human" (2020, p. 112). My goal is to explicate the melancholic sequelae of malignant familial and societal events and to ponder what might enable a child to nurture a capacity for imagining self as agentic and creative or even as deserving of the right to exist. I will conclude by exploring the potential of notions of radical performativity, critical relationality, and mutual interdependence to redress this suffering.

Embedded in a matrix of parental desire and societal strictures and expectations, a challenge exists for all children to figure out how to inhabit and then exceed these intertwined interpellations. The problem is particularly acute for children who experience what I describe below as metabolic excess due to living in a situation where emotional processing is occluded. Discussing family situations where children are exposed to material they cannot absorb, in his book *What is a child?*, Michael Gerard Plastow suggests that this unassimilable material will inevitably leak from the child in the form of symptoms, a phenomenon well understood by child psychoanalysts (cf., Mannoni, 1970; Mathelin, 1999). As Plastow notes, "[t]he symptom is the means by which the child is able to accede to his or her own truth, through an experience that exceeds the place reserved for the child by the mother and father" (2015, p. 101). While finding one's own truth is a challenge for children raised in emotionally turbulent families, the level of precarity is escalated for those who are raised in societies or groups where political repression, intergenerational trauma, or other forms of social hazard such as neoliberal social formations render the child's emotional experiences and creative impulses unnamable and unspeakable, and where the privilege of experiencing being may be denied.

FAILURE OF THE MIRROR: THE CONSEQUENCES OF FORECLOSURE, OCCLUSION, AND MISRECOGNITION

Entering the symbolic and cultural world presents risk for all infants. Jean Laplanche (1999) has noted the primacy of alterity in the formation of the unconscious. Our sense of ourselves as subjects can only come through experiencing an Other. Mirroring[2] is a fraught process because, in addition to overt intersubjective engagement, a caregiver also imparts unconscious knowledge to the infant or child.[3] The adult possesses an unconscious while the infant's is in formation. The inherent asymmetry of the caregiver-infant relationship means that there is a metabolic excess—that the infant necessarily takes in material that it is beyond its capacity to process (cf., Stack, 2005, p. 65). As Jean Wyatt noted, "the internalized trace of the parental other is never fully assimilated" (2006, p. 191). Laplanche states that the enigmatic nature of the signifiers that are beyond the child's capacity to metabolize form the basis of an unconscious—a residue that resists symbolization. In something as simple as unconsciously stroking an infant and experiencing pleasure from doing so, a mother for example, will deliver an enigmatic communication of erotic pleasure that the infant cannot process and that will leave an imprint on the emerging unconscious. Precarity increases when a caregiver has experienced considerable psychic trauma or has inherited such trauma intergenerationally. The psychoanalytic literature is replete with illustrations of the complexity for a child when a caregiver, either due to their own present emotional difficulties or due to inherited unmourned melancholy, transfers an emotional occlusion to their child instead of promoting the kind of symbiosis that would allow the child to experience agency and pleasure, to engage in reciprocal emotional exchange, and to begin to experience themselves as a formulator of thoughts. So, for every child, there is work to be done, but for a child with a misrecognizing parent, the burden is greater: These enigmatic signifiers that portend nameless dreads, foreclosure, and ungovernable inhibitions and desires do not lend themselves to easy formulation or understanding and can constrain a child's capacity to be free.

The term "ghost" is often used in the clinical literature to describe potentially malignant spectral remnants absorbed by an infant or child. Prophecy Coles (2011), for example, discussing the arrival of a sibling to replace one who has died, uses the term "sibling ghosts." Any unmourned loss, Coles states, is likely to transmit across generations and manifest as emotional blockage in descendants. Coles suggests that a replacement child is burdened with two impossible tasks: "to comfort the mother, and assuage her longing that the dead child might live" (2011, p. 29). The inherently social nature of subject formation is evident in Coles's formulation. Describing a child whose "sense of himself was forged upon the death of his brother," she says, "his self-identity was linked to his generational history" (p. 38). In "Ghosts in the nursery," Fraiberg, Adelson, and Shapiro capture the intergenerationality of this process:

> The intruders from the past have taken up residence in the nursery, claiming tradition and rights of ownership. They have been present at the christening for two or more generations. While no one has issued an invitation, the ghosts take up residence and conduct the rehearsal of the family tragedy from a tattered script. (1975, p. 388)

There is extensive documentation of the difficulties children of Holocaust survivors, for example, have experienced due to the undiscussability of their parents' losses.[4] Edward Emery links misrecogntion of a child's difference to confusional states on the mother's part that originate in unmourned losses:

> The intersubjective became a prison in which the ghost-within is the warden. The work of haunting foreclosed difference and instills in its place, mutual but oscillating confusional states . . . there is a deformation and ultimate breakdown of potential space. (2002, p. 173)

Nowhere is this discussed more clearly than in André Green's paper on the dead mother phenomenon (Green, 1972; Kohon, 1999). For a child in the presence of a psychically dead mother, Green suggests, that mother is transformed from a potential source of vitality into "a distant figure, toneless, practically inanimate" (1972, p. 142). This leads to severe impairment in the child's capacity for the kind of symbiosis that is so vital to the development of subjectivity. Such a child, instead of developing vitality and a robust capacity to reciprocate, will absorb the mother's mourning and develop a blankness at the core of its being. The infant will first respond by seeking meaning through reanimating the mother, Green says. When such efforts fail, the child will experience anxiety and dis-ease, and if no response is forthcoming, the child will "decathect the maternal object"[5] (1972, p. 150) and abandon all hope of reciprocity and meaning. The consequences for a child's capacity to develop future emotional relationships can be catastrophic:

> In truth, he will encounter the inability to love, not only because of ambivalence, but because his love is mortgaged to the dead mother. The subject is rich but he can gain nothing in spite of his generosity, for he does not reap enjoyment from it. (Green, 1972, p. 156)

In extreme cases, these dynamics can lead to psychosis (Aulagnier, 2001). In *One foot wrong,* Sofie Laguna (2008) presents an account of the life of a fictional child, Hester, whose capacity for being was so foreclosed by her disturbed parents that she descended into limitless psychosis. I worked for several years with a boy who was enmeshed with a mother who had been severely traumatized as a child. This mother was recovering from a recent hospitalization for psychosis. She attempted to keep this ten-year-old boy in a baby-like state so that he would not endure a painful childhood like the one she had experienced. In his first session with me, he drew a self-portrait with the word "SOS" emblazoned on the corner of the page, portending urgent knowledge of his precarity. Later, he drew a stick figure in a womb and captioned it "The boy who could not grow up." This boy's love was mortgaged to his psychically dead mother and his capacity for finding his own way was suspended if not foreclosed.

Renowned children's author, Maurice Sendak, grew up melancholic and preoccupied with death. When Sendak was a child, his parents explained to him the efforts they had made to abort him. While Sendak was fortunate to have an older brother and sister who mitigated the occlusion by serving as surrogate parents, he developed a melancholic disposition. His loss was compounded due to a particular recognition he was denied: Despite a happy relationship with his gay partner of fifty years, Maurice regretted being born gay because the blank refusal of his parents to acknowledge his queer identity left him profoundly melancholic.[6]

My life, too, has been shadowed by what Julia Kristeva (1982) refers to as "inaugural losses," and my life story illustrates the intertwining of familial and sociohistorical occlusions. I was born into a family genealogy in which my parents were descended from the poorest class of Irish people. They were only a few generations removed from the catastrophic losses of Ireland's Great Hunger. Living in abject poverty, in the shadow of colonialism and carrying an unsymbolized excess from their ancestors, they developed dispositions of fatalism and stoicism to endure their unmourned losses. My mother once remarked that there wouldn't be any point in talking with me about her life as she could not discuss "the bad things" as they were "too awful." I spent much of my first two years in hospital with a serious illness, and the hospital finally advised my parents to purchase a coffin and prepare for my death. In desperation, my father took me to the only other hospital in town where, in due course, I recovered. What did living with the knowledge of my potential death do to my mother, a woman whose own mother had died during her childhood, and who was prone to lifelong anxiety? How did my undoubted absorption of her unspeakable mortal anxiety affect my going-on-being? Could this be the root of the "nameless dread" I have periodically experienced? Wilfred Bion (1962) refers to nameless dread as a kind of free-floating anxiety that comes from a failure of emotional containment—in my case no doubt due to my mother's anxious preoccupation with death and my own knowledge of my dying. On the other hand, what of my father's bold action that insisted I should live? Could this have served as a source of vitality? Could it explain my persistence in the face of adversity? I grew up to be a cerebral, tentative, and hesitant child—holding thoughts and aspirations tightly but not daring to name them. Dutiful and parentified as a child, to this day I continue to labor in the shadow of "the tyranny of the should" (Horney, 2013)—an inexhaustible desire to do more and do it better—to make reparations for my existence.

The publication of my partly autobiographical book *The subject of childhood* (2009) was a coming-out moment for me. I was finally ready to render an account of myself and my origins. Unanimous rejection of the book by my family threw me into a tailspin. Finally, my siblings proposed that relations could resume if we agreed to forget that I ever wrote the book. Much like Sendak, I have found strands of recognition and mirroring elsewhere, but that primal loss resists resolution.[7]

PIERA AULAGNIER: BRIDGING FAMILIAL, SOCIAL, AND POLITICAL CONSIDERATIONS IN SUBJECT FORMATION

Mariana Wikinski (2021) notes that Piera Aulagnier's work is of particular interest because Aulagnier not only offers a description of the lacuna at the core of subjectivity when a child is subjected to metabolic excess within a family, but her work also allows us to understand how ideological systems such as colonialism, forced migration, state terror, etc., can erase genealogical filiations and leave humans bereft of capacity to anchor meaning and think freely.

Aulagnier begins with an analysis of how subjectivity is situated in discourse: The mother as "Speaking I" offers herself to the infant who, lacking a capacity to decode meaning, develops a pictographic representation of self from the tone, flow, and reciprocity of the mother's utterances. By her speech the mother "indicates to him the limits of the possible and the allowable" (2001, p. 11). If the child can receive the mother's speech pleasurably, Aulagnier suggests, these representations will form the core of subjectivity. However, if the mother's speech is violent and produces unpleasure, these inhospitable utterances will work against the consolidation of an I and the child will experience a blank space where intersubjectivity ought to reside. A certain kind of speech is prosthetic in the formation of an I. The outcome of the communication hinges on the mother's relative pleasure or unpleasure in being a mother. As the child enters the world of symbols, imposition of external cultural meanings is inevitable. The crux, Aulagnier notes, is whether the appropriation of culture can be accomplished in a way that leaves the child with a sense of agency; whether the child will accumulate unmetabolized material that will reappear later through deferred action;[8] or whether, in the most extreme case, occlusion is so totalizing and negating that the seeds of psychosis are set in place. As Aulagnier notes, when signification collapses "insanity is the extreme form of the only refusal acceptable to the I" (2001, p. 91). Judith Butler (1997) characterized this dilemma of subject formation as the tension embodied in the striving for emancipatory subjectivity in the context of societal constraints that delimit subjective possibilities and demand conformity and ultimately subjection.

If a child feels pressure to incorporate an alien and unpleasurable discourse, this will result in "the amputation of the subject's own psychical space" (Aulagnier, 2001, p. 52). The word-bearer of the family either demands conformity or, alternately, invites a child into a symbiotic dance in the play space of childhood (Mannoni, 1999). This potential space can be eroded even before the child's arrival if the child's genealogical destiny is foreclosed by those who "demand that the child conform to an image of the child that occupied the cradle long before the body was placed in it" (Aulagnier, 2001, p. 52).

RISKS IN THE ENTRY INTO FILIATION AND SOCIAL BELONGING

For the emerging subject, Wikinski notes, entry into "filiation, belonging, or social continuity" is essential and a major risk is that systems of occlusion such as colonialism and state terror sever these genealogical links and produce muteness, constriction, and lack of agency in the subject (2021, p. xvi).[9] Second to the word-bearing mother, the father serves as guarantor of societal continuity. Aulagnier points out that the linkage between psychic aspects of childrearing and the imperatives of cultural indoctrination is inescapable:

> Every society privileges what encourages the status quo and its models, a status quo that is defended at first by those who are privileged by those models. But it must be understood that no society would succeed in doing so if it could not use the force of violence that it exerts . . . in order to preserve the illusion that what, in fact, is in the service of conservative intentions conforms to the needs of the psychical structure. (2001, p. 107)

Summarizing the "narcissistic pact" through which a child gains a sense of belonging by entering a totalizing identification with a group, Stefania Pandolfo underlines both the necessity and risk of this pact for the infant and child:

> The "narcissistic pact" permits the subject to project herself or himself into an ideal community, to have a place and title through which she or he can articulate a singular voice within a chorus of other voices. But there are situations in which the pact is "falsified at the outset" by the dynamics within the family or by the group, which refuses to grant what Aulagnier calls a "*droite de cite*" (a right to belong)—or proposes an exploitative, slavish, or unacceptable contract. The subject is thus arbitrarily dispossessed of the place that would have been her own, through a history of exclusions within the family, a history that is often enough mirrored in the social world. (2018, p. 49)

Access to historicity and ancestral lore is critical to cultural regeneration (Atkinson, 2002). The question of interest in the remainder of this essay is what happens when this genealogical continuity is ruptured by alien ideological forces and the meaning-making capacity of a child is silenced or erased. With respect to sovereign authority, a danger is that a child's own desires will be annulled as the child learns that "an Other decides in all sovereignty the order of the world and the laws according to which its own psyche ought to function" (Aulagnier, 2001, p. 182). While there is a risk of "the collapse of a future tense" (Aulagnier, 2001, p. 114) for any child, the risk is much greater for those born into states of exception than for those born into privilege. The latter may use education, mobility, therapy, cultural capital, etc., to find their way to a position of desire and narrative possibility. The picture is far bleaker for those for whom the sovereign has sought to foreclose subjective possibilities.

DISPOSSESSION: EFFECTS OF SEVERANCE OF GENEALOGICAL FILIATIONS AND SOCIAL LINKS

It is hard to miss precarity writ large in the lives of children. One need only think of those children hovering between life and death as they seek to make the perilous ocean journey from Turkey or Libya to Greece. There is the searing image of a migrant toddler, face down on a beach in Bodrum, Turkey, and an equally harrowing image of a father and daughter drowned in the Rio Grande. Migrant children have been detained in inhumane conditions at borders across the world. Some children live their entire lives in refugee camps, as do their children, and their children's children. Others are victims of genocides, wars, and the devastation increasingly wrought by climate change.[10] Leonor Arfuch quotes Judith Butler on the striking asymmetry in the life chances of people:

> [c]ertain lives will be highly protected, and the abrogation of their claims to sanctity will be sufficient to mobilize the forces of war. Other lives will not find such fast and furious support and will not even qualify as "grievable." (Butler, 2004, quoted in Arfuch, 2020, p. 112)

Jacqueline Bhabha (2011, 2014) has documented the legal precarity of children who are othered by sovereign authorities. Anthropologists and political scientists have characterized such outcast persons as disposable, as rubbish, as vermin, as living in a state of exception or bare life or social death. Achille Mbembe (2019) draws our attention to the explicitly necropolitical intention of sovereigns who develop policies that ensure the continuance of extreme inequality for out-groups.[11] In *Dispossession,* Athena Athanasiou engages Judith Butler in a conversation about the losses that produce a sense of dispossession—a state of non-being—in a person. Butler and Athanasiou focus particularly on "processes and ideologies by which persons are disowned and abjected by normative and normalizing powers" (2013, p. 1). The authors are very clear that the logic of dispossession is one in which sovereigns allocate precarity by violently imposing non-being on selected others, deciding

> who can be wasted and who cannot; it distinguishes those who are disposable from those who are not . . . by rendering certain communities or populations unintelligible, by eviscerating them of the conditions of possibility for life and the "human" itself. (p. 20)

This precarity is enacted through a process of "subjugation, surveillance, and interpellation" (p. 12). Both in the colonial order and in the contemporary neoliberal social order, Butler and Athanasiou note, subjectivity for the privileged is brought about by desubjectifying their Others, "rendering them usable, employable, but then eventually into waste matter" through systems that normalize privilege for some and sanction precarity for others (p. 27). For participants in out-groups, seeking recognition as fully human the price of admission is high: "[c]onferred recognition as humans according to the established norms of recognizability" is only granted, they note, "on the condition of and at the cost of conforming to these norms" (p. 36). An insidious part of this process is interpellating such persons with a belief in the necessity of their own precarity:

> Precarity . . . describes the process acclimatizing a population to insecurity. It operates to expose a targeted demographic to unemployment or to radically unpredictable swings between employment and unemployment producing poverty and insecurity about the economic future, but also *interpellating that population as expendable.* [Emphasis added] (p. 43)

Invoking Frantz Fanon's (1967) reference to the impossibility of recognition in the colonial context, Butler and Athanasiou suggest that emancipation is foreclosed:

> The indigenous colonized subject—as a discursive byproduct of the colonialist historical condition—is absolutely deprived of any of the kind of mutuality that the very possibility of formulating the political claim of recognition would require. (p. 78)

Sovereign authority sets out to rupture genealogical filiations and erase ancestral and historical memory to produce paralyzing self-abasement and ideological interpellation. The result is a subjectivity severed from history and characterized by melancholy.[12]

ALGERIA: AN ILLUSTRATIVE CASE OF ERASURE OF SUBJECTIVE POSSIBILITIES

Karima Lazali (2021) explores the subjectivity of contemporary Algerians, meditating on their brutal colonial history as well as continuing suffering under a fundamentalist Islamic regime.[13]

The core of the wound to subjectivity, Lazali notes, is a lack of a sense of belonging that is rooted in a severance from genealogical histories. Subjected to totalizing ideology, language erasure, religious fundamentalism, and political authoritarianism, Algerians internalized amnesia and a sense of absoluteness that chokes their capacity for meaning. French colonial authorities adopted a version of what came to be known in Australia as *terra nullius* (Coleman, 2017)—a declaration that nothing existed prior to the arrival of the colonists:

> The rich history embodied in the land's languages, myths, poetry, and traditions had been abandoned. Designating the autochthonous population *"indigènes"* attests to this fantasy of a people without history—the founding myth of coloniality. (Lazali, 2021, p. 33)

There were also physical massacres and forced displacements designed to rupture social links and destroy genealogical continuity in storytelling, religious practices, childrearing, etc. As Lazali observes, "the '*indigènes*' were treated like beasts" (p. 37). More pernicious still, the colonial regime set out to erase its own origins, interpellating its colonial subjects with an ideology of racial inferiority and a demand that they adopt the role of supplicants in a colonial capitalist economy. Torture, starvation, internment, and deportation reduced humans to "nameless bodies . . . held in constant suspicion on religious and racial grounds" (p. 41). A way out for some was through *mimicry* of their colonial masters (H. Bhabha, 1994):

> French nationality was reserved for a select group of "*indigènes*," most frequently French-speaking individuals who had strayed from their social traditions. Nationality was therefore granted to individuals who were seen to be linguistically close to France, and more important still, who were seen as having severed ties with the language and traditions they were associated with. (Lazali, 2021, p. 41)

By dismantling the symbolic system of shared cultural values and by forcing Algerians to adopt Francophone names, the colonizers created genealogical wreckage that yielded a collective dispossession of subjective identity. The narcissistic pact was thereby falsified and Algerians had to identify with a narrative of dispossession:

> The colonial practice of unnaming bodies and land could have no other effect but this. It imposed itself on the bodies and places of the autochthonous population while stripping the land of its historical and linguistic past. Dispossession is thus complete, triggering a widespread phenomenon of depersonalization. . . . This shows the scale of colonialism's destruction of the symbolic order. It didn't so much repress history as *preclude* it, which is to say erase it irremediably. [Italics in original] (p. 54)

Toward the end of her study, Lazali discusses how children in Algeria have disappeared at an alarming rate in recent years and how mutilated corpses of children were discarded as trash. Lazali interprets this as an internalization in the psyche of a spectral remnant of the violence and forced disappearances indigenous Algerians have suffered:

> Disappearance, sexual abuse, dismemberment of bodies, and the way some bodies have been discovered (in trash bags, at the bottom of wells), attest to the treatment of the body as a worthless object, worse even than a corpse, no longer worthy of burial. . . . How can one explain this cruelty unleashed on children, where History "becomes flesh"? How can the living be concerned with anything except disappearance and mutilation? (pp. 204–5)

In *History Beyond Trauma*, Davoine and Gaudillière (2004) point to psychosis as a logical outcome of catastrophic occlusion. As I noted elsewhere,

> Davoine and Gaudillière argue for an artfully attuned listening that recognizes the historical and ancestral communication that is potentially embedded in psychic disturbance: "Sometimes," they write, "a fit of madness tells us more than all the news dispatches about the leftover facts that have no right to existence" (2004, p. xxviii). They describe psychosis as destruction of "autobiographic consciousness." Lacking an Other with the capability to respond truthfully to the knots of their souls, persons experiencing psychosis are destined to experience "an interiority invaded by annihilation, anxiety, and stress" (p. 129). Drawing on the work of Lionel Bailly, Davoine and Gaudillière conceptualize childhood psychosis, for example, as bringing back the voices of the dead—Derrida's (2006) spectral *revenants*—that haunt them:
>
> As the child psychiatrist Lionel Bailly puts it, when "children hear the voices of the dead "they are most often the voices of those who died without burial, without a rite. This brief hallucination will cease as soon as it is heard by a therapist in whom the voices of the dead can resonate instead of remaining in a dead letter. If the voice finds no echo, he says, "we have the seed of psychosis." (p. 145) (O'Loughlin, in press)

RADICAL PERFORMATIVITY, CRITICAL RELATIONALITY, AND INTERDEPENDENCE AS MODES OF REDRESS

Becoming a subject with an interior life, embodying a capacity for creativity and critical thought, and gaining a sense of belonging to a group requires an environmental provision that allows the child to absorb alterity without annihilating occlusion. It also requires the growing child to insert her- or himself into a lineage and a history. How might a child be invited into a situation of invigorating mutuality or critical relationality if occlusions—due to parental shortcomings, political repression, or a severance of genealogical lineage—have caused that child to take refuge in foreclosure? From a clinical perspective, André Green (1972) argues for the importance of revivifying experiences to create a transitional space in which a person might be invited into mutuality and experience the possibility of recognition and pleasure in such reciprocity.[14] Butler and Athanasiou, despite acknowledging the hazards of totalizing foreclosure, frame this question in terms of the possibility of radical performativity. Is it possible for us to be present to each other, they ask, in ways that are not delimited by the occlusions of our familial and societal circumstances? Is it possible to refuse to stay "in our proper place" (p. 21)? Is it possible to push back against norms in ways that "imply a dislocation of the sovereign subject" (p. 69)? The complication, of course, is that expecting an I that has been shaped by emotional foreclosure or forced amnesia to ask questions and to imagine her or himself otherwise is a tall order:

> So much depends on how we understand the "I" who crafts herself, since it will not be a fully agentic subject who initiates the crafting. It will be an "I" who is already crafted, but also who is compelled to craft again her crafted condition. (p. 70)

Agentic social engagement calls for an impulse toward mutuality, toward "becoming-with-one-another" and "beside ourselves" (p. 71) that allows us to absorb new alterities and expand our subjective possibilities. It is an open question as to whether this might be achievable. On the one hand, Butler and Athanasiou reiterate Fanon's pessimism—also echoed in Lazali's work in Algeria—that the colonial yoke can ever be lifted to allow for an aspiration of liberation. Narration of the self through a "self-poietics" (p. 93) matters, Butler and Athanasiou note, but they are wise enough to understand that this may not be sufficient to call the subject into an emancipatory or agentic position. A certain environmental provision is called for:

> . . . certain conditions for my aliveness and for my capacity to question have already to be opening me onto the world prior to any question of how I best ought to open myself. (p. 109)

As Butler and Athanasiou note, what is at issue here is "the vexed thematics of agency" (p. 14): Can the apparatus of recognition and normalization ever be disorganized so that individuals might experience a "performative proclamation of a self that has been undone and redone" (p. 65)? Or, as they also suggest, can we ever overcome "the cunning of recognition" (p. 75)? This is, of course, a pedagogical question, immortalized, as Butler and Athanasiou note, in Fanon's plea: "O, my body, make of me always a man who questions" (quoted on p. 80). Can we, then, imagine pedagogical systems that would enable children to begin to give an account of themselves (cf., Butler, 2001), in ways that would allow them to begin to deconstruct the systems of recognizability embedded in the familial, cultural, and political matrices within which they are embedded, and indeed from which they are constituted?[15] The potential of moving children from mere existence or subservience to ethical relationality and agentic possibility suggests that we should pursue this question with some urgency.

REFERENCES

Abraham, N., and Torok, M. (1994). *The shell and the kernel: Vol. 1*. N. Rand (Trans.). University of Chicago Press.

Agamben, G. (1998). *Homo Sacer: Sovereign power and bare life*. D. Heller-Roazen (Trans.). Stanford University Press.

Agamben, G. (2005). *State of exception*. K. Attell (Trans.). University of Chicago Press.

Ahmed, A., and Semple, K. (2019). Photos of drowned migrants captures pathos of those who risk all. *New York Times*. www.nytimes.com/2019/06/25/us/father-daughter-border-drowning-picture-mexico.html.

Ahmed, S. (2004). *The cultural politics of emotion*. Edinburgh University Press.

Anisfeld, L., and Richards, A. (2000). The replacement child: Variations on a theme in history and psychoanalysis. *The Psychoanalytic Study of the Child*, *55*, 301–18.

Apfelbaum, E. (2002). Uprooted communities, silenced cultures, and the need for legacy. In V. Walkerdine (Ed.), *Challenging subjects: Critical psychology for a new millennium* (pp. 78–87). Palgrave.

Arfuch, L. (2020). *Memory and autobiography: Exploring at the limits*. C. MacSweeney (Trans.). Polity Press.

Atkinson, J. (2002). *Trauma trails: Recreating song lines: The transgenerational effects of trauma in Indigenous Australia*. Spinifex Press.

Auerhahn, N., and Prelinger, C. (1983). Repetition in the concentration camp survivor and her child. *International Review of Psychoanalysis, 10*, 31–46.

Aulagnier, P. (2001). *The violence of interpretation: From pictogram to statement.* A. Sheridan (Trans.). Brunner-Routledge.

Bangs, L., and Jonze, S. (2009). [Directors]. *Tell them anything you want: A portrait of Maurice Sendak.* Oscilloscope.

Barlow, K. (2004). Critiquing The "good enough" mother: A perspective based on the Murik of Papua New Guinea. *Ethos, 32*(4), 514–37.

Bauman, Z. (2003). *Wasted lives: Modernity and its outcasts*. Polity Press.

Bernard, A., and Shoumali, K. (2015, Sep. 3). Images of drowned Syrian, Aylan Kurdi, 3, brings migrant crisis into focus. *New York Times*. www.nytimes.com/2015/09/04/world/europe/syria-boy-drowning.html.

Bhabha, H. (1994). *The location of culture*. Routledge.

Bhabha, J. (Ed.). (2011). *Children without a state: A global human rights challenge.* MIT Press.

Bhabha, J. (2014). *Children migration and human rights in a global age*. Princeton University Press.

Bion, Wilfred R. (1962). "A theory of thinking." *International Journal of Psycho-Analysis (43)*, 306–10.

Butler, J. (1997). *The psychic life of power: Theories in subjection.* Stanford University Press.

Butler, J. (2001). Giving an account of oneself. *Diacritics, 1*(4), 22–40.

Butler, J. (2004). *Precarious life: The powers of mourning and justice*. Verso.

Butler, J., and Athanasiou, A. (2013). *Dispossession: The performative in the political.* Polity Press.

Carrington, D. (2021, Aug. 20). A billion children at 'extreme risk' from climate impacts—Unicef. The Guardian. ttps://www.theguardian.com/environment/2021/aug/20/a-billion-children-at-extreme-risk-from-climate-impacts-unicef.

Caviston, P. (2016). *The mother in psychoanalysis and beyond: Matricide and maternal subjectivity*. Routledge.

Coleman, C. (2017). *Terra nullius*. Hachette Australia.

Coles, P. (2011). Sibling ghosts. In *The uninvited guest from the unremembered past* (pp. 27–42). Karnac.

Danon-Boileau, L. (2002). *The silent child: Exploring the world of children who do not speak.* Oxford.

Davoine, F., and Gaudillière, J-M. (2004). *History beyond trauma: Whereof one cannot speak, thereof one cannot stay silent*. Other Press.

Derrida, J. (2006). Hospitality. In G. Anidjar (Ed.), *Acts of religion* (pp. 356–420). Routledge.

Dickerson, C. (2019), June 21. 'There is a stench': Soiled clothes, no baths for migrant children at Texas Center. *New York Times*. www.nytimes.com/2019/06/21/us/migrant-children-border-soap.html.

Eigen, M. (1999). *Toxic nourishment*. Karnac.

Emery, E. (2002). The ghost in the mother: Strange attractors and impossible mourning. *Psychoanalytic Review, 89(2),* 170–94.

Erikson, K. T. (1976). Loss of communality at Buffalo Creek. *American Journal of Psychiatry, 133*(3), 302–5.

Ettinger, B. (2020). *Matrixial subjectivity, aesthetics, ethics.* G. Pollock (Ed.). Routledge.

Fanon, F. (1967). *Black skin, white masks*. Grove Press.

Fraiberg, S., Adelson, E., and Shapiro, V. (1975). 'Ghosts in the nursery,' *Journal of the American Academy of Child Psychiatry, 14,* 387–421.

Freud, S. (1950/1895). Project for a scientific psychology. In J. Strachey (Ed. and Trans.), *Standard edition of the complete psychological works of Sigmund Freud: Vol. I* (pp. 283–397). London, UK: The Hogarth Press. (Original work published 1895.)

Green, A. (1972). The dead mother. In *On private madness* (pp. 142–73). International Universities Press.

Greenspan, S., and Wieder, S. (2009). *Engaging autism: Using the Floortime Approach to help children relate, communicate, and think.* Da Capo Lifelong Books.

Hollway, W. (2016). Feminism, psychology, and becoming a mother. *Feminism & Psychology, 26*(2), 137–52.

Horney, K. (2013). *Neurosis and human growth.* Routledge.

Kaplan, L. (1996). *No voice is ever wholly lost: An exploration of the everlasting attachment between parent and child.* Simon & Schuster.

Khanna, R. (2009). Disposability. *Differences: A Journal of Feminist Cultural Studies, 20*(1), 181–98.

Khanna, R. (2003). *Dark continents: Psychoanalysis and colonialism.* Duke University Press.

Kohon, G. (1999). *The dead mother: The work of André Green.* Routledge.

Kristeva, J. (1982). *Powers of horror: Essays on abjection.* Columbia University Press.

Kristof, N. (2017, Jan. 6). As Donald Trump denies climate change, these kids die of it. *New York Times.* https://www.nytimes.com/2017/01/06/opinion/sunday/as-donald-trump-denies-climate-change-these-kids-die-of-it.html.

Lacan, J. (1994). *The four fundamental concepts of psychoanalysis.* J-A. Miller (Ed.). A. Sheridan (Trans.). Routledge.

Lacan, J. (2006). The mirror stage as formative of the *I* function as revealed in psychoanalytic experience. In J. Lacan, *Écrits* (pp. 75–81), B. Fink (Trans.). W. W. Norton.

Laguna, S. (2008). *One foot wrong.* Other Press.

Laplanche, J. (2017). *Après coup.* J. House and L. Thurston (Trans.). Unconscious in translation.

Laplanche, J. (1999). *Essays on otherness.* J. Fletcher (Trans.). Routledge.

Laub, D. (1995). Truth and testimony: The process and the struggle. In C. Caruth, *Trauma: Explorations in memory* (pp. 61–75). Baltimore: Johns Hopkins University Press.

Layton, L. (2010). Irrational exuberance: Neoliberal subjectivity and the perversion of truth. *Subjectivity, 3*(3), 303–22.

Lazali, K. (2021). *Colonial trauma.* M. W. Smith (Trans.). Polity Press.

Mannoni, M. (1970). *The child, his "illness," and the others*. Karnac.

Mannoni, M. (1999). *Separation and creativity: Refinding the lost language of childhood.* Other Press.

Margonis, F. (2016). Opting out of neocolonial relationality. *Philosophy of Education,* 1–13.

Mathelin, C. (1999). *Lacanian psychotherapy with children: The broken piano.* Other Press.

Matziaraki, D. [Director]. (2018). *4.1 miles.* https://www.youtube.com/watch?v=hjnj5B2GCvc.

Mbembe, A. (2019). *Necropolitics*. Duke University Press.

Mignolo, W. (2007). Delinking. *Cultural Studies, 21,* 449–514.

Mohdin, A. (2015), Nov. 30. When refuge camps last three generations, we must accept they're not going anywhere. *Quartz*. www.nytimes.com/2019/06/25/us/father-daughter-border-drowning-picture-mexico.html.

O'Loughlin, M. (2007). On losses that are not easily mourned. In L. Bohm, R. Curtis, and B. Willock (Eds.), *On deaths and endings: Psychoanalysts' reflections on finality, transformations, new beginnings* (pp. 103–20). New York: Routledge.

O'Loughlin, M. (2009). *The subject of childhood.* New York: Peter Lang Publishing.

O'Loughlin, M. (2010). Ghostly presences in children's lives: Toward a psychoanalysis of the social. **[AU: incomplete information]**

O'Loughlin, M. (2012). Trauma trails from Ireland's Great Hunger: A psychoanalytic inquiry. In L. Bohm, R. Curtis, and B. Willock (Eds.). *Loneliness & yearnings* (pp. 233–50). Routledge.

O'Loughlin, M. (2013). Reclaiming genealogy, memory and history: The psychodynamic potential for reparative therapy in contemporary South Africa. In C. Smith, G. Lobban, and M. O'Loughlin (Eds.), *Psychodynamic psychotherapy in contemporary South Africa: Contexts, theories, practices* (pp. 242–71). Johannesburg, SA: Wits University Press.

O'Loughlin, M. (2017a). The emergence of the speaking subject: Child therapy and the subject of desire. In B. Seitler (Ed.), *From cradle to couch: A remembrance of the work of Sylvia Brody* (pp. 360–83). New York: International Psychoanalysis Books.

O'Loughlin, M. (2017b). The possibility of nurturing a kernel of creativity in a child. In D. Caracciolo and C. L. Weida (Eds.), *The swing of the pendulum: The urgency of arts education for healing, learning, wholeness* (pp. 69–86). Rotterdam: Sense Publishers.

O'Loughlin, M. (2020). Whiteness in the psychoanalytic imagination. *Contemporary Psychoanalysis, 56*, 2–3, 353–74.

O'Loughlin, M. (2021). Western democracy and the necessity of the "illegal traveller." In A. Samuels and T. Singer Eds.)., ARAS Collections [Archive for Research in Archetypal Symbolism], Special Edition: 2020 Analysis and Activism/Presidency Conference proceedings. Available online at: aras.org/newsletters/aras-connections-special-edition.\.

O'Loughlin, M. (In press). Cultural ruptures and their consequences for mental health across generations: The case of Ireland. In I. Lambrecht and A. Lavis (Eds.), *Culture and psychosis.* Routledge.

O'Loughlin, M., and de Assis, R. (2021). The reduction of children to bare life: The case of child migration. In G. Cannella and T. Kinard. (Eds.), *Childhoods in more just worlds: An international handbook* (pp. 3–19). Myers Education Press.

O'Loughlin, M., and Johnson, R. (Eds.). *Imagining children otherwise: Theoretical and critical perspectives on childhood subjectivity* (pp. 49–74). New York: Peter Lang Publishing.

O'Loughlin, M., and Merchant, A. (2012). Working obliquely with children. *Journal of Infant, Child & Adolescent Psychotherapy, 11,* 149–59.

Pandolfo, S. (2018). *Knot of the soul: Madness, Psychoanalysis, Islam.* University of Chicago Press.

Patterson, O. (1982) *Slavery and social death: A comparative study*. Harvard University Press.

PBS. (2013). Maurice Sendak on "Being a kid": https://www.pbs.org/video/blank-blank-maurice-sendak-being-kid/.

Piontelli, A. (1992). *From fetus to child: An observational and psychoanalytic study.* Routledge.

Plastow, M. G. (2015). *What is a child? Childhood, psychoanalysis, and discourse.* Karnac.

Rogers, A. (2006). *The unsayable: The hidden language of trauma.* Random House.

Rothschild, L. (2017). Review of C. Yates: *The play of political culture, emotion and identity. Psychoanalysis, Culture & Society, 22*(4), 448–51.

Rothschild, L. (In preparation). *Rapprochement between fathers and sons: Breakdowns, reunions, potentialities.* Phoenix Publishing House.

Scheper-Hughes, N. (1997). People who get rubbished. *New Internationalist*, 295. https://newint.org/features/1997/10/05/people.

Stack, A. (2005). Culture, cognition and Jean Laplanche's enigmatic signifier. *Theory, Culture & Society, 22*(3), 63–80.

Stone, A. (2012). *Feminism, psychoanalysis and maternal subjectivity*. Routledge.

Wikinski, M. (2021). Foreword In K. Lazali, *Colonial trauma* (pp. viii–xviii). M. W. Smith (Trans.). Polity Press.

Winnicott, D. W. (1960a). The theory of the parent-infant relationship. *The International Journal of Psychoanalysis, 41,* 585–95.

Winnicott, D. W. (1960b). Ego distortion in terms of true and false self. In *The Maturational Process and the Facilitating Environment: Studies in the Theory of Emotional Development* (pp. 140–57). International Universities Press.

Winnicott, D. W. (1971). Mirror-role of mother and family in child development. In *Playing and reality* (pp. 149–59). Routledge.

Winnicott, D. W. (1974). Fear of breakdown. *International Review of Psychoanalysis, 1*, 103–7.

Wyatt, J. (2006). Laplanche's reconstruction of Freud's other-centered subject: The enigmatic signifier and its political uses. *Psychoanalysis, Culture & Society, 11*, 190–98.

Yates, C. (2015). *The play of political culture, emotion and identity*. Macmillan.
Zembylas, M. (2020). From the ethic of hospitality to affective hospitality: Ethical, political and pedagogical implications of theorizing hospitality through the lens of affect theory. *Studies in Philosophy of Education, 39*, 37–50.

NOTES

1. I wish to express my gratitude to Paula Salvio and Shilpi Sinha for valuable feedback on an earlier draft of this chapter.

2. For mirroring see, for example, Lacan (2006), Laplanche (1999), Winnicott (1971).

3. I employ the term "caregiver" here. Although there are dependencies between prenatal and postnatal life for mother and infant that privilege mother-infant interaction (cf. Hollway, 2016; Piontelli, 1992), feminist writers suggest that the common psychoanalytic notion of mothering denies the agency of the maternal subject. For critique and alternative theorizations of maternal subjectivity see, for example, Barlow (2004); Caviston (2016); Ettinger, (2020); Hollway, (2016); Stone (2012). In discussing authors such as Aulagnier, Emery, and Green, I will employ the term "mother," which is their term of art. Aulagnier, for example, sees quite different roles for fathers and mothers and Hollway (2016) discusses the elision of the mother's subjectivity through a shift in usage from "mothering" to "parenting." More work needs to be done in elucidating maternal and paternal dynamics in child subject formation.

4. See for example Anisfeld and Richards (2000); Auerhahn and Prelinger (1983); Kaplan (1996); Laub (1995); Rogers (2006).

5. Decathect = withdraw all attachment.

6. These notes on Maurice Sendak's childhood are drawn from a documentary by Bangs and Jonze (2009) as well as from a US public television animated video (PBS, 2013).

7. My published autobiographic and genealogical explorations include O'Loughlin, 2007, 2009, 2010, 2012, 2017a, b, 2020, in press.

8. This notion of deferred action, in which a traumatic event is stored unprocessed and can only be experienced later when the psyche may be able to handle it is referred to by Freud (1950/1895) as *Nachträglichkeit.* Lacan (1994) and Laplanche (2017) explore deferred action as *après coup,* while Winnicott (1974) speaks of *fear of breakdown* to describe a similar phenomenon.

9. For related writing on consequences of rupture of genealogical filiation and severance of social linkages see Abraham and Torok (1994), Atkinson (2002), Apfelbaum (2002), Davoine and Gaudillière (2004), Erikson (1976), O'Loughlin, (2013; in press).

10. For the Mediterranean passage see Matziaraki (2018). For Bodrum, see Bernard and Shoumali (2015); for Rio Grande, see Ahmed and Semple (2019); for migrant children at US border, see Dickerson (2019); for refugee camps that continue across generations see Mohdin (2015); for effects of climate change see Carrington (2021); Kristof (2017).

11. See Scheper-Hughes (1997) on people who get rubbished: Bauman (2003) and Khanna (2009) on disposable people; for state of exception and for bare life see Agamben (1998, 2005); for social death see Patterson (1982). For an overarching theory of necropolitics see Mbembe (2019). For an application of these ideas to international migration, including child migration, see O'Loughlin (2021), O'Loughlin and de Assis (2021).

12. See Abraham and Torok (1994), Khanna (2003), Lazali (2021), and Pandolfo (2018) for further discussion of the melancholic effects of rupture of social links.

13. The illustrative case presented her concerns the persistence of political repression and emotional occlusions in postcolonial Algeria. I should note that the argument has broader implications and there is considerable scholarship around the deleterious effects of neoliberal capitalism on the development of subjectivity and the elicitation of modes of performing subjectivity that are bogus and relationally hollow, as the work of Layton (2010), Rothschild (2017), and Yates (2015) as well as the foregoing discussion of Butler and Athanasiou's dialogue (2013) suggest. Further, in his forthcoming book, Louis Rothschild (In preparation) offers a nuanced psychoanalytic understanding of performativity. Drawing on Winnicott's (1960b) notion of *false self* and Eigen's (1999) discussion in *Toxic nourishment*, for example, he notes that while a child learns to smile early enough, they may also learn early to smile in bad faith.

14. See Danon-Boileau (2002), Greenspan and Wieder (2009), and O'Loughlin and Merchant (2012) for clinical examples of an invitation to symbiotic engagement and aliveness for children with difficulties in emotional communication.

15. Writing by educational philosophers drawing on Jacques Derrida's (2006) notion of hospitality, Walter Mignolo's (2007) notion of delinking from colonial legacies, and Sara Ahmed's (2004) work on the cultural politics of emotion, point toward the possibility of hospitable relationality as creating conditions for development of the kind of critical and ethical subjectivity under discussion here. See, for example Margonis (2016) and Zembylas (2020) for discussion.

Index

ADA. *See* Applied Behavioural Analysis
Abraham, N., 208n1, 258n9, 259n12
adhesiveness, 44, 47
adolescence, xiii, 5, 6, 12, 63–72, 75, 79–86, 89, 91
affectless states, 147
Africans, 185, 187, 188, 196
Afro-Italians, 176, 188
Agamben, G., 2, 241, 259n11
agency, 4, 5, 27, 144, 146–48, 168–70, 184, 241, 243, 246–47
agony, 151
aggression, 31, 43, 193–94, 198–99
Ahmed, S., 229, 258n10, 259n15
Alcorn Jr., M. W., 38
alpha function, 40, 42
alterity, 242, 252
Altman, N., 23, 197
Alvarez, A., 144, 146–48, 151, 154–55
ambivalence, 64, 72, 244
American Association of Pediatrics, 139
anaclitic depression, 143, 145
Anisfeld, L., & Richards, A., 194, 258n4
anorexia, 67
Aotearoa, 12, 109–15, 120–22
Apfelbaum, E., 258n9
Apollon, W., 54–55
Appiah, K. A., 203
Applied Behavioural Analysis, 15, 226, 227, 229
après coup, 246
Archangelo, A., 11, 42, 200
Arfuch, L., 242, 248, 253
Aristotle, 238
Aron, L., 235
Asian American, 148
Asperger's syndrome, 104, 226
asylum-seekers, 13, 133
asymbolic, 228, 230, 233
asymmetrical splitting, 203
Atkinson, J. 3, 247, 258n9
Auerhahn, N., 258n4
Aulagnier, P., 244, 246–47, 258n3
Auschwitz, 196
Austen Riggs Center, 216
Austria, 185, 196–97,
autism, 15, 104, 112, 145, 225–36
autosensuousness, 14
Ayman-Nolley, S., 163

Badiou, A., 12, 86
Baldwin, J., 201
Barad, K., 126, 133–34
Bass, A., 202
Baudendistel, R., 192n9, 198
Baudrillard, J., 6, 112–14, 122
Bauman, Z., 70, 259n11

Beck, U., 99, 106
Beebe, B., 154
Beghetto, R. A., 163
behaviorism, 227, 235
being without, 144, 146, 148, 151, 153, 155–56
Ben-Ghiat, R., 177–78
Benjamin, J., 194, 197, 199, 203
Benjamin, W., 28
Bernstein, R., 176, 180–81, 192n6, 207
Bertiglia, A., 13, 175–76, *177*, 179, *180*, 180, *182*, 183, 185, *186*, 192n6
betwixt and between, 75
Bhabha, H. K., 134, 250
Bhabha, J., 248
bilingualism, 127
Bion, W. R., 8, 14, 38–41, 44, 46–47, 149–53, 209–11, 230, 245
biopolitical, 80, 187, 229
black hole, 144, 150
Black, M. I., 14, 194, 195, 200–2
Black Skin, White Masks, 27, 30
Bond-Stockton, C. B., 181
Bonomi, C., 193–94
boredom, 30, 80, 83–86, 120
Branch Street children, 160, 165–69
bridge, 11, 39, 41–48
bullying, 52, 197
Burman, E., 11, 19–20, 24–25, 29–30
Butler, J., 4, 6, 164–65, 168, 203, 229, 247, 249, 252
Byatt, A. S., 209, 212–16

Callaway-Cole, L., 125, 136
capitalism, 5, 12, 25, 26, 63, 70, 71, 86–87, 90, 124, 169, 198, 207, 226, 259n13
Captain America, 198–99
Carlo Erba, S. A., 175, 190
catastrophic, 3, 4, 149, 152, 211, 218, 231, 244–45, 251
Catholic, 4, 179, 184, 189
cave paintings, 233
Cederman, K., 12, 109, 203
Charles, M., 14, 32, 209, 211–13, 216
Chen, V. H., 26, 34
cherubs, 14, 97, 107, 176
child: as method, 11, 15, 19, 25–26, 32, creative, 13, 159–60, 162–63, 166–68, 170–71, economically useless, 96, 103, labour, 95, 98, 'perfect,' 102
childhood: as cultural construction, 34, bourgeois, 159, creativity, 159, 160, 170, criminalisation of, 104, 'disorders' of, 104, 112–13, 156, 157, drawings, 120, 149, 150, 156, 233, 236, 'found,' 11, 19, 20–25, 27–28, 30, 32, 33, inherent creativity of, 160, 163, 171, innocence, 1, 14, 176, 179, 181–89, medicalization of, 104, normalized, 170, 'perfect,' 12, 95, 96, as 'spectacle,' 97, 103, 104, 107, super–saturated, 96, 98, 101
childing, 95–96, 98, 100–6
childrearing, 161, 247, 250
Christ, 234n3
Cindy, 155
citizenship, 176–77, 181, 187–89
city project, 11, 53, 55
civil rights, 189, 197
Civil War, 137, 196
Coates, T.-N., 197–202
code: noir, 197, switching, 198
cognitive: deficits, 144, 148, 154, development, 127, 148
cohabitation, 187
Coles, P., 243
Colonial: discourse, 233, natives, 179, *180*, 180, 184, 186, postcards, 13–14, 175–76, *177*, 179, *180*, 180–83, *182*, 185–87, *186*, 188–89
colonies, 197
comic books, 195, 198
commodity fetishism, 97
containment, 2, 145, 150–51, 234–35, 245
Corbett, K., 195
countertransference, 8, 28, 232–33
Crenshaw, K., 196
critical theory, 130

Cropley, A., 163, 170
Cross, G., 162
Cyrulnik, B., 3, 44, 49

Davoine, F., & Gaudillière, J.-M., 3, 57, 251
De Decca, E., 42
dead mother, 16, 244–45
deferred action, see *après coup*, 246
Deleuze, G. &. Guattari, F., 6, 90–91, 178, 236
Deligny, F., 235–38
Delpit, Lisa D., 126
denudation, 152
Dermott, E., 100
Dewey, J., 163
developmental: deficits, 15, 226, norms, 166, 170, phases, 23, psychology, 33, theories, 24, 134
Diamond, M. J., 203
disavowal, 19, 200, 202, 215
disengaged, 30, 143, 144
disintegration, 113, 150
disobjectalization, 152
'disorders' in children. *See* childhood, 'disorders' of
disorganized, 29, 90, 153
dispossession, 15, 248, 250
dissociation, 156, 193–94, 199, 120
distillation, fractional, 14, 15, 225–26
Ducat, S., 203
Durban, J., 144, 145–49, 154–56
dust bowl, 200

echo-praxia, 233
echolalia, 83, 229
effraction in being, 56
Eggers, D., 136–37
Eigen, M., 8–9, 143, 200, 203, 208n1
Ekman, S., 103, 106
Emery, E., 208n1, 243
emotional: labour, 12, 95, 98, 100–1, 105, work, 12, 95–96, 99, 102
entry into filiation, 247
epistemology, 33, 235
etiological theory, 228
eugenics, 161, 182
'event,' 12, 83–86
eye contact, 146, 226

family history, 129, 134
Fanon, F., 27, 30–34, 35n3, 200–2, 255
fantasy, 5, 13–14, 27, 54, 58, 97, 104, 106, 127, 131–32, 137–38, 207, 213–15, 219, 233, 250
Farley, L., 181
fascist, 13–14, 175–80, 183–89
Fass, P., 161
fatherhood, 106, 204,
fatherlessness, 199
fathers, 14, 72, 100, 179, 193–96, 199, 203, 242, 247, 258n3
Faulkner, J., 176, 181–84
Ferenczi, S., 193–95
Ferlinghetti, L., 195,
fetish, 87, 183
Fhadi, story of, 144–47, 149, 152, 154–55
folktales, 126, 137
Fonagy, R., 14, 213
foreclosure, 2–4, 143, 242–43, 252
foreigner, 12, 79–81, 84–86, 90
Foucault, M., 110, 136, 229
found objects, 11, 19, 22, 24
fracking, 14, 225–26
fractional distillation. *See* distillation, fractional
Fraiberg, S., 243
Freire, P., 2, 134, 140
Freud, S., 6, 8, 14, 26, 30, 48–49, 54, 66, 78n2, 79–81, 85, 89, 113, 193–94, 196 97, 201, 230, 258n8
Fromm, E., 195
frozen time, 60–61

Gaige, A., 38
gemeinschaft, 105
Geneva Protocol, 177
geopolitical, 5, 11, 21, 24–26, 29
Germany, 111, 176, 196, 208n2

Gherovici, P., 105–6
'ghost,' 227, 243–44
ghostbuster, 128
Glaveanu, V., 163
"going on being," 15, 241, 245
good objects, 43
Grand, S., 196
Green, A., 4, 152–54, 241, 244, 252, 258n3
Grotstein, J. S., 146, 149

Hague Declaration, 185
Han, B.-C., 84–87
hand flapping, 234
Harris, A., 195, 201, 208n1
Haslam, N., 197
Hayles, K., 116
Head Start, 129
Hebrew, 154
heteronormative, 26, 69
heteropatriarchal, 26
Hinshelwood, R. D., 50n1
Hitler, A., 197
Hmong people, 127, 129–30
Hochschild, A. R., 100–1
holding environment, 143
homelessness, 111, 120, 145, 148–50, 156
homoeroticism, 186
hooks, b., 196, 202
Howard University, 201
Hulbert, A., 160–61, 168
hydraulic metaphors, 227

imaginaries, 21, 31, 175–76, 179, 181
imaginary, 13, 30, 71, 176, 179, 212, 215, 218, 227–28
inaugural losses, 245
infant, 26, 35n2, 66–67, 82–83, 115–16, 118, 129, 132, 143–44, 154–56, 230, 241–44, 246–47, 258n3
I-ness, 147
innocence, childhood. *See* childhood, innocence
intergenerational, 3–4, 12, 117, 127, 130, 137, 167, 193, 196, 200, 241–42, transmission, 167, sequelae, 241
intermarriage, 187
intermittence, 11, 37, 39, 44–49
internal links, 145, 148
intersectionality, 198
'intimate fathering,' 100
introjecting, 150
invisible economies of sentiment, 101
Italo-Ethiopian war, 14, 175–77, 183, 191n1
Italy, 175–80, 182–89

Jamieson, L., 99
Jews, 178, 187, 196–97, 208n2
Jouissance, 67, 70–71, 73–75, 80, 112, 114

Kaplan, L., 258n4
Katz, C., 96–98, 103–4, 223
Khanna, R., 259nn11–12
Kim, KyungHee, 163
King, Dr. Martin Luther, 52
Klein, M., 14, 46
Knafo, D., 195
Kovel, J., 103–5
Kristeva, J., 113, 121, 245
Kupers, T. A., 203

Lacan, J., 5–7, 14, 53, 62–63, 70–71, 73, 106, 117, 209–11, 218–19, 235, 258n2, 258n8
(De) Lajonquière, L., 81–82, 85
Lakoff, G., 196
Laos, 13, 127
Lancey, D., 97
Laplanche, J., 211, 242, 258n2, 258n8
Lareau, A., 98, 101
Lasch, C., 105
Layton, L., 194, 259n13
Lazali, K., 4, 249, 250–51, 252, 259n12
League of Nations, 178, 185
Lévinas, E., 14, 210, 214–15, 219

libidinal economies, 12, 95–96, 98, 100–2, 105–6, horizontal, 96, 98, vertical, 96, 98
liminal, 5, 11–12, 53, 55, 57–59, 61–62, 64, 66, 69–75, 78n2
liminal hotspot, 70
liminal space, 11, 53, 55, 57–59, 61–62, 69
limit point, 46, 48–49
Lindenmeyer, K., 161
linear development, 13, 159, 163, 166
linking, attacks on, 40, 156
literacy, 13, 126–30, 133, 142n2
Lo Bosco, R., 195
Louisiana, 197

manic denial, 227, 230
Mann, T., 197, 206
Mannoni, M., 120, 242, 246
masculinity: hegemonic, 195, 199, toxic, 194, 196, traditional, 194, 200–2
material social practices, 98
maternal attention, 147
Mathelin, C., 120, 242
Mbembe, A., 248, 256, 259n11
McDougall, J., 143
McLean, E., 180
melancholic sequelae, 242
Meltzer, D., 40, 46–47
memorywork, 29
metabolic excess, 242, 246
metapsychology, 231
Mexico, 132
migration, 3, 12, 111, 125–26, 128–32, 135–38, 176, 200, 246, 259n11
Millar, A., 43, 160, 169
mini adults, 160
mirroring, 103, 245, 258n2
mirror-stage, 53–54
misrecognition, 15, 53, 157, 211, 241–42
misrecognizing parent, 243
missionary, 233–35
Mitchell, S., 235
Möbius strip, 81
multigenerational, 200
Mussolini, B., 14, 175–79, 183–85, 187–89, 191n2, 192n7

Nakba, 200
name-of-the-father, 71
nameless dread, 151, 243, 245
narcissism, culture of, 105
narcissistic pact, 247, 250
Native American, 196, 200
naturalized assumptions, 159
Nazi, 196
necrophobia, 14, 193, 195, 199
negative hallucination, 146–47
Nelson, C., 162, 170
Nelson, K. 134–35
neoliberal: capitalism, 5, consumer society, 194, ideology, 199, social formations, 242, 249
neoliberalism, 71
neontocracies, 99
neuronormative, 234
neuroscience, 127
neurotypical, 226, 228–31
New Orleans, 9, 197
New York Times, 200, 204
Nietzsche, F., 30
no K, 41, 150, 152
non-experience, 143
normalization, 170, 253
not-me objects, 146
Note on the Child, 73
nowhere-ness, 13, 144–52, 154–56

Obama, B., 198
object-relations, 45–47, 50n1, 66, 76, 105
occlusion, 242–43, 245–47, 251–52
Oedipal Complex, 66, 72
Offer, A., 99
Ogata, A., 170
Ogden, T. H., 143, 147, 151
O'Loughlin, M., 42, 181, 200, 204, 241, 251, 258n7, 258n9, 259n11, 259n14
O'Shaughnessy, E., 150, 152

ontological insecurity, 95, 169
Other: Big, 71, parental, 241–42, sovereign, 15, 241
Owens, C., 1, 7, 12, 63, 71, 78n4

Pahekeheke, 12, 121
Palacios, M., 203
Palestinian refugees, 200
pandemic, 9, 11–12, 37, 39, 41, 44, 47–48, 73, 79–80, 89–91, 110, 115
Pandolfo, S., 247, 259n12
Paneth, M., 160, 164–69
Pankhurst, R., 178, 183–86
panoptic, 229
parasitic relationship, 47
parental anxiety, 12, 95, 104
parentified child, 245
parenting, 95–96, 100–6, 111, 159, 161, 171, 212, 258n3, normative, 96, positive, 96, 101, 102, 104
Parnell, W., 134
Patterson, O., 259n11
pauses, types of, 39–40
persecutory states, 144
Peterson, J. B., 199
phallogocentrism, 229
phenomenon, continuous, 45, intermittent, 44
Phillips, A., 97
philosophy, 181, 184, 199
phobic Constructions, 71
physical deformities, 153
Plastow, M. G., 242
playing, 8, 29, 61–62, 106, 158, 185, 196, 203, 229, 235
playroom, 50, 152
postcolonial, 25–26, 259n13
posthuman, 20, 116, 123
postindustrial, 21
poststructural, 134, 230, critique, 229, potential, 38, 51, 53, 80, 82, 87, 89, 103–4, 106, 162, 183, 197, 215, 232, 235–36, 242, creative, 51, 53
predatory capitalism, 198
Prelinger, C., 258n4
progressive education, 162–63
propaganda, 176, 181, 185–86, 189
Prose, F., 137, 141
psychic: deadness, 143, 156, reduction, 152–53
psychoanalysis, xiii, xv, 1, 6, 15, 24, 65, 71, 91, 119–20, 156, 159, 162, 204–5, 209–12, 221, 225–27, 232–36
psychotic depression, 143
psychological catastrophe, 230
psychotherapy, 10, 122, 156, 195, 204, 216
puberty, 66, 68, 85

'quality time,' 96, 99–100
qualitative methods, 130
Quintero, E. P., 125, 128–29, 131–32, 134

racism, 12, 81, 109, 111, 120–22, 197
racist projections, 200
rage, 31, 47, 151–52, 185, 187
real, the, xiii, 14, 62, 73, 80, 83, 84–85, 90, 98, 113, 117, 194, 231
Red Cross, 178, 185
refugee, xiv, 1, 4, 13, 15, 125, 127, 129–30, 137, 241, 248, 258n10
Refugee Council, UK, 130
relational: approach, 156, psychoanalysis, 232, theorists, 235, tradition, 235, work, 101, 122
repetition compulsion, 231
revivifying experiences, 252
Rosales, C., 168
Rothschild, L., 9, 14, 196–97, 203, 259n13
Rozmarin, E., 193–94

Salazar, A., 139
Salomonsson, B., 153–55
Salvio, P. M., 13, 181, 191n5, 158n1
Sandy Hook, 201
Santa Claus, 126
Sapountzis, I., 13, 153
SARS-cov-2, 79, 89

Scherer, L., 169
school life, 133
Sealander, J., 161
Self-mutilation, 153
self-reproach, 193–94, 208n1
Sennett, R., 105
separation, 25, 45, 47, 64, 67, 71, 74, 83, 85, 138, 143, 194, 226, 230–32
Shalaby, C., 169
shame, 195, 214
signifier, xiii, 5, 10–11, 60, 66, 70, 80, 91, 117, 229, 243
silence of the beaten, 42
Silicon Valley, 118–20, 122
sinthome, 64, 211
slavery, 181–83, 200
Smuts, A., 161
Soler, C., 114, 124
social bond, xiv, 7, 12, 27, 63–64, 71, 113–15, 118–19, 121
social death, 248, 259n11
social link, 53, 55, 57–58, 61–62, 248, 250, 259n12
social networks, 87, 89
social relationships, 113, 120, 184
Somalia, 13, 127
Sovereign: other, 15, power, 184, 253
spaces of exclusion, 171
Spitz, R. A., 143–45
squiggle game, 150
"state of exception," 15, 241, 248, 259n11
state of non-being, 248
status, legal, 184
Steiner, J., 143, 153
Stenner, P., 70
Stiegler, B., 116–19, 203
storying, 125–26
Solnit, R., 203
Strathern, M., 21, 25
subjectivity: child, 4, 96
Sudan, 137
suicide, xiv, 64, 68, 110, 118, 145
Suomi, S., 212, 219
Sweden, 185
Switzerland, 185
symbolic, the, 26, 71, 119, 228, 233, 235, 238, 242
symbolic order, 7, 70–71, 117, 226, 238, 250
sympathetic magic, 233
systems of occlusion, 247

teacher, 39, 41–46, 51–52, 55, 65, 128–34, 136, 179–80
teenagers, 86, 105, 196
teens, 72–73
testimonio, 135–37
Thailand, 129
The Exorcist, 235, 240n3
The Little Mermaid, 229
theory: curriculum, 181, 188–89, etiological, 228, feminist, 136, 205, literary, 181, of mind, 231, 235
Torok, M., 204, 208n1, 258n9, 259n12
trail of tears, 200
trans, 1, 66
transformative experiences, 155
transitional object, 45, 68, 117, 231
trauma, xiv, 2–3, 12, 15, 53–54, 56, 62, 69, 110, 113, 131, 133, 137, 146, 148, 152, 193, 199, 204–5, 208n1, 213–14, 216, 218, 221, 242–43, 251
trauma, early experience of, 56
Trump, D., 196, 198
Turner, V., 75
Tustin, F., 143–44, 146–47, 155, 226, 230–35
tweenies, 12, 63–65, 75
Twitter, 198–99

uncanny, the, 24, 80
unconscious, the, xiii, 27, 38, 44, 47, 50n1, 54, 56–57, 62, 81, 116, 120, 146, 152, 184, 186, 200, 210–11, 230, 241, 242–43
unconscious knowledge, 184, 242
undrawn, 147
unfathomability of child, 52

unheimlich, the, 12. *See also* uncanny, the
UNICEF, 4, 112, 138, 154
United Kingdom, 130
United States, 2, 64, 133, 139, 176, 192n6, 196, 198–201
unsayable, the, xiii, 57–58, 120

Vanier, A., 70
Vanier, C. *See* Mathelin, C.
Vaughans, K. C., 200
Vietnam, 13, 127
Villela, F. C. B., 11, 42, 45, 50
virtuality, 80, 83, 86–87
virtual bond, 12, 79–80, 88–90
virus, 89–90
Voela, A., 203
Volkan, V. D., 208n2
vulnerability, 30, 32, 65, 69, 160, 164–65, 184n193, 195–203
Vuong, O., 51, 52, 54–55, 61

war, 3–4, 14–15, 58, 121, 129, 137–38, 160, 164–65, 175–78, 182–86, 188–89, 191n1, 191n4, 193, 196–97, 202, 241, 248
weaponization, 14, 176, 179
Wells, K., 169
West, C., 198
westernized cultures, 95
whiteness, 197, 199
Wikinski, M., 246–47
Williams, M. H., 203
Winnicott, D. W., 6, 8, 14, 30, 35n2, 38, 42, 44, 45–47, 50, 70, 117–18, 143–44, 150–54, 210–11, 258n2, 258n8
World War One, 193, 197
World War Two, 191n4, 196
Wyatt, J., 242

Yates, C., 199, 259n13
Yergeau, M., 226, 227–30, 238

Zelitzer, V., 96
Zembylas, M., 259n15

About the Contributors

Ana Archangelo is associate professor at the University of Campinas (UNICAMP) Faculty of Education in Brazil. Author of several academic papers and books, her latest book is *The Capacity Not to Learn* (2021). She has undertaken psychoanalytic training with the Brazilian Psychoanalytic Society of São Paulo. She has been a member of the editorial board of the journal *Psychoanalysis, Culture & Society*, as well as a member of the Association for the Psychoanalysis of Culture & Society.

Erica Burman is professor of education at the University of Manchester, associate fellow of the British Psychological Society, and a United Kingdom Council of Psychotherapists registered Group Analyst (and full member of the Institute of Group Analysis). A past chair of the Psychology of Women (now Psychology of Women and Equalities) section of the British Psychological Society, in 2016 she was awarded an Honorary Lifetime Fellowship of the British Psychological Society in recognition of her contribution to psychology. Erica is well-known as a critical developmental psychologist and methodologist specialising in innovative and activist qualitative research, about which she has lectured and taught courses all over the world. She is author of *Developments: child, image, nation* (Routledge, 2020, 2nd edition), *Fanon, education, action: child as method* (Routledge, 2019), and *Deconstructing Developmental Psychology* (Routledge, 3rd edition, 2017), and is an Associate Editor of the *SAGE Encyclopaedia of Childhood and Childhood Studies* (2020). Erica co-founded the Discourse Unit (www.discourseunit.com), a transinstitutional, transdisciplinary network researching the reproduction and transformation of language and subjectivity. Erica's research has focused on critical developmental and educational psychology, feminist and postcolonial theory, childhood studies, and on critical mental health practice (particularly around gender and cultural issues). Her recent work addresses the connections between emotions, mental health and (social as well as individual) change, in particular as anchored by representations of, and appeals to, childhood. She has co-led transnational research projects on conceptualising and challenging state and interpersonal violence in relation to minoritised women and children, on educational and mental health impacts of poverty and "austerity," on superdiversity and "traditional" Muslim healing practices, and she is a co-investigator on a crossnational project exploring postsocialist childhoods. She sees debates about children and childhood as central to current theories and practices around decolonisation, as indicated by her current working elaborating what she calls "child as method."

Kaye P. Cederman is research fellow at Trinity College, Dublin, Psychoanalyst and Supervisor with specific focus on the child clinic. Kaye teaches at the Centre for Lacanian Analysis, Aotearoa/NZ. Current research includes a critical feminist understanding of contemporary Aotearoa, Jean Baudrillard's philosophy, and child and adolescent psychoanalysis. Key work: *Child Psychoanalysis and the Psycho-Technologies of Consumer Capitalism* (2018), *A Baudrillardian Reading of Education in the Hyper-Industrial Era: A Renewable Course?* (2009), *The child.com in NZ Early Childhood Pedagogies* (2008), *Synergy—High Quality Early Intervention for Children with Special Needs* (2006), *Homesick in Hyperreality* (2002).

Marilyn Charles, PhD, ABPP, is a psychologist and psychoanalyst at the Austen Riggs Center, Co-Chair of the Association for the Psychoanalysis of Culture and Society (APCS), and Scholar of the British Psychoanalytic Council. Affiliations include Chicago Center for Psychoanalysis; Universidad de Monterrey; Harvard Medical School; and Boston Graduate School of Psychoanalysis. Books include *Working with Trauma*; *Psychoanalysis and Literature;* and *Introduction to Contemporary Psychoanalysis.*

Anne-Marie Cummins is senior lecturer in sociology at the University of the West of England, Bristol, UK, where she is a member of the Psycho-Social Studies & Therapeutic Practices Research Group. She is former UK editor of the journal *Organisational and Social Dynamics* and co-founder of Foundation Degree in Therapeutic Child Care in partnership with the Mulberry Bush School, Oxfordshire. Anne-Marie has a practice background in Group Relations, Group Analysis, and Listening Post methodology.

Katherine Martin is a doctoral candidate at Rutgers University (USA) in the Childhood Studies department. She holds an MA in childhood studies from Rutgers-Camden, and a BA in contemporary art history from Ramapo College. She is a founding member of the Childhood Studies Racial Justice Initiative at Rutgers-Camden and volunteers her time at a local youth art center. Her research is focused on Depression Era community art programs in the US and the UK, histories of art education and arts-based youth reform programs, and early twentieth-century visual and material culture.

Ben Morsa is a graduate of the George Washington University Professional Psychology Program and he currently teaches psychological assessment at the Wright Institute. Ever polymathic and autodidactic, his clinical work and writing is rooted in psychoanalytic theory and wanders divergently through several SPINS including: the educational assessment of bilingual children, queer and transgender theory and experience, neurodiversity and neuro-affirming approaches to assessment and psychoanalysis, historical and contemporary constructions of masculinity, critical autism studies, ecology, and mycology. Benjamin is also the owner of Tide Pools, a psychological corporation, which offers psychotherapy, psychoanalysis, psychological assessment, and consultation to clinicians on affirming work with gender diverse and neurodivergent patients.

Michael O'Loughlin is professor in the College of Education and Health Sciences and in the programs in Clinical Psychology and School Psychology at Adelphi University, New York. He is co-editor of the journal *Psychoanalysis, Culture & Society* and he is a scholar of the British Psychoanalytic Council. He founded the Adelphi Asylum Project, and he has a private practice for psychotherapy and psychoanalysis on Long Island, New York. Website: *michaeloloughlinphd.com.*

Carol Owens is a psychoanalyst and Lacanian scholar in Dublin, Ireland. A member of the APCS, APPI, and affiliate member of CPUK, she is also the founder and convenor of the Dublin Lacan study group. Her most recent book is *Psychoanalysing Ambivalence with Freud and Lacan* (with Stephanie Swales, 2020); she is the series editor for *Studying Lacan's Seminars* at Routledge.

Elizabeth Quintero's research, teaching, and service has focused on early childhood studies collaborating in communities with migrating families. After receiving her EdD at New Mexico State University, she designed and implemented programs at University of Minnesota Duluth, and New York University. From 2007 to 2019 she was Chair of Early Childhood Studies at California State University Channel Islands. She is now active with asylum-seekers in southern California. Her publications include *Making Space for Storied Leadership in Higher Education: Learning with Migrant and Refugee Populations in Early Childhood and Teacher Education Contexts* (Quintero, E. P., Callaway-Cole, L., and Taha-Resnick, A., 2021) and *Storying*

Learning in Early Childhood: When Children Lead Participatory Curriculum Design, Implementation, and Assessment (Quintero, E. P., 2015).

Louis Rothschild, PhD, is a clinical psychologist in Baltimore County, Maryland. Specializing in psychoanalytic psychotherapy, he also provides supervision, writes, and occasionally reviews manuscripts. His publications have ranged from quantitative to qualitative, social-cognitive to psychoanalysis, and clinical to philosophical. He is presently writing a book to be published with Phoenix Publishing House entitled *Rapprochement between Fathers and Sons: Breakdowns, Reunions, Potentialities*. Outside of his professional life, he has a fondness for tennis, triathlon, and chasing a rather elusive sourdough starter in the kitchen.

Paula Salvio is professor of education and affiliate professor of Classics, Humanities, and Italian Studies at the University of New Hampshire. Along with her numerous articles and book chapters, she is the author of *The Story-Takers: Public Pedagogy and Contemporary Italy's Non-Violent Resistance Against the Mafia* (Univ. of Toronto Press, 2017); *Anne Sexton: Teacher of Weird Abundance* (SUNY Press, 2007); *Community-based Media Pedagogies: Relational Practices of Listening in the Commons* (written with Bronwen Low and Chloe Brushwood Rose, Routledge Press, 2016); *Love's Return: Psychoanalytic Essays on Childhood, Teaching and Learning* (Co-Edited with Gail Boldt, Routledge, 2006). Her current scholarship focuses on anti-fascist education, transnational memories, and transitional justice.

Rosiane Cristina dos Santos (1976–2021) was a Portuguese language and literature teacher at a public school in São Paulo State. She was completing a doctorate in education at the State University of Campinas Faculty of Education and was an invited teacher on the Cultural Diffusion course: "The Psychic Survival of the Teacher in Times of Crisis: Affective Aspects of the Teacher-Student relationship," at the same university. Sadly, she passed away on November 17, 2021, and is mourned by her colleagues.

Ionas Sapountzis is associate professor at the Derner School of Psychology of Adelphi University and the director of its School Psychology program. He is a faculty member and supervisor in the Psychoanalytic Psychotherapy and in the Child, Adolescent and Family Psychotherapy programs of the Derner School of Psychology. His articles have been published in the journals of *Psychoanalytic Psychology*, *Psychoanalytic Review*, *Psychoanalytic Perspectives*, and in the *Journal of Infant, Child and Adolescent Psychotherapy* (*JICAP*). He maintains a private practice in Garden City, New York.

Aileen Schloerb, PhD, has worked with the Schools Initiative of the Chicago Psychoanalytic Institute for the past fourteen years serving as project director, clinician, and clinical consultant. She is also a clinical consultant for the school's project of a community mental health organization in the city and collaborates with a group of colleagues in Quebec on the creation of psychoanalytically informed interventions with adolescents. Having previously worked abroad with humanitarian and human rights organizations serving refugees in France and the Middle East, she has long been interested in bringing psychoanalytic principles to bear on collaborations with marginalized communities and has published several book chapters on such projects.\

Liora Stavchansky, PhD, psychoanalyst, was born in Mexico City. Her practice is divided between the psychoanalytic clinic and teaching at Universidad Iberoamericana (among other universities and clinical institutions). Her research is focused on childhood, infancy, subjectivity, writing, and psychoanalysis. She is a founding member of the FCLM (Forum of Lacanian Field Mexico). She has published many psychoanalytic books and papers in Mexico, Argentina, and the United States. Her books include *Lacanian Psychoanalysis between the Child and the Other* (2015); *Exploring the Cultures of Childhood* (2018); and *Autismo y cuerpo. El lenguaje en los trazos de la perfección.* México (2013).

Fábio Camargo Bandeira Villela is assistant professor at the São Paulo State University and permanent professor on the Professional Master's Program in Inclusive Education. He does research on psychoanalysis and education and is co-author of the collection "The Meaningful School" (published by Loyola).

Jamieson Webster is a psychoanalyst in New York City. She is the author of *The Life and Death of Psychoanalysis* (2011), *Conversion Disorder* (2018), and *Disorganisation and Sex* (2022). She writes regularly for *Artforum*, *The New York Review of Books*, *The New York Times*, and *Spike Art Quarterly*. She teaches at the New School for Social Research and is a member of Das Unbehagen and IPTAR.

Praise for The Holiness of Doubt

"It was a pleasure to engage on this journey of questions and answers, doubt and faith, through the Torah with Rabbi Joshua Hoffman as a guide. He helps us explore our own questions and doubts, leaving lots of room to think and reflect along the way. Bring an open mind and heart, and start reading!"

—**Rabbi Jacob Blumenthal**, CEO,
United Synagogue of Conservative Judaism

"Rabbi Hoffman's unique focus of methodically examining the questions *within* Torah, rather than the questions we may have *about* Torah, reveals a 'face' of Torah we might otherwise overlook. This opens important conversations about inquiry, faithfulness and doubt that are most relevant and grounded in our sacred text."

—**Rabbi Rachel Bovitz**, executive director,
Florence Melton School of Adult Jewish Learning

"One of my best Talmud teachers told us that the questions in the Talmud were often better than the answers. A professor of mine told us graduate students in philosophy that a philosopher is a five-year-old child who never stopped asking 'Why?' Being willing to ask questions and not expect totally satisfactory answers is the mark of the epistemological humility that we all should have, for God may know everything, but no human being does. This does not mean, though, that we should not ask questions and seek answers. On the contrary, questions are absolutely critical in seeking meaning in life, as this book amply demonstrates. So ask away, and let Rabbi Hoffman and the Torah itself spur you to more questions!"

—**Rabbi Elliot N. Dorff**, rector and distinguished
service professor of philosophy, American Jewish University

"This is a wonderful book for anyone who wants a deeper mode of Torah study. Rabbi Hoffman explores the world of the Torah through the questions found in the text and helps us ask our own questions of ourselves, God, and the world."

—**Rabbi Denise L. Eger D.D.**, founding Senior Rabbi of Congregation Kol Ami in West Hollywood, CA, author, and past president of the Central Conference of American Rabbis

"The one who questions and doubts is a person of faith. Scattered throughout the Torah are prompts—questions that help guide our lives. In Rabbi Joshua Hoffman's masterful book, he seeks to answer those questions. And in doing so, he provides us with direction for our own lives while also helping us to probe the depths of wisdom that Torah has to offer. At the same time, Rabbi Hoffman offers us his own torah so that we may deepen and widen our learning even further."

—**Dr. Kerry M. Olitzky**, former executive director of Big Tent Judaism

"In the sacred text of the Torah to which so many turn for answers and clarity, the presence of abundant questions challenges us to probe deeper. Hoffman's book thoughtfully and insightfully invites us to embrace the blessing of uncertainty in our studies and spiritual life journey."

—**Rabbi Ari Sunshine**, Senior Rabbi, Congregation Shearith Israel, Dallas, TX

"A beautiful reading and rereading of the Torah, offering readers elegant insights, inspiration, and guidance in these difficult days."

—**Rabbi David Wolpe**, Senior Rabbi, Sinai Temple, Los Angeles, CA